Political Partisanship
in the American Middle Colonies,
1700–1776

Political Partisanship
in the American Middle Colonies,
1700–1776

Benjamin H. Newcomb

Louisiana State University Press
Baton Rouge and London

Copyright © 1995 by Louisiana State University Press

All rights reserved

Manufactured in the United States of America

First printing

04 03 02 01 00 99 98 97 96 95   5 4 3 2 1

Designer: Glynnis Phoebe

Typeface: New Baskerville

Typesetter: Moran Printing, Inc.

Printer and binder: Thomson-Shore, Inc.

Library of Congress Cataloging-in-Publication Data

Newcomb, Benjamin H., 1938–

    Political partisanship in the American middle colonies, 1700–1776

 / Benjamin H. Newcomb.

      p.   cm.

    Includes bibliographical references and index.

    ISBN 0-8071-1875-3 (cl.)

    1. United States—Politics and government—To 1775.   I.   Title.

E195.N493   1995

320.973'09'033—dc20

94-39764

CIP

The letter of January 27, 1769, from Peter Van Shaack to Henry Van Shaack is from the Hawks Manuscripts of the New-York Historical Society and is quoted courtesy of the New-York Historical Society.

For Benjamin and Laura

Contents

Acknowledgments

Many institutions have kindly contributed financial and scholarly support to my research for this book. Texas Tech University provided state-supported research grants in the summers of 1967, 1968, and 1974, when this project was in its earliest stages. The American Council of Learned Societies awarded me a fellowship for seven months of 1975. Library staffs were also very helpful. Particularly I am greatly indebted to the Texas Tech University Library, the Library of the Historical Society of Pennsylvania in Philadelphia, the Library of the American Philosophical Society in Philadelphia, the Free Library of Philadelphia, the New York Public Library, the Library of the New-York Historical Society, and the libraries of the University of Pennsylvania, Princeton University, Rutgers University, and Rowan College. I also consulted material belonging to the Franklin D. Roosevelt Library, Hyde Park, New York. The able criticism of numerous anonymous readers made this a much better book. The editorial staff of Louisiana State University Press helped make it presentable.

Abbreviations

Am. Arch.	Peter Force, ed., *American Archives.* Fourth Series. 6 vols. Washington, D.C., 1837–53.
AHR	*American Historical Review.*
APS	American Philosophical Society Library, Philadelphia.
DCHNY	E. B. O'Callaghan, ed., *Documents Relative to the Colonial History of the State of New York.* 15 vols. Albany, 1853–87.
HSP	Historical Society of Pennsylvania Library, Philadelphia.
JAH	*Journal of American History.*
Labaree *et al.*, eds., *Franklin Papers*	Leonard W. Labaree *et al.*, eds., *The Papers of Benjamin Franklin* (New Haven, 1959–).
LP	Livingston-Redmond Papers, Franklin D. Roosevelt Library, Hyde Park, New York. Includes Philip Livingston General Correspondence, 1701–49; Robert Livingston, Jr., General Correspondence, 1724–90; and Peter R. Livingston General Correspondence, 1760–95. Consulted on microfilm belonging to the New-York Historical Society, New York City.
MP	Robert Morris Papers, Rutgers University Library, New Brunswick.

NJA

William A. Whitehead *et al.*, eds., *Archives of the State of New Jersey, First Series: Documents Relating to the Colonial History of the State of New Jersey.* 41 vols. Newark *et al.*, 1880–1949.

N.J. Prov. Cong. Votes

Extracts from the Journal of Proceedings of the Provincial Congress of New Jersey, Held at Trenton the Months of May, June, and August 1775. Burlington, 1775. *Journal of the Votes and Proceedings of the Provincial Congress of New Jersey, Held at Trenton in the Month of October 1775.* Burlington, 1775. *Journal of the Votes and Proceedings, as Well of the Committee of Safety, of a Sitting in January, 1776, as the Provincial Congress of New-Jersey, at a Sitting in New Brunswick, Begun January 31, and Continued to the Second Day of March Following.* New York, 1776. *Journal of the Votes and Proceedings of the Convention of New Jersey Begun at Burlington the 10th of June 1776, and Thence Continued by Adjournment at Trenton and New Brunswick to the 21st of August Following.* Burlington, 1776.

N.J. Votes

The Votes and Proceedings of the General Assembly of the Province of New Jersey. Philadelphia *et al.*, 1738–76. *Journal and Votes of the House of Representatives of the Province of Nova Caesarea or New Jersey . . . Begun . . . 1703.* Jersey City, 1872. Votes and Minutes of the House of Assembly of the Colony of New Jersey. Records of the States of the United States. Microfilm. Washington, D.C., 1941.

N.Y.C. Poll List, 1761

New York (City and County). *A Copy of the Poll List of the Election for Representatives from the City and County of New-York; Which Election Began on Tuesday the 17th Day of February and Ended on Thursday the 19th of the Same Month, in the Year of Our Lord MDCCLXI.* New York, 1880.

N.Y.C. Poll List, 1768	New York (City and County). *A Copy of the Poll List of the Election for Representatives for the City and County of New York; Which Election Began on Monday the 7th Day of March and Ended on Friday the 11th of the Same Month, in the Year of Our Lord MDCCLXVIII.* New York, 1880.
N.Y.C. Poll List, 1769	New York (City and County). *A Copy of the Poll List of the Election for Representatives for the City and County of New York; Which Election Began on Monday the 23rd Day of January, and Ended on Friday the 27th, of the Same Month, in the Year of Our Lord MDCCLXIX.* New York, 1769.
NYHS	New-York Historical Society Library, New York City.
NYHSC	*Collections of the New-York Historical Society,* vols. 1–4, vols. 1–5, vols. 1–73. New York, 1811–1940.
NYHSQ	*New-York Historical Society Quarterly.*
N.Y. Laws	*The Colonial Laws of New York from the Year 1664 to the Revolution, Including the Charters to the Duke of York, the Commissions and Instructions to Colonial Governors, the Duke's Laws, the Laws of the Dongan and Leisler Assemblies, the Charters of Albany and New York and the Acts of the Colonial Legislature from 1691 to 1775 Inclusive.* 5 vols. Albany, 1894–96.
NYPL	New York Public Library, New York City.
N.Y. Votes	*Journal of the Votes and Proceedings of the General Assembly of New York.* 2 vols. New York, 1764–76. *Journal of the Votes and Proceedings of the Colony of New York from 1766 to 1776, Inclusive.* Albany, 1820.
Pa. Col. Recs.	*Minutes of the Provincial Council of Pennsylvania, from the Organization to the Termination of the Proprietary Government* [also titled *Colonial Records of Pennsylvania*]. 10 vols. Philadelphia and Harrisburg, 1851–52.

Pa. Hist.	*Pennsylvania History.*
Pa. Votes	*Votes and Proceedings of the House of Representatives of the Province of Pennsylvania.* 6 vols. Philadelphia, 1752–76. [The later edition, Gertrude McKinney, ed., *Pennsylvania Archives*, Eighth Series, Harrisburg, 1931–35, contains some inaccuracies.]
PMHB	*Pennsylvania Magazine of History and Biography.*
TPP	Thomas Penn Papers, Historical Society of Pennsylvania, Philadelphia.
WMQ	*William and Mary Quarterly.*

In quotations, old-style dates have not been converted to new style. The year of old-style dates between January 1 and March 24 inclusive is hyphenated in citations but given in new style in the text. The thorn has been converted to "th."

Introduction

The dimensions of historical study have vastly expanded since earlier prac-
titioners treated history as merely past politics. As part of this expansion and
reformulation has come a new political history. Not just great men but ordinary voters of varied social groups take major roles. Not just momentous decisions of state but the mundane doings of caucus and committee and polling
place count in the historical narrative. Not just the motives of the principal
actors but the attitudes and behavior of common human beings—the political culture of the society—determine the course of the state. Both the
drama of spirited conflict and the prosaic rigor of quantitative analysis drive
this new historical expression. Nineteenth- and twentieth-century American
parties, on which voluminous statistical and biographical records have been
compiled, provide the most accessible subjects for studies that have contributed to a new understanding of American politics. For colonial America,
although a comparable quantity of election data and detailed public records
is lacking, the same kind of new political history is also possible; what follows
is an attempt to apply it to a portrayal of party politics in its earliest American stage.

Unlike the later United States, the colonies had no "national" politics that
provided unifying themes for the study of local and state parties and elections. A single study of the history of partisan politics of the thirteen colonies
that would explain the developments in all of them would involve such divergent themes, multiple exceptions to generalizations, procrustean cate-
gorizations, and meaningless contrasts that it could not highlight the major developments that several of the colonies experienced.[1] A study of a

1. Jack P. Greene, "Changing Interpretations of Early American Politics," in *The
Reinterpretation of Early American History*, ed. Ray A. Billington (New York, 1968), 175–77,
classifies factionalism in most of the colonies. Bernard Bailyn, *The Origins of American
Politics* (New York, 1968), traces the ideological roots to eighteenth-century British
politics and provides capsule summaries of politics in several colonies. Alison G. Olson, *Anglo-American Politics, 1660–1775: The Relationship Between Parties in England
and Colonial America* (New York, 1973), attempts to link politicians and parties in Britain
and America. Marc Egnal, *A Mighty Empire: The Origins of the American Revolution* (Ithaca,

limited area, the middle colonies, refines the historical understanding of colonial politics and reveals important developments in the origin of national
partisan politics. Studying New York, Pennsylvania, and New Jersey together
avoids too narrow a focus and treats three colonies that constitute a coherent
unity because they were intertwined in various ways. Their common conditions were more notable and more significant than their differences. New
York and Pennsylvania experienced much the same economic growth, fostered by merchants who traded highly demanded foodstuffs, produced by
thriving farms, to Britain, Europe, and the West Indies. Although New York
City and Philadelphia were rivals in the export of forest and farm products,
important commercial links connected them. New Jersey did not grow as fast
as its neighbors, for it had no great port, but its prosperity derived from many
of the same products. New York was the commercial capital for the eastern
part of the colony and Philadelphia for the west. Dutch merchants of New
York City had interests in New Jersey. As well, merchants of Perth Amboy did
business from New York. Religion played as great an interconnecting role as
did commerce. Philadelphia, the Quaker city, was central for the Society of
Friends. That city and Burlington were the homes of the Yearly Meeting for
Pennsylvania and New Jersey. Public Friends from that area journeyed to visit
and to attend to Quakers in Long Island and Westchester County. Anglicans
had strength in both New York and New Jersey. They founded King's College
over determined partisan opposition. Thomas B. Chandler, rector at Elizabethtown, attempted to coordinate New Jersey, New York, Pennsylvania, and
Connecticut clergy in the effort to obtain a bishop. The two cities were also
important centers of Presbyterianism and for a time housed rival synods. Sit-
uated between them was the Presbyterian college at Princeton.[2]

Prominent individuals and families had connections with more than one
of these colonies and sometimes with all three. The Morris family of New
York contributed to that colony assemblymen, councillors, and justices; to

1988), 52–68, 83, 92–93, 348–54, exhibits the difficulties and insufficiencies of an over-
broad treatment.

2. For commercial connections, Virginia D. Harrington, *The New York Merchant on
the Eve of the Revolution* (New York, 1935), 224. On the role of the two cities for New
Jersey, Larry R. Gerlach, *Prologue to Independence: New Jersey in the Coming of the Revolu-
tion* (New Brunswick, 1976), 9, 29–30. On religion, *ibid.*, 26–27, and Carl Bridenbaugh,
Mitre and Sceptre: Transatlantic Faiths, Ideas, Personalities, and Politics, 1687–1775 (New
York, 1962), 179–80, 246–48.

New Jersey a governor, councillor, and chief justice; and to Pennsylvania a governor. The Alexander family was also very important in New York and New Jersey. The Smith family of Burlington conducted its mercantile business from Philadelphia as well and contributed assemblymen to both colonies' representative bodies. William Trent and John Kinsey, Jr., served in both the Pennsylvania and New Jersey assemblies as Speakers.[3]

Because of these economic, personal, religious, and familial links, political leaders in these three colonies kept abreast of political policies or techniques adopted by their neighbors. Governor John Montgomerie of New York and New Jersey in 1729 lamented to the Board of Trade that the New York Assembly would undoubtedly imitate New Jersey's passage of a triennial act unless the act were voided in Britain. New York began publishing the roll call votes of its legislature in 1737; New Jersey followed the next year, perhaps because Lewis Morris, who had favored the New York innovation, was governor of New Jersey in 1738. The New York House in 1739 moved to limit the duration of the appropriation of the governor's salary to one year; New Jersey adopted the same limitation in 1741. New Jersey Quakers, in their dispute with Governor Morris in 1744 and 1745, sought advice from their Pennsylvania counterparts about how best to confront the governor. The model of the legislatively powerless Pennsylvania Council probably inspired the New Jersey Assembly in 1748–1751 to attempt to deprive the council of the colony of its authority to review tax bills. Political leaders in all three colonies attempted to implement good behavior tenure for judges in 1759–1760. The assemblies of the three colonies in 1769–1770 responded to the push of constituents, or anticipated their pressure, in admitting the public to hear House debates, though Pennsylvania revoked the privilege after a year. These efforts at enlarging popular liberties and refining legislative procedure be-

3. The Morris family activities in these colonies can best be seen in the family papers, particularly those letters of Robert Hunter Morris at Rutgers University Library. The papers of James and William Alexander in the NYHS illustrate their activities. For the Quaker connections, see the Pemberton Papers and the John Smith correspondence at the HSP. For Trent, Samuel Smith, *The History of the Colony of Nova-Caesaria, or New Jersey; Containing an Account of the First Settlement, Progressive Improvement, the Original and Present Constitution, and Other Events to the Year 1721* (Burlington, 1765), 419. For Kinsey, Joseph S. Walton, *John Kinsey, Speaker of the Pennsylvania Assembly and Justice of the Supreme Court of the Province* (Philadelphia, 1900). Gerlach, *Prologue to Independence,* 31–32, discusses the important family connections extending from New Jersey into New York and Pennsylvania.

came common to the middle colonies and contributed to the "Rise of the Assembly" that marked eighteenth-century British colonial development.[4]

A second general common attribute was the great internal diversity of the middle colonies. They had within them larger variations in both economic activity and ethnic backgrounds than did other groups of colonies. These three colonies had higher proportions of non-British inhabitants than did any other British colony, and each contained from eleven to fifteen religious denominations. Ethnic and religious pluralism encouraged these very diverse peoples to participate in political activity, both to forward the principles of their group and for self-protection. In the middle colonies the largest urban sites in eighteenth-century British America were coupled with both backcountry subsistence farming areas and very profitable commercial agriculture. These different economic interests were interdependent parts of a flourishing economy that expanded the land under cultivation and marketed its products widely in the Atlantic trading area. The middle colonies remained generally prosperous during this period, experiencing only brief economic dislocations. The flourishing economy encouraged a large part of the society to be involved and interested in political matters; people were not too overwhelmed by privation to care about such things. At times merchants, large landowners, and small farmers competed for political benefits, but many issues brought two or more of the economic interests together.[5] Partisan

4. Governor John Montgomerie to the Lords of Trade, Apr. 20, 1729, in *NJA,* V, 236; *N.Y. Votes,* June 15, Nov. 16, 1737; Oct. 16, 1739; Apr. 4, 8, Dec. 6, 1769; *N.J. Votes,* Oct. 29, 1741; Oct. 12, 1769; *Pa. Votes,* Oct. 18, 1770; Governor George Clarke to the Duke of Newcastle, Nov. 30, 1739, in *DCHNY,* VI, 149–50. On aid from Pennsylvania political leaders to New Jersey, Thomas Penn to Ferdinand John Paris, Apr. 24, 1741, in TPP; Richard Smith, Jr., to John Smith, Mar. 22, 1744–5, in John Smith Correspondence, HSP; Richard Partridge to Richard Smith, Jr., June 1, 1745, in Pemberton Papers, HSP. On good behavior tenure of judges, Benjamin H. Newcomb, *Franklin and Galloway: A Political Partnership* (New Haven, 1972), 61; Larry R. Gerlach, "Anglo-American Politics in New Jersey on the Eve of the Revolution," *Huntington Library Quarterly,* XXXIX (1975–76), 296, 298; Jerome J. Nadelhaft, "Politics and the Judicial Tenure Fight in Colonial New Jersey," *WMQ,* 3rd ser., XXVIII (1971), 46–63; Milton M. Klein, "Prelude to Revolution in New York: Jury Trials and Judicial Tenure," *WMQ,* 3rd ser., XVII (1960), 439–62.

5. Douglas Greenberg, "The Middle Colonies in Recent American Historiography," *WMQ,* 3rd ser., XXXVI (1979), 397, 411, 422, notes that the middle colonies reflect the "varied character of colonial life" better than does any other group of colonies;

leaders in these colonies incorporated these varied interests into manageable political groups in both legislatures and the electorate by developing techniques that resembled those of modern political parties.

This book uses the techniques of the new political history in examining this politically lively region to explore political activity that became over the course of the middle fifty years of the eighteenth century very like that of

---

that geographical variations determined diversity within the middle colonies, as did the aims of early colonizers and promoters, the abilities of local leaders, and the arrival of various ethnic and religious groups; and that the middle colonies saw more rapid changes than other colonies did. Milton M. Klein, "New York in the American Colonies: A New Look," in *Aspects of Early New York Society and Politics*, ed. Jacob Judd and Irwin H. Polishook (Tarrytown, 1974), 11, finds heterogeneity the central fact of that colony's history. Jacob Judd, "New York: Municipality and Province," in *Aspects of Early New York Society*, ed. Judd and Polishook, 5, claims that New York is atypical and not a middle colony. Peter O. Wacker, *Land and People: A Cultural Geography of Preindustrial New Jersey: Origins and Settlement Patterns* (New Brunswick, 1975), 158, notes that "New Jersey exhibited the maximum cultural diversity of any American colony or state before 1800." Africans, Dutch, Germans, Scotch, Scotch-Irish, Swedes, and Swiss made up its non-English population. For denominational variety in New York and New Jersey, see Richard W. Pointer, *Protestant Pluralism and the New York Experience: A Study of Eighteenth-Century Religious Diversity* (Bloomington, 1988), 3; and Smith, *History of New-Jersey*, 489–500. For Pennsylvania, Rev. William Smith to Archbishop Thomas Secker, Nov. 27, 1759, in *DCHNY*, VII, 407, which notes six denominations and omits Jews; and Robert Proud, *The History of Pennsylvania, in North America, from the Original Institution and Settlement of That Province, Under the First Proprietor and Governor William Penn, in 1681, Till After the Year 1742* (2 vols., Philadelphia, 1797–98), II, 340n. The number and diversity of German denominations is summarized in Sidney Ahlstrom, *A Religious History of the American People* (New Haven, 1972), 230–59. For a brief summary of economic conditions, see James M. Henretta, *The Origins of American Capitalism: Collected Essays* (Boston, 1991), 167–71. Gary Walton and James F. Shepherd, *The Economic Rise of Early America* (New York, 1979), 147–48, notes that wealth was more evenly distributed in the middle colonies than in the South or New England. Robert J. Gough, "The Myth of the 'Middle Colonies': An Analysis of Regionalization in Early America," *PMHB*, CVII (1983), 393–419, denies any middle-colony homogeneity equaling that which marked the South and New England. Countering this view is Wayne Bodle, "The Myth of the Middle Colonies Reconsidered: The Process of Regionalization in Early America," *PMHB*, CXIII (1989), 527–48, who finds important political connections among the three colonies in William Penn's time.

the mass political parties of the nineteenth century. Many historians have recognized some link between middle-colony politics and modern parties, but they have not been in agreement on whether the resemblance of middle-colony political groups to modern parties was very pale or clear and strong. Recent studies of these colonies most commonly term the political groups "factions," "loose coalitions," "interest groups," and "juntos" but do not define these terms or explain how these political groups were unlike parties. Some find rudimentary parties in Pennsylvania but not in the other two colonies. Leaders of these groups were "ideological chameleons," interested only in holding office, a "narrow political elite," who did not compete for office but were "swapping assembly terms among themselves."[6]

6. Marc Egnal, in *A Mighty Empire*, 6, 60, 124, termed the New York and Pennsylvania groups "loose coalitions" and "loose political groupings." Earlier, Egnal, in "The Pattern of Factional Development in Pennsylvania, New York, and Massachusetts, 1682–1776," in *Party and Political Opposition in Revolutionary America*, ed. Patricia U. Bonomi (Tarrytown, 1980) 46, portrayed them as "factions" that "were long lived and cohesive." Patricia U. Bonomi, *A Factious People: Politics and Society in Colonial New York* (New York, 1971), 13, finds "at least a dozen more or less identifiable factions whose membership and allegiance were forever changing." Michael C. Batinski, *The New Jersey Assembly, 1738–1775: The Making of a Legislative Community* (Lanham, 1987), 99, characterized the politics of that colony as "unstable and milling factionalism." In his "Quakers in the New Jersey Assembly, 1738–1775: A Roll-Call Analysis," *Historian*, LIV (1991–92), 67, Batinski terms the Quakers a "formidable interest group" but "not a political party in the modern sense." Thomas L. Purvis, *Proprietors, Patronage, and Paper Money: Legislative Politics in New Jersey, 1703–1776* (New Brunswick, 1986), 95–97, 136–37, identified a proprietary "coalition" and several other blocs in the New Jersey Assembly. Gerlach, *Prologue to Independence*, 20, asserted that the New Jersey "factions or juntos which did coalesce from time to time were largely *ad hoc;* their leadership, diffuse and unstructured." Gary B. Nash, in *The Urban Crucible: Social Change, Political Consciousness, and the Origins of the American Revolution* (Cambridge, Mass, 1979), chap. 10, characterized some of the most heated 1760s Pennsylvania party activity as "factional politics." Alan Tully, "Quaker Party and Proprietary Politics: The Dynamics of Politics in Pre-Revolutionary Pennsylvania, 1730–1775," in *Power and Status: Officeholding in Colonial America*, ed. Bruce C. Daniels (Middletown, 1986), 76, viewed that party as "one of the very few colonial political organizations that, from a modern perspective, deserves the term party." Richard A. Ryerson, *The Revolution Is Now Begun: The Radical Committees of Philadelphia, 1765–1776* (Philadelphia, 1978), 251, saw the Quaker-Assembly party as not truly modern but merely a "stable but narrow political elite [that] contended over issues that did not vitally affect most Penn-

Although several American colonial historians see society in the colonies as developing in an ordered, sequential fashion, those studying the middle colonies have not formulated a view of party development that links the rudimentary political groups of the early colonial period with those of the 1790–1850 period. This book asserts that in the middle colonies political parties arose from small and limited factions to become large, diverse alliances of both legislators and voters. Party development occurred in marked stages, though not in an unbroken line of progression. Those political groups active before 1725–1735 were factions. They were simple, one-dimensional partisan groups that had very narrow and particular aims, often merely attainment of office; were socially homogeneous to a high degree; were led by small cliques, often composed of relatives; employed closed, secretive, and often corrupt methods; and were short-lived. By about 1735–1740 they were becoming organizations with wider appeal and purpose, taking on the character of political parties. Identifiable parties in the middle colonies first centered in the elected assemblies. Members of the middle-colony legislatures

---

sylvanians." Jackson T. Main, *Political Parties Before the Constitution* (Chapel Hill, 1973), 6–15, found that Pennsylvania had continuous and somewhat organized parties led by avid campaigners, New Jersey had no parties but only voting blocs in the legislature, and New York had parties or factions. Michael G. Kammen, *Colonial New York: A History* (New York, 1975), 205, 192, discovered "ideological chameleons" leading the New York "protoparties." Edward Countryman, *A People in Revolution: The American Revolution and Political Society in New York, 1760–1790* (Baltimore, 1981), 78, identified parties active there as "small groups of men whose main concern was to hold office themselves or to control the men holding it." John M. Murrin, "Political Development," in *Colonial British America: Essays in the New History of the Early Modern Era,* ed. Jack P. Greene and J. R. Pole (Baltimore, 1984), 444, suggested that New Jersey assemblymen swapped assembly terms. Other recent works noting the importance of middle-colony politics include Greenberg, "Middle Colonies in American Historiography," 425–26; Patricia U. Bonomi, "The Middle Colonies: Embryo of the New Political Order," in *Perspectives on Early American History: Essays in Honor of Richard B. Morris,* ed. Alden T. Vaughan and George A. Billias (New York, 1973), 65, 86; Robert Kelley, *The Cultural Pattern of American Politics: The First Century* (New York, 1979), 105; H. James Henderson, "The First Party System," in *Perspectives on Early American History,* ed. Vaughan and Billias, 361; William N. Chambers, "Party Development and the American Mainstream," in *The American Party Systems: Stages of Political Development,* ed. Chambers and Walter Dean Burnham (2nd ed.; New York, 1975), 88.

began to band together in voting blocs that were united by agreement on policy but did not merely reflect an economic, religious, regional, or personal interest. These groups maintained their membership and policy aims for long periods. In New York and New Jersey in most legislative sessions, roll calls identified the party groups for constituents and for leaders of the assemblies. Legislative parties forged coalitions by distributing posts and benefits according to political calculations. These were truly parties in the legislature—a major manifestation of the modern political party. These parties applied names, sometimes vague and sometimes specific, to the legislative members and to the constituents. They made planned, coordinated, and open efforts to attract voters and rally them at election time. Often writing newspaper pieces and pamphlets and sometimes even controlling a newspaper, they cultivated and aroused an electorate that was ordinarily uninterested in politics, and they succeeded in raising a sporadic but passionate political consciousness among voters. In important election campaigns, the legislative parties thus became parties in the electorate—another major manifestation of the modern party. The third manifestation—party as organization—was a temporary rather than sustained aspect, unlike the modern party.[7]

7. Jack P. Greene, "Interpretive Frameworks: The Quest for Intellectual Order in Early American History," *WMQ*, 3rd ser., XCVIII (1991), 526, 530, notes the importance of sequential models of development. Although taking no notice of partisanship, Alison G. Olson, "Eighteenth-Century Colonial Legislatures and their Constituents," *JAH*, LXXIX (1992–93), 543–67, notes the sequential development of several legislatures in responding to constituents. The best general discussion of types of parties, though it fails to include Third World one-party states, is Maurice Duverger, *Political Parties: Their Organization and Activity in the Modern State* (2nd ed.; New York, 1963), 45, 53, 61, 65, which makes European and American comparisons. Also see Giovanni Sartori, *Parties and Party Systems: A Framework for Analysis* (Cambridge, Eng., 1976), 27, 62–63. Jean Charlot, "Political Parties: Toward a New Theoretical Synthesis," *Political Studies*, XXXVII (1989), 352–61, summarizes recent theories concerning categorizing and analyzing parties. The tripartite characterization of parties used here—party as organization, party in the electorate, party in the legislature—is that of Frank J. Sorauf, "Political Parties and Political Analysis," in *American Party Systems*, ed. Chambers and Burnham, 37–39, 53. For the post-1790 period, David A. Bohmer, "The Maryland Electorate and the Concept of a Party System in the Early National Period," in *The History of American Electoral Behavior*, ed. Joel H. Silbey, Allan G. Bogue, and William H. Flanagan (Princeton, 1978), 146; Ronald P. Formisano, "Deferential-Participant Politics: The Early Republic's Political Culture, 1789–1840," *American Political Science Review*, LXVIII (1974), 474–75; and Paul Kleppner, *The Third Electoral System, 1853–1892:*

Middle-colony political leaders undertook much of this effort without publicity and without much mention in private letters. Politicking was sometimes embarrassing for them to acknowledge. These leaders relied on British ideas and examples to guide their practices, and from British thought and practice they drew ambivalent moral lessons about parties. No eighteenth-century British ministry viewed itself as derived from party. Party in opposition was a common mode of speech, but those in opposition to a ministry generally deprecated partisan activity.[8] Most British political thinkers believed parties improper or dangerous to the polity. They argued that permanent parties were a mistake; temporary alliances among good men were the proper means to effect reform. In this vein James Harrington criticized parties; his intellectual descendants, Bolingbroke and James Burgh, later agreed. The principal opposition publicists of the early 1720s, John Trenchard and Thomas Gordon, authors of "Cato's Letters," attacked the party mode of political behavior because parties or factions were all too readily manipulated by party leaders. They and their audience saw parties as artifacts or tools—unnatural to society. Designing men created two parties in order to rule them both at the same time.[9]

Parties, Voters, and Political Cultures (Chapel Hill, 1979), 13, apply Sorauf's categories. John F. Hoadley, *Origins of American Political Parties, 1789–1803* (Lexington, Ky., 1986), 17–18, sees party in the legislature, party in the electorate, and party as organization as stages of party development—polarization, expansion, and institutionalization. Lester G. Seligman, Michael R. King, Chong Lin Kim, and Roland E. Smith, *Patterns of Recruitment: A State Chooses Its Lawmakers* (Chicago, 1974), 454, finds that party organization in Pennsylvania and Oregon varied according to population density. Malcolm E. Jewell and Samuel C. Patterson, *The Legislative Process in the United States* (New York, 1966), 424–25.

8. J. C. D. Clark, "A General Theory of Party, Opposition, and Government, 1688–1832," *Historical Journal*, XXIII (1980), 296–97, 300–301, 317; Geoffrey Holmes, *British Politics in the Age of Anne* (New York, 1967), 410. Holmes (*ibid.*, 47) argues the British of the early eighteenth century had a "guilt complex" about parties.

9. For Harrington, J. R. Pole, *Political Representation in England and the Origins of the American Republic* (New York, 1966), 11. Bolingbroke's work on parties is *A Dissertation on Parties* (1734); Burgh's is *Political Disquisitions* (1775). Also see Sartori, *Parties and Party Systems*, 6–7. "Cato's Letters," Letter 16, Feb. 11, 1720, Letter 17, Feb. 18, 1720, in David L. Jacobson, ed., *The English Libertarian Heritage* (Indianapolis, 1965), 48, 53–54; H. T. Dickinson, *Liberty and Property: Political Ideology in Eighteenth Century*

A few British authors of the early eighteenth century gave favorable treatment to partisanship. Political writers John Toland, Walter Mayle, and Edward Spelman commented on the important aid that party divisions gave to free government. They believed that the partisan techniques and tactics of the opposition, despite its disclaimers of partisanship, were the only methods useful in attacking those who in its view were subverting the constitution. These authors were exceptions; doubts about the rectitude of party activity dominated British political views until the early nineteenth century.[10]

Inhabitants of the middle American colonies accepted the idea of partisanship earlier and more readily than did Britons or most other colonials. Their political ideas were closer to those of the later British radicals, who emphasized broad suffrage and strict limits on executive power. They saw the advantage of political organizations that would mobilize the populace and check the administration. Politicians of the time made infrequent but clearly evident pro-party comments, showing that they were not ashamed to be known as partisans. A 1738 declaration in the *Pennsylvania Gazette* that there is "no liberty without faction" was perhaps the strongest early public presentation of the idea. Benjamin Franklin in 1731, although believing that parties often broke apart because "each Member becomes intent upon his particular interest," saw nothing inherently harmful in parties and optimistically hoped for the organization of a "united party for Virtue." Twenty-five years later political parson William Smith, engaged in hot contention with Franklin and his allies, not surprisingly viewed parties as natural and necessary. The New York *Gazette* in 1734 saw parties as a needful check on one another, keeping the ambition of political contenders within bounds—a sentiment that resembles James Madison's view in *The Federalist* No. 51. William Livingston, writing in the *Independent Reflector* in 1753, believed parties were no danger to lib-

---

Britain (London, 1977), 180–81; and Caroline Robbins, "Discordant Parties: A Study of the Acceptance of Party by Englishmen," *Political Science Quarterly,* LXXIII (1958), 507–509.

10. Toland wrote in 1705, Mayle in 1726, and Spelman in 1743. Robbins, "Discordant Parties," 525–27. For general views on British party development, Michael Wallace, "Changing Concepts of Party in the United States: New York, 1815–1828," *AHR,* LXXIV (1968), 472; J. H. Plumb, *The Origins of Political Stability: England, 1675–1725* (Boston, 1965), 131; Paul Langford, *The Excise Crisis: Society and Politics in the Age of Walpole* (Oxford, 1975), 114–15; John Brewer, *Party Ideology and Popular Politics at the Accession of George III* (Cambridge, Eng., 1976), 14–15, 66–67.

erty but rather checked any "Combination of Roguery" among rulers. Peter Van Schaack of New York in 1769 propounded the necessity of parties as balancing forces.

> In a Constitution like that of Great Britain, there ever will be (I wish never to see the Day when their shall *not* be) Parties—the Bulk of the People will be divided & espouse one or other Side—from the very Temper of Man when he gets power he will be inclined to abuse it, especially when he is irritated by the Reflection of past Opposition—Hence the prevailing Party forgets a becoming Moderation—the unsuccessful Party on the contrary are little disposed to submit to any Exercise of Superiority even tho intended for their Benefit from a Set of People they hate: but while each Party continues formidable to the other & upon an equal Footing neither will dare to attempt because neither can oppress—.

The two principal political managers of Pennsylvania politics, Assembly party leader Joseph Galloway and his foe the Proprietary party boss Samuel Purviance, Jr., revealed how master politicians truly conceived of partisanship in 1766 when each, candidly writing to colleagues, separately described his political organization as "our Party." [11]

Deprecatory remarks about partisan behavior voiced in the middle colonies rarely evinced genuine concern about division in the body politic; more

---

11. *Pennsylvania Gazette* (Philadelphia), Mar. 21–30, 1737-8, quoted in Bailyn, *Origins of American Politics*, 127; Benjamin Franklin, *Autobiography*, ed. Leonard W. Labaree *et al.* (New Haven, 1964), 161; William Smith, *American Magazine and Monthly Chronicle for the British Colonies*, Oct., 1757, p. 34, quoted in George Dargo, "Parties and the Transformation of the Constitutional Idea in Revolutionary Pennsylvania," in *Party and Political Opposition in Revolutionary America*, ed. Bonomi, 101; New York *Gazette*, Mar. 11–18, 1733-4, quoted in Bailyn, *Origins of American Politics*, 126. Also see *ibid.*, 127–30, for other similar views of New Yorkers. James Graham to Robert Hunter Morris, July 10, 1735, in MP; William Livingston, "Of Party-Divisions," in *The Independent Reflector, or Weekly Essays on Sundry Important Subjects More Particularly Adapted to the Province of New York*, ed. Milton M. Klein (Cambridge, Mass., 1963), Feb. 22, 1753, 148; Peter Van Schaack to Henry Van Schaack, Jan. 27, 1769, in Hawks Manuscripts, NYHS, quoted by permission; Galloway to William Franklin, Sept. 13, 1766, in Franklin Papers, APS; Purviance to Ezra Stiles, Nov. 1, 1766, in Franklin B. Dexter, ed., *Extracts from the Itineraries and Other Miscellanies of Ezra Stiles, D.D., LL.D, 1755–1794, with a Selection from His Correspondence* (New Haven, 1916), 556.

frequently they expressed resentment toward contentious underlings daring to challenge authority or constituted one party's railings against the activities of another while conveniently forgetting that it was a kettle as black as the pot. Of the rarer sort, high-principled Pennsylvania Quakers are the chief example. These appear in the heated elections of 1742 and 1764 but are scattered and do not indicate widespread reprobation of partisanship.[12] Condemnations of party spirit were very often condemnations of the *other* party for allegedly subverting liberty while the "friends of the people" endeavored only to protect it. In Pennsylvania and New York political broadsides and newspaper articles warned about the other side's "immoderate Party-Zeal," claimed that their opponents were "more under the Government of Passion than Reason," and contrasted their side's "Spirit of Liberty" with the adversary's "Faction." When James Duane complained that "we are now run mad with Faction & Party," he was voicing his fears that his opponents were about to end his party's domination of New York City politics.[13] Governors and their associates roundly condemned any parties that animated the legislatures into contention against them but said nothing against parties that supported their side. Lewis Morris in 1740, while governor of New Jersey, denounced assemblymen for "Supporting and Uniting of a Party" rather than working for the public good. Cadwallader Colden, when acting governor of New York

12.   The Philadelphia Library Company spoke out in 1742, as reported by Dietmar Rothermund, *The Layman's Progress: Religion and Political Experience in Colonial Pennsylvania, 1740–1770* (Philadelphia, 1961), 59 n. 3. For antiparty sentiment among Quakers, Thomas Clifford to Mildred & Roberts, May 12, 1764, in Clifford Correspondence, HSP. Also William Logan to John Smith, [Sept., 1764?], in John Smith Correspondence, HSP. For a contrary view, Alan Tully, *William Penn's Legacy: Politics and Social Structure in Provincial Pennsylvania, 1726–1755* (Baltimore, 1978), 122, 139.

13.   *Pennsylvania Journal* (Philadelphia), Sept. 30, 1756; "Portius," untitled broadside (New York, 1732), 3; "Robt. Dissolution," *A Letter from a Gentleman in the Country to His Friend in Town* (New York, 1732); *A Letter to the Freemen and Freeholders of the Province of New-York, Relating to the Approaching Election of Their Representatives* (New York, 1750), 10; *An Answer to a Pamphlet, Entitled A Letter to the Freemen and Freeholders of the City of New York: Wherein Is Fully Shewn, the True Causes of the Defection of the Six Nations of Indians, with Some Historical Collections Never Yet Made Publick* (New York, 1752), 3–4; John Cruger, *To the Freeholders and Freemen, of the City and County of New-York* (New York, 1769); Duane to Robert Livingston, Jr., Feb. 19, 1770, in LP; here Duane criticized Alexander McDougall and his adherents. For a contrary view, Bonomi, *Factious People*, 12.

in 1770, castigated his adversaries as "the Party in the Assembly"; the other side was the "Friends of Government." Lewis' son Robert Hunter Morris excused his engagement in party contentions by explaining that it was only "in Opposition to a Faction." Despite the criticisms and disclaimers of the defeated or timid, middle-colony political leaders and voters took consciously partisan roles, just as they fully participated in religious and occupational groups.[14]

American, particularly middle-colony, partisanship was a well-marked descendant of British politics but at the same time an important variant, if not a new species, of political activity. The lines of descent are not completely understood, for Britain did not admit to parentage, and the colonies after 1776 did not claim an inheritance.[15] An Anglo-American political system existed only in bare outline. When colonial political life began, ideas and practices were borrowed or derived from the home country, but by the middle of the eighteenth century British and American partisan systems were on separate paths.

Parties in America were slower and more halting in their progress than those in Britain, but they developed into strong competing groups by the late eighteenth century, while during the same period British parties became less cohesive. Middle-colony partisanship evolved from less stable, narrow factionalism in the 1720s and 1730s. In the middle colonies in the early eighteenth century no great crises convulsed the people and sent them tumbling into the streets. It was, rather, when voters gradually repudiated narrow, self-interested elite leaders and coalesced around generally clear principles and positions on vital issues that they began to become partisans. In other colonies such development occurred as late as the aftermath of the Revolution.

Two circumstances—the method of electing representatives in Britain and

14. *N.J. Votes,* Apr. 16, 1740; Colden to the Earl of Hillsborough, Jan. 6, 1770, in Colden Letter Books, *NYHSC,* X, 200; Morris to Admiral Clinton, Jan. 10, 1754, in MP. William E. Gienapp, "'Politics Seems to Enter into Everything': Political Culture in the North, 1840–1860," in *Essays on American Ante-Bellum Politics, 1840–1860,* ed. Stephen E. Mazlish and John J. Kushna (College Station, 1982), 44, comments that "antiparty and antipolitical sentiments have been commonplace throughout American history."

15. Clarence L. Ver Steeg, *The Formative Years, 1607–1763* (New York, 1964), 253–54, asserts that "the political factions developing in the American colonies looked to the English party system as the example to imitate." As he notes, the actual connection between British and American partisanship "is somewhat intangible."

the colonies and colonial familiarity with British partisan practice—led colonial Americans to adapt some features of the British partisan model. The similarity of the electoral and legislative systems meant that the partisan systems of Britain and America would also be similar. Because legislators in Britain and America were elected by simple majority on a single ballot, Maurice Duverger's "sociological law" that such an electoral practice "favors the two-party system" and creates a "natural political dualism" appears to explain the shape of the party systems. Britain developed two national party organizations in the thirty years after the Exclusion Crisis of 1679–1681.[16] Dualism was sharp in early eighteenth-century British politics, despite the antiparty rhetoric and pose of political leaders and writers. Nearly every member of Parliament had a clearly marked political identity. In Commons, only one-eighth of the members voted against party views or party leaders. Parties cohered especially tightly in the election of the Speaker. Each party had its own coffee house and practiced "strict political segregation." Americans who involved themselves in shaping partisan groups in the first half of the eighteenth century knew about these rigid divisions. Middle-colony political leaders were not infrequently immigrants or persons who had spent time in Britain on business, for education, amusing themselves, or lobbying for place. Colonists also learned about British party politics from London news reports included in colonial newspapers and from British political pamphleteers.[17]

Middle-colony Americans adapted British party practices of the first fifteen years of the eighteenth century to their own conditions, refining and correcting them when the practices suited particularly American purposes. They

16. Duverger, *Political Parties,* 217, 215. This "law" does not seem to apply to the Canadian or to the contemporary British political systems. See David Sills, ed., *International Encyclopedia of the Social Sciences* (New York, 1968), s.v. "Party Systems," by Harry Eckstein. The origins and chronology of the British party systems are in Clark, "General Theory of Party," 296–97. Mark Kishlansky, "The Emergence of Adversary Politics in the Long Parliament," *Journal of Modern History,* XLIX (1977), 625–26, dates the beginnings of partisanship in the 1640s.

17. Duverger, *Political Parties,* 215–17. Clark, "General Theory of Party," 306; Holmes, *British Politics in the Age of Anne,* 22, 34, 40–41; B. W. Hill, *The Growth of Parliamentary Parties, 1689–1742* (London, 1976), 24–25, 211; Brewer, *Party Ideology and Popular Politics,* 149. Isaac Norris, Sr., noted to James Logan, Nov. 11, 1707, in Edward Armstrong and Deborah Logan, eds., *Correspondence Between William Penn and James Logan, Secretary of the Province of Pennsylvania, and Others, 1700–1750* (2 vols.; Philadelphia, 1870–72), II, 250–51, the great excitement in London concerning parliamentary politics.

found electoral corruption distasteful. Especially dismaying was the political manipulation *à la* Walpole. Young John Dickinson was appalled by the bribery and jobbery of the parliamentary election of 1754, colonial newspaper pieces criticized rotten-borough abuses, and Benjamin Franklin took considerable pains to criticize corrupt practices for his correspondents.[18] Middle-colony Americans were inspired by British reformers who opposed corruption to try to eliminate it from their elections. Although no middle colony halted every corrupt practice, middle-colony elections were by the 1730s much more often the expression of voters' views rather than dominated by a few leading officials.

Nor did the colonists quickly copy Britain's polarized political divisions. They did not adopt the basic party names of Whig and Tory. No group was ever called Tories until 1774; the term *Whig* was employed rarely and ambiguously until the 1770s, when it came to mean an advocate of American rights. Whig and Tory could not be used by colonial parties because they did not refer to internal colonial issues. Tories were closely identified with High Anglicanism in Britain, a religious view probably not extant in the colonies, so the term was not relevant. The terms *Whig* and *dissenter* were linked in England; consequently, the name *Whig* would signify little in colonial America, where so many were dissenters.[19]

Only occasionally did middle colonials employ the informal partisan terms *court* and *country* because they understood these as meaningful designations that in some respects could be attached to both American and British political systems. The terms described attitudes toward government, not parties. Middle-colony political leaders to some extent accepted the term *Country*

18. Milton E. Flower, *John Dickinson, Conservative Revolutionary* (Charlottesville, 1983), 19; *Pennsylvania Gazette* (Philadelphia), Apr. 30, 1772; Franklin to Joseph Galloway, Mar. 13, 1768, Feb. 25, 1775, in Labaree *et al.*, eds., *Franklin Papers*, XV, 79–80; XXI, 509. J. C. D. Clark, *The Dynamics of Change: The Crisis of the 1750s and English Party Systems* (Cambridge, Eng., 1982), 8–9, offers a description of the characteristics of British politics with which many colonials would have concurred: "behind the scenes intrigues," "maneuvers," "pursuit of power."

19. Plumb, *Origins of Political Stability: England*, 131, and other authors divide the Whigs and Tories into Court and Country groups. Holmes, *British Politics in the Age of Anne*, 121–22, 222, 249–51, 253–59, 270, 279–80, discusses Court Whigs, Country Whigs, Country Tories, Court Tories, high Tories, Jacobites, and Hanoverian Tories. Reed Browning, *Political and Constitutional Ideas of the Court Whigs* (Baton Rouge, 1982), 12–20, classifies only five groups.

party as identifying their general partisan viewpoint. They related the ideas of the British Country party or parties, as they understood them, to the American situation.[20] They generally saw themselves closest to the Country or "real" Whigs, the opposition group during the Walpole ministry. The basic tenets of this group were fair and direct representation and elimination of corruption. Landholders would govern. The independence of the virtuous gentleman landholder would preserve the constitution. Triennial elections would ensure more direct contact between representative and constituent. Place acts would restrain the corruption of patronage. Honest, noncoercive elections, the secret ballot, and the elimination of pocket and rotten boroughs would guarantee direct, actual representation. Constituents would instruct their representatives, and the representatives should be responsive to those instructions.[21] Americans in the middle colonies agreed with many, though not all, of these reforms. Some were instituted in the early period of colonial founding, some were sought over the course of the eighteenth century and occasionally achieved, and others, particularly antiparty implications of the term *Country*, were ignored in some colonies.

American politics included something resembling a court, for in many of the colonies there existed what was sometimes termed a set of courtiers—the small group that surrounded the governor and provided his political support. Lacking extensive patronage and a true aristocratic base, it could hardly approximate the political might of the British court. Although the term *Court party* was hung on the middle-colony courtier group by its opponents, it was not of itself a party and could not attract supporters using that name.[22] The

20. Governor Robert Hunter to the Lords of Trade, May 7, 1711, in *NJA*, IV, 59, referred to one New Jersey political group as the "country party" and its opponents as the "other party." James Alexander of New York to Cadwallader Colden, Apr. 6, 1739, in *NYHSC*, LI, 194, termed his side the "country party." Tully, "Quaker Party and Proprietary Politics," 104, notes that the Quaker party of Pennsylvania had both court and country characteristics.

21. Bailyn, *Origins of American Politics*, 52–58; J. G. A. Pocock, *The Machiavellian Moment: Florentine Political Thought and the Atlantic Republican Tradition* (Princeton, 1975), 506–509; Pocock, *Politics, Language, and Time: Essays on Political Thought and History* (New York, 1971), 133–35; Dickinson, *Liberty and Property*, 104, 111–117, 173–74, 183–84, 188–91; Holmes, *British Politics in the Age of Anne*, 129, 132–33; Brewer, *Party Ideology and Popular Politics*, 206; Pole, *Political Representation in England*, 404–406.

22. Aaron Leaming, a New Jersey assemblyman, castigated courtiers in his Diary, Mar. 28, 1761, in HSP. James Logan told William Penn, Oct. 3, 1704, in Armstrong and

group often wisely attempted to appeal to a larger constituency by de-emphasizing its interest in place and patronage and by taking a principled stand in support of prerogative, or of impartial economic policies, or of common defense. Such political strategy frequently won adherents.

Because the sources of support for middle-colony parties were not analogous to those in Britain and because the party programs differed from their British counterparts, the term *Court* and *Country* are not appropriate. Possible alternates, employed by some political historians, are *center* or *core* and *periphery*. These seem unsatisfactory because they do not clearly connote partisan goals or functions. Jack P. Greene notes that the terms indicate respectively "the dominant (and usually older) areas and subordinate (and usually newer) areas." Greene's characterizations are one-dimensional. Dominance in the legislatures shifted among parties; those without executive power did not regard themselves as outsiders but sometimes saw themselves as central and their opponents as the interlopers. Opposing partisans in the middle colonies were often neighbors. Both the urban centers and the up-country areas were politically divided. Partisan differentiation among regions was based on other characteristics, not merely date of settlement.[23]

On occasion middle-colony partisan groups adopted or responded to labels; often they avoided using them. This book will employ the names that the groups called themselves, or that described their supporters, or that iden-

---

Logan, eds., *Penn-Logan Correspondence,* I, 323, that his supporters on the Pennsylvania Council "are looked on as ill here as the Court party at home." Works that use the "court-country" terminology include James K. Martin, *Men in Rebellion: Higher Governmental Leaders and the Coming of the American Revolution* (New Brunswick, 1973), 25; Eugene R. Sheridan, *Lewis Morris, 1671–1746: A Study in Early American Politics* (Syracuse, 1981), 121, 158, 185; and John M. Murrin, "The Great Inversion, or Court Versus Country: A Comparison of the Revolutionary Settlements in England (1688–1721) and America (1776–1816)," in *Three British Revolutions, 1641, 1688, 1776,* ed. J. G. A. Pocock (Princeton, 1980), 384–85.

23. Jack P. Greene, *Peripheries and Center: Constitutional Development in the Extended Politics of the British Empire and the United States, 1607–1783* (Athens, Ga., 1986), ix. Ronald P. Formisano, *The Transformation of Political Culture: Massachusetts Politics, 1790s–1840s* (New York, 1983), 5–7, 149–54, applies "center" and "periphery" to state politics in the early national period. Thomas E. Jeffrey, *State Parties and National Politics: North Carolina, 1815–1861* (Athens, Ga., 1989), 160, sees the urban Whigs as the periphery party and the country Democrats as the core in this state.

tified their main programs, or that were based on the names of the chief leaders of the group. For example, the terms *Proprietary party*, or *Country party*, or *DeLanceys*, or *contrary party* have been commonly used in historical studies and by contemporaries, even though the description or family name might not precisely reflect the features of the partisan group. Because they were employed in middle-colony politics and are reasonably precise descriptors, they and other similar ones will be applied in this book. The most accurate and useful terms appear to be *administration*—denoting support generally for executive power, for the council, for the civil list, and for full compliance with imperial demands—and *opposition*—denoting curtailment of the power of governor and council, the control of appropriated money, the taxing of the great landholders more heavily, and the maintenance of the privileges of religious minorities.

The absence of general party names illustrates that middle-colony inhabitants did not feel the same partisan spirit that prevailed in early eighteenth-century England. Party spirit grew slowly, developing in three particular stages. First came the emergence of a competitive party system from weaker and narrower groups; this is outlined in Chapter 1. Chapter 2 explores the ideological and social bases of partisanship. The influence of adherence to political principles, support of economic interests, and affiliation with cultural, regional, and economic groups will be evaluated. The next chapters trace successive political realignments that occurred almost simultaneously in each of the colonies. Such issues as defense, finance, and imperial policy fostered these realignments. The last chapter analyzes how the political groups were either destroyed or greatly reshaped by the tremendous crisis caused by the separation of the empire and what they contributed to the future development of partisanship in the United States.

1

From Factionalism to Partisanship, 1700–1737

In the middle colonies in 1700 partisanship meant combats between ephemeral and narrow factions. By 1735–1739 political organizations that closely resembled modern political parties were operating in the legislatures and beginning to draw the support of groups in the electorate. These parties developed in stages. Out of rudimentary groupings came clearly marked factions in all three middle colonies. From the late 1720s to the mid-1730s these factions refined their political practices and developed into broader, more structured, and more influential political groups.

From the beginning of settlement in the middle colonies through the first twenty years or so of the eighteenth century, all political divisions were factional. Political leaders were self-aggrandizing, changed sides readily, and were mainly concerned with obtaining office. Their small groups of followers pursued only narrow or temporary interests such as ousting a bad governor; they employed trickery or fraud in elections; they enunciated little ideological commitment; and they had no endurance but rapidly waned.

Faction leaders were sometimes very able, but their major qualification was, according to William Penn, an "excess of vanity." This quality attracted the small groups they dominated but few others. Lewis Morris of New York and New Jersey was resilient, determined, and imperious. Other factional leaders of New Jersey claimed no particular talent, for, according to one, "the people of this province being a Rebellious people I do think and I always thought it was an easy thing to raise a party amongst them against the Government." David Lloyd of Pennsylvania was litigious to a fault. His colleague William Biles of Bucks County possessed a confrontational and berating style of dealing with proprietary governors that was popular with his constituents. Leaders and members of factional groups shifted direction almost as often as the wind. From the beginnings of the government in Pennsylvania, some Quakers changed from the proprietary side to the opposition, as their particular interests dictated. Several of the great families of New York also shifted factional position without strong cause. The three principal "landed" leaders—Livingston, Morris, and Colden—were not party managers but allies of convenience.[1]

1. William Penn to Roger Mompesson, Feb. 17, 1704-5, in Edward Armstrong and Deborah Logan, eds., *Correspondence Between William Penn and James Logan, Secretary of the Province of*

The elite factional leaders practiced varieties of political chicanery. Mostly they manipulated elections. The New York City elections of 1698 and 1701, though fervently fought, were blatantly rigged. Women, servants, and minors voted, not in class protest but because they were induced to do so by candidates and permitted to by corrupt officials. In 1695, to ensure victory for his candidates, Governor Benjamin Fletcher sent British soldiers with bayonets and sailors with clubs to the polls. The voters quickly fled. Seven years later Governor Lord Cornbury called out the garrison for the same purpose. In Pennsylvania, political leaders either attempted to deny the vote to certain segments of the electorate or to rig the balloting. In 1696 the new frame of government raised property qualifications to exclude most immigrants, who were not Quakers. Isaac Norris, Sr., of Pennsylvania reported to James Logan how his allies swept the 1710 assembly election: "the use of tickets is managed" by the election inspectors, therefore "a man cannot take or reject less than the whole." New Jersey suffered the most factional election manipulation of this early period. The sheriff of Middlesex refused to take a poll at the Amboy contest in 1703, and at the Burlington county election of 1706 the sheriff refused the votes of Quakers. In both instances they cheated the rightful victors out of election. In 1708, to prevent an opposition from organizing, Governor Lord Cornbury did not provide due notice of the election. Governor Robert Hunter attempted to control the 1711 election by appointing cooperative magistrates and sheriffs. The Middlesex sheriff engineered a victory for his candidates in 1713. The Amboy marshal stopped the 1722 election, in which both sides allegedly used floating and ineligible voters. Because his votes were not fairly counted, the ordinary inhabitant at times made little effort to come to the polls. In 1711 Salem County voters complained that the wrong candidate was chosen, "many of us being Neglidgent in the last Election." [2]

Pennsylvania, and Others, 1700–1750 (2 vols.; Philadelphia, 1870–72), I, 374, Sheridan, *Lewis Morris*, 94–121; Journal of the Governor and Council, Mar. 25, 1721, in *NJA*, XIV, 151–52; James Logan to William Penn, Oct. 3, 1704, Oct. 2, 1702, Nov. 22, 1704, Feb. 12, 1704-5, Dec. 1, 1702, July 25, 1706, Aug. 10, 1706, Penn to Logan, Sept. 8, 1701, all in Armstrong and Logan, eds., *Penn-Logan Correspondence*, I, 323, 139, 344, 362, 150–51, II, 138, 147, I, 54; Kammen, *Colonial New York*, 141–42.

2. More than the known number of male taxpayers voted in the New York City 1701 election (Nash, *Urban Crucible*, 88–91). For the 1695 election, Grievances at New York for Primo September 1692 to 31 October 1695, in *DCHNY*, IV, 218. For the 1702 election, John M. Murrin, "English Rights as Ethnic Aggression: The English Conquest, the Charter of Liberties of 1683,

Legislative expulsion was another device faction leaders employed whole-sale in New York and New Jersey in this period. Two members suffered ex-pulsion from the New Jersey House in 1711 and nine were thrust out in 1716. This latter was their reward for attempting another factional trick—absent-ing themselves to prevent a quorum. New York legislators also expelled their rivals frequently.[3]

In none of the middle colonies did the factions endure; rather, they faded out in the period from 1717 to 1723. By 1717 Governor Robert Hunter of New York found "perfect harmony reigning among all parties," and when he de-parted in 1719 the colony appeared at political peace. James Alexander re-ported in 1722 that "Opposition is So very much Diminished that that [mer-chant] Party can Scarcely carry four Votes in the Assembly Even with the addition of Mr. Philipse to that body."[4] After 1720 New Jersey factionalism also had spent its weak force. James Alexander told Robert Hunter in 1722 that "I believe [there] never was less division or disquiet in Jersey." In 1725 Gover-nor William Burnet reported "the most unanimity that I ever knew." In this period New Jersey, like New York, had experienced a rise and decline of fac-tional infighting among elites, not party politics.[5] In Pennsylvania from

---

and Leisler's Rebellion in New York," in *Authority and Resistance in Early New York*, ed. William Pen-cak and Conrad Edick Wright (New York, 1988), 94, n. 98. Gary B. Nash, *Quakers and Politics: Pennsylvania, 1681–1726* (Princeton, 1968), 207; Isaac Norris to Logan, Aug. 29, 1710, in Arm-strong and Logan, eds., *Penn-Logan Correspondence*, II, 427; Robert Quary to the Lords of Trade, Dec. 20, 1703, in *NJA*, III, 14–15; Affidavit of George Ingoldsby, July 16, 1706, *NJA*, III, 153; William Slope, Memorial to the Board of Trade, Feb. 14, 1705-6, in *NJA*, III, 135; Petition of Middlesex County, [Dec. 1713], in *NJA*, IV, 186–89; Alexander to Hunter, [Oct. 1722?], in *NJA*, V, 58–62; Address from Salem Inhabitants to Governor Hunter, May 25, 1711, in *NJA*, IV, 113.

3. [?] to William Dockwra, [1711], in *NJA*, IV, 125–26; Governor Hunter to the Lords of Trade, June 16, 1716, in *NJA*, IV, 256–57; J. M. Sosin, *English America and Imperial Inconstancy: The Rise of Provincial Autonomy, 1696–1715* (Lincoln, 1985), 214–29.

4. Hunter to Secretary William Popple, Nov. 22, 1717, in *DCHNY*, 493; Alexander to Robert Hunter, [Oct., 1722?], in *NJA*, V, 56. Bonomi, *Factious People*, 75–76, 82–87, ably summarizes Hunter's contributions and notes the decline of New York City opposition in this period. For Morris' role, Sheridan, *Lewis Morris*, 94–121. Lawrence H. Leder, *Robert Livingston, 1654–1728, and the Politics of Colonial New York* (Chapel Hill, 1961), 241–46.

5. Alexander to Hunter, May 5, 1722, in *NJA*, V, 63; Burnet to the Lords of Trade, Nov. 24, 1725, in *NJA*, V, 104. Thomas L. Purvis, "'High-Born, Long-Recorded Families': Social Origins of New Jersey Assemblymen, 1703 to 1776," *WMQ*, 3rd ser., XXXVII (1980), 608–609, argues that New Jersey was becoming less democratic in the royal period, with fewer elections and higher property qualifications. He reflects the view of Jack P. Greene, "The Growth of Political Stabil-ity: An Interpretation of Political Development in the Anglo-American Colonies, 1660–1760,"

1710 to the early 1720s factional contentions largely disappeared as the leaders left the House to pursue other interests. Anglicans raised only desultory opposition. In the years 1717 to 1721 James Logan could find no factional activity. For the two decades after 1700, factions cycled from disruption to quiescence, providing no direction to politics.[6]

Although these early middle-colony political groups were no more than factions, they used some of the same techniques, albeit rudimentary ones, that are often associated with parties. Daniel Coxe, West Jersey Anglican and chief factional leader, won election in 1715 using a modern approach. He appealed to those "link'd to him by land purchases" and brought an "inundation of Swedes" to the polls. But Coxe, on finding his allies unable to control the legislature, quickly reverted to the factional tactic of preventing a quorum. New York City factions employed patronage, had platforms and a fairly consistent ideology, set up prearranged tickets, and issued pamphlets to attract voters. But their election management tactics and their short duration indicate that they were not parties. They were primarily interest groups and family alliances.[7]

Middle-colony factions in the period before 1725 declined because they served only narrow interests affecting small groups, had shallow popular bases, practiced electoral corruption, and lacked ideological consistency. A narrow elite based on family connections was not adequate for, or competent to manage, a political system of growing size and greater economic and social complexity. The voters were not content with electoral manipulation and chicanery, with bribing the sheriff or rigging the poll. After 1725 the political groups in the middle colonies changed character, becoming factions in transition to parties. They still lacked strong organizational structure and were

in *The American Revolution: A Heritage of Change*, ed. John Parker and Carol Urness (Minneapolis, 1975), 48, that the colonies in this period generally experienced a "contraction in the role of the electorate." Richard P. McCormick, *The History of Voting in New Jersey: A Study in the Development of Election Machinery* (New Brunswick, 1953), 33, 38–40, 62–63, asserts that electoral participation was small in the proprietary period before 1702, that Governor Cornbury intervened in elections, that after 1709 in practice a liberal freehold suffrage requirement opened up elections, and that the highest turnouts in colonial New Jersey were later in the royal period.

6. Nash, *Quakers and Politics*, 328–33; Joseph E. Illick, *Colonial Pennsylvania: A History* (New York, 1976), 94–96; Sosin, *English America and Imperial Inconstancy*, 129.

7. Hunter to the Lords of Trade, Mar. 28, May 12, 1715, in *NJA*, IV, 207, 210; Stanley N. Katz, *Newcastle's New York: Anglo-American Politics, 1732–1753* (Cambridge, Mass., 1968), 39; Bonomi, *Factious People*, 13.

generally dependent on the personal magnetism of particular leaders. These leaders now learned new techniques, developed more honest and popularly acceptable means of winning assembly votes and elections, and incorporated more of the provincial elite and the diverse interest groups into their political activity.

Pennsylvania was the first of the middle colonies in this period to move from an elemental factionalism to a stage in which transitional factions began to behave like parties. The first perceptible shift from the placidity of the period since 1710 was the singularly large turnover of assemblymen in the election of 1723. David Lloyd returned to the House after a five-year absence. Joining him were five others from Chester County, four from Bucks, and three from Philadelphia, all of whom were new to the House. This turnover was the largest the assembly experienced in any one election from 1710 to 1776. Lloyd and William Biles, Jr., served as Speakers in the 1720s, but their faction was not merely renewing an ancient quarrel. The old Lloyd group and the new members were now pursuing a new, popular policy: supplying Pennsylvania with paper money. A loan officer, instituted in May, 1723, had aroused the ire of some Philadelphia merchants and agents of the Penn family. These interests, fearing for their debts, condemned paper money as a device by which the poor, suffering as a result of their own sloth, extravagance, and viciousness, would plunder the diligent and provident. These denunciations had the unintended effect of rallying the political supporters of paper bills of credit to ally with others in what looked very much like a political party.[8]

The supporters of paper money soon tied their cause to that of the renegade governor Sir William Keith. Keith, taking advantage of the confused state of proprietary authority, planned to recoup his fortunes by becoming royal governor of Pennsylvania and gaining control over land sales. It is likely that most of the new members elected in 1723 were favorably disposed toward Keith, who agreed with the House on paper money issues. The Keith party included "abt. four or five sycophant creatures that he had modelled to

8. There were twelve new assemblymen (46.2 percent), three with prior service (11.5 percent), and eleven incumbents (42.3 percent) (*Pa. Votes, passim,* for the assembly rosters of each year). Tully, *William Penn's Legacy,* 181–82; Jack P. Greene, "Legislative Turnover in British America, 1696 to 1775: A Quantitative Analysis," *WMQ,* 3rd ser., XXXVIII (1981), 446–47; James Logan, *The Charge Delivered from the Bench to the Grand Jury, at the Court of Quarter Sessions, Held for the County of Philadelphia, the Second Day of September 1723* (Philadelphia, 1723), 10–11. Logan to Joshua Gee, Oct. 8, 1724, in Logan Papers, HSP, criticized the continued issue of paper money, which would "in a little time sink the whole to almost nothing."

his own heart" in the Philadelphia delegation in the House. The two assemblymen from Philadelphia city, or burgesses as they were called, appear to have been elected in an Anglican middle-class reaction against rich Quaker merchants, who were their predecessors before 1722.[9] Keith and his assembly cohorts in 1724 took the offensive in the controversy, denouncing the proprietary instructions to the governor that attempted to prevent paper money issues by requiring Keith to get the consent of his council to such legislation. Playing on the stubbornness and intransigence of proprietary agent James Logan and the rich merchants who opposed paper money, the governor and assembly made the economic controversy about paper money into a constitutional one: arbitrary proprietors against the people. They calculated correctly that such a transformation, an incorporation of clear ideological principle, would broaden the appeal of their side.[10]

Keith's major political innovations and achievements were in mustering the populace. Borrowing the tactics used in British boroughs such as Westminster, he and his supporters organized political clubs to contest elections. One club was for the elite, though opponents characterized the members as debtors; the other was the Tiff Club for artisans. For James Logan, such a strategy was proof that "there are no arts to which he does not stoop in order to ingratiate himself with the Common People." In the Tiff Club the "Common People" had some power, for both clubs were involved in the selection of assembly candidates. Very likely the Tiff Club was responsible for the riotous aftermath of the 1726 election in Philadelphia, when the stocks, pillory, and, probably accidentally, some butchers' stalls were burned; James Logan was mobbed; and his house was attacked. The political organizations appear to have remained active only through the 1727 Philadelphia election.[11] Violence likely damaged the reputation of the clubs and led to their decline; clubs would return again to Pennsylvania politics in the 1760s.

9. Thomas Wendel, "The Keith-Lloyd Alliance: Factional and Coalition Politics in Colonial Pennsylvania," *PMHB*, XCII (1968), 295–96, 298. The five Keithians were almost certainly John Kearsley and Thomas Tress, Anglican burgesses of the city, and county members John Swift, Job Goodson, and Francis Rawle, who originated the 1722 proposal for a loan office. Swift was a Baptist, the other two were Quakers. Rawle and Swift were longtime Lloyd supporters. Jeremiah Langhorne to Andrew Hamilton and Clement Plumsted, Feb. 10, 1724–5, in Society Collection, HSP; Nash, *Quakers and Politics*, 298–300.

10. *Pa. Votes,* Jan. 15, Feb. 6, 9, 1724–5; Roy N. Lokken, *David Lloyd: Colonial Lawmaker* (Seattle, 1959), 212.

11. James Logan to Joshua Gee, June 5, 1725, in Logan Papers, HSP. On British clubs, Hill, *Growth of Parliamentary Parties*, 71. Logan, in *Advice and Information to the Freeholders and Freemen of*

Keith as well made a special ethnic appeal to the Pennsylvania Germans. His effort to settle German Palatines on Indian land was part of his campaign among that group. He also cultivated the support of a German merchant, Ludovick Christian Sprogle, of unsavory reputation but popular enough to serve three terms in the House as a Keith ally.[12] The wily governor, more familiar with the techniques of British politics than were most colonials, was one of the first in the middle colonies to envision how a multi-interest and culturally pluralistic political group might be formed.

The tactic that the anti-Keith, anti-paper-money, proprietary supporters believed that they knew and could wield best was propaganda. James Logan, Isaac Norris, Sr., and others of that group thought that superior arguments, coming from superior people, would overawe assemblymen and constituents and squelch all support for Keith. This was mistaken strategy because it encouraged Keith and Lloyd to address their propaganda to the generality. The debate in the pamphlet war at first concerned the constitutional issue of the power of the assembly and the impotence of the council but during 1725 shifted to a concern with the political roles of economic groups. As one of the pamphlets written by the proprietary side put it, *The Conspiracy of Catiline* was again afoot; it alleged that "the Views of *Plebians, however elevated above their own Dirt* by accidental promotions, are *sordid* and *grasping*, and the Rule of their Proceedings is always to grasp at other Men's Properties to swell their own Fortunes higher."[13] Lloyd, replying to Logan's claim that councillors deserved to possess real authority because of their social and economic status, asserted that "a mean Man, of small Interest, devoted to the faithful dis-

---

the *Province of Pennsylvania* (Philadelphia, 1727), 3, accused Keithians of bringing unqualified voters to the polls—a familiar plaint of an elite opposition. Wendel, "Keith-Lloyd Alliance," 299–300, 305, cites Franklin's *The Busy-Body No. 4* in concluding the clubs were defunct after 1728. Also see Nash, *Quakers and Politics,* 334; Nash, *Urban Crucible,* 152.

12. Isaac Norris, Sr., to John and Thomas Penn, Nov. 15, 1731, in TPP. James Logan to John Penn, Oct. 22, 1727, in Logan Papers, HSP, accused Sprogle and his brother of cheating the German Frankford (Frankfurt) Company out of its land grant. Samuel Powell, Jr., told Thomas Hyam, July 1, 1727, in Samuel Powell Letter Book, HSP, that Sprogle would not pay debts and was dishonest. Also see Nash, *Urban Crucible,* 151–54.

13. "Brutus," *The Conspiracy of Catiline; Recommended to the Serious Consideration of the Authors of Advice and Information to the Freeholders and Freemen of the Province of Pennsylvania: And Further Information, Dated October 2, 1727* (Philadelphia, 1727), 2. Andrew Hamilton, "Narrative," *Memoirs of the Historical Society of Pennsylvania,* Vol. 2, Pt. 2, p. 37, also claimed that the poor of the colony were out to plunder the rich.

charge of his Trust and Duty to the Government, may do more good to the State, than a Richer or more Learned Man, who by his ill Temper and aspiring Mind becomes an opposer of the Constitution by which he should act." [14] Even though Keith made appeals to the lower orders, his rhetoric was cautious; it was not calculated to stir the mob to the destruction of provincial or private property. Keith in a 1726 pamphlet pleaded merely for equal treatment of high and low by the government. Programs favoring equality of treatment and curtailing the power of a small, selfish interest resembled the "real" or "independent" Whig views that were gaining currency in Britain a few years before these Pennsylvania debates. The *Independent Whig* and "Cato's Letters" of John Trenchard and Thomas Gordon, published in Britain in 1720–1723, were known to and probably sources for the antiproprietary pro-paper-money partisans. [15]

Neither Pennsylvania partisan group assumed a clear party label. The term *Keithian*, although used, was inconvenient because the label also referred to an earlier group of Quaker schismatics. Nor did the label *proprietary* reflect all the purposes of the other side, though it fit better. The elite leaders and the members of the clubs understood what they had in common but did not have in mind or see the need for a popular, all-embracing term or slogan that would describe their group. The difficulty of the Pennsylvania propagandists in finding suitable labels should not be surprising, for modern American party labels are not descriptive but traditional.

The elections in Pennsylvania in 1726 and the two following years were far

14. Logan began the barrage of propaganda with his *Charge to the Grand Jury* of 1723, condemning paper money; he continued with *A Memorial from James Logan, in Behalf of the Proprietary's Family, and of Himself, Servant to the Said Family* (Philadelphia, 1725), which attempted to answer Keith's and the assembly's attacks on the council and the proprietary instructions. Lloyd's quoted answer is from *A Vindication of the Legislative Power* (Philadelphia, 1725), 3. This and other pamphlets by Logan, Keith, and Lloyd of 1725 are identified and summarized in Lokken, *David Logan*, 214–24. Important propaganda pieces of 1726 and 1727 are noted in Wendell, "Keith-Lloyd Alliance," 300, n. 44.

15. [Sir William Keith], *The Observator's Trip to America* (Philadelphia, 1726). Franklin's employer Samuel Keimer reprinted numbers 1–53 (1720–1721) of the *Independent Whig* in 1724. For propaganda by Keithians, [John Kearsley?], *A Letter from a Gentleman in Philadelphia to His Friends in Bucks* (Philadelphia, 1728), and Edward Horne *et al.*, *A Defence of the Legislative Constitution of the Province of Pennsylvania as It Now stands Confirmed and Established by Law and Charter* (Philadelphia, 1728). Ronald Schultz, "The Small-Producer Tradition and Artisan Radicalism in Philadelphia, 1720–1810," *Past and Present*, CXXVII (1990), 96–98, emphasizes the rhetoric of class conflict in the election propaganda of 1725–1729.

different from previous political events in the province. In 1726 Keith's clubs got out the vote for their leader, now ousted as governor and seeking an assembly seat, and for his allies in the Lloyd–paper money group. Keith led a parade of gentlemen on horseback and the leather-apron Tiff Club on foot through the city to rouse voters of all ranks. The victory celebration, in which the demonstrators burned stocks and pillory and attacked James Logan, made the proprietary group determined to counter the "most unhappy Wicked Party" by organizing its own election machinery. In 1727 it tried to bring the electorate in from Philadelphia County outside the city. But it found only fair weather supporters; heavy rain prevented or discouraged voters from coming to the polls. In 1728 the two sides attempted other means of persuading the Philadelphia electorate. They adopted an extensive practice of British elections, treating the voters. The thirsty electorate imbibed some forty-five hundred gallons of free beer, courtesy of the candidates and their backers. The elite also employed its position and resources to intimidate voters, according to an election broadside of 1728. It related that one of the "*Great Men* (as they are now called) came into our Neighborhood last Week, and told Us he had been all over the county" soliciting votes, but "many of Us were afraid to speak our Minds freely to him, because he threatened to sue some of Us, if we did not agree to what he proposed and told Us that others in Town would do the same." Pennsylvania political leaders, now more organized and more ideological, were also becoming supplicatory, ingratiating, and threatening.[16]

Despite the introduction of new election techniques, the factions were flawed and immature. The antiproprietary opposition came unraveled when Keith unsuccessfully contested with Lloyd for the speakership of the assembly in 1726 and 1727. Keith's scheme to convulse proprietary Pennsylvania and present himself to Britain as the prime candidate for royal governor was too self-serving for many of his allies. Early in 1728 the mercurial politico sailed back to London, abandoning the political faction he had helped to or-

16. James Logan to John, Thomas, and Richard Penn, July 29, 1728, in Logan Papers, HSP. Logan to John Penn, Oct. 27, 1727, *ibid.*, for the election of that year. On the 1728 election treating, Carl Bridenbaugh, *Cities in the Wilderness: The First Century of Urban Life in America* (1938; rpr. New York, 1964), 431; James H. Hutson, *Pennsylvania Politics, 1746–1770: The Movement for Royal Government and Its Consequences* (Princeton, 1972), 151; Milton M. Klein, "Corruption in Colonial America," *South Atlantic Quarterly*, LXXVIII (1979), 67. On intimidation, "Timothy Telltruth," *To Morris Morris, On the Reasons Published for His Conduct in Assembly, in the Year 1728* (Philadelphia, 1728), 1.

ganize.[17] The group stayed very much alive for another year. A cry for more than doubling the paper money supply became the single issue of the election of 1728, pushing the broader constitutional issues raised by Keith and Lloyd into the background. In the Philadelphia contest of that year seven of eight incumbents, all supporters of Keith and paper money, were reelected.

A strong proprietary faction rose up after 1728 and outmaneuvered the Keith-Lloyd faction. Proprietary supporters and merchants organized it to counter the threat of popular violence against opponents of paper money. In April, 1729, James Logan reported that "about 200 Countrymen had agreed to come to this town with Clubs, and with such of the place as would joyn them of whom they might have had large numbers, to apply first to the Assembly and then storm the Governor, but with the Council at least some of them it was to have gone the hardest." Andrew Hamilton, a Philadelphia lawyer, who was elected assemblyman from Bucks County in 1727 by proprietary management, understood better than did Logan or the Lloyd group the need for compromise: "to make the people easy about paper money (wherein they seem to be mad) without giving offence to the proprietors family." The assembly retreated from a demand for a £50,000 issue to a more moderate £30,000. Governor Patrick Gordon agreed to this in April, 1729.[18]

The principal result of the settlement of 1729 was the increased popularity and cohesion of Hamilton's proprietary faction. Although its leaders would never admit its partisan nature, the proprietary side in the 1730s was making a more determined transition from a faction to an organization that resembled a party than was the antiproprietary group. What gave this group an advantage over its rival and made it more like a party was that its leaders were important county magnates, united by ideological commitment despite their religious diversities. Hamilton and Quaker Jeremiah Langhorne captured Bucks County by 1730. At least four other assemblymen from that district, out of eight, stood with them. With the aid of Anglican William Moore of Chester County the proprietary side made some inroads there. James Hamilton, Andrew's son, represented Lancaster and strengthened proprietary influence among Scotch-Irish voters. Wealthy Presbyterian merchant William Allen led a small Philadelphia contingent. The proprietary side could count on

17. Logan to John Penn, Oct. 27, 1727, in Logan Papers, HSP; *Pa. Votes*, Aug. 9, 1728; Lokken, *David Lloyd*, 228.

18. Logan to John, Thomas, and Richard Penn, Apr. 29, 1729, Hamilton to David Barclay, Oct. 27, 1728, copy, all in TPP; *Pa. Votes*, Aug. 15, 1728, Jan. 1, 1728–9, May 10, 1729; Lokken, *David Lloyd*, 233–34.

about thirteen or fourteen supporters in the House and about five neutrals who did not interfere.[19]

Meanwhile, Lloyd's retirement in 1729 weakened the antiproprietary group; it lost its former clear majority in the House and now held two or three fewer seats than its rival. It remained strong in Philadelphia; four of its five key members were based there. New representatives from Philadelphia—John Kinsey, Jr., formerly of New Jersey and its House Speaker, and Isaac Norris II, who unlike his father opposed the proprietors—acted as party leaders rather than factional contenders, although they were not as accomplished as was Hamilton. The issues that had provoked violence were now settled, but political rivalry burst forth frequently during the 1730s. Isaac Norris II and John Kearsley attacked Hamilton viciously in the 1733 election campaign. They accused him of defrauding widows and orphans, of managing the loan office corruptly, of wasting money in the construction of the State House, and of using his slaves rather than the unemployed of the city as laborers on that project. The barrage forced Hamilton from office for a year, but his party continued to gain strength and he was soon back as Speaker. Proprietor Thomas Penn in 1736 expressed his annoyance at the "Contrary Party," which would by the end of the decade be no longer a faction but a party and more contrary than he would dare to imagine.[20]

Factions in New York developed many of the same practices and moved toward becoming parties at the same time as did the Pennsylvania factions. Both

19. Langhorne was a longtime proprietary supporter. Cohorts from Bucks County included the very wealthy Lawrence Growden, Joseph Kirkbride, Jr., Christian Van Horne, and Benjamin Jones. From Chester came John Parry, from Philadelphia Jonathan Robeson, from Lancaster Andrew Galbraith. The vote totals for Lancaster elections, *American Weekly Mercury* (Philadelphia), Oct. 5, 1737, Oct. 6, 1738, show that the proprietary side's candidates were the most popular in that county.

20. Thomas Penn to John Penn, Sept. 10, 1736, in TPP, identified the "Contrary Party" leaders as Kinsey, Norris, Edward Warner, and John Kearsley from Philadelphia and Joseph Pennock of Chester. Other probable members, as compiled from past affiliations or those known after 1738, were William Monington, Job Goodson, and Israel Pemberton, Sr., from Philadelphia; Joseph Harvey, John Owen, and William Hughes from Chester; and William Biles, Jr., Abraham Chapman, and John Watson of Bucks. Also see Isaac Norris, Sr., to John and Thomas Penn, Nov. 15, 1731, in TPP. For anti-Hamilton propaganda, "Paul Veritt," *To My Friends in Pensilvania* (New York, 1733?), 2–3; Katherine D. Carter, "Isaac Norris II's Attack on Andrew Hamilton," *PMHB*, CIV (1980), 139–61. Disputes about the State House construction are in *Pa. Votes*, Aug. 5, 11, 14, 1732. Walker Lewis, "Andrew Hamilton and the He-Monster," *WMQ*, 3rd ser., XXXVIII (1981), 268–94, exculpates Hamilton from some of the charges against him.

economic interests and ideological stances sharpened divisions in these colonies. In both colonies the factions made fervent appeals for the electorate's favor, with one group in each taking what it attempted to make appear to be the more popular side. Soliciting voters resulted in raucous, hard-fought elections. Even though the issues were different—paper money and proprietary policy in Pennsylvania, regional economic clash and an insufferable governor in New York—the pattern of party development was similar.

As in Pennsylvania, the early glimmers of partisanship in New York came with changes in the composition of the assembly that, although slight, upset a stable configuration. In 1725 the seventeenth assembly was in its tenth year; it had sat some seven years longer than any previous one and reflected the quiescent politics that had settled on the colony. By-elections in that year brought in members who chafed under the domination of Robert Livingston, Lewis Morris, Sr., and their faction. When Livingston retired as Speaker in 1725, his opponents engineered a coup that observers thought would bring about a "great turn to the Councils of that house"; they made Adolph Philipse, chief opponent of the Livingston-Morris faction, the Speaker. The assembly brusquely rebuffed the logical claimant to the post—Morris, who had served in the House for fifteen years; it installed a Speaker who had served only three years and had entered the House only after the governor had suspended him from the council.[21]

Old factional rivalries and accumulated personal differences had much to do with the revival and perpetuation of political strife after 1725. Philipse demanded vindication for his suspension; Governor William Burnet denied him relief in chancery court. Morris advised Burnet not to qualify Stephen DeLancey as assemblyman in 1725 (though he had served in previous Houses), for DeLancey was allied with Philipse. By 1729 the Morrises were themselves victims of the personal pique of their opponents. The House reduced Lewis, Sr.'s, salary as chief justice by £50 on the excuse that it was excessive. When his son Lewis, Jr., complained in council about the reduction, he was quickly suspended, further heating up the feud.[22]

Economic and regional interests overshadowed the personal differences.

21. George Clarke to Horace Walpole, Nov. 24, 1725, in *DCHNY*, V, 768–69. Bonomi, *Factious People*, 296–316, lists service of assemblymen and councillors.

22. Burnet to the Lords of Trade, Nov. 26, 1720, Dec. 21, 1727, in *DCHNY*, V, 578–79, 847; Cadwallader Colden to Alexander Colden, [n.d], Jan. 13, 1760, in Letters on Smith's History, *NYHSC*, I, 210–13, 221–22; Lewis Morris, *The Chief Justice's Speech to the General Assembly of the Province of New York, the Third of May 1726* (New York, 1726), 2; Bonomi, *Factious People*, 99–100.

Merchants feared adverse legislation of all sorts, particularly discriminatory taxation. Lewis Morris, Sr., in his unpublished "Dialogue Concerning Trade," exemplified attitudes of landholders toward merchants. He upheld the interests of the "river," meaning his large landholder allies, while castigating the merchant "partie" as composed of profiteers and swindlers of simple country folk. Merchants did not bear their fair share of government expenses, Morris claimed, and were always seeking some government favor or complaining when they failed to receive one. The merchants were a "partie" in the pejorative sense; the "river" evidently did not apply that term to itself. The latter group considered itself public-spirited in its efforts to encourage direct trade with the Canadian Indians, thereby weakening the French; this policy also enhanced the value of members' speculative landholdings. According to Morris, the conflict of interests was primarily over what sort of economic activity should be most prized and least hampered by the government. He believed that the ordinary shopkeeper and artisan of the city would forge a union with the landholding interest against exploitative merchants; he hoped for a partisan coalition of interests rather than continued narrow factionalism.[23]

Personal and interest alignments were potent vestiges of the old factional strife in New York; they were compounded in the late 1720s by cultural alliances and ideological positions that emerged when electoral politics resumed. After the long hiatus, elections came rapidly; three were held in 1726–1728 because of Burnet's dissolution of the House, the death of George I, and the arrival of new governor John Montgomerie. The elections of 1726 and 1727 were only mildly contested and put neither group in firm control; by 1728 the political leaders concluded that the House could no longer be permitted to drift to one side or the other. Both groups set about obtaining a solid majority.

The "river" or Morris-landholder side mounted a campaign in five counties at least; it concluded that, because in these assemblymen had been recently turned out and the electorate seemed volatile, it had a good chance of

---

23. [Lewis Morris, Sr.], "'Dialogue Concerning Trade': A Satirical View of New York in 1726," ed. Edmund Dale Daniel, *New York History,* LV (1974), 208–13, 222–23. The editor inserts the word "party" after "river." The landed interest wished to close down the Indian trade through the French; Albany and New York City merchants opposed this plan. Milton M. Klein, *The Politics of Diversity: Essays on the History of Colonial New York* (Port Washington, 1974), 14–15; Leder, *Robert Livingston,* 265–66; Alice P. Kenney, *Stubborn for Liberty: The Dutch in New York* (Syracuse, 1975), 136.

capturing additional seats. Some Morris ally, perhaps James Alexander, sought Adolph Philipse's New York City seat. The Morris group also enlisted the aid of Cadwallader Colden in Ulster County, attempted to join with Henry Beekman in Dutchess County, and combined with Isaac and Benjamin Hicks, uncle and nephew who were assemblymen from Queens County. In Westchester County an ally of Adolph Philipse challenged Lewis Morris, Sr.; Lewis Morris, Jr., "Spent Some weeks amongst the people" to canvass for voters. One important group from which the Morris side sought support was the Quakers of Westchester and Queens. Lewis Morris, Sr.'s uncle was a noted Quaker, and in New Jersey during the Cornbury years Morris had established good relations with them. The Morris allies in Queens, the Hicks family, were related to Quakers and perhaps Friends themselves. Although Morris' supporters developed political techniques in working to combine religious and economic interests, as well as personal loyalties, in a broad coalition, his faction lacked a clear unifying, overarching principle or ideological cause, in contrast to the strong platforms enunciated by the Pennsylvania parties of the time. Instead of promoting particular policies, it criticized the conduct of Speaker Adolph Philipse; he allegedly cheated a poor widow, attacked the chancery court only because it ruled against him, wrote a pretended committee report against chancery courts, and tricked the House at the last half-hour of its final session into passing the report. These were pallid issues on which to build a colony-wide campaign, the hallmark of a neophyte political effort. With some organization and electoral strategy, but without a clear conception of public purpose, the Morris group was becoming a political party but had not yet reached that stage.[24]

The Philipse-DeLancey or merchant-city group paralleled its opponents in activity. It was organized sufficiently to contest some county elections; more important and different was that it mounted a campaign based on ideological principle. Under Philipse's leadership and because of his earlier quarrel with Burnet it attacked the court of chancery. Because the court rendered judgments in cases involving quitrent arrears, attacking it was a popular stance among landowners; because it was actually the executive making judicial decisions, attacking it as an exercise of arbitrary power was popular generally. James Alexander noted ruefully that the issue won reelection for Philipse from New York City, although this hard-fought contest did not change the fac-

24. James Alexander to Cadwallader Colden, May 5, 1728, in *NYHSC*, L, 260; *To the Honourable Adolph Philipse, Esq.* (2 Pts.; New York, 1728). See Bonomi, *Factious People*, 98–99, 303–304, for assemblymen, 1726–1728.

tional balance in the House or cost any political leaders their seats. Alexander also took note of the lesson in Philipse's electoral campaign; shortly after the election he reported that "the people begin to Clamour agt. Philipse & say that they—it was only Selfishness that induced him to what's just & that they will never have him again." The two political sides were learning that candidates had to commit themselves convincingly to "what's just" to gain popular backing.[25]

The Morris group did not long lack for ideological issues; during Governor Montgomerie's term, 1728–1732, several of its supporters were ejected from appointive office, and during Governor William Cosby's tenure, the next four years, abuses multiplied. Cosby attempted to revive an equity court; removed officers as he wished, including Lewis Morris, Sr., as chief justice; tried to dominate the council and ignored its privileges; grabbed at land; and, most notably, tried to censor the criticism that James Alexander and others printed in John Peter Zenger's newspaper. Cosby cooperated best with the DeLancey-Philipse group, siding with it in its claims to the "Oblong" land strip, ceded to New York by Connecticut and ripe for speculators. He angered the "river" by attempting to grab one-third of all land grants that he issued and by interfering with Albany's land claims.[26]

The governor entrenched his friends in office and dismissed those who crossed him or the DeLancey-Philipse group, as did Assemblyman Vincent Matthews of Orange County. When officials of that county complained in print about the treatment of their representative, they were also thrown out of office, in a particularly crude display of political punishment. Cosby's influence made the DeLancey-Philipse group the stronger in the assembly. The Morris group was compelled chiefly to nibble away by contesting by-elections and local elections, to raise the attention of the electorate using Zenger's newspaper, and to press for a dissolution and a general election.[27]

25. Alexander to Peter Graeme, Oct. 10, 1728, in James Alexander Papers, NYHS. On the chancery court issue, Joseph H. Smith and Leo Hershkowitz, "Courts of Equity in the Province of New York: The Cosby Controversy, 1732–1736," *American Journal of Legal History*, XVI (1972), 12–15.

26. James Alexander to Cadwallader Colden Aug. 12, Sept. 11, 1729, Jan. 12, 1730–1, Lewis Morris, Jr., to Colden, Jan. 17, 1734, Daniel Horsmanden to Colden, Mar. 25, 1734, all in *NYHSC*, L, 293, 296–300, LI, 18, 101, 106–108; Katz, *Newcastle's New York*, 63–83. *Ibid.*, 82, suggests that Cosby may have burned a deed to Indian land to conciliate the Indians, not for his own profit. Bonomi, *Factious People*, 116–21; Philip J. Schwartz, *The Jarring Interests: New York's Boundary Makers, 1664–1776* (Albany, 1979), 68–72.

27. On patronage, William Smith, Jr., *Continuation of the History of New York*, in *NYHSC*, IV, 17; "Speech of Vincent Matthews," Oct. 21, 1735, in *NYHSC*, LXVII, 233.

The Morris side and Governor Cosby both sought primary political support in New York City. The DeLancey-Philipse side organized the Hum-Drum Club, composed of New York merchant supporters. The Morris side made its headquarters the Black Horse Tavern, to recruit and entertain allies. Most important in party development was the founding of Zenger's New York *Weekly Journal* in November, 1733. It was designed to be both a party newspaper and an ideological rallying point, emulating the British *Independent Whig*. Its articles, chiefly written by James Alexander, adopted the views of the British "real" Whigs in stating the case against arbitrary and corrupt government. As William Smith, Jr., later remarked, it was "filled with extracts from the spirited papers of Trenchard, Gordon, and other writers on the popular side." In broadsides from Zenger's press "John Sydney" outlined a platform including a triennial act, appointment of judges on good behavior, popular election of mayors and councilmen in New York City and Albany, popular nomination of sheriffs, encouragement of schools, and economic programs; and "Robt. Dissolution," whose pseudonym signified a principal demand of the Morris group, echoed the same ideas, claiming they were coming from a "Gentleman in the Country," not from a corrupt court. The Morris group now had both a clearly enunciated ideology, which included a largely familiar set of ideas and some broad programs, and also the vehicle for wide dissemination of its views. These the DeLancey-Philipse group could counter only with the other newspaper in New York City and, when it failed to persuade, with the infamous prosecution of printer Zenger.[28]

In the heat of two crucial elections during the Cosby period partisanship in New York entered a new stage of development, for the political leaders worked out techniques for mobilizing the electorate. In October, 1733, came a by-election in Westchester County to replace a deceased assemblyman who had been a longtime Morris supporter. The previous year Lewis Morris, Jr., had regained for his side the Westchester Borough seat that had been lost in 1728; the Morris party believed it was accumulating support and determined to solidify its hold on the county. Lewis, Sr., now stood for this vacancy. The Philipse-DeLancey side, having lost the borough seat, was likewise determined to get even by capturing a seat formerly held by its opponents. Most of the campaign effort was concentrated in the month before election day. The Morrises probably canvassed the county more avidly than they did in

---

28. On clubs and taverns, Katz, *Newcastle's New York,* 69; Smith, *Continuation of the History of New York,* 7; "John Sydney," untitled broadside (New York, 1734), 1–4; "Robt. Dissolution," *A Letter from a Gentleman in the Country to His Friend in Town* (New York, 1734).

1728. By election day they had persuaded some three hundred to come to the polls, the largest contingent for a candidate ever to appear at a Westchester election. These voters assembled and paraded around the town, led by a band of trumpets and violins, to arouse any laggards to join their side. The opposition paraded also, but instead of musicians the party bosses themselves marched in front. Chief Justice James DeLancey and incumbent county assemblyman Frederick Philipse, nephew and heir of Speaker Adolph, led their party's parade of about 170 backers, expecting the populace to fall in behind them in awe and trembling. The music and the anti-Cosby stance of the Morris campaign proved more appealing. Outnumbered, Philipse and DeLancey resorted to an old-style factional device. They demanded a poll and then induced the sheriff to refuse the votes of 38 Quakers because Quakers had long been Morris supporters. But the politics of mass appeal triumphed over narrow factionalism, for the poll ended with Morris at 231 votes and his rival some 80 less. The proportion of the county's white adult males that voted, 32.8 percent, was probably the largest ever for Westchester. The determined canvassing, the appeals of influence and pageantry, and the ideological clash all roused the ordinary sort and showed how partisanship was shifting from factional manipulation to involvement of the major part—in this election 65.6 percent—of the electorate.[29]

The other important electoral contest of this period that greatly contributed to party development was the September, 1734, New York City local election. Its meaning was chiefly symbolic, for it did not increase the Morris group's strength in the House. The opposition to Cosby believed it essential to demonstrate that he had no popularity and that his supporters could be beaten in New York City, where they had always been the strongest. The spark for the contest was the presentation by the city corporation board on June 3, 1734, of an address to Cosby praising his administration. This was a direct affront to the Morris side, which immediately began recruiting supporters and found them among the artisans and laborers.[30]

29. New York *Weekly Journal*, Nov. 5, 1733; Rip Van Dam, *Heads of Articles of Complaint by Rip Van Dam, Esq; Against His Excellency William Cosby, Esq., Governor of New-York, &c.* (Boston, 1734), 19; Smith, *Continuation of the History of New York*, 7. Thomas Willett to Robert Hunter Morris, Dec. 1, 1734, in MP, identifies the deceased assemblyman as a Morris supporter. Bonomi, *Factious People*, 114–15, ably describes the election. Nash, *Urban Crucible*, 148, dates political mobilization in New York from this time. For numbers and proportions of voters, see Appendix III.

30. Untitled broadside containing address to Governor Cosby from New York City merchants, freeholders, and inhabitants, June 3, 1734 (New York, 1734); Nash, *Urban Crucible*, 144.

Campaigners for the Morris party directed election propaganda toward the ordinary voter; "Timothy Wheelwright" complained about the dominance of the wealthy and called for the election of an "*honest poor* or *middling Man.*" In an attempt to influence workmen, Lewis Morris, Sr.'s son-in-law brought his Royal Navy ship into New York for a £900 refitting job just before the election.[31] The election results show the strong grasp that each of the parties had on their supporters. Both succeeded in persuading their backers to vote straight tickets in most instances. In five of the seven wards, including one in which the alderman candidate was unopposed, the alderman and common council candidates of each party garnered the same number of votes. The Morris side won most of the wards and turned out a larger number of voters than had ever before appeared in a municipal contest. The 25.3 percent of the white adult males who voted was not as high a proportion as would appear for later assembly elections, but it constituted a strong partisan showing and a major political turning point for New York City politics.[32] By 1735 the Morris group understood that its organizing of election campaigns, propaganda assaults, petitions to the king against Cosby, and subscriptions to send Lewis Morris, Sr., to London to complain in person were in effect putting together an "Opposition" or "party," as Morris' son-in-law termed it. It was composed of persons with varied backgrounds and interests—the Livingstons of Albany, the Hicks family and future assemblyman Thomas Cornell of Queens, about equal numbers of English and Dutch—all united behind the program of curtailing arbitrary gubernatorial power.[33]

The attitude and actions of Lewis Morris, Sr., in this critical period exemplify how far New York factionalism had come, and how far it still had to go, in moving toward more stable partisanship. He and his allies had constructed out of a faction a political party that could rally an electorate, reinforce a faltering representative body, and confront an executive. Morris showed considerable understanding of the tactic of forging coalitions with similar in-

31. "Timothy Wheelwright," untitled broadside (New York, 1734); Nash, *Urban Crucible*, 143.

32. New York *Weekly Journal*, Sept. 30, 1734. Jon C. Teaford, *The Municipal Revolution in America: Origins of Modern Urban Government, 1650–1825* (Chicago, 1975), 32, terms this a unique contest for the colonial period. Cosby to the Lords of Trade, Dec. 6, 1734, in *DCHNY*, VI, 20–24, ascribed the defeat to "a mislead [*sic*] populace."

33. Mathew Norris to Lewis Morris, Nov. 6, 1735, in MP; Lewis Morris, Jr., to Robert Hunter Morris, June 3, 1735, in MP; Katz, *Newcastle's New York*, 95; Bonomi, *Factious People*, 126–27. Nash, *Urban Crucible*, 458, n. 56, identifies 46 percent of the signers of pro-Morris petitions as English, 44 percent Dutch, and 7 percent French.

terests. Yet he still held to old factional habits. He relied only on his own personal leadership; he claimed that he could determine whether the colony would violently resist council president George Clarke's attempt to take acting governorship of the colony after the death of Cosby in March, 1736, or pursue peaceful politics; and he showed only shallow commitment to the ideological principles espoused by his party. Morris was no hero of the real whig cause, as his later career as New Jersey governor proved, but he sparked the development of administration-opposition party conflict in New York.[34]

Political strife revived in New Jersey after 1725, about the same time as in the other middle colonies. The election reform law of that year, sparked by the Burlington sheriff's trick of moving the election to a remote corner of the county, eliminated many of the corrupt electoral practices of the factional leaders. Later elections were seldom if ever rigged. Both Governors Burnet and Montgomerie by 1728–1729 detected new party activity in the assembly—the rise of a Quaker group, "unadvisable and ungovernable." This group was led by John Kinsey of Middlesex County and his son of the same name, later a Pennsylvania assemblyman. It allied with the antiproprietary group of Monmouth County, some of whose leaders were also Quakers, and who were demanding quitrent exemptions. Another ally was proprietor Peter Sonmans, who was locked in battle with the East Jersey proprietors over land claims. The Quaker group was particularly interested in correcting the political abuses that had become common during the previous intense factional struggles in the colony and in ensuring that executive power did not increase. These efforts stemmed from the old tradition of lax government in the western section of the province, from general Quaker ideas about government, and from the "real" Whig views then current in Britain. This group sought a triennial act, a place act, and only short-term support for the governor.[35] In opposition

34. For assembly attitudes toward Cosby and the dispute over his successor, *N.Y. Votes*, May 22–23, June 7, 12, 20–21, Oct. 17–18, 22, 29, Nov. 7, 1734, Oct. 21, 27, Nov. 6, 1735; "Speech of Vincent Matthews," in *NYHSC*, LXVII, 237; Smith, *Continuation of the History of New York*, 2–3, 12–13; Philip L. White, *The Beekmans of New York in Politics and Commerce, 1647–1877* (New York, 1956), 173–78; *Copy of a Letter from Rip Van Dam, Esq; to the Several Members of That General Assembly of New York, That Stood Adjourned to the Last Tuesday of March, 1736* [and] *At a Meeting of the Members of That Assembly That Stood Adjourned; by Their Own Adjournment, to the Last Tuesday of March Last* (New York, 1736), 4. Katz, *Newcastle's New York*, 134–38, follows Colden and Clarke in recounting events and asserting that civil war was imminent. Lewis Morris to the Lords of Trade, Nov. 5, 1737, in *NJA*, V, 473–74, notes that he forbore violence. Morris was probably fearful that Clarke would take political revenge against his side, as Clarke suggested to Newcastle, Oct. 7, 1736, in *DCHNY*, VI, 76–77.

35. On the election law, McCormick, *History of Voting in New Jersey*, 49–51, and Burnet to the

was a "contrary party" led by Dr. John Johnstone, proprietary leader of East Jersey and an old-time factional politician. His group, which backed the governor, was slightly smaller in assembly representation than was the Quaker side and its allies, but it impelled compromise. None of the political reforms were blocked, but Johnstone's group pushed through a bill for five years' support for the governor. These groups in the New Jersey House were not by 1729 as organized as the parties in New York or Pennsylvania, but they were identified as major forces and were beginning to take ideological positions.[36]

Only meager shreds of evidence give indication of New Jersey legislative behavior in this period; less is known about elections. One change indicates a shift from a factional to a more partylike system: fewer new men were elected to the assembly. In the elections from 1716 through 1727 over 60 percent of the assemblymen were newly elected each year, and most of those served only one term. Great turnover occurred because the assemblymen made no true organized party commitment to remain in the House and advance particular policies. By 1730, after two identifiable political groups contested and compromised in the 1729 assembly, assemblymen and constituents changed their views toward intermittent assembly service. Electoral patterns show that they recognized the value of continuity in service that would enable an experienced corps of dedicated members to accomplish particular tasks. Instead of assemblies having a few incumbent factional leaders and many inexperienced followers, as had been the case before 1729, members would remain in the House, learn how to work within it, and forge enduring political bonds with like-minded members. Consequently, the electorate in 1730 expected continuous service from the representatives, if prior service was satisfactory, and refused to make the customary wholesale changes. In that year only nine new

---

Lords of Trade, Nov. 24, 1725, in *NJA*, V, 104. Burnet to the Lords of Trade, July 3, 1728, in *NJA*, V, 195; Montgomerie to the Lords of Trade, Apr. 20, 1729, in *NJA*, V, 234–35. On the Kinseys, John Smith to William Logan, June 2, 1750, in John Smith Correspondence, HSP. On Monmouth County, William Lawrence to James Alexander, Jan. 1, 1734–5, in James Alexander Papers, NYHS; John E. Stillwell, *Historical and Genealogical Miscellany: Data Relating to the Settlement and Settlers of New York and New Jersey* (5 vols.; New York, 1903–32), I, 220–22. On Sonmans, Journal of the Governor and Council, Apr. 30–June 4, 1726, in *NJA*, XIV, 309–17. Samuel Neville, comp., *The Acts of the General Assembly of the Province of New Jersey* (2 vols.; Philadelphia, 1752–61), I, 195–96.

36. James Alexander to Robert Hunter, Feb. 3, 1729–30, in *NJA*, V, 262–63. The above account differs from that in Purvis, *Proprietors, Patronage, and Paper Money*, 95–97, who credits the proprietors for political reform and political stability in this period, asserting that "native elites" acted similarly in other colonies.

men (37.5 percent) were elected, and all but one of the fifteen new members elected in 1727 were retained. These continuing members would become the cores of the parties that would develop by the end of the 1730s. By the election of 1738 only one-third of the House would be new, after no general election for eight years; and the incumbent majority would rapidly manifest the same partisan characteristics that New York and Pennsylvania had already put into practice.[37]

By neglecting New Jersey, Governor Cosby spared it political controversy during his stormy years in New York. The Morris party, employing some of the family members resident in New Jersey, attempted to involve the New Jersey Assembly in its campaign against Cosby, but without evident success. Because there were no general elections and only one session of the House between 1730 and 1738, it is a wonder that any political interest was sustained. Nevertheless it was. Inhabitants continued to speak critically of the "Court Party," meaning the East Jersey proprietors' faction. With a separate governor for the province and new elections in 1738, New Jersey political leaders immediately commenced partisan activity in the electoral campaigns and in the House.[38]

A growing elite group, intercolonial contact, and the importation of new and vigorous political ideas brought about changes in the system of political partisanship in the middle colonies in the late 1720s and early 1730s. By this time the colonies contained a considerable number of prosperous elite leaders who found it practical to engage in serious politics. A sufficient condition for partisanship is that there be leaders who are willing to unite on a common basis and as well disagree peaceably according to rules. The elite must be sizable enough so that like-minded individuals can join together. It must be prosperous enough so that a large number have leisure time. No one leader was the totality of the group. The Morris party was much more than Lewis Morris, Sr., who retained an opportunistic and factionalist outlook. Its inclusion of leaders such as James Alexander, William Smith, Vincent Matthews,

---

37. Thomas L. Purvis, "The New Jersey Assembly, 1722–1776" (Ph.D. dissertation, Johns Hopkins University, 1979), 256–312, lists assemblymen and dates of service. The second election in 1716, in which the Coxe faction was replaced, was disregarded in counting terms for the new members of the first 1716 assembly. In that election the seven new members that replaced the Coxe partisans all served only one term.

38. Fenwick Lyell to [Robert Hunter Morris, 1733], in MP; Michael Kearney to Robert Hunter Morris, Apr. 5, 1735, in MP; Jonathan Holmes, "Diary," Feb. 26–Mar. 3, 1736–7, in Stillwell, *Historical and Genealogical Miscellany*, III, 365–66.

other assemblymen, and ordinary New Yorkers, who were now beginning to give parties fuller electoral support, meant that the party had superseded the factional attitudes and conduct of its predecessors. Likewise, the Pennsylvania Keithian–paper money group was more than Sir William. Parties were a more mature response to political alternatives that now the elite leaders were prepared to use.

Intercolonial contacts among the elite alerted them to important political developments in the other middle colonies. Political principles that attracted support in one colony soon crossed colonial boundaries to inspire partisanship in another. John Kinsey, Jr., represented a significant intercolonial transfer. He learned his political trade in New Jersey and had no difficulty applying those lessons in his longer and more noteworthy career in Pennsylvania. The Morris family began political involvement in New Jersey, became even more active in New York, and yet retained its influence and commonly exerted its power in New Jersey as well. Leaders readily perceived the political processes that worked well for their neighbors. These processes in each colony began to take on a life of their own as they proved their worth; they would be almost automatically employed in elections and in the assemblies. Once propaganda drew out the electorate and broad canvassing brought voters to the polls, these tactics could hardly be discarded.

Probably most significant in bringing about changes in partisanship at this time was that a greater number of persons than the factions could formerly command were now attentive to the ideas and programs that motivated the party leaders. A web of circulating information—newspapers at coffee houses and backcountry inns, merchants' letters, peddlers' reports, porters' gossip— all brought more people into the information network. Here they encountered appealing ideas—particularly ideas derived from Britain—that the government could be ordered so as to remove corruption and gross inequity, give all who deserved it a role to play, and produce benefits for the greater number in society, such as paper money issued by a loan office. From this time partisan spirit would grow in intensity, partisan practices would become more adeptly used, and partisan activity would knit the diverse groups to produce organized competition rather than political fragmentation.

2

The Determinants of Partisanship

As middle-colony factions became parties after 1735 and as these parties continued to polish techniques and to extend their influence into the electorate, they preserved and expanded their relationships with religious, regional, ethnic, occupational, and economic groups. In the context of these relationships, they also developed ideological positions that were attractive to voters and fostered group cohesion. This chapter presents an overview of the motivating factors of partisanship: ideology and the demands of social groups. Noting how these factors were important to middle-colony parties will provide a base for the ensuing discussion of how party development took place in the forty years before independence.

The determination of partisan affiliation and biographical data about legislators form the basis of the study of partisanship and social groups. For New York and New Jersey, both cluster-bloc analysis of legislative roll calls and the voting patterns of individual assemblymen revealed partisan affiliation. For Pennsylvania, where roll calls are lacking, enough literary and inferential evidence exists to determine partisan affiliation in many instances. Partisanship of legislators was cross-tabulated with their most salient social characteristics: religion, ethnicity, wealth, occupation, and regional affiliation. Determination of the relationship between partisan assemblymen and their social group gives us some clues as to the basic relationship between that group and a particular partisan persuasion but does not clinch identification of party with social group in the electorate. It can be validly assumed that legislators of particular religions or ethnic groups were representing a considerable number of voters of that persuasion or background. An analogous assumption cannot be made about individual legislators of specific economic status that will cover most cases. Very likely a legislator of the middling orders—of farmer or artisan status—was representing constituents of like status and had similar political ideas. But these were rare; nearly all representatives had substantial wealth, and many were engaged in occupations not reflective of the society at large. Cautious, conditional judgments about the connection of economic circumstances with partisanship in the legislature and in the electorate are all that are warranted.[1]

1. See Appendix I, Analysis of Roll Call Voting, for a discussion of method and statistics.

The two social group characteristics that were most important to middle-colony partisanship were, first, religious affiliation, and second, regional location. Statistical evaluation, as reported in Tables 1 through 8, shows that in the period 1737–1776 region was overall a slightly stronger determinant of partisan affiliation in the New York and New Jersey assemblies than was religion, with occupation a distant third and wealth having very little influence on assembly partisanship. Despite the slightly greater significance of region in New Jersey and New York in the forty-year period, this study concludes that religion was generally the most important determinant of partisanship in the middle colonies. In New York and New Jersey religion was less significant than region at first, but it became more important than regional residence in the later colonial period. Tables in the succeeding chapters show that in New Jersey from 1754 to the Revolution, and in New York from 1759 on, religion had the most influence on party affiliation. Religion was strongly associated with partisanship when controlling for region, occupation, or wealth. For Pennsylvania, for which statistical evidence is lacking, religion appears to have had the most influence on party divisions. The well-known east-west split in the colony indicates that regionalism had a strong influence in politics, but the powerful Quaker party, its successor, and its rivals testify to the very great religious divisions that marked partisanship.[2]

TABLE 1

Religion and Partisanship: New Jersey, 1738–1775

(*All tabulated figures are assembly terms*)

	Administration	Opposition	Middle	Indeterminate
Anglican	38	1	0	1
Quaker	34	77	5	8
Presbyterian	34	22	3	
Dutch Reformed	18	26	5	
Baptist	4	24	2	1
Lutheran	0	7	0	
Unknown	4	1		

lambda-b = 0.34
chi-square, opposition and Quaker = 10.88;   phi = 0.19
chi-square, opposition and Baptist = 7.72;   phi = 0.16
chi-square, administration and Presbyterian = 6.61;   phi = 0.14
chi-square, administration and Anglican = 50.53;   phi = 0.40

2. Each term that a reelected assemblyman served was counted. Midterm replacements are counted as a term. Information on the religion of Pennsylvania assemblymen is from Tully, *William*

TABLE 2

Religion and Partisanship: New York, 1737–1775
(All tabulated figures are assembly terms)

	Administration (*DeLancey*)	Opposition (*Livingston*)	Indeterminate
Anglican	58	28	3
Presbyterian	2	14	
Dutch Reformed	57	50	2
Congregational	2	7	
Lutheran	1	2	
Quaker	1	3	2
Unknown	16	10	1

lambda-b = 0.19
chi-square, opposition, and Presbyterian = 11.29;   phi = 0.21
chi-square, administration and Anglican = 7.46;   phi = 0.17

Partisanship and religion became closely related in the middle colonies for several reasons. First, religion was not superfluous or merely decorative but was important in the lives of large numbers of colonists. As much as three-fourths of the population may have considered itself members of a religious denomination. Middle-colony inhabitants sought an ideological component in their lives, offered by both the doctrinal principles of religious groups and the policy aims of parties. Religion also offered the social satisfaction of gath-

Penn's Legacy, 170–73, 225–27; and Wayne L. Bockelman and Owen S. Ireland, "The Internal Revolution in Pennsylvania: An Ethnic-Religious Interpretation," *Pa. Hist.,* XLI (1974), 125–59, which shows the post-1776 religious influence on partisanship. William Wade Hinshaw, *Encyclopedia of American Quaker Genealogy* (Ann Arbor, 1938), vols. II–III; Purvis, "N.J. Assembly," 256–312; and scattered biographical notes in *NJA* furnish data on the religion of assemblymen. James S. Olson, "The New York Assembly, the Politics of Religion, and the Origins of the American Revolution, 1768–1771," *Historical Magazine of the Protestant Episcopal Church,* XLIII (1974), 21–28; E. T. Corwin, comp., *Ecclesiastical History of the State of New York* (7 vols.; Albany, 1901–16); Abstracts of Wills on File in the Surrogate's Office, City of New York, in *NYHSC,* vols. 25–39; "Old New York and Trinity Church," *NYHSC,* III, 174–408; Hinshaw, *Encyclopedia of Quaker Genealogy,* vol. III; and scattered sources identify the religions of assemblymen. Contrary to this study, Purvis, *Proprietors, Patronage, and Paper Money,* 117, argues that "neither regionalism nor religion strongly influenced voting in the lower house" in New Jersey. John A. Phillips, *Electoral Behavior in Unreformed England: Plumpers, Splitters, and Straights* (Princeton, 1982), 309, concludes that partisanship in late eighteenth-century Britain was influenced chiefly by ideology and religion. See also James E. Bradley, *Religion, Revolution, and English Radicalism: Nonconformity in Eighteenth-Century Politics and Society* (Cambridge, Eng., 1990).

ering with like-minded individuals. Those who shared religious sentiments looked to each other for companionship and support. They came to regard their group as giving them a common identity. Its goals and doctrines deserved public understanding and appreciation; but more important, these deserved protection from rivals. Those who belonged to different groups, perhaps with beliefs and values that appeared to challenge another group, were perceived as hostile. Nearly all middle-colony religious groups tacitly agreed to respect the existence of each other but were simultaneously determined not to let another group gain any advantage over them. Challenges hurled by one group to another and recriminations among the groups abound in the political polemics of the time. Propaganda attacks raked up exotic or remarkable or suspect features to emphasize the differences among groups and to generate suspicion of outsiders. Parties capitalized on these divisions, yet as they matured they also came to appreciate the value of combining religious groups that possessed a modicum of compatibility. Moving beyond denominational exclusiveness to combination was more difficult than was binding a party to a particular religious view, but it created a much stronger and much more appealing political organization.[3]

Of all the dozen or so religious groups in the middle colonies, the one exhibiting the most partisan effort and drive, cohesion in politics, successful leadership, clear political purpose, financial sacrifice, and shrewd techniques was the Quakers. Quakers either dominated or were a major component of one of the contending parties in Pennsylvania; were, as Table 1 indicates, statistically associated with the opposition party in New Jersey; and in New York, though small in number, generally voted with the opposition side. Most important for the Quakers' success in politics was their commitment to widely shared principles. Richard Smith, Jr., who resented spending cold weeks at

3. Pointer, *Protestant Pluralism and the New York Experience*, 31, calculates that 73.6 percent of New Yorkers were church adherents in 1750 and 59.2 percent were in 1775. *Ibid,* 51, 68, reports that various denominations accepted religious pluralism by the 1760s, and some "conservatives" even favored continuing the Anglican establishment. He corrects the conclusions of Patricia U. Bonomi and Peter R. Eisenstadt, "Church Adherence in the Eighteenth-Century British American Colonies," *WMQ,* 3rd ser., XXXIX (1982), 272–74. Sally Schwartz, *"A Mixed Multitude": The Struggle for Toleration in Colonial Pennsylvania* (New York, 1987), 252, 256, 293–94, points to toleration and cooperation among Pennsylvania Anglicans and Lutherans, but this cannot be generalized to include Quakers and Presbyterians. Douglas G. Jacobsen, *An Unprov'd Experiment: Religious Pluralism in Colonial New Jersey* (Brooklyn, 1991), 73–74, 142–47, notes that in that colony before 1740 consciousness of denominational distinctiveness was tempered by toleration and cooperation.

assembly meetings among unfriendly "politicos," clearly stated the dedication to principle that many Quakers held. As he wrote his son in 1744, "Our Cause appears Just, and necessary at this time, which is the only Inducement that I Know of to persist In it for other wise we deale very Much In disagreeables to me."[4] Quaker political ideology was based on the highest standards of religious conviction and ethical idealism, as well as on individual rights and liberties. Ideological unity impelled Quakers to act in concert and encouraged others to join with them. Non-Quakers, who might be basically inimical to Quaker religious views, were attracted to vote for those who supported Quaker ideals because they recognized in them an inherent political justice. Quaker principles had been forged in the English crises when commonwealthmen and Whigs confronted and battled royalists and Tories who upheld the prerogative. Quakers contributed to these struggles, learned much, and transmitted a blend of religious and whig principles that upheld the protection of the rights of the subject.

Religious liberty was a high-ranking principle of middle-colonial America to all except satisfied members of the established church. Quakers both observed and defended this principle most scrupulously and avidly. At many times religious consciousness and religious jealousies reached a high pitch in the middle colonies, as the examples of warring Anglicans and Presbyterians in New York in the 1750s and 1760s and contentious Quakers in New Jersey and Pennsylvania attest. Quakers earned political support because they were perceived by many non-Quakers as opposed to the religious supremacy of any group, including their own, and because they were trusted not to abuse political power by practicing religious discrimination. Out of both principle and expediency they never became concerned about the religious practice, or lack thereof, of useful allies like Benjamin Franklin. Their imposition of particular Quaker practices, such as affirmations, or of Friends' codes of behavior, were not seen as infringements on important liberties.[5]

The important liberties were the political ones. Those that Quakers strongly supported included the ballot, frequent elections, and the general expansion of legislative power. Pennsylvania used the ballot because Quakers in-

4. The relationship of Quakers to the opposition side was significant when controlled for region and occupation. Richard Smith to John Smith, Nov. 26, 1744, Mar. 22, 1744–5, in John Smith Correspondence, HSP.

5. Tully, *William Penn's Legacy*, 62, 85, concurs with this view of Quaker toleration. On early Pennsylvania legislation on morality, personal behavior, and affirmation, see J. William Frost, *A Perfect Freedom: Religious Liberty in Pennsylvania* (Cambridge, Eng., 1990), 16–19, 22–25.

stituted this protection, and in 1769 Quakers in New York joined the Livingston party in demanding ballot voting rather than *viva voce* polls. New Jersey and New York both viewed the Pennsylvania annual election system as ideal. Both colonies made unsuccessful efforts to institute triennial elections; in New Jersey Quakers pushed this reform. Conflicts wherein the assemblies upheld their privileges and practices—indeed, what they thought were basic popular liberties—against executive assertion of the prerogative occurred frequently in Pennsylvania and New Jersey. Much of the conflict centered on provision for defense, but important controversies also concerned paper money expansion, which Pennsylvania and New Jersey Quakers demanded; the taxation of proprietary estates; revision of proprietary land policies in Pennsylvania; reducing fees and salaries in New Jersey; and disciplining the East Jersey treasurer for negligence leading to the treasury's robbery. John Wright of Lancaster County, Pennsylvania, fought back in 1741 when, because of his opposition in the House to Governor George Thomas, he was removed from his judgeship. He published a rousing *Speech . . . to the Court and Grand Jury,* asserting that for defending "the Cause of *English liberty,* for standing in the Civil Defence of Right and Property, are we dismissed."[6]

Quakers appear to have been particularly good Whigs, both ideologically and in their political behavior. Although they supported popular expression in politics and the power of the legislature to put that expression into action, they were cautious in pushing to extremes. Pennsylvania Speaker John Kinsey, who in 1740 strongly denounced defense measures, compromised with Philadelphia merchants in supporting such efforts in 1747. Both his successor Isaac Norris II and Israel Pemberton, Jr., became willing to compromise with the proprietors on the issue of royal government in 1764. Most New Jersey Quaker assemblymen in 1751 and 1752 voted against bypassing the council in forwarding the support bill directly to the governor, a very radical constitutional maneuver. Quakers sometimes lapsed into self-righteousness, bigotry, and self-interest. Israel Pemberton, Jr., termed his opponents "ungodly." His brother James displayed an un-Friendly, sour attitude toward his political adversaries, characterizing them as "disagreeable to the People," of "mean Character," and one as an "Envious Pres——n." Richard Smith, Jr.,

6. Peter R. Livingston to Robert Livingston, Jr., Dec. 25, 1769, in LP; *N.J. Votes,* Dec. 12, 1738, Jan. 19, Feb. 13, 1738-9; Wright, *The Speech of John Wright, Esq; One of the Magistrates of Lancaster County, to the Court and Grand-Jury, On His Removal from the Commission of the Peace at the Quarter Sessions Held at Lancaster for the Said County in May 1741* (Philadelphia, 1741), 4; Proud, *History of Pennsylvania,* II, 220–21.

of New Jersey peevishly opposed authorization of a lottery to aid the College of New Jersey: "Theres to [*sic*] many of the prespaterian Clergy Concernd Indeed all their Trustees Except Andw. Johnston & Jno. Kinsey are Such the one Designd to Decoy the Church and the other the Quakers to send their Children to be Educated prispeterians So that in time they'll have the rule & governing the province." Perhaps Ebenezer Miller of Cumberland County, New Jersey, exhibited the most characteristic self-interest. He owned 420 acres at the site where he planned that the county courthouse would be built and used his influence to have it located at that site. Miller and the Quaker merchant assemblymen of Philadelphia who helped to vote themselves government contracts during wartime were acting no differently, no more Quakerly, than did other legislators. They seem not to have damaged the reputation of the more scrupulous Quaker political leaders or Quaker political efforts generally. The combination of solid whiggery and sensible discretion powerfully attracted non-Quakers to support Friends in politics.[7]

Radical Quaker social views were less popular politically than was Quaker insistence on political liberties, but they also helped to unite Quakers and to attract support from outside the society. No one held against Quakers politically their calls for fairer and more equitable treatment of women, the poor, and African-Americans, though few allied with them to pursue these ends. The peace testimony and the concurrent efforts to have Native Americans treated humanely at first attracted support from non-Quakers. These policies for many years provided two important benefits for inhabitants of Pennsylvania and New Jersey: less chance of Indian attack and no compulsory military service. Pennsylvania had no militia before 1755, and that of New Jersey was in practice voluntary. But non-Quaker settlers who demanded Indian land, non-Quaker proprietors who grabbed it, and the French, who claimed they were helping the Native Americans defend it, ruined Quaker peacekeeping efforts and made pacifism unpopular.[8]

---

7. *American Magazine and Monthly Chronicle*, Feb., 1758, p. 211; *Pa. Col. Recs.*, July 13, 1747, May 26, 1748, V, 91, 251; Hutson, *Pennsylvania Politics*, 129–33, 170; *N.J. Votes*, Oct. 11, 1749, Oct. 21–22, 1751, Feb. 8, 1752; Israel Pemberton, Jr., to Samuel Wily, Dec. 2, 1758, Israel Pemberton, Jr., to Edmund Peckover, Oct. 19, 1748, James Pemberton to William Logan, Nov. 11, 1760, James Pemberton to John Fothergill, Dec. 18, 1765, all in Pemberton Papers, HSP; Richard Smith, Jr., to John Smith, Nov. 23, 1748, in John Smith Correspondence, HSP; Thomas Cushing and Charles E. Sheppard, *History of the Counties of Gloucester, Salem, and Cumberland, New Jersey, with Biographical Sketches of Their Prominent Citizens* (Philadelphia, 1883), 526.

8. Frost, *Perfect Freedom*, chap. 2, is the best account of Quaker pacifism and its consequences.

Quakers in politics matched the strength of their ideological commitment with a lack of ethical inhibitions in their employment of political tactics. Although historian Alan Tully has depicted Friends as striving to implement the ideals of community and harmony in political practice and attempting to avoid contention, in actuality Quakers readily confronted opponents and employed nearly all the tactics common to determined partisans. From the time when Quakers participated in the exclusion crisis in England, through their earliest political activity in America, in Maryland, they were in the thick of controversy. As do many political leaders, Quaker politicians compartmentalized their political practices from their ideological stance. Friends' partisan political style included manipulation and fierce contention, though their principles were justice, fair dealing, and harmony.[9]

Quakers developed very effective techniques and strategies for winning election campaigns. Their efforts were often exclusive, closed, and contentious, rarely Friendly or saintly, and on occasion suspect if not dishonest. Quaker meetings or informal caucuses nominated candidates and planned election strategy. During the election campaigns of the 1730s in Pennsylvania, Quakers cooperated with "diverse Inhabitants of other Perswasions" to form county tickets. In the next decade, in Philadelphia at least, a caucus of Quaker leaders, held in conjunction with the Burlington-Philadelphia yearly meeting, set the ticket. After Quakers partially withdrew from Pennsylvania politics in 1756, members of that denomination no longer dominated the process, but prominent Quaker merchants served as part of a nominating "juncto." New Jersey Quakers were also competent election strategists and organizers. In Monmouth County in 1738, where Quakers and Baptists "bear the greatest Sway," the "heads of the 2 towns" were notified at "our Quaker meeting" to gather to choose or endorse candidates. In Cumberland County

---

Gov. Robert Hunter Morris to Gen. William Shirley, Aug. 19, 1755, in *Pa. Col. Recs.*, VI, 553; Lewis Morris to the Earl of Sunderland, Feb. 9, 1707-8, in *NJA*, III, 80.

9. Tully, *William Penn's Legacy*, 141, argues that Quakers had "a whole set of values, procedures, and traditions [that] operated to promote both good harmony between Quakers and those of different religious views and unity among Friends." Herman Wellenreuther, "The Quest for Harmony in a Turbulent World: The Principle of 'Love and Unity' in Colonial Pennsylvania Politics," *PMHB*, CVII (1983), 557, notes that Quakers observed these principles when seeking supporters. Douglas R. Lacey, *Dissent and Parliamentary Politics in England, 1661–1689* (New Brunswick, 1969), 112–14; David W. Jordan, "God's Candle Within Government: Quakers and Politics in Early Maryland," *WMQ*, 3rd ser., XXXIX (1982), 641–44, 647–51; Jordan, *Foundations of Representative Government in Maryland, 1632–1715* (Cambridge, Eng., 1987), 85–86.

in 1772 the Quakers organized to put up both a Quaker nominee and a Presbyterian candidate and employed "money and unity" to carry the contest.[10]

Their production of political propaganda illustrates that Quaker politicians were little hampered by religious meekness. Quakers had a long tradition of contending in the public press with their religious rivals, and they challenged political rivals in the same vein. Isaac Norris II launched an attack on the character of proprietary side leader Andrew Hamilton in 1733. Anonymous New Jersey pamphleteers, almost certainly Quaker political leaders, rebutted the contentions of the administration side in the 1740s disputes. Israel Pemberton, Jr., in 1754 wrote a "political harrangue . . . [delivered] at the Court house to some hundreds of people" before the Philadelphia election. This was printed and distributed in the back counties to stir up the voters. In the 1764 and 1765 campaigns, Isaac Hunt, a Quaker lawyer and probably a paid propagandist, outdid all other colonial propagandists with an amazing, shocking set of tirades containing the vilest personal abuse. He blasted Franklin's opponents with charges of widespread bastardy and eating vomit and ordure. Official Quakerdom took little notice of the propaganda prepared by Quakers, nor were Quakers called to account for it. Quaker meetings dutifully expelled members for marrying outside the faith, personal immorality or misbehavior, debt, and other assorted transgressions, but never for publishing defamatory political opinions. Quakerism provided no sanctions against political activity unless the cause were opposed to Quaker tenets.[11]

10. *Pa. Votes*, Sept. 2, 1740, Aug. 11, 1744 (Appendix); Richard Hockley to Thomas Penn, Nov. 1, 1742, in TPP; James Logan, *To Robert Jordan, and Others the Friends of the Yearly Meeting for Business, Now Conven'd in Philadelphia* (Philadelphia, 1741), 4; Rothermund, *Layman's Progress*, 84–85. Robert J. Dinkin, *Voting in Provincial America: A Study of Elections in the Thirteen Colonies* (Westport, 1977), 81, notes a 1750 caucus. Tully, *William Penn's Legacy*, 86–89; Edward Shippen, Jr., to Edward Shippen, Sept. 19, 1756, in Thomas Balch, ed., *Letters and Papers Relating Chiefly to the Provincial History of Pennsylvania* (Philadelphia, 1855), 64; *Pennsylvania Gazette* (Philadelphia), Sept. 27, 1770; Jacob Dennis to Robert Hunter Morris, Nov. 11, 1738, in MP; Larry R. Gerlach, "'Quaker' Politics in Eighteenth-Century New Jersey: A Documentary Account," *Journal of the Rutgers University Library*, XXXIV (1970), 1–12.

11. Richard Hockley to Thomas Penn, Oct. 1, 1754, in TPP. Hunt's propaganda pieces include *A Letter from a Gentleman in Transilvania* (New York, 1764); *The Scribbler* (Philadelphia, 1764); *A Humble Attempt at Scurrility* (Philadelphia, 1765); and *The Substance of an Exercise Had This Morning in Scurrility-Hall*, numbers 1–7 (Philadelphia, 1765). Gary B. Nash, "The Transformation of Urban Politics, 1700–1765," *JAH*, LX (1973–74), 618–20, notes the use of paid writers and the increase in personal attacks. The Philadelphia Monthly Meeting, in the *Pennsylvania Gazette* (Philadelphia), Jan. 1, 1756, condemned *Tit for Tat, or the Score Wip'd Off* (Philadelphia, 1755), written by non-Quakers William Franklin and George Bryan and lapsed Quaker Joseph Galloway,

Quakers in and out of the assemblies contributed party work at election time. New Jersey Quaker Richard Smith, Jr., took avid interest in election developments in his own and other districts and led his supporters to the polls. Pennsylvania Quaker assemblymen brought the issues directly to their constituents. Five of them and several non-Quakers were assigned by Joseph Galloway in August, 1764, to distribute his *Speech* as election propaganda in Philadelphia, Bucks, Chester, and Lancaster counties. Spreading this pamphlet meant answering pointed questions and justifying the conduct of the party. In these circumstances Quaker House members probably could not sidestep confrontation.[12]

Two Philadelphia Quakers, Israel Pemberton, Jr., and Thomas Wharton, seemed to welcome confrontation, were politicians but not elected officials, and donated much time and resources to bringing out the voters and to broadcasting the programs of the Quaker party. Their political activities were much like those of the modern campaign manager or back room broker—they sought control by directing party activities, not by holding office. Pemberton flourished chiefly in the 1740s and 1750s, becoming less prominent after 1764; Wharton contributed importantly in the 1760s, but his influence declined as the Assembly party dwindled after 1770. Pemberton may have had ambitions for high position in the assembly, but he found his niche outside the House. His major contributions were made in the Burlington-Philadelphia Yearly Meeting and on the streets at election time.[13] Many of Pemberton's political activities exhibit extraordinary contentiousness, but none more so than his most un-Quakerly impulse to fight on election day. In the 1741 election he scuffled with James Hamilton, who demanded further satisfaction. Pemberton answered that "he Did not fear him any Time nor Place." The near-duelist Quaker was ready for trouble in the "knock-down" election of the next year. Down the street he chased the ship captain whose

---

as a libel. Tully, *William Penn's Legacy*, 197–206, tabulates charges and disownments made by various meetings before 1756.

12. John J. Thompson, ed., "Poll Book of an Election in 1739 [-40], Burlington County, New Jersey," *PMHB*, XVIII (1894), 185–93. Abel James, Israel Jacobs, John Jacobs, Joseph Pennock, and Samuel Foulke are the five Quakers listed in the Beale Collection, HSP.

13. James Hamilton to Thomas Penn, Oct. 13, 1753, Richard Peters to Penn, Sept. 11, 1753, in TPP. Although Pemberton and Norris were seen as potential rivals to succeed Kinsey in 1750, they cooperated well. *Pa. Votes*, 1750–51, for Pemberton's numerous committee assignments. Jack D. Marietta, *The Reformation of American Quakerism, 1748–1783* (Philadelphia, 1984), 44, suggests that Norris and Pemberton tacitly divided Kinsey's political and religious offices.

crew started the riot. Merchant Joseph Turner tried to stop the fight between Pemberton and the captain, whereupon Israel grabbed Turner and fought with him.[14]

Thomas Wharton, like Pemberton a wealthy Quaker merchant, was less contentious and remained more behind the scenes. He held only local office, but House candidates of the Assembly party often owed their success to his assistance. As in British elections of the period, wealthy party members defrayed campaign expenses. Wharton's most vigorous campaigning occurred in 1765 in the effort to get the Assembly party leadership under Joseph Galloway back into the House. The merchant politician wrote to Benjamin Franklin that he had never before worked harder in an election. One of his major contributions was paying naturalization fees for Germans so they would be eligible to vote. In 1766 he and Galloway began the *Pennsylvania Chronicle,* printed by William Goddard, to broadcast party propaganda. After the collapse of the Assembly party in Philadelphia in 1770 and Galloway's retreat to Bucks County, Wharton became less active, but he still retained his interest. His principal motive seems to have been to serve his allies and friends, particularly Franklin and Galloway, in their electoral and policy endeavors. Like James Pemberton, Richard Smith, Jr., and many other Quakers, he distrusted Presbyterians and by his political efforts hoped to keep them from power. Wharton and Pemberton were the apex of the party pyramid in Pennsylvania; many nameless party workers toiled in election campaigns. Some of them expected tangible patronage, but the major reward for all was the satisfaction of contributing to a worthy cause.[15]

When Quakers faced direct challenges to their ideals, could call upon leaders adept at party organization, and enjoyed a receptive electorate, they were able to organize a "Quaker Party." This occurred only in Pennsylvania in 1740–1755, when they made up 20 percent of the electorate. In New York Quakers were hardly numerous enough and in New Jersey they did not, ex-

14. Samuel Noble to John Smith, Oct. 3, 1741, in John Smith Correspondence, HSP; *Pa. Votes,* Jan. 6, 1742-3, Aug. 13, 1743. Pemberton here averred that he did not pursue the captain and that Turner started the fight. Marietta, *Reformation of American Quakerism,* 43.

15. Wharton to William Fisher, Jan. 14, 1762, in Pennsylvania Provincial Congress Papers, HSP; Wharton to William Franklin, May 29, 1767, in Beale Collection, HSP; Wharton to Benjamin Franklin, Oct. 5, 1765, Feb. 9, 1768, in Labaree *et al.,* eds., *Franklin Papers,* XII, 290–91, XV, 39–41. William Franklin to Wharton, Sept. 12, 1771, in Society Collection, HSP; William Goddard, *The Partnership* (Philadelphia, 1770), 63. On financing British parties, Hill, *Growth of Parliamentary Parties,* 116.

cept for a short period, face the direct confrontation to their ideals that occurred in Pennsylvania. Traditional popular issues—preventing any extension of the proprietary prerogative, maintaining peace and avoiding any military defense activities, and emitting more paper money—were the major programs of the Quaker party. Kinsey, Norris, and Pemberton provided expert leadership. All Quaker assemblymen whose political affiliation can be determined, except for one, were Quaker party supporters in these years. Not only did the group have solid unity but also nearly complete dominance of the House. Through these sixteen elections the number of Quaker assemblymen elected from the five original and largest districts was either twenty-four or twenty-five out of thirty. Quakers ensured their dominance by making united, determined election efforts to bring out their coreligionists to support Quaker candidates. Results in Lancaster and Philadelphia counties demonstrate the effects of Quaker electoral efforts. During Lancaster County's first ten years, 1729–1738, Quaker assemblymen made up 22.5 percent of the delegation. From 1740 to 1755 the proportion of Quaker assemblymen from that county was 75 percent. The Quaker proportion of the population there was probably no higher than 10 percent. In Philadelphia County from 1740 to 1755, where the Quakers made up about 25 percent of the population, either seven or all eight of the assemblymen were Quakers. In both thickly settled areas and remote back counties, Quakers exerted disproportionate political influence.[16]

Franklin and his non-Quaker allies after 1755 created the political heir of the Quaker party, known as the Assembly party. While drawing its leadership from a broader spectrum of opinion, this organization still incorporated a large proportion of Quakers. The number in the House reached its lowest during the war years 1757–1760 but increased during the 1760s. It was hyperbolic for Governor John Penn in 1766 to term Quakers a "Macedonian Phalanx," but he captured the essential basis of their success—an emphasis on unity that had served them well for thirty years.[17]

16. Jeremiah Langhorne was the one Quaker who supported the proprietors. Rev. William Smith to Archbishop Thomas Secker, Nov. 27, 1759, *DCHNY,* VII, 407; Tully, *William Penn's Legacy,* 85–86, 170–73, 225–27; *Pa. Votes,* May 9, 1739, Apr. 5, 9, 11, May 8, Aug. 9, 13, 1754; Carl Bridenbaugh and Jessica Bridenbaugh, *Rebels and Gentlemen: Philadelphia in the Age of Franklin* (2nd ed.; New York, 1962), 16.

17. John Penn to Thomas Penn, Nov. 12, 1766, in TPP; Bockelman and Ireland, "Internal Revolution in Pennsylvania," 157–58. Quakers were not more numerous in the assembly because they were wealthier than the average citizen. They constituted a larger proportion of the wealth-

Quakers were never a majority in the New Jersey House and so never exercised the hegemony over politics that the Pennsylvania Quakers did in 1740–1755. It seems a reasonable assumption that the oppositionist stance of Quaker assemblymen, as noted in Table 1, represented the general views of most Quakers. They were only one part, along with Baptists and landowners of rural East and West Jersey, of the oppositionist group. In close communication with Philadelphia Friends, they absorbed party spirit from the Pennsylvania political contests. They shared with their Philadelphia brethren the real whig demands for fuller powers for the assembly and the suspicion of Anglicans and Presbyterians. Several New Jersey Quaker leaders shifted sides; although skilled party managers, they were not political zealots like Pemberton and Wharton.

Both ideology and political skills contributed to Quaker success in New Jersey, as in Pennsylvania. They elected a larger proportion of the House than their population, about 17 percent at midcentury, would have entitled them to. Quakers were in a minority in Monmouth County, but it was often represented by one Quaker. Salem County, 16.4 percent Quaker, sent at least one and sometimes two Quaker representatives to the House. Hunterdon and Cape May counties, each less than 5 percent Quaker, on occasion elected Quaker assemblymen. In Monmouth and Hunterdon, Friends allied with the Baptists; Baptist assemblymen, who were in several instances from Quaker families, were also generally oppositionist, as Table 1 notes. Baptists believed themselves in competition with larger religious groups and adopted real whig views for many of the same reasons that Quakers did.[18]

Although New York Quakers were only about 5 to 8 percent of the population and were politically discriminated against, they showed both unity and determination. Very possibly four Quakers served as assemblymen. Three members of the Hicks family, notable in Quaker history, were elected from

---

ier group in 1774, when they had become less active in politics, than in 1754, when they were dominant. See J. William Frost, *The Quaker Family in Colonial America: A Portrait of the Society of Friends* (New York, 1973), 205.

18. "Number of People in the Western and Eastern Divisions of New Jersey," *NJA*, VI, 242–43; Wacker, *Land and People*, 183; Batinski, "Quakers in the New Jersey Assembly," 68. There is no evidence that non-Quakers were ineligible to vote in such proportions as to ensure minority Quaker hegemony. New Jersey had a proportionately larger representation of Baptists in the House than did the other middle colonies—9.8 percent of all assembly seats. Batinski, *New Jersey Assembly*, 31, 38–39, 74, identifies Baptist assemblymen differently than I do.

Queens, as was Zebulon Seaman, who was born a Quaker. New York required an oath of its officials and refused to accept an affirmation; such a regulation would ordinarily bar Quakers from service. These assemblymen may have left the Society or taken the oath regardless. New York Quakers usually supported the Morris and Livingston sides because Lewis Morris came from a Quaker background and because those groups were more ideologically compatible with whiggish Quaker views. Because few Quakers could or would stand for election, that denomination threw its combined vote to ideologically satisfactory non-Quaker candidates. In the 1728 elections in Queens and Westchester, in the 1733 election in Westchester, and in the 1750 election in Dutchess Quakers unified behind one side. Henry Beekman, political leader of Dutchess County, believed them important enough to court in crucial elections. The thirty-eight Quaker voters whom the Philipse-De-Lancey sheriff rejected in Westchester constituted only about 9 percent of the electorate but as bloc voters could turn an election. In 1775–1776 they were very influential in Queens in promoting neutrality toward the war with Britain. Quakers could not give direction to New York politics, as they did in Pennsylvania and New Jersey, but within one of the emerging parties they were a major group that had influence greater than its size warranted. Quakers in all these colonies were strong partisans; the degree of party organization depended on particular issues, leadership, and numbers.[19]

The Quaker situation in New York points up one important tactic used by Friends in politics: to arrange a coalition with others that enabled both Quakers and the other leaders in the coalition to share power. Statistical analysis of the leadership of the Pennsylvania House indicates that Quakers did not dominate the assembly as leaders out of proportion to their numbers. As in Pennsylvania, Quaker political leaders in New Jersey adopted the strategy of sharing power and working in tandem with reliable and like-minded non-Quakers. Quakers shrewdly shared leadership in the legislature with political allies and thereby cemented party unity more solidly.[20]

19. Data in Pointer, *Protestant Pluralism and the New York Experience*, 4, show the proportion of Quaker meetings as 8.5 percent of churches in 1750 and 9.2 percent in 1775. For the Dutchess election see Bonomi, *Factious People*, 170. Isaac Hicks, married to a Quaker, served in the House 1716–1739. His brother Benjamin served 1716–1737. Their nephew Thomas served 1759–1761. See Sister Mary Martin Mass, "The Hicks Family as Quakers, Farmers, and Entrepreneurs" (Ph.D. dissertation, St. John's University, 1976), 301–305; Hinshaw, *Encyclopedia of Quaker Genealogy*, III, 446; Joseph S. Tiedemann, "A Revolution Foiled: Queens County, New York, 1775–1776," *JAH*, LXXV (1988–89), 422.

20. For the determination of leadership see Appendix II. Chi-square for the relationship be-

Ideology was the strongest lever that Quaker politicians possessed in persuading non-Quakers to side with them, but it also eventually proved to be the most negative aspect of Quaker political appeal. The coming of the Revolution ended Quaker political power. Quaker ideology could not encompass the resistance to British authority after 1764. The peace testimony inhibited Quakers from joining the prerevolutionary protests and boycotts. They also feared that their social and economic gains would be jeopardized by extremist politics that would probably prevail in any revolutionary situation. Philadelphia merchants who were Friends protested the Stamp Act in company with nearly all other merchants but then dropped out of resistance activity. Eleven of the fifteen Quakers in the Pennsylvania Assembly opposed sending strongly anti-British delegates to the Stamp Act Congress. The Philadelphia Quaker Meeting opposed nonimportation and the tea boycott. The nonimportation committee of 1769 was 40 percent Quaker, but only 27 percent of the Association committee of 1774 was of that denomination. The number of Quaker assemblymen declined from an average of seventeen in 1766–1770 to fewer than fifteen in 1771–1775. The change came about primarily in the Philadelphia delegation; by 1775 only three of those ten members were Quakers (two of these were probably lapsed or disowned) because the city was a hotbed of anti-British resistance. By late 1775 Pennsylvania Quakers were the targets of revolutionaries who accused them of too easily and readily shirking the military obligations required of all patriots. The proportion of Quakers in the New Jersey Assembly likewise declined from 37.5 percent in 1769–1772 to 23.3 percent in 1772–1775. New Jersey Quakers also withdrew from committee activity in 1774–1775. The one likely Quaker assemblyman in New York serving in 1775 retired from politics about the time war broke out.[21]

---

tween leadership and Quakerism in Pennsylvania was calculated to be 0.00 and for New Jersey, 0.51, indicating that there was no significant relationship.

21. The Pennsylvania Assembly vote on the Stamp Act Congress delegation is in Donald F. Durnbaugh, ed., *The Brethren in Colonial America: A Source Book on the Transplantation and Development of the Church of the Brethren in the Eighteenth Century* (Elgin, 1967), 385, quoting an election broadside of Christopher Sauer, Jr. On Quaker merchants see Robert F. Oaks, "Philadelphia Merchants and the Origins of American Independence," *Proceedings of the American Philosophical Society*, CXXI (1977), 418–30. Robert Gough, "Can a Rich Man Favor Revolution? The Case of Philadelphia in 1776," *Pa. Hist.*, XLVIII (1981), 244, notes that religion was "probably the most important characteristic influencing the position of the wealthy toward the Revolution." Gerlach, *Prologue to Independence*, 232. Tully, "Quaker Party and Proprietary Politics," 105, and Richard

No other middle-colony religious or ethnic group could match the Quakers in political activity, though many were larger and some needed political power to protect themselves. Presbyterians were overall the most numerous of middle-colony denominations, constituting about 15–20 percent in New York and 25–30 percent in both New Jersey and Pennsylvania. In the ten years before the Revolution they became very significant in politics and very anti-British. Yet before 1750 they were not readily aroused to denominational political endeavor. The Great Awakening seems not to have been directly important in drawing Presbyterians into politics in these colonies (though it may have been elsewhere). The New Side–Old Side division had no political meaning. When Freehold, New Jersey, was gripped by intense religious revivalism from 1730 to 1745, it was Quakers, Baptists, and Dutch who contested in politics there; Presbyterians were inert.[22] New to the colonies, beset by internal religious turmoil, feeling no strong rivalry with other groups in this period, they threw their support to more activist allies. Most Presbyterians of New Jersey who sought office followed the lead of Anglicans in supporting the administration side. These two religious groups mutually believed that their principal challengers were the more vigorous and, from their religious viewpoints the more outlandish, Quakers and Baptists. Moreover, no Anglican establishment threatened New Jersey Presbyterians. The back counties of Pennsylvania, from which the majority of Presbyterian assemblymen in the middle colonies were elected, chose them because they were local leaders, not because they were expected to pursue policies that were related to their religious views. In Pennsylvania politics before 1755 the Presbyterians liked Quaker government and made no challenges against it.[23]

In New York in the 1750s and in Pennsylvania in the 1760s Presbyterian po-

Alan Ryerson, "Portrait of a Colonial Oligarchy: The Quaker Elite in the Pennsylvania Assembly, 1729–1776," in *Power and Status*, ed. Daniels, 134, argue that Quaker domination in Pennsylvania was doomed by increases in the non-Quaker population.

22. Pointer, *Protestant Pluralism and the New York Experience*, 4; Tully, *William Penn's Legacy*, 55; Smith, *History of New Jersey*, 489–500; Ned Landsman, "Revivalism and Nativism in the Middle Colonies: The Great Awakening and the Scots Community in East New Jersey," *American Quarterly*, XXXIV (1982), 158. Tully, *William Penn's Legacy*, 64, notes that the Great Awakening did not intrude into Pennsylvania politics. Patricia U. Bonomi, "A Just Opposition: The Great Awakening as a Radical Model," in *The Origins of Anglo-American Radicalism*, ed. Margaret Jacob and James Jacob (London, 1984), 253, argues that the Awakening fostered a "more assertive political culture."

23. Bockelman and Ireland, "Internal Revolution in Pennsylvania," 139, find the Scotch-Irish "preoccupied with the process of settlement and religious divisions." Frost, *Perfect Freedom*, 51,

litical activity increased. Middle-colony Presbyterians by the 1760s became second only to Quakers in the significance and intensity of their partisanship. Presbyterianism became strongly related to the opposition side in New York, as Table 2 indicates, and in Pennsylvania became primarily associated with the Proprietary party. In New Jersey, as shown in Table 1, it was significantly but only moderately associated with the administration side. Presbyterians differed in response in each of these colonies because they were reacting negatively to differently positioned opponents.[24]

New York Presbyterians reacted very negatively to a major issue which Anglicans brought forward into that colony's politics: the founding of Anglican-dominated King's College. William Livingston—Presbyterian, lawyer, brother to the lord of Livingston Manor, and New York's first litterateur—assisted by William Smith, Jr.—Presbyterian, lawyer, and son of a councillor—and by John Morin Scott—Presbyterian and lawyer—made the Anglican college proposal a *cause célèbre* in his *Independent Reflector* of 1752–1753. Not only was it antithetical to liberty to permit an established church to dominate the training of youth and the intellectual life of the colony, the *Reflector* argued, but it gave Anglicans a decided political advantage. Livingston addressed the danger of Anglican power in politics in a 1754 pamphlet, inquiring whether "a Corporation worth £2,000 a Year Sterling, and that of *Trinity* Church, which is, or will be perhaps five Times as opulent, joined in and swayed by one Common Interest, will not be able so powerfully to influence all Elections in this City, as to destroy their proper Freedom, and hence forward exclude all other Protestants, *Dutch* as well as *English, from every elective Office?*" Livingston as well feared that the sectarian college would be granted public funds by the assembly if lottery receipts pledged to its support proved insufficient.[25]

---

asserts that "the incessant wrangling and splits that stemmed from the Great Awakening" inhibited Presbyterian political activism. Alan Tully, "Ethnicity, Religion, and Politics in Early America," *PMHB*, CVII (1983), 498, 531, posits (I think correctly) that the Scotch-Irish supported the Quakers on common ideological grounds and for political services rendered. Presbyterians held 8.9 percent of the assembly seats in Pennsylvania, 1729–1754, and 13.5 percent of the seats in New Jersey, 1738–1754. No known Presbyterians held seats in the New York House, 1728–1752; the religion of 10.9 percent of the seat holders is unknown.

24. For partisan determination and sources on biographical data, see note 2, this chapter. Presbyterian affiliation with the administration side in New Jersey was significant when controlling for region.

25. Livingston, *Independent Reflector,* ed. Klein, Mar. 22, 29, Apr. 5, 12, 19, 1753. Also see Klein's

Livingston's articles began a determined campaign to arouse the Presbyterians throughout the colony to the danger of encroachments on religious liberty and to warn the assembly to reject any that might be attempted. He and his allies circulated petitions in the back counties against using public funds to support the college. Propaganda sparked what William Smith, Jr., termed "dissentions" throughout the colony. Presbyterian ministers proclaimed against the plan. The outcry both prevented the assembly from granting public money to the college and encouraged its Anglican managers to refrain from blatant sectarianism.[26]

The college controversy encouraged greater Presbyterian political activity. Presbyterians allied with the Livingston group, which in the 1750s was becoming the political party in opposition to Governor James DeLancey and his allies. As a result, several members of the Livingston family entered the assembly in 1759, including William, his brother Philip, and cousins Robert R. and Henry. The latter two ousted the assemblymen from Dutchess County who had supported public funding for the college. Nephew Peter R. Livingston came into the House in 1761. Three other Presbyterians who were allied with the Livingston party were elected in 1768 and 1769. This family and its allies, capitalizing on a religious issue, gave New York Presbyterians, by midcentury second in number to Dutch Reformed church members, political visibility and inspiration.[27]

In the 1760s Presbyterians in New York City formed a self-conscious, albeit

---

introduction, *ibid.*, 7–10. Livingston, *The Querist: or, a Letter to a Member of the General Assembly of the Colony of New-York, Containing a Variety of Important Questions Occasioned by a Charter Lately Granted for the Establishment of a College* (New York, 1754), 10. Donald F. M. Gerardi, "The King's College Controversy, 1753–1756, and the Ideological Roots of Toryism in New York," *Perspectives in American History*, XI (1977–78), 150. David C. Humphrey, *From King's College to Columbia, 1746–1800* (New York, 1976), 50; Dorothy R. Dillon, *The New York Triumvirate: A Study of the Legal and Political Careers of William Livingston, John Morin Scott, William Smith, Jr.* (New York, 1949), 33. On the lottery, *N.Y. Votes,* June 13, July 3, 1753.

26. Smith, *Continuation of the History of New York,* 213. President Samuel Johnson asserted in June, 1754, that the college would not impose particular sectarian tenets on the students but only those of "common Christianity" (New York *Gazette, or the Weekly Post Boy,* June 3, 1754).

27. Presbyterian assemblymen numbered four (14.8 percent) in 1761, five (18.5 percent) in 1768, and six (22.2 percent) in 1769. Brothers William, Philip, and Peter V. B. and nephew Peter R. Livingston were Presbyterians, as were most others of the family; manor lord Robert, Jr., was Dutch Reformed, and Robert R. of Clermont was Anglican. See Robert Livingston, Jr., to James Duane, Mar. 9, 1772, in Duane Papers, NYHS.

small, electoral force. Those voters recorded on the poll lists for the 1761, 1768, and 1769 elections who bore Scotch-Irish names showed, by the latter two elections, a strong preference for Presbyterians Philip Livingston, Jr., and John Morin Scott. They gave much less support to Presbyterian James Jauncey, who was a candidate of the DeLancey party set up to draw votes from Scott to the DeLancey ticket. In the 1769 election Livingston and Scott garnered over 60 percent of the Scotch-Irish vote, though capturing only 42 to 44 percent of the general electorate. Jauncey's vote totals were almost the reverse; he received just under 60 percent of the votes of the electorate generally but only a bit more than 40 percent of the Scotch-Irish vote. Presbyterians failed to pull the 1769 election to their candidates because they lacked the political sophistication and discipline of the Quakers in New Jersey and Pennsylvania, but they showed that they were a strong minority that might be crucial in a close contest.[28]

In Pennsylvania, Benjamin Franklin and the other leaders of the 1756 transformation of the old Quaker party into the Assembly party incorporated some Presbyterians in the revamped political group. Such calculated ticket balancing strengthened Franklin's party, especially in Philadelphia. Another group of Presbyterians from the back counties entered the House in the mid-1750s; these were proprietary supporters who took their cues from William Allen, Presbyterian opponent of the Quakers and the Assembly party. This Proprietary party bloc included ten of the fourteen Presbyterians in the assembly in the 1760s. When Franklin and his Assembly party allies proposed in 1764 to change the government from proprietary to royal, they aroused the opposition of many Presbyterians and lost the backing of most of that denomination. The Pennsylvania Presbyterian clergy issued a circular letter blasting the scheme, and Presbyterians joined with proprietary supporters and officeholders to form what was termed the Proprietary party. Presbyterians stood for assembly election in 1764 to try to block the change. From 1764 through 1766 the Proprietary party continued the battle against the Assembly party. After its second successive failure to make substantial gains against the Old Ticket, in the 1766 election, this combination gave up most political campaigning.[29]

28. Percentages are based on the total electorate and on the total identified as Scotch-Irish. Names and votes are recorded in the *N.Y.C. Poll List, 1761; N.Y.C. Poll List, 1768;* and *N.Y.C. Poll List, 1769.* All those with common Scotch-Irish names were tallied. See Forrest McDonald and Ellen Shapiro McDonald, "The Ethnic Origins of the American People, 1790," *WMQ,* 3rd ser., XXXVII (1980), 190–97; and Thomas L. Purvis, "The European Ancestry of the United States Population, 1790," *WMQ,* 3rd ser., XLI (1984), 93–96.

29. *Pa. Votes,* Oct. 20, 26, 1764, Oct. 15, 1765, Jan. 13, 20, Feb. 11, 12, 18, 24, 25, Dec. 16, 17, 24, 1773; TPP, *passim;* Bockelman and Ireland, "Internal Revolution in Pennsylvania," 157–58.

James Hutson and other historians of prerevolutionary Pennsylvania have asserted that a "Presbyterian party" organized in Philadelphia and fought elections after 1766. In fact, Presbyterians in Pennsylvania made little effort to take full political advantage of the imperial crises from 1767 through 1773 and of the failure of the Assembly party to respond quickly and determinedly to these. That party divided on the questions of what the imperial connection should be and how best to resist British encroachments, but no group of Presbyterians tried to take power from Assembly party leader Joseph Galloway and his allies. Neither Philadelphia nor Lancaster County elected any Presbyterians to the assembly in the nine elections from 1766 through 1774. Even with the addition of five back county seats to the House in 1771–1774, the proportion of known Presbyterians in the assembly was virtually the same in 1766–1775 as it had been in 1756–1765—10.6 percent in the latter period and 10.3 percent in the earlier. Prominent Presbyterians such as Samuel Purviance, Jr., and George Bryan turned their attention away from party politics. Purviance, who led the Proprietary party election campaign efforts in 1764–1766, left Philadelphia. John Dickinson, the Proprietary party leader whom Presbyterians had strongly backed in the elections of 1764–1766, was not a Presbyterian, showed no interest in organizing Presbyterians, and had only occasional electoral success. As the imperial crises became more acute, some Presbyterians began to take a more active part in the movement for resistance to Britain. Dickinson, joining with Presbyterians Charles Thomson and William Goddard, helped to found a new ideologically based anti-British group in 1772, which called itself the Patriotic Society. This was not primarily Presbyterian nor a very vigorous party. A Presbyterian party was only the bogey of some Quakers and Anglicans, not an organized group that fought elections or spurred resistance.[30]

30. Hutson, *Pennsylvania Politics,* 208–31; Bockelman and Ireland, "Internal Revolution in Pennsylvania," 141; Frost, *Perfect Freedom,* 61–62. Purviance wrote to Ezra Stiles, Nov. 1, 1766, in Dexter, ed., *Itineraries and Miscellanies of Ezra Stiles,* 554, about the partisan efforts of "Our Friends the Presbyterians," but he meant here those who had attached themselves to the Proprietary party. Many prominent opponents of the Assembly party, including Allen, Bryan, Goddard, and the Bradfords of the *Pennsylvania Journal,* were Presbyterians, but these men did not group themselves as a Presbyterian organization. Boyd Stanley Schlenther, *Charles Thomson: A Patriot's Pursuit* (Newark, Del., 1990), 57, 93, 96, notes that Thomson was first an Assembly party supporter who joined Dickinson in a "patriot party" and the Patriotic Society. Schlenther does not identify a Presbyterian party. Assembly party leaders frequently called their opponents a Presbyterian party because the term aroused the political temper of Quakers and Anglicans. The opposition to the Assembly party, still active in Lancaster County, was not a Presbyterian party but a coalition of various groups that made specific efforts to attract Presbyterians by putting some on local tickets. William Atlee to James Burd, Sept. 20, 1768, in Shippen Family Papers, APS; Wayne L. Bockelman, "Local Politics in Pre-Revolutionary Lancaster County," *PMHB,* XCVII (1973), 71.

No significant religious issues aroused New Jersey Presbyterians to heightened political activity. They remained subordinate to the administration supporters, who were Anglicans, siding with them because both were suspicious of Quaker aims. By the 1770s the denomination increased in size enough to dominate some districts and to defend its political interests. In the 1772 Quaker-Presbyterian election confrontation in Cumberland County, a clergyman led his flock in setting up Presbyterian candidates and issuing anti-Quaker propaganda. In that year the assembly added seats from three heretofore unrepresented counties; from them four new Presbyterian assemblymen entered the House. The proportion of Presbyterians increased from five of twenty-four in 1754 to one-fourth by 1769 and one-third after 1772.[31]

Opportunity rather than calculation placed Presbyterians in a much more politically powerful situation during and after the Revolution. The efforts of Presbyterian leaders to raise religious consciousness for political purposes focused on matters such as Quaker pacifism or Anglican bishops and colleges, not on the major issues that divided Britain and America. Presbyterians, however, had no religious grounds for opposing the Revolution, as did Quakers and Anglicans. When the latter groups abandoned politics in revolutionary crisis situations, Presbyterians stepped into the vacuum. Their prominence after 1776 was fortuitous rather than the result of political growth in the period before the outbreak of war in 1775.[32]

Anglicans, who in each of the middle colonies made up about 10 percent of the population, were less a partisan force than were Quakers and were less self-conscious, defensive, and negative toward opponents than were Presbyterians. Anglicanism was significantly related to partisanship in New York and New Jersey, as Tables 1 and 2 indicate; it was probably not related to either political party in Pennsylvania. New Jersey Anglicans in the House were significantly and strongly related to the administration side, that of the East Jersey proprietors. Anglicans wanted a special relation with the administration; the Church of England, unestablished and vulnerable in the colony, had to retain its attachment to the home government to preserve its status. For many of its adherents the church was a symbol of British authority and

31. Gerlach, " 'Quaker' Politics in Eighteenth-Century New Jersey," 1–5, 8–9, quotes a supposedly Quaker broadside, but it appears to be of non-Quaker origin, meant to embarrass the Quaker candidates.

32. Bockelman and Ireland, "Internal Revolution in Pennsylvania," document the domination of the Pennsylvania legislature by Presbyterians after 1776. Owen S. Ireland, "The Crux of Politics: Religion and Party in Pennsylvania, 1778–1789," *WMQ,* 3rd ser., XLII (1985), 454–58, shows the Presbyterian identification with the Constitutionalist party.

order. The association of Anglicans with the home government and over-bearing authority became an important propaganda argument early in New Jersey's political history. In the 1738 Monmouth election, Quakers and Baptists condemned alleged Anglican plans for "bringing in a Bishop, and Tythes." Although these issues were completely trumped up, they apparently served well to rally voters against Anglican candidates.[33]

Anglicans in New York were not as politically active as their New Jersey counterparts. When under attack by the dissenters for proposing the appointment of a bishop, they rallied together and voted for coreligionists. But their efforts were not very strenuous, for they felt secure against most challenges. Their church was established in the four southern counties of the colony, and its members held social and economic leadership posts. The largely Anglican DeLancey party did not respond using the same tone of strident accusations that marked the propaganda of its Livingston rivals in 1769. Rather, the DeLancey side pointed out carefully that its ticket contained Anglicans, a Presbyterian, and a Dutch Reformed candidate. When friction with Britain heightened after 1773, Anglicans in New York tended to take the imperial side. In Jamaica, Queens County, 65 percent of the Anglicans became tories. The DeLancey party, whose leaders and followers were largely Anglican, was the loyalist nucleus by 1775.[34]

In Pennsylvania both of the contending parties appealed to the Anglicans for support on a political, not a religious, basis. No religious issue pushed them to either side. Some had supported the Quaker party before 1755; Anglicans were elected from Philadelphia as Quaker party stalwarts. Thomas Leech served continuously as Philadelphia representative from 1739 to 1750 and again later in the decade. He organized the counterattack of Quakers and Germans against the riotous sailors in the 1742 election. When Quakers retired in 1755 and 1756, several Anglicans who had been "poysoned" by Franklin's political blandishments succeeded them in the Philadelphia delegation and in leadership posts. The Proprietary party used Rev. William Smith as its chief propagandist in the 1750s and 1760s and also had scattered

33. Pointer, *Protestant Pluralism and the New York Experience*, 4; Rev. William Smith to Archbishop Thomas Secker, Nov. 27, 1759, in *DCHNY*, VII, 407; Smith, *History of New Jersey*, 489–500. Anglicans were most numerous in the central capital-town region of New Jersey; Anglicanism proved to be a significant determinant of partisanship, when controlling for region. Anglican association with the administration side was stronger than was that of proprietors and great landholders. See Jacob Dennis to Robert Hunter Morris, Nov. 13, 1738, in MP.

34. For determination of religion and political affiliation, see note 2, this chapter; New

Anglican support from Philadelphia merchants and back county leaders. In the absence of numerous roll calls in the Pennsylvania House, no precise statistical determination of the relationship between Anglicanism and partisanship is possible. Assuming constant divisions between the two parties based on the 1764–1765 roll calls, I find no significant relationship between Anglicanism and partisanship.[35]

Religion did much to determine the modes of political action of prominent laymen but only rarely encouraged clergymen to participate. The exceptions to this rule probably prove that clergymen were not welcome in politics. Nothing came of the organization of ministers that was to promote the aims of dissenters in New York City in 1769. Rev. William Smith reduced his stature in Pennsylvania by writing political polemics and engaging in debates with opponents. Only one clergyman is recorded to have been a candidate for a middle-colony assembly seat. Abraham Keteltas, Presbyterian minister and Yale graduate, stood from Queens in 1768. He was a brother-in-law of Livingston partisan William Smith, Jr., and probably was a party candidate opposing two Anglicans. Keteltas finished lowest in the poll, about four hundred votes behind the winners.[36] That the clergy were prevented from playing a large role, or failed in the attempt, shows that the political leaders and the electorate feared that if clergymen were active candidates or political managers, they might push issues to extremes, exacerbating religious differences.

Regional residence, next in importance to religion in determining political affiliation, is a somewhat arbitrary category. The middle colonists usually

York *Gazette and Weekly Mercury,* Jan. 16, 1769; Joseph S. Tiedemann, "Communities in the Midst of the American Revolution: Queens County, New York, 1774–1775," *Journal of Social History,* XVIII (1984), 58.

35. Tully, *William Penn's Legacy,* 170–73; William T. Parsons, "The Bloody Election of 1742," *Pa. Hist.,* XXXVI (1969), 298–99; Richard Peters to Thomas Penn, Apr. 25, 29, 1756, in TPP; Ralph Ketcham, "Benjamin Franklin and William Smith: New Light on an Old Philadelphia Quarrel," *PMHB,* LXXXVIII (1964), 142–63. In 1764–1765, the House split nineteen Assembly party members to eleven Proprietary partisans; fourteen Anglicans sided with the former and eight with the latter. Projecting these proportions, I calculate a chi-square for the relationship between Anglicanism and the Proprietary party of 0.05, insignificant at the 0.05 level with 1 df.

36. New York *Mercury,* Mar. 21, 1768; Benjamin F. Thompson, *History of Long Island From Its Discovery and Settlement to the Present Time* (3rd ed., 3 vols.; New York, 1918), II, 608. Franklin B. Dexter, *Biographical Sketches of the Graduates of Yale College, with Annals of the College History* (6 vols.; New York, 1885–1912), II, 289–90.

defined regions as east and west or city and country. In each of the middle colonies, distant geographical sections saw themselves as different, and urban centers and town districts had an identity separate from their rural surroundings or hinterland. The delineation of the several urban and rural areas that is employed here is based on geography, identity of settlers, economic activities, and common antagonism to another region. Regional residence was related to religious denomination in cases in which a denomination clustered in one region, but generally denominations were spread throughout these three colonies.[37]

Pennsylvania's east-west conflict is one of the most famous in the history of early America because of its bloodthirstiness and revolutionary potential. Westerners were so alienated and alarmed by what they considered an unrepresentative government, dominated by easterners who held antiwestern or uncaring views, that they took drastic measures. Sectionalism emerged dramatically when in November, 1755, John Hambright led some three hundred to seven hundred backcountrymen in a march on Philadelphia to demand firmer defense measures against the French and their Native American allies. In late 1763 came the most ferocious rural uprising in the middle colonies, the Paxton Boys' rampage. These unruly, desperate, and thuggish Lancaster County settlers, after murdering twenty innocent Native Americans in and near Lancaster in December, 1763, marched on Philadelphia demanding equal representation and more defense measures. In March, 1765, they wreaked further revenge on the capital by attacking the wagons of Philadelphia merchants at Sideling Hill in central Pennsylvania. Politically the western discontent over the Quaker peace policy helped to rejuvenate the Proprietary party; in 1756 Philadelphia proprietary supporters were elected as assembly representatives from the back counties and became the mainstays of a small western–Proprietary party delegation in the House. The coalition remained intact to contest the eastern-dominated Assembly party in the elections of 1764–1766. Rambunctious defiance by westerners continued after these elections; in 1768 a mob rescued from the Carlisle jail two Germans accused of murdering ten Native Americans. Political frustration, hatred for Native Americans and Quakers, and suspicion of eastern economic activities let loose the most atrocious villainy.[38]

37. Pointer, *Protestant Pluralism and the New York Experience*, 5–7, provides maps of the location of churches in New York in 1775.

38. Robert Hunter Morris to Thomas Penn, Nov. 28, 1755, in Labaree *et al.*, eds., *Franklin Papers*, VI, 280–82; *Pa. Votes*, Nov. 23, 1755; Hutson, *Pennsylvania Politics*, 25–26; Franklin, *Nar-*

Westerners got little recognition from the government. The western counties' demands for equal representation and the remedy of other grievances received only a perfunctory hearing in 1764 and no immediate or full action. In succeeding years the establishing of circuit courts and the increasing of back county representation met these demands only partially. In the roll calls of the 1764–1765 period and in those commencing in 1772, when the House began regular reporting of record votes, the Assembly party representatives from the eastern counties generally voted together in opposition to the proprietary supporters from the remote districts. This division obtained whether the issue was proprietary government, equitable taxation, or payment of salaries. Philadelphia merchant William Allen was careful to vote with his allies, the back county Proprietary party assemblymen, on most of these roll calls.[39] Both cultural and economic differences inspired the seaboard-backcountry conflict; cultural differences—of religion and attitude toward Native Americans—seem the stronger inspiration.

New York and New Jersey also split regionally, but into more than two sections. New York divided into six regions. As Table 3 shows, New York City, the two counties on the east shore of the Hudson River between New York and Albany, and the two counties on the west shore were significantly related to a particular partisan group: the city and the east shore to the administration side, the west shore to the opposition. These divergent political views appear to have resulted largely from regional economic differences. The interests of the city included not only those of the merchants who dominated the assembly delegation, the city corporation, and the Chamber of Commerce, but also those of artisans, shopkeepers, bakers, and others of the middling orders who supported the trading interest. The leaders who best articulated these interests were affiliated with the Philipse-DeLancey administration side. The Philipse family received the allegiance of its neighbors, the large landholders on the east shore. Small farmers on the Hudson

---

rative of the Late Massacres, in Lancaster County, of a Number of Indians, Friends of This Province, by Persons Unknown, in Labaree et al., eds., Franklin Papers, XI, 45–47. For the march on the city, Labaree et al., eds., Franklin Papers, XI, 69–75; For other incidents see Stephen H. Cutcliffe, "Sideling Hill Affair: The Cumberland County Riots of 1765," Western Pennsylvania Historical Magazine, LIX (1976), 45–47; G. S. Rowe, "The Frederick Stump Affair, 1768, and Its Challenge to Legal Historians of Early Pennsylvania," Pa. Hist., XLIX (1982), 259–88.

39. Pa. Votes, Feb. 25, May 25, Oct. 20, 1764, Oct. 25, 1765, Sept. 28, Dec. 16, 17, 24, 1773, Jan. 4, 1774.

TABLE 3

Regions and Partisanship: New York, 1737–1775

(All tabulated figures are assembly terms)

	Administration	Opposition	Indeterminate
New York City	29	11	
Albany	22	23	1
East shore	40	14	2
West shore	11	27	1
Long Island, Staten Island	31	38	4
Back counties	4	0	

lambda-b = 0.22
chi-square, opposition and west shore = 10.67;   phi = 0.20
chi-square, administration and east shore = 8.93;   phi = 0.19
chi-square, administration and New York City = 6.40;   phi = 0.16
chi-square, opposition and Long Island, Staten Island = 2.70

west shore voted for the opposition and Livingston parties. Albany and the small farm region composed of Long Island and Staten Island were divided in party affiliation, and the distant back counties were too new to characterize.

Important regional issues flared up on occasion, but only one persisted to become a party issue. After 1750 the inspection of products, the restriction of auction sales, the maintenance of a lighthouse, and the regulation of port pilots were all uncontested, though they had occasioned some differences before that time. Representatives of the landholding interests and city assemblymen clashed over the assizes of victuals of New York City—the regulation of food prices—in 1763. When price controls were imposed, representatives from Queens and Richmond, producers of farm produce, attempted to retaliate against the city by regulating firewood sales there. The rural representatives finally pushed through a bill voiding the assizes, which the council ignored. Controversy over these economic issues was only occasional. Much more important to politics was the unequal taxation of the regions, which became a party matter when the colony had to raise funds for defense against the French in 1744, 1746, and 1755.[40]

In New Jersey, regional factors were more significant than in New York.

40. *Examiner, No. 2* (New York, 1769), 2; *N.Y. Votes,* Oct. 24, 26, 1750, Dec. 5, 7–8, 16–20, 22–23, 1763. See William Alexander to John Provoost, Nov. 16, 1750, in William Alexander Papers, NYHS, on back county representatives' opposition to economic legislation.

TABLE 4

Regions and Partisanship: New Jersey, 1738–1775

(*All tabulated figures are assembly terms*)

	Central capital-town	West Jersey rural	East Jersey rural
Administration	78	37	17
Opposition	23	81	54
Middle	2	8	5
Indeterminate	2	8	

lambda-*b* = 0.37
chi-square, administration and central = 65.86;   phi = 0.46
chi-square, opposition and West Jersey rural = 9.18;   phi = 0.17
chi-square, opposition and East Jersey rural = 16.41;   phi = 0.23

The traditional view of sectional division in New Jersey is that of the barrel tapped at both ends, the west attached to Philadelphia and the east to New York. Smaller regions based on geographic factors and ethnic settlement can also be located, but identifying three regions seems both realistic and useful.[41] In the central part of the colony lay the capitals and the major towns— Perth Amboy and Burlington, Elizabethtown and Newark. As Table 4 shows, assemblymen from this central capital-town region were affiliated with the administration side; those from the eastern and western rural counties, which because of their commercial attachments and cultural characteristics should be regarded as two separate regions, were affiliated with the opposition. These relationships were significant when controlled for religion and occupation.

These towns in the central region were the largest local trading centers of the colony; their interests were in bringing order to trade and reducing competition. Their representatives in 1743 and 1744 supported a duty on wheat, the regulation of flour exports, and restrictions on the trade in cedarwood by nonnative merchants; the landowner majority defeated these measures. Antagonism over economic policy did not last, for within a few years, as trade increased, the House became more amenable to regulation. A flour act was passed in 1751, and regulation of auction sales was imposed in 1763 and 1768. During the postwar depression of the 1760s the central capital-town region supported debtor relief and the appropriation of £200 for distressed farmers in rural Sussex County.[42] The merchants and professional men at the cap-

---

41. Wacker, *Land and People,* 410, divides New Jersey into six settlement regions.
42. *N.J. Votes,* Nov. 4, 1743, Oct. 16, 26, 1744, Oct. 4, 1751, Dec. 6, 1763, June 15–18, 1765, Apr.

TABLE 5

Occupation and Partisanship: New York, 1737–1775

(*All tabulated figures are assembly terms*)

	Administration	Opposition	Indeterminate
Great landholder	38	20	
Landowner	24	19	2
Farmer	11	19	3
Merchant	36	28	
Manufacturer-shopkeeper	11	4	
Lawyer	3	8	1
Unknown	14	16	2

lambda-b = 0.13
chi-square, administration and great landholder = 4.15; phi = 0.13
chi-square, administration and manufacturer-shopkeeper = 1.87
chi-square, administration and merchants = 0.23
chi-square, opposition and lawyers = 1.75
chi-square, opposition and farmers = 2.22

itals also sought the patronage and friendly association of the officers of administration; in exchange, they allied with these officials in the party that supported them.

Occupation ranked statistically behind religion and region in influencing partisan choice in both New York and New Jersey. For Pennsylvania, lack of data makes it impossible to measure the importance of occupation so that colony will be omitted from the discussion, though there is no reason to believe that occupation was an important determinant there. Although it might appear from a casual glance at Tables 5 and 6 that farmers, merchants, artisans, and lawyers sided with one party or the other, none of those groups was significantly related to partisanship. Merchants, probably more than any other group, profited from legislative regulation of commerce, but this was rarely a partisan matter. As these tables show, the major occupational group related to partisanship in both colonies was the great landholders—the proprietors of large tracts or manors, often thousands of acres and often with tenants. In New Jersey lesser landowners—those with a few hundred acres—were also significantly associated with partisan positions, when con-

25, 1768. James H. Levitt, *For Want of Trade: Shipping and the New Jersey Ports, 1680–1783* (Newark, N.J., 1981), 35–38, blames the assembly for lack of mercantile encouragement, without considering whether the New Jersey merchants wished to shift their activities from the larger neighboring ports.

TABLE 6

Occupation and Partisanship: New Jersey, 1738–1775
(*All tabulated figures are assembly terms*)

	Administration	Opposition	Middle	Indeterminate
Great landholder	31	13	2	
Landowner	37	85	4	4
Farmer	17	25	4	
Merchant	25	22	3	3
Manufacturer-shopkeeper	7	6	0	1
Lawyer	14	7	2	
Unknown	1			2

lambda-*b* = 0.20
chi-square, administration and great landholder = 13.17;   phi = 0.20
chi-square, opposition and landowner = 19.46;   phi = 0.25
chi-square, administration and lawyer = 2.88
chi-square, opposition and farmer = 0.38

trolling for region. Only the smaller landowners and the farmers with even less acreage could be considered to be representing the economic status of their constituents. The great landholders, a minuscule part of society, chiefly pursued their personal aims.[43]

In New Jersey the substantial and well-to-do landholders consisted of two groups: the East and West Jersey proprietors and the landowners who possessed more than merely the holdings of a small, semisubsistence farmer. The proprietors were associated with the administration side, but the lesser landowners joined with the oppositionists. The core of the the administration supporters was composed of the East Jersey proprietors, who unanimously backed that side. Every characteristic of the East Jersey proprietors led them to join the administration. They needed the support and patronage of the executive against their adversaries in land disputes, particularly so they could control the judiciary. They were wealthy and Anglican without exception. West Jersey proprietors divided between the administration and opposition sides. Those who did not ally with the administration were mostly Quaker or Baptist mavericks.[44]

43. Thomas M. Doerflinger, *A Vigorous Spirit of Enterprise: Merchants and Economic Development in Revolutionary Philadelphia* (Chapel Hill, 1986), 59–60, 182, notes that his subjects were largely apolitical or took political positions based mainly on religious affiliations.

44. Proprietors in the assembly are identified in scattered biographical footnotes in the *NJA*, and in Purvis, "N.J. Assembly," 256–312. Purvis, *Proprietors, Patronage, and Paper Money*, 130–31,

Members of the East Jersey proprietors' council were aristocratic and haughty because they served for life terms in a closed corporation and comprised a family compact of blood and marriage relatives. Richard Peters' characterization of Morris ally James Alexander probably applied equally to the other East Jersey proprietors: Alexander had "the most immoderate Thirst for Land of any man I know." In Alexander's case, his whig principles in New York politics left him when he crossed the Jersey border, and greed took over. Perhaps more revealing was the example of Lewis Morris Ashfield—grandson of Morris, proprietor, and member of the New Jersey Council—who arrogantly cursed a constable: "God Damn you with your King's Laws." For good measure, Ashfield also horsewhipped the constable. The councillor was, of course, exonerated.[45] The East Jersey proprietors were as contentious as they were overweening. Determined to protect their land rights, they confronted the challenges of squatters of interlopers who claimed their land by right of Indian title, of recalcitrant purchasers who refused to pay quitrents, and of timber poachers. The Indian title land claimants—the Clinker Lot Right men from Elizabethtown, or, as the proprietors called them, the rioters—were their greatest bane. These adversaries refused to move or pay rents, they took up clubs to deter collectors and sheriffs, and they massed to deliver their fellows from jail. To safeguard their property the proprietors sought political power in both the council and the assembly. Samuel Neville, perhaps the wealthiest proprietor, preferred to serve in the assembly rather than the council and also as Supreme Court justice. Almost invariably proprietors like Neville occupied the two Perth Amboy assembly seats. They often contested for the Middlesex County seats as well but had to share these with antiproprietary assemblymen.[46]

---

notes the importance of patronage for the proprietor bloc in the legislature. For their business affairs, John E. Pomfret, *The New Jersey Proprietors and their Lands, 1664–1776* (Princeton, 1964), 108.

45. Lewis Morris to [?], July 18, 1728, in MP; Peters to Thomas Penn, June 20, 1752, in TPP; Journal of the Governor and Council, Oct. 3, 1751, May 23, 1753, in *NJA*, XVI, 324–26, 401–402.

46. Thomas L. Purvis, "Origins and Patterns of Agrarian Unrest in New Jersey, 1735 to 1754," *WMQ*, 3rd ser., XXXIX (1982), 600–627; Edward Countryman, "'Out of the Bounds of the Law': Northern Land Rioters in the Eighteenth Century," in *The American Revolution: Explorations in the History of American Radicalism*, ed. Alfred F. Young (De Kalb, 1976), 37–69; Gary S. Horowitz, "New Jersey Land Riots, 1745–1755," in *Economic and Social History of Colonial New Jersey*, ed. William C. Wright (Trenton, 1974), 24–33. Quitrent collections were £15,000 in arrears in 1746, according to "Statement of the Council of Proprietors, March 25, 1746," in *A Bill in the Chancery of New-*

In contrast to their wealthier colleagues, the lesser landowners of the New Jersey Assembly appeared to lend a peaceful, bucolic cast to politics. Critics such as Lewis Morris, Sr., made fun of their petty concerns: landowner-dominated assemblies busied themselves with

> great debates, of piggs and fowl,
> what bigness Stallions ought to Stroul?
> if hogs should run at large.

A Bolingbrokian might believe that these landowners exemplified the ideal of the independent country gentleman who disdained party allegiance. Such independent legislators may have been numerous in Britain, outside the tory peer's imagination, but not in the middle colonies. In New Jersey and also in New York landholders took partisan stances in nearly all instances. Great landholders, landowners, and farmers who were consistently partisan held 96.4 percent of the total seats held by those groups in the New York Assembly; in the New Jersey House they held 93.6 percent. In New Jersey and Pennsylvania the well-to-do landowners opposed the expansion of proprietary claims. New Jersey landowners, fearful of the lordly proprietors, were compelled to protect their rights to their holdings and to assert their liberty to expand them. Consequently, they joined the opposition side, as noted in Table 6. William Lawrence and his son Robert, later New Jersey Assembly Speaker, claimed that Monmouth County farmers possessed the landholding rights of "Sons of Adam" and castigated the East Jersey proprietors for invading these. In Pennsylvania, the 1759 effort to pass a warrants and surveys act was an attack on the Penns' land office on behalf of the landowners.[47]

As did the New Jersey proprietors, the manor lords and other great land-

---

Jersey, at the Suit of John, Earl of Stair, and Others, Proprietors of the Eastern Division of New-Jersey, Against Benjamin Bond, and Some Other Persons of Elizabeth-Town, Distinguished by the Name of the Clinker Lot Right Men (New York, 1747), 6. Proprietors held twenty-one of the twenty-four places from Perth Amboy, 1738–1775, but only five of twenty-four from Middlesex County.

47. [Lewis Morris], "The Mock Monarchy or the Kingdom of Apes. A Poem by a Gentleman of New Jersey in America," in MP. "Apes" refers to Speaker Adolph Philipse of New York; the piece was probably written in 1726–1728. Also see [Morris], "'Dialogue Concerning Trade,'" ed. Daniel, 203, n. 9; William Lawrence to James Alexander, Jan. 1, 1734–5, in James Alexander Papers, NYHS; Stillwell, *Historical and Genealogical Miscellany,* I, 220–22; Isaac Norris to Benjamin Franklin, Aug. 22, 1759, in Labaree *et al.,* eds., *Franklin Papers,* VIII, 428–29.

holders of New York secured their political power by serving in the assembly. Three of the manors, Rensselaerwyck, Livingston, and Cortlandt, had their own representatives in the House; the representative was often the manor lord himself. The lords of the manors of Philipseburg and Islip always represented their counties also. The son of the owner of Clermont Manor served two terms, the owner and the son of the owner of Morrisania sought assembly seats in most elections, and the son-in-law of Sir William Johnson, who desired a patent for his vast frontier holdings, represented that remote area. Even the owners of the comparatively insignificant manors of Fox Hall and Bentley sat in the House for their counties. Henry Beekman, a very great landowner with status equal to that of a manor lord, also was a representative. In the thirty-eight years before the Revolution, nineteen manor lords or equivalently important great landholders served 22.4 percent of all assembly terms.[48]

The manor lords, as Table 5 shows, generally lined up on the administration side because they were anxious to protect their holdings from title challenges made by the British government, from rebellious tenants, and from envious interlopers or squatters. Some of the purchases that constituted the origins of the great manors were of very questionable legality; the founders had obtained titles from the Native American occupants by fraud and had run extensive and unwarranted boundaries. When officials such as Lieutenant Governor Cadwallader Colden criticized the origins of the enormous landholdings, the manor lords became understandably nervous. In reality there

---

48. From Rensselaerwyck: lord Jeremiah and heir John Baptist Van Rensselaer; from Livingston Manor: lord Robert, Jr., and heir Peter R. Livingston; from Cortlandt: Philip Verplanck and Pierre Van Cortlandt; from Philipseburg representing Westchester County: the Frederick Philipses II and III; from Islip representing Suffolk County: the William Nicolls II and III; from Morrisania representing or standing for election from Westchester: the Lewis Morrises, Sr., Jr., and III; from Clermont: heir Robert R. Livingston; from the Johnson Grant in Tryon County: Guy Johnson; from Fox Hall and Ulster County: Abraham Gaasbeck-Chambers; from Bentley on Staten Island: Christopher Billop. Beekman was from Dutchess County. Manor lord Adolph Philipse represented New York City. Biographical data compiled from Abstracts of Wills, in *NYHSC*, vols. 25–39; Bonomi, *Factious People*, 288–92; Sun Bok Kim, *Landlord and Tenant in Colonial New York: Manorial Society, 1664–1775* (Chapel Hill, 1978), 416–17; George Dangerfield, *Chancellor Robert R. Livingston of New York, 1746–1813* (New York, 1960); Jacob Judd, "A Loyalist Claim, the Philipse Estate," in *The Loyalist Americans: A Focus on Greater New York*, ed. Robert A. East and Jacob Judd (Tarrytown, 1975), 104, 111; Martha B. Flint, *Long Island Before the Revolution: A Colonial Study* (1896; rpr. Port Washington, 1967), 259; Ina K. Morris, *Morris' Memorial History of Staten Island, New York* (2 vols.; New York, 1898–1900), I, 142–43.

was little likelihood that the British government would overset a land grant on the grounds that its proprietors swindled some Indians, but it was wise to possess political power that might forestall any such effort.[49] Challenges from tenants who disliked the terms of their leases and from interlopers who moved west from New England to seize what appeared to them to be vacant land were more immediate and personally threatening. Great landholders needed political power and influence because the might of the government was the most effective means of suppressing these upstarts. The manor lords received all the support they could have hoped for when British troops put down tenant and squatter riots in 1766.[50] The support the New York manor lords gave to the parties drew from ideology and economic self-interest, not from a tight family compact. James Alexander's assessment of Robert R. Livingston's potential as a partisan ally precisely compares the significance of family and ideology: despite Livingston's close "relations in blood to the C[hief Justice James DeLancey] & J Livingston & H Beekman, which indeed are near and which staggered me a little . . . upon the whole we believe that RRL's good Sense Spirit and independence, could over ballance that relation."[51]

Partisanship was not strongly related to wealth holdings in the middle colonies, as Tables 7 and 8 show. Using the categories of wealthy, well-to-do, middling, and poor, I found that wealthy assemblymen in New York and New Jersey were usually on the administrative side, but the wealthy group was not related to that party when great landholders were excluded. Wealthy assemblymen did not band together to uphold their specific interests. They believed that they were obligated to attend to the interests of constituents who elected them to represent, not to aggrandize. Although historian Robert J. Dinkin asserts that the "Esquire" vote in the 1769 election in New York

49. Klein, "Corruption in Colonial America," 59–60; Bonomi, *Factious People*, 209.

50. Kim, *Landlord and Tenant*, 188–90; Irving Mark, *Agrarian Conflicts in Colonial New York, 1711–1775* (2nd ed.; Port Washington, 1965), 136–45. Robert Livingston, Jr., noted concern about interlopers' attacks on his manor and whether the government would defend him, to William Alexander, Mar. 26, 1753, in William Alexander Papers, NYHS; to Henry Van Rensselaer, Aug. 14, 1753, in Van Rensselaer–Fort Papers, NYPL; to James Duane, Feb. 15, 1762, Sept. 20, 1769, in Duane Papers, NYHS.

51. James Alexander to Cadwallader Colden, Dec. 5, 1751, in *NYHSC*, LIII, 303–304. Bernard Friedman, "The New York Assembly Elections of 1768 and 1769: The Disruption of Family Politics," *New York History*, XLVI (1965), 7–8, concludes that family politics had been important until the prerevolutionary crisis, when ideology came to be a more powerful political determinant.

TABLE 7

Wealth and Partisanship: New York, 1737–1775

(*All tabulated figures are assembly terms*)

	Wealthy	Well-to-do	Middling	Unknown
Administration—DeLancey	73	47	8	9
Opposition—Livingston	48	43	16	7
Indeterminate	1	3	2	2

lambda-b = 0.07
chi-square, administration and wealthy = 4.14;   phi = 0.12;
    (omitting great landholders, chi-square = 0.81)
chi-square, opposition and middling = 2.86

TABLE 8

Wealth and Partisanship: New Jersey, 1738–1775

(*All tabulated figures are assembly terms*)

	Wealthy	Well-to-do	Middling	Unknown
Administration	61	54	8	9
Opposition	54	83	19	2
Middle	5	6	2	2
Indeterminate	3	4	1	2

lambda-b = 0.05
chi-square, administration and wealthy = 4.40;   phi = 0.12;
    (omitting great landholders, chi-square = 0.08)
chi-square, opposition and middling = 1.75

chiefly went to the DeLancey party, in fact there is no statistically significant difference between the "Esquire" vote for the DeLanceyites and the vote of the electorate generally. In Pennsylvania, however, the richest citizens may have inclined to the administration side. Thomas Penn snobbishly rejoiced that the opposition to obstreperous Quakers in the Pennsylvania House in 1741 came from "many of our wealthy Inhabitants." In 1756 Proprietary party leaders in Philadelphia were taxed slightly higher than was a group of leading Quakers. There was no significant relationship between partisanship and the other categories of wealth. Differences in economic status did not divide assemblymen or voters into parties nearly as much as did religious and regional differences.[52]

52. For estimates of wealth holdings of assemblymen, Abstracts of Wills, in *NYHSC*, vols. 25–39; Olson, "New York Assembly," 21–28; Calendar of New Jersey Wills, Administrations, Etc.,

As recent research has made clear, a sizable inequality in the distribution of wealth marked the middle colonies in the latter half of the eighteenth century. In New Jersey 30 to 40 percent of the populace was classified as poor or landless; in southeast Pennsylvania 27 to 41 percent were landless. New York City and Philadelphia were compelled to increase their appropriations for poor relief substantially. This had little meaning for politics. The lower sort protested particular economic actions they deemed harmful but did not demand that the legislatures redress inequality. They did not comprehend general problems with the economic system and so remained mostly inarticulate. The parties in the legislature sometimes offered aid to relieve specific economic suffering but could generally ignore most needs of the lower orders without much protest.[53] The lesser role of economic characteristics, particularly wealth status, in partisanship did not mean that wealth differences had little part to play in the formation of parties or their operations. Political leaders used the inequalities of wealth to exploit the political activities of those of less means. Many of these men could vote, but they had to be brought into political activity. The traditional rhythm of the daily life

---

in *NJA*, vols. 30, 32–42; Batinski, *New Jersey Assembly*, 252–300; Tully, *William Penn's Legacy*, 174–75; Ryerson, *The Revolution Is Now Begun*, 260–62; Oaks, "Philadelphia Merchants and the Origins of American Independence," 407–36. The categories of wealthy, well-to-do, and middling, adapted from Jackson T. Main, *The Social Structure of Revolutionary America* (Princeton, 1965), are employed here to provide a base for comparison among the middle colonies. Olson, "New York Assembly," uses these categories. Purvis, *Proprietors, Patronage, and Paper Money*, 53–54, uses percentile categories. He ranks 70.1 percent in the top 5 percent, equivalent to the "wealthy" category; this study finds 39.0 percent of New Jersey assembly terms served by the wealthy. The discrepancy arises from different interpretations of landholding amounts given in New Jersey wills. Making estimates for 40.6 percent of Pennsylvania assemblymen, I conclude that 28.5 percent of these were wealthy and 8.9 percent were of the middling category. Using the compilations of Dinkin, *Voting in Provincial America*, 200, and the *N.Y.C. Poll List, 1769*, chi-square for the relationship of "Esquire" voters to the DeLancey side is calculated at 0.06, insignificant at the 0.05 level with 1 df. See Thomas Penn to Ferdinand John Paris, Mar. 27, 1741, in TPP; Stephen Brobeck, "Revolutionary Change in Colonial Philadelphia: The Brief Life of the Proprietary Gentry," *WMQ*, 3rd ser., XXXIII (1976), 422–23.

53. Dennis P. Ryan, "Landholding, Opportunity, and Mobility in Revolutionary New Jersey," *WMQ*, 3rd ser., XXXVI (1979), 575–77; James T. Lemon, *The Best Poor Man's Country: A Geographical Study of Early Southeastern Pennsylvania* (Baltimore, 1972), 94; Nash, *Urban Crucible*, 252–56, 321–23, 402; Billy G. Smith, *The "Lower Sort": Philadelphia's Laboring People, 1750–1800* (Ithaca, 1990), 91. Smith, 121, notes economically motivated political action of laborers and sailors in Philadelphia, but this occurred chiefly after 1776.

of the middling sort—plant, harvest, go to market, labor at the bench—allowed little opportunity for deep commitment to politics. Persuading them was the task of election canvassers. Canvassing was a consequence of the people's desire not to trouble themselves ordinarily with matters out of their routine, unless individually persuaded otherwise.

All parties canvassed; some became very proficient and gained an important advantage over their rivals. The best at canvassing was the Assembly party of Pennsylvania. The party in Philadelphia used a group called the White Oaks that included ship carpenters and other middling artisans who supported the Assembly party. The organization worked for the Franklin-Galloway ticket from before 1764 to 1769, rounding up voters, drumming up spirit for campaigns, and guarding against disorders. It helped to suppress an incipient Stamp Act riot in 1765. These artisans had no particular economic aim in allying with the Assembly party. They admired their fellow artisan Franklin because of his name and fame, and they favored the stance of the Assembly party against the elite proprietary supporters who dominated Philadelphia's local government.[54]

Elite political leaders in New York and New Jersey also put considerable effort into garnering voters. In New York City they often employed door-to-door solicitation. In the 1737 election there, gentlemen sent their carriages to convey voters of the lesser orders to the polls. In the 1748 election, instead of providing gentlemanly favors, the canvassers fraternized with the humble while dressed in old clothes. Governor George Clinton reported before the 1750 election that "several Yorkers & others had been canvassing for Members from this Place [New York City] up to Albany (as they expect a dissolution) working up the People to their own seditious way of thinking, among them was Robt. Livingston of the Mannor, James Livingston, John Livingston, Nich. Bayard, Coll Gosbeck [Gaasbeck-Chambers], and Coll Mathews [sic]." Allies of the wealthy Livingstons offered Abraham Yates £50 to cover canvassing expenses if he would stand in the Albany assembly election of 1761. Councillor Oliver DeLancey canvassed for his nephew and allied can-

54. Historiographical debate about the White Oaks can be followed in James H. Hutson, "An Investigation of the Inarticulate: Philadelphia's White Oaks," WMQ, 3rd ser., XXVIII (1971), 3–25; Jesse Lemisch and John K. Alexander, "The White Oaks, Jack Tar, and the Concept of the 'Inarticulate,'" WMQ, 3rd ser., XXIX (1972), 109–34; Simeon J. Crowther, "A Note on the Economic Position of Philadelphia's White Oaks," WMQ, 3rd ser., XXIX (1972), 134–36; Hutson, "Rebuttal," WMQ, 3rd ser., XXIX (1972), 136–42; Charles S. Olton, Artisans for Independence: Philadelphia Mechanics and the American Revolution (Syracuse, 1975), 38.

didates in 1768. Richard Smith, Jr., assemblyman of Burlington, New Jersey, led a contingent from the town to the county election site in a hard-fought election in 1740.[55]

Demonstrations and entertainments, sometimes combined with canvassing, constituted an important mode of communication to those of the middling sort who wished to experience political excitement rather than merely read about issues. The parades on or immediately before election day were in effect marches of unity to the polls, calculated to get bystanders to admire the displays and to join them. Party leaders might use musicians to attract attention and arouse emotion, as did the Morrisites in the 1733 Westchester Borough election. Demonstrators might show ethnic solidarity by marching or singing, as did German voters in Philadelphia and New York. The most elaborate demonstration in the middle colonies before the revolutionary crisis was the celebration of the king's birthday in Philadelphia in 1766. Joseph Galloway and his party allies planned this event to whip up renewed affection for Britain after the repeal of the Stamp Act and to call the attention of their constituents to the moderate stance taken by the Assembly party. Bands, a parade, food and drink, patriotic toasts, and fireworks all served to attract and entertain a large, happy crowd and, judging by the election results later that year, to revitalize Galloway's party.[56]

Treating the electorate, a British custom, was another way that the elite political leaders hoped to draw the middling sort to the polls. It was practiced frequently enough: in Philadelphia in the 1720s and 1760s and in New York in various elections, particularly that of 1768. Undoubtedly the promise of refreshment drew some voters to the polls. Politicians worried enough about the advantage treating might give to wealthy opponents that they criticized each other for treating and tried to halt it. In the New York election campaign of 1769 the Livingston party sought agreement with the De-Lancey side to stop treating, but the DeLancey side rejected the proposal. Perhaps the Livingstons protested too much, for a broadside writer in 1768 conveyed a more hardheaded sentiment toward treating:

55. Nicholas Varga, "Election Procedures and Practices in Colonial New York," *New York History*, XL (1960), 263; Bridenbaugh, *Cities in the Wilderness*, 435; Nash, *Urban Crucible*, 228; Clinton to Cadwallader Colden, Feb. 9, 1749–50, in *NYHSC*, LII, 189; Nicholas Varga, "The Development and Structure of Local Government in Colonial New York," in *Town and County: Essays on the Structure of Local Government in the American Colonies*, ed. Bruce C. Daniels (Middletown, 1978), 198; Thompson, ed., "Poll Book of an Election in 1739 [–40], Burlington County," 185–93.

56. *Pennsylvania Gazette* (Philadelphia), June 12, 1766.

Since sundry moneyed Gentlemen of this City, have been generous enough to open the Strings of their Purses, to furnish Belly-Timber during the present Election; Let us Eat heartily, tho' temperately; Drink liberally, tho' cautiously; Sing jovially, tho' modestly; Applaud disinterestedly, tho' generously: And under the protection of Bacchus, let those Gentlemen know, that we love their Bread and Wine, but despise the imputation of being influenced by Either, to vote for any Person who appears so extremely anxious of advancing himself to a P[ost] where the same Motives that induced him to contribute so generously to multiply Votes, would doubtless prevail with him to concert Schemes, whereby we shall be obliged to reimburse Tenfold as much when the most painful Subordination or Slavery shall command our beloved Interests.[57]

During the 1720s and 1730s, at the inception of partisan politics, the upper class tried to appeal to the economic interest of the middling sort. Elite leaders explained that their side was the friend of the middling voter and their policies would curtail the dominance of the wealthy. In the 1727 election in New York City all candidates promised to tax the wealthy more heavily. A broadside of the early 1730s complained of tax inequity: "How unreasonable is it, that Gentlemen should possess large Tracts of uncultivated Lands, without paying Taxes, and yet these Tracts undeniably increase in Value by the Industry of the poorer Sort, and other Inhabitants who pay Taxes." In its campaign against Cosby, Chief Justice DeLancey, and their supporters, the Morris-Alexander party appealed to New York artisans to join it against what its propaganda portrayed as grasping merchants and unscrupulous lawyers. In 1734 "Timothy Wheelwright" urged that the electorate choose a common councilman from the lower sort, not exclusively from the New York City merchants. Sir William Keith and David Lloyd used the paper money controversy in Pennsylvania to frame class appeals to city artisans.[58]

Appeals to economic interests became less important from the 1740s to the 1770s, probably because political leaders came to realize that they were effective only in special circumstances. During the 1768 and 1769 New York City elections "Messrs. Axe and Hammer" in their broadsides from "Trades-

57. The proposed rules also included a ban on demonstrations and a guarantee of free access to the stairs at the polling place (*To the Freeholders* [New York, 1769]). "Bibibus," *A Toothful of Advice* (New York, 1768).

58. "John Sydney," untitled broadside; "Timothy Wheelwright," untitled broadside; Nash, *Urban Crucible,* 140–41, 143, 147, 150–51.

man's Hall" argued that mechanics and merchants should join their common interest in trade against conniving lawyers, but they focused on only one
candidate—John Morin Scott. Artisans in Philadelphia only occasionally emphasized political differences between themselves and the upper class. "A
Brother Chip," ship carpenter and spokesman for Philadelphia artisans in
the 1770 election, lamented that "a certain Company of leading Men nominate Persons, and settle the Ticket . . . without ever permitting the affirma-
tive or negative voice of a mechanic to interfere." This outburst helped to
gain greater political power for artisans, but another of the middling sort
had no success in his appeal. A candidate for sheriff of Philadelphia in 1770,
apparently otherwise unemployed, addressed an election broadside to the
"Tradesmen, Artificers, Mechanics, & c." in hopes that they would elect
him rather than "pamper Luxury, by adding to the Abundance of the Rich."
This was a tactical error for the times; the electorate rejected him. Artisans
did not promote an impractical class antagonism; they principally demanded
an equal chance with the opulent to participate in political life. They cared
much less for treats than for righting wrongs and maintaining liberties.[59]

Despite its cooperation and activity, the middle class received from the elite
in exchange little power or position in politics. As Table 9 indicates, middle-class petitioners did not fare well in getting petitions accepted. Some
artisan petitions that reflected special demands, particularly those of rope-
makers, silversmiths, and cordwainers to the Pennsylvania House in the 1760s,
were ignored. Spinners, shoemakers, tanners, and bakers petitioned the New
York Assembly from 1761 to 1768 for various regulations and bounties and
got no action. Legislatures were more responsive to petitioners pleading for
relief from imprisonment for debt—these included many middling farmers
and tradesmen who slipped over the edge in the postwar depression of the
1760s. Assemblies passed various relief acts benefiting all classes of debtors.
The political system helped to protect the middling sort from privation but
bestowed on it no favors that might come at the expense of the superior orders.[60]

59. "Mr. Axe and Mr. Hammer," *A Card* (New York, 1768); "Messrs. Axe and Hammer," *A Card,
to the Freeholders and Freemen, of This City and County* (New York, 1769); *Pennsylvania Gazette* (Philadelphia), Sept. 27, 1770; Robert Kennedy, *To the Worthy Tradesmen, Artificers, Mechanics, &c., Electors for the City and County of Philadelphia* (Philadelphia, 1770). Schultz, "Small-Producer Tradition and Artisan Radicalism," 98–116, does not discuss efforts to appeal to class interest in colonial
Philadelphia elections after the 1720s.

60. Petitions were tallied from *N.J. Votes*, 1738–1775, *N.Y. Votes*, 1729–1775, and *Pa. Votes*,

TABLE 9

Proportions of Petitions Accepted by Assemblies (in percent)

	Middle class	Merchant	Total
New York, 1729–1775	27.2	77.8	51.6
New Jersey, 1738–1775	13.3	(1 of 1)	57.7
Pennsylvania, 1726–1776	33.3	42.9	46.2

Artisans and small farmers were elected to the assemblies on occasion, but most of the middling sort who held office occupied local posts. Elite leaders did not ordinarily invite middle-class officeholders to rise higher. In the posts they held, middle-class officeholders generally demonstrated their competence in vain, for they gained no friends by serving as tax assessors or constables. The middling sort would have to be satisfied with their role as voters because political activity rarely led to higher office.[61]

Ethnic group affinity was not as strong or as significant for political unity as was religious cohesion or economic factors. Few members of the major

---

1726–1776. See also Purvis, *Proprietors, Patronage, and Paper Money,* 186; Alan Tully, "Constituent-Representative Relationships in Early America: The Case of Pre-Revolutionary Pennsylvania," *Canadian Journal of History,* XI (1976), 145. Artisan petitions from Philadelphia were received more favorably than the Pennsylvania average: eight of sixteen were acted on. New York city artisan petitions got a 17.6 percent (three of seventeen) favorable response. For artisan petitions, Olton, *Artisans for Independence,* 14–15, 17–18, 20; *N.Y. Votes,* Dec. 10, 1761, Oct. 3, 1764, Dec. 11, 1766, Jan. 14, 18, 1768. For debtor relief, *Pa. Votes,* Feb. 2, Sept. 20, 1765, Feb. 21, 1767, Feb. 18, July 30, 1769, Feb. 24, 1770; *N.Y. Votes,* Dec. 16, 1763, Dec. 15, 1766, June 3, 1767; *N.J. Votes,* Dec. 6, 1763, June 15, 18, 1765, May 2, 1768.

61. For New York, 26 of 256 terms were filled by middling-sort assemblymen; in New Jersey, 30 of 315 were. Insufficient data exist for Pennsylvania. See note 52, this chapter, for sources on wealth of assemblymen. Tully, *William Penn's Legacy,* 116–17; Clair W. Keller, "The Rise of Representation: Electing County Officeholders in Colonial Pennsylvania," *Social Science History,* III (1979), 139–66; Town Book of Newton, N.J., in HSP; Patricia U. Bonomi, "Local Government in Colonial New York: A Base for Republicanism," in *Aspects of Early New York Society and Politics,* ed. Judd and Polishook, 118–31. In New York City, 61 percent of the lower offices and 30 percent of the common council seats were held by craftsmen, as were 46 percent of Philadelphia lower offices (Nash, *Urban Crucible,* 363). Bruce Wilkenfeld, "The New York City Common Council, 1689–1800," *New York History,* LII (1971), 255–56, notes that the proportion of artisans fell since the earlier eighteenth century. Kenneth Prewitt, *The Recruitment of Political Leaders: A Study of Citizen-Politicians* (Indianapolis, 1970), 48, finds that local office candidates in late twentieth-century America come from the "white collar level"; this appears to be a narrower recruiting range than in the middle colonies.

non-British groups, except for the Dutch, served in the assemblies. It was not the Dutch but the Germans in Pennsylvania who were the most political ethnic minority group in the middle colonies. They acted as an important voting bloc, much to the dismay of proprietary sympathizers. Governor James Hamilton termed them an "ignorant, sordid people . . . yet they are become the most busy at all Elections, which they govern at pleasure, in almost all the counties of the Province with a degree of Insolence heretofore unknown to us." Confronted with such negative attitudes and outright bigotry, Germans reacted negatively and defended themselves politically. In the York County election of 1750, Scotch-Irish squatters, who had recently moved into the area, tried to prevent Germans from voting. Incited by one of their leaders, Coroner Nicholas Ryland, the German electors rushed the courthouse, drove away the sheriff and election inspectors, and appointed Ryland to conduct the election for his countrymen.[62]

The dominant Quaker party quickly perceived that its success depended on controlling German electoral power. It encouraged the Germans to become conscious of their ethnic identity and of their particular needs and to unite to gain their ends. The party was almost always successful in holding German allegiance. It bargained perhaps unscrupulously to obtain German votes. In the 1740s Chief Justice and Assembly Speaker John Kinsey, Jr., allegedly permitted a "knott" of German counterfeiters to be "excused for trifling fines" because of his "great dependence . . . upon them for His Election." In 1755 Franklin, as agent for General Edward Braddock, procured good contracts for Germans who supplied wagons and other equipment for that ill-starred expedition. For years afterward Germans were reminded of Franklin's favors to them. Christopher Sauer, Dunker and publisher of a German-language newspaper in Germantown, advised his countrymen to become politically active on the side of their friends in the Quaker-Assembly parties.[63] Consequently, the Germans rarely deviated from following and supporting the leaders of those parties. They stood shoulder to shoulder with the Quakers when the sailors swooped down on the Philadelphia courthouse in the election riot of 1742 and wanted to retaliate with violence: "The Dutch

62. Hamilton to Thomas Penn, Sept. 24, 1750, in TPP. Richard Peters to Penn, Oct. 26, 1749, in TPP, claimed that the Germans "carry the Elections in all the Counties except Chester." *Pa. Col. Recs.*, Oct. 6, 1750, V, 468; *Pa. Votes*, Oct. 16–18, 1750.

63. James Hamilton to Thomas Penn, Nov. 18, 1750, TPP; *Ein Anrede an die Deutscher Freyhalter der Stadt und County Philadelphia* (Philadelphia, 1764), 5; Rothermund, *Layman's Progress*, 87, 90–91.

were for getting Guns but were prevented." In 1764, when the change of government issue convulsed Pennsylvania politics, the Proprietary party collected many German voters and tried to keep their favor in 1765 by granting church charters, but that alliance did not endure. By June, 1766, as Joseph Galloway informed Benjamin Franklin, the prodigal allies "are now generally come over to the Assembly party, and have lost their former Prejudices." Defeat of the Proprietary party in 1765 and publication in German of Franklin's Examination in Commons, denouncing the Stamp Act, regained German votes for the Assembly party.[64]

In most election campaigns German voters understood why they were voting with the Quaker-Assembly parties. They had become well aware that these parties supported religious liberty and unintrusive government. Some propagandists asserted that the Germans were ignorant and manipulated. A New York political broadside, arguing the elite case against election by ballot, claimed that in Pennsylvania the Germans were "in general so unacquainted with our Language that they are incapable of knowing whose Name is inserted in the Ticket they deliver, and are thereby frequently the Means of electing Persons, whom they detest in their Hearts." Such was reportedly the case in the Bucks County election of 1770, where Germans, illiterate in English, tried to repudiate Joseph Galloway but were given and turned in tickets with his name on them. It is possible that some Germans were hoodwinked, but they could not have been fooled more than once and would have raised challenges to such electoral practices had they occurred frequently.[65]

Ideology must have counted for a great deal with the Germans, for the Proprietary party had no luck in winning them over, save in 1764 and 1765. Germans gave no heed to pleas that unless they deserted their false allies, the pacifist Quakers, the colony must fall to the French. Thomas Penn hoped that requiring German children to attend charity schools would mean that "the Germans will in a few years be undeceiv'd, and drawn off from the attachment they now have to the Quakers." The assembly gave this plan no sup-

64. Richard Hockley to Thomas Penn, Nov. 1, 1745, John Penn to Thomas Penn, Oct. 14, 1765, in TPP; Galloway to Franklin, June 7, 1766, in Labaree *et al.*, eds., *Franklin Papers*, XIII, 296.

65. "J.W.," *The Mode of Election Considered* (New York, 1769); "A Bucks County Man," *A True and Faithful Narrative of the Modes and Measures Pursued at the Anniversary Election . . . for the County of Bucks . . . 1770* (Philadelphia, 1771), 5. Laura L. Becker, "Diversity and Its Significance in an Eighteenth-Century Pennsylvania Town," in *Friends and Neighbors: Group Life in America's First Plural Society*, ed. Michael Zuckerman (Philadelphia, 1982), 202, 211–13, notes the unfamiliarity of Reading Germans with both the language and the political system.

port and it failed; the Quakers had convinced the Germans of their common affinity, and until 1774 the alliance remained fundamentally intact.[66]

Colonial political leaders soon discovered that Germans were very sensitive about ethnic slurs and insults. If one group made careless or thoughtless remarks about the Germans, its opposition would quickly expose the derogatory statements to embarrass the detractors. In the 1764 Philadelphia election the Proprietary party gleefully publicized Franklin's description of German immigrants as "Palatine Boors." Philadelphia election propaganda of 1770 trumpeted that Galloway had called them "damn'd Dutchmen." New York Germans in propaganda issued during the 1769 election were told that John Morin Scott had referred to them as "firebrands" and that Germans "were publicly identified by Scott's party as stubborn, stupid, and obstinate people." [67] Insults aroused Germans to action in both Philadelphia and New York. Germans turned out en masse in 1764 and 1765 in Philadelphia; in 1765, six hundred Germans met at the Lutheran church and marched in a body to the polls to vote for Henry Keppele, Lutheran candidate on the Proprietary ticket. In 1769 Germans made their first political appearance in New York, marching through the streets singing a song in praise of the DeLancey candidates.[68] Germans were learning from English-speaking political groups how to get attention, how to use ethnic issues to unite their group, and how to make their votes count. Their importance as officeholders was primarily local in all three of the middle colonies, but in the 1760s the competing Pennsylvania parties responded to their expanding political presence by nominating Germans as Philadelphia representatives to the assembly. By 1775 Germans were active on revolutionary committees.[69]

Unlike the Germans, the Dutch inhabitants of New York and New Jersey

66. Walton, *John Kinsey*, 20–24; Penn to Richard Peters, Feb. 21, 1755, in TPP; *Pa. Votes*, Feb. 15, Dec. 10, 1754.

67. *An die Freyhalter und Einwohner der Stadt und County Philadelphia, Deutscher Nation* (Philadelphia, 1764); Goddard, *The Partnership*, 11; *A German Freeholder, to His Countrymen* (Philadelphia, 1770); Peter Van Schaack to Henry Van Schaack, Jan. 27, 1769, in Hawks Manuscripts, NYHS. *Nutzlich Gegen Nachrichte, an die samtliche Hoch-Teutsche in der Stadt New-York, von zwey Wohlmeinended Lands Leuten* (New York, 1769).

68. Rothermund, *Layman's Progress*, 104; *Nun Will Ich Valedieren Nun So Will Ich* (New York, 1769).

69. Bockelman and Ireland, "Internal Revolution in Pennsylvania," 139, 157–59; Tully, *William Penn's Legacy*, 63–64, 118; Bockelman, "Politics in Lancaster County," 70; Becker, "Diversity in Eighteenth-Century Pennsylvania," 201; Ryerson, *The Revolution is Now Begun*, 49–51, 229, 268.

were feeble partisans. Statistical computation of the relationship of the Dutch assemblymen to partisanship shows that it was insignificant. The Livingston party's vigorous efforts in New York City in 1769 to politicize the Dutch came to nothing. Dutch assemblymen readily changed sides or abandoned temporary alliances.[70] Dutch disdain for partisanship appears to have been a part of that group's legislative inactivity and cultural circumstances. In New Jersey and New York inactive legislators were more likely to be Dutch than of any other social or economic group. Legislators from predominantly Dutch districts such as Albany were only weakly tied to party positions. Cultural circumstances placed Dutch assemblymen in an awkward position, dissuading them from activity. The Dutch were rapidly assimilating. Those in New Jersey and New York were abandoning their language in the mid-eighteenth century. Dutch legislators, however, still had difficulty with the English language. They too wanted to assimilate, but they feared embarrassing themselves by participating fully in politics using clumsy, unpolished language. The Dutch faced no specific threat to their power or privileges except occasionally in certain localities where non-Dutch moved in and asserted themselves politically. Even in such districts, when a small majority or a large minority of Dutch voters had to contest some other group to get Dutch representatives elected, the Dutch showed little interest in supporting a Dutch slate. Unlike the Germans and some religious groups, they were rarely targets of public insults (although non-Dutch correspondence contains numerous private castigations). Ever since the early eighteenth century, they had been divided into religious factions of the Dutch Reformed Church; for this reason they balked at joining Livingston party efforts in New York City in 1769. They found more reasons to stay out of partisan activity than to get involved.[71]

 As evinced by the importance of religion for party affiliation, by the de-

70. Chi-square for the relationship between New Jersey Dutch assemblymen and the opposition side = 1.69; for the relationship between New York Dutch assemblymen and the administration side, chi-square = 0.03.

71. Chi-square for the relationship between inactivity and being Dutch for New Jersey assemblymen = 9.84, phi = 0.27. For New York assemblymen, chi-square = 11.38, phi = 0.32. In New York, 24.0 percent of the Dutch assemblymen were leaders, compared with 36.5 percent of all assemblymen; in New Jersey, 13.6 percent were leaders, compared with 29.9 percent of all assemblymen. On leadership, see Appendix II. *N.Y.C. Poll List, 1761; N.Y.C. Poll List, 1768; N.Y.C. Poll List, 1769.* Randall Balmer, *A Perfect Babel of Confusion: Dutch Religion and English Culture in the Middle Colonies* (New York, 1989), 119, 142–44, notes that English was prominent among the Raritan Valley Dutch in the 1730s and prevailed in New York by the mid-1760s. On local rivalry

termination of the Germans to assert their identity, and by the statements of those who claimed that family connections would not prevail over "good Sense Spirit and independence," ideology and principle counted for much in partisanship. Propaganda, particularly that appearing during the most contested and crucial elections, was replete with ideological arguments. As the party leaders had already discovered by the 1730s and 1740s, appeals to political liberties and constitutional rights, interspersed with demands based on religious principles and for religious freedom, had greater effect than did economic ones. The examples of ideological statements are legion; they are found in the writings of nearly all the prominent political leaders of the middle colonies. One must, of course, be immediately suspicious of the truth value, or the evidentiary worth, of self-serving pronouncements appearing in the midst of political campaigns. That is why one of the best demonstrations of ideological commitment by partisan leaders is a statement unrelated directly to electoral politics, presented in a factual context, and prepared not by capital-city lawyers but by two relatively unknown rustic assemblymen.

Aaron Leaming and Jacob Spicer, from the tiny county of Cape May, in 1755 compiled *The Grants, Concessions and Original Constitutions of the Province of New Jersey*, not as merely a reference work but as a statement of belief. Its origin and use illustrate how the opposition side in the New Jersey House put its whig ideals into practice. When Leaming visited the office of the provincial secretary in October, 1750, he found there a book containing "the Concessions and agreements of the Lords Proprietors of the Province of New Caesarea or New Jersey & c." He may have intended this historical research or stumbled into it; in any event, he was surprised and fascinated by his findings. Leaming discovered grants of important political and property rights: annual elections, provisions for an assembly more independent of executive authority than was the current House, and limitations on land resur-

in Schenectady, Bonomi, *Factious People,* 27. On Dutch Reformed divisions, Peter R. Livingston to Robert Livingston, Jr., June 15, 1769, in LP. See also Balmer, *A Perfect Babel of Confusion,* 127–33, 137–40, 146–50; and Adrian C. Leiby, *The Revolutionary War in the Hackensack Valley: The Jersey Dutch and the Neutral Ground* (New Brunswick, 1962), 19–23. New Jersey assemblyman David Demarest told Pastor Henry Melchior Muhlenberg in 1751 as noted by Jacobsen, *Unprov'd Experiment,* 83–85, that Dutch pastors ought to be united rather than contentious, evincing a nonpartisan viewpoint. Adrian Howe, "The Bayard Treason Trial: Dramatizing Anglo-Dutch Politics in Early Eighteenth-Century New York City," *WMQ,* 3rd ser., XLVII (1990), 89, claims that repercussions from Leisler's rebellion taught the Dutch in New York to be inactive, but this fails to explain why New York and New Jersey Dutch behaved much the same politically.

veys after seven years' possession. His colleagues and constituents, Leaming believed, were not fully aware of these entitlements. He decided that these old charters and laws should be published to provide a claim to rights against the exertions of authority by governors or proprietary landholders. On his motion, undoubtedly backed by his oppositionist colleagues, Leaming procured authorization for himself and his Cape May oppositionist associate Spicer to inspect the laws, records, and fundamental constitution.[72]

Living remote from the capitals, the two assemblymen were slow in their compiling. The House, perhaps at the behest of the administration side, in 1754 nearly turned the job over to two proprietor-assemblymen. Yet Leaming and Spicer kept on, and in 1755 the work appeared, published at provincial expense. It was not a bland, neutral documentary reference work; its preface showed that the compilers had political axes to grind. Leaming and Spicer wrote that the work was necessary for both protecting property rights and providing a model of good government. The original proprietors of New Jersey, of quite different attitude than that held by the current East Jersey crew, had secured the "Religion, Liberties, and Properties of the Adventurers and their latest Posterity." The compilers concluded with advice for current circumstances: "if our present System of Government should not be judged so equal to the Natural Rights of a Reasonable Creature, as the one that raised us to the Dignity of a Colony, let it serve as a Caution to guard the Cause of Liberty." The "sagatious and publick Spirited . . . may learn some useful hints to guard them against every Attempt of innovation."[73]

Leaming and Spicer grounded rights not in legality but rather in a philosophical system, that of John Locke, familiar to all literate and reflective contemporaries. In the same breath, admonishing their readers to guard against innovation, they were echoing one of the favorite maxims of the commonwealthmen of the late seventeenth century. Robert Molesworth's famous and widely known *Account of Denmark* (1693) was the foremost example of the commonwealthmen's argument that allowing prerogative power to make alterations in the constitution would destroy representative institutions and erect absolutism, as happened in Denmark in 1660. Leaming and Spicer blended these two arguments, both solidly grounded in the British Whig tra-

72. Leaming, Diary, Oct. 8, 1750, in HSP; *N.J. Votes*, Feb. 2, 1750-1.
73. *N.J. Votes*, June 15, 1754, Aug. 13, 1755. The *Pennsylvania Gazette* (Philadelphia), Feb. 11, 1755, advertised the publication. Leaming and Spicer, *Grants, Concessions . . .* (Philadelphia, 1755), preface. Purvis, *Proprietors, Patronage, and Paper Money*, 25–49, describes the gentry lives of Leaming and Spicer but says little about their views expressed in this publication.

dition, because they felt the particular need to assert a strong defense against the combination of administrative and proprietary power. Against prerogative they upheld the natural right to property because of its importance for the general community, not just for themselves and their fellow wealthy and well-to-do assemblymen.[74]

A "sagatious and publick Spirited" assemblyman put the compilation to use when it was hot off the press. In March, 1755, a few weeks after its publication was advertised, John Wetherill, landowner and adversary of the East Jersey proprietors, employed its arguments in a political dispute in New Brunswick. He asserted that all freeholders of the town, not merely the few made freemen by the town corporation, were entitled to vote in a crucial election. Wetherill based his argument on Magna Carta and the "fundamental *Constitutions of East and West Jersey*." There can be no doubt where he consulted the latter.[75]

Partisan leaders often forged sincere ideological appeals and adopted positions, not necessarily to their own advantage, that they presumed would enable them to reach across class and interest boundaries to bring in the literate, informed, and like-minded of other groups. Their strategy was activistnot backbencher, partisan not disdainful of politics, Whig not Country. Middle-colony parties, although influenced by the social and economic factors recounted here, served primarily to uphold a religious orientation adopted or prominent in one party and to support an ideology that reflected both the self-interested and the public-interested views of leaders and voters of that party.

74. For Molesworth and his *An Account of Denmark as It Was in the Year 1692* (London, 1693), see Caroline Robbins, *The Eighteenth Century Commonwealthman: Studies in the Transmission, Development, and Circumstance of English Liberal Thought from the Restoration of Charles II Until the War with the Thirteen Colonies* (2nd ed.; New York, 1968), 98–102. Spicer argued against prerogative infringements, and for a contractual relationship between king and people, more fervently during assembly sessions than he had in his editorial comments. He stated in 1754 that "Kings are but men, and as such may Err, and when they do their actions are liable to a modest Censure. . . . For what is a King more than the people's Delegate to Transact affairs of government as head of the State, for which we render obedience, and to which he is Bound by Oath, the Breach of which dissolves the people's allegiance." Furthermore, "the purse strings are known to be the Grand check we have upon our Superiors, and no Government shou'd be without its Checks" (Anthony Nicolosi, "Colonial Particularism and Political Rights: Jacob Spicer II on Aid to Virginia, 1754," *New Jersey History*, LXXXVIII [1970], 80, 83, 87).

75. New York *Gazette or the Weekly Post Boy*, Mar. 7, 1755.

3

The First Partisan Alignment, 1737–1753

The first period of party activity began with the emergence of partisan alignments in all the middle colonies in 1737–1740 and ended just before major
realignment in 1753–1755. The issues of government reform and defense inspired two parties, with specific agendas and determined leaders, to take form
in each of the colonies' lower houses. They began to reach out to create bases
of support in the electorates of the three colonies. These parties did not
develop identically in all three colonies, but the course of their partisan activities and the timing of major shifts were strikingly parallel.

A defense crisis and executive demands generated strong partisan responses
in both Pennsylvania and New Jersey. In Pennsylvania the Quaker party rose
to power. This boldest and best organized of all middle-colony parties began
as an undercurrent of opposition to the prerogatives of proprietorship
during the mid-1730s, became a highly polarized party in 1739–1740, gained
domination of the legislature, and effectively mobilized both traditional and
new voters. Opponents of the Penns stirred more vigorously than in recent
years before the October elections in 1738, anticipating that the arrival of a
new governor and the expiration of the paper money legislation in 1739 would
occasion sharp partisan conflict. A Philadelphia merchant lamented that the
colony was "much divided in Parties and Factions." The 1738 election turnout
in Philadelphia was the highest since the 1728 struggle, and the results strengthened the positions of some of the staunchest antiproprietary assemblymen.
Bucks and Chester counties each elected three Quakers, either new to the
House or returning from absences, who, judging from their later records of
service, were sent to the assembly to firm up an antiproprietary front. This
election gave the House an enlarged, vigorous, and determined antiproprietary delegation, ready to contest the governor and proprietors on the major
issues that it believed likely to be raised in the near future.[1]

When the Penns and their governor refused to reissue provincial paper
money on the old terms, the most extreme members of the antiproprietary

---

1. Samuel Powell, Jr., to David Barclay and Son, Oct. 14, 1738, in Samuel Powell Letter Book,
HSP. For election figures, Appendix III. Turnover statistics and religious affiliation are from tables in Tully, *William Penn's Legacy*, 177–82.

minority in the House refused to compromise. They were so anxious to publicize the administration's extreme position that they demanded a procedure that had never before occurred in the Pennsylvania Assembly and was most un-Quakerly: a published roll call. These antiproprietary Quakers ignored Friendly ideals of harmony and consensus. They believed that it was to their constituents that they should be true. Voters had chosen them not to back off or compromise with the proprietors but to hold to the paper money system that had been established in the 1720s. The roll call forced legislators to reveal to their constituents what side they were supporting. It also helped to create a visible legislative solidarity that became the core of the Quaker party.[2]

The roll call and the paper money controversy served to identify the Quaker party and rally its supporters, but even more polarizing was the imminent war between Britain and Spain in the late summer of 1739. The Burlington-Philadelphia yearly meeting circulated the peace testimony of the Quakers in September, 1739, shortly before the October election and probably as a campaign document. A nominating caucus of Quaker leaders and sympathizers convened to choose candidates who would uphold the testimony and an antiproprietary stance. This election, the House later claimed, saw "less struggle and less Division amongst the Inhabitants . . . than has happened in many other Years." The proprietary supporters did not wage much of an election campaign; the Quaker side encountered little resistance in pushing its party message among the voters. Of eight nonincumbent assemblymen elected, six were antiproprietary, and they replaced four assemblymen who either favored the proprietors or were nonpartisan.[3] The antiproprietary side now numbered about twenty—a clear majority, probably including six of seven from Chester, eight from Philadelphia, and four from Bucks. It was composed of the extremist antiproprietary core and a smaller moderate element. The core had nearly enough power to vote down any grant for defense purposes

2. *Pa. Votes,* Jan. 20, 1738-9, May 19, 1739, make it clear that Governor Thomas was attacking the legal tender provision of the proposed emission. The tally, *ibid.,* May 9, 1739, was seventeen to nine for compromise; Quaker leader John Kinsey, Jr., did not vote, probably torn between compromise and taking an antiproprietary stance. The extreme antiproprietary minority claimed that Thomas had misappropriated £50 and tried to deduct it from his salary (Thomas Penn to John Penn, May 31, 1739, in TPP).

3. Thomas upbraided the Quakers for holding "Consultations"; the House replied that a caucus may have been held, and it was "usually done every Year" (*Pa. Votes,* Aug. 26, Sept. 2, 1740). Also see Herman Wellenreuther, "The Political Dilemma of the Quakers in Pennsylvania, 1681–1748," *PMHB,* XCIV (1970), 158–59.

or other executive demand. The moderates, including new Speaker and Quaker meeting clerk John Kinsey, Jr., and a minority of the Quakers, combined with the proprietary supporters to grant conditional support for the military expedition against the Spanish Main, but, joining with the extreme Quaker pacifists, they refused to establish a defense force.[4]

The proprietary supporters now recognized that failure to campaign in 1739 was a strategic error. If the Quakers could organize, issue election propaganda, and nominate candidates faithful to their party, the Proprietary party, of greater social accomplishments, ought to be able to do the same to greater effect. William Allen in Philadelphia, Jeremiah Langhorne in Bucks, and James Hamilton in Lancaster were probably responsible for putting together full slates of proprietary supporters for the 1740 contest. The Quaker group, meanwhile, lined up all the Philadelphia incumbents in its camp, as well as five from Bucks and three from Lancaster. In Chester it set up an opponent to Assemblyman William Moore, who was probably the lone Proprietary party candidate in that hotbed of Quaker oppositionism. For the first time in Pennsylvania, except perhaps for the 1710 election, there was a colony-wide effort by two partisan groups to elect candidates and institute major policy revisions.

Almost everywhere the solidly organized and vigorous Quaker party trounced its opponents. In Philadelphia city and Chester the Quaker party won easily; in Lancaster, Proprietary party leader James Hamilton and his allies were decisively repudiated. Defects in strategy still plagued the Proprietary party, particularly in Lancaster. Here its candidates split some four hundred votes among them, while the three incumbents commanded almost universal support and the new Quaker candidate got about five hundred votes more than his rivals. The voter turnout in Lancaster was about the same as two years before, showing that the Proprietary party had failed to poll additional voters, while the Quaker party held fast to its constituents.[5]

Philadelphia and Bucks counties experienced the closest contests. Here the Proprietary party traditionally had considerable strength. In Philadelphia

4. *Pa. Votes,* Jan. 5, 19, 1739-40, Aug. 9, 1740; *American Magazine and Monthly Chronicle,* Feb., 1740-1, p. 64. The House made a modest appropriation of £3,000 for the expedition, conditional upon return of indentured servants who had attempted to escape their masters by enlisting in the army.

5. Moore was ousted in Chester. The incumbents—a Quaker and an anti-Hamilton Anglican—won in Philadelphia city. Lancaster vote totals in Tully, *William Penn's Legacy,* 227. Vote totals noted in Appendix III.

the retirement in 1739 of its best candidates cost them the advantages of incumbency. Only two, Allen and William Monington, attempted to return in 1740; the other five candidates on the Proprietary ticket had never been assemblymen. They challenged the seven incumbent Quakers; one Anglican, although he sided with the Quaker party, was not opposed. Party organization and discipline were the hallmarks of this election. Both sides brought to the Philadelphia polls voters with strong commitment. Together they turned out over 60 percent of the qualified. Each did about as well in bringing in voters and holding them to the party line as any political machine could expect to do. Statistical analysis of the electoral support for both tickets shows how sharp a party contest this was. The cohesion index for the seven incumbents was a very strong 0.991, meaning that a solid bloc of party voters supported the whole ticket. That for the Proprietary party was a strong 0.968, showing that very few of its voters failed to vote the whole ticket. The turnout figures, the vote results, and its 59 percent majority demonstrate that the Quaker party made an extremely effective electoral appeal in Philadelphia. In Bucks County, it was almost as effective but ran into stiffer opposition. Here the cohesion index for the Quaker party candidates was 0.950, that for the Proprietary party was 0.924. Bucks voters clearly perceived that the candidates were running on party tickets. Given the rural circumstances, the cohesion of voters and a 50 percent turnout of eligible voters mark a significant party effort. Despite Quaker labors, one of the most prominent Proprietary party leaders, Jeremiah Langhorne, squeezed by the lowest vote-getter on the Quaker ticket by one vote.[6]

The Quaker minority in Pennsylvania organized this full-fledged Quaker party by expanding its alliance with other groups. Combining with the Germans was particularly effective in Philadelphia and Lancaster, as despondent proprietary supporters frequently remarked. Despite religious differences, Anglicans and some Presbyterians also allied with the Quaker political group. The peace testimony did not alienate these allies, and secular issues—the antiadministration appeal, the insistence on the discharge of indentured servants who had enlisted in the Cartagena expedition—attracted many to coalesce and cooperate. The Quaker party in this election initiated skillful electoral politics that would be the strongest and most enduring feature of it and its successor.

6. Vote totals in Tully, *William Penn's Legacy,* 225–26. Turnout calculations are noted and the cohesion index is explained in Appendix III.

With the Quaker leaders fortified by a mandate and all assemblymen but Langhorne from Bucks and one or two others firmly within the embrace of the antiproprietary party, the scene was set for political deadlock. No bills were passed, no support for the government was approved, and, despite petitions from Philadelphia merchants led by Andrew Hamilton, no defense provisions were made. To combat Quaker party dominance, Thomas Penn and his supporters in 1741 decided to abandon electoral opposition and to stake all on complaints to the home government. Penn arraigned the assembly before the Board of Trade, and in the summer of 1741 a petition to the Crown signed by about 260 Philadelphia merchants went off to London. The petitioners desired imperial intervention that would force defense appropriations and perhaps even disqualify Quakers from office. The decision to appeal to Britain epitomizes the weakness and frustration of the Proprietary party. They had organized their supporters well, but they simply did not have enough voters to combat a more resourceful and better equipped opposition. The governor's distribution of patronage failed to attract many and only provided a basis for additional propaganda efforts in support of those Quakers who were dismissed. Administration parties did not characteristically give up; in New Jersey and New York the governors and proadministration groups persisted in attempting to win seats, even when confronted by an overwhelming opposition, in the belief that their efforts would eventually erode the adversary's strength. To quit electoral campaigning was an understandable decision, but not a wise one.[7]

Only James Logan and William Allen attempted to "make an opposition" in the election of 1741. Allen "took all the pain I was able with our friends to induce them to indeavour to get others chose into the Assembly but could not prevail upon Jeremiah Langhorne nor hardly any others to Join me, their answer was we have petitioned his Majesty and we will await the issue of that petition." In the Philadelphia city election, Provincial Secretary Richard Peters showed his frustration with and contempt for the electoral process when he "carried in two tickets was opposed & struck." Tempers flared further when "Young Israel [Pemberton] went to Part them & [James] Hamilton beat him in the face & swore by his Maker the next time he was by himself he would have full satisfaction. Israel answered him that he Did not fear him any Time nor Place." Gentlemanly behavior and Quaker decorum (if Israel, Jr.,

7. The petition is in John Smith Correspondence, HSP. On patronage, Wayne L. Bockelman, "Local Government in Colonial Pennsylvania," in *Town and County: Essays on the Structure of Local Government in the American Colonies,* ed. Bruce C. Daniels (Middletown, 1978,) 232.

had any) were quickly forgotten as both sides bristled at the neck. The feeble and bad-tempered Proprietary party efforts resulted in the ejection of its last remnants from the House. Langhorne was ousted; Bucks now sent a solid Quaker party delegation, though not entirely of that denomination. All incumbents returned from Chester and Philadelphia counties. In Lancaster James Logan and Conrad Weiser tried to lure the Germans from their alliance with the Quakers. They failed completely; the election results were numerically about the same as in the previous year. The Quaker party did not relax merely because the Proprietary party appeared to retire but kept its grip on the electorate.[8]

Continued deadlock between governor and assembly led the proprietary supporters to realize that they had made a grave political error in 1741, which they should not repeat in 1742. The election had to be contested. This time William Allen saw a chance for victory, hoping to refute the Quaker party contention that it had the overwhelming support of Pennsylvanians. He told Thomas Penn three months before the polling, "We are resolved to have another tryal with them this next election they shall not have it to say that they were chose without opposition they will I believe have a warm one if we can secure the germans or divide them I believe we shall outnumber them." The petition effort had stalled; there was no indication that the home government would intervene against the Quakers. Evidence of dissatisfaction with the Quakers among their constituents might jar it moving again. Allen and his allies put up full slates in Bucks County and probably in Philadelphia city, contested four seats in Philadelphia County, and sought one in Lancaster. Winning all these contests would give the Proprietary party just enough assembly votes to break the impasse between governor and assembly.[9]

The Proprietary party faced a very difficult rebuilding task, both in persuading the electorate and in getting out the vote. It tried a propaganda attack to arouse potential voters for its side; its broadsides blamed the House for allowing useful legislation to expire during the deadlock with the governor, for economic depression, for filching public funds, and for trying to bring in a royal government in place of the proprietors.[10] When these arguments

8. Allen to Thomas Penn, Oct. 24, 1741, in TPP; Samuel Noble to John Smith, Oct. 3, 1741, in John Smith Correspondence, HSP; Logan to Weiser, Sept. 18, 1741, in Logan Papers, HSP; Tully, *William Penn's Legacy*, 30, for the Lancaster election totals.

9. Allen to Thomas Penn, July 8, 1742, in TPP.

10. "T.B.," *To the Freeholders of the Province of Pennsylvania* (Philadelphia, 1742); "T.B.," *The Letters to the Freeholders of the Province of Pennsylvania, Continued* (Philadelphia, 1742).

proved lackluster and unconvincing, the Proprietary party leaders decided to employ more tangible persuasion—a show of force to prevent the Quakers from intimidating Germans at the Philadelphia polls. With the aid of ship captains then in port, they recruited some fifty sailors, who were to appear early on election day morning at the courthouse polling place with clubs. Anti-Quaker prejudice fired up the sailors. To give cowardly pacifists a thrashing, as revenge for refusal to do their patriotic duty by providing for defense, was probably its own reward for sailors who constantly risked their lives on the seas during wartime. When the "Govs. Friends" dropped hints about their plans, giving some Quakers an inkling that violent confrontation might ensue, the Quaker party leaders tried to avoid provocation by discouraging their side from bringing clubs to the election. But the sailors showed no such restraint; they swooped down on the election site, and as soon as Quaker party election inspectors were chosen over Proprietary party members, they attacked the assembled voters and drove them away from the courthouse. Quaker party supporters rallied, Germans from the outlying towns came up, a cooper cut up hog-driving poles into clubs, and they counterattacked. Even some Quakers joined the affray. The Quaker party defenders drove the sailors back to their ships and hauled some off to jail.[11]

The personal and property damage done by the riot was negligible; the political damage done to the Proprietary party was huge. Although William Allen appeared to have a good chance in either the county or the city race, his erstwhile supporters at the election, on hearing reports blaming him for the riot, immediately scratched his name from their tickets. He finished more than 1,100 votes behind the leading vote-getter of the Quaker party. The winning party turned out a solid bloc of almost 1,500 voters out of 1,843 appearing at the polls. Not only was the Proprietary party completely routed in Philadelphia, but the riot provided the antiproprietary side with propaganda ammunition that lasted as long as did the proprietorship. In 1776 Philadelphians still bitterly recalled the "knock-down" election of 1742.[12]

11. Allen to Thomas Penn, July 8, 1742, Richard Hockley to Thomas Penn, Nov. 1, 1742, in TPP; *Pa. Votes,* Appendix, Aug. 11, 1744; Isaac Cornly, "Sketches of the History of Byberry in the County of Philadelphia, with Biographical Notices of Some of the First Settlers, and Other Distinguished Inhabitants of the Neighborhood," *Memoirs of the Historical Society of Pennsylvania,* II (1827), Pt. 1, p. 193.

12. Richard Hockley to Thomas Penn, Nov. 1, 1742, TPP; Parsons, "The Bloody Election of 1742," 300; Tully, *William Penn's Legacy,* 226, for vote totals; Charles P. Keith, *The Provincial Councillors of Pennsylvania Who Held Office Between 1733 and 1776, and Those Earlier Councillors Who Were Some of the Chief Magistrates of the Province, and Their Descendants* (Philadelphia, 1883), 148.

The 1742 elections in the other Pennsylvania counties followed the same patterns that they had since 1740. The cohesion index for the Quaker party candidates in Lancaster was 0.997, showing that its supporters, including many Presbyterians, hardly deviated from their straight ticket voting. These candidates all got about 1,100 more votes than did James Hamilton, the one Proprietary party candidate. In Bucks County again both parties were well organized, had their adherents out in force on election day, and persuaded their voters not to split tickets. The cohesion indices testify to the success of each: for the Quaker party, 0.981, and for the Proprietary party, 0.973. As in the other counties, the Quaker party turned out the majority of these strongly committed voters—about 100 more than the opposition—and won all the seats.[13]

Those proprietary supporters who previously had advocated abandoning the electoral wars had, after the 1742 debacle, the more convincing arguments. The group determined to do little or nothing in future elections, even though in the late 1740s and early 1750s issues arose that might have provided political capital. The report of Richard Peters to Thomas Penn in 1748 best summed up the views of the Penns' allies on elections: the assembly was "re-elected without opposition it appearing manifest that had there been a Contest there would be no hope of Success, they are now firmer than ever & cannot be removed unless they quarrel with one another." Only one identifiable proprietary supporter was elected to the House after 1741, a representative from Bucks County elected in 1747 perhaps because the defense issue reemerged. Until 1754, in nearly all election districts, the Proprietary party suspended partisan politics. It showed both ineptitude and loss of nerve; its opponents were shrewd, skillful, and bold.[14]

Neither personnel changes nor ideological differences within the House seem to have shaken the solidarity of the Quaker party. In 1744 Israel Pemberton, Jr., made some effort to promote a more determinedly pacifist slate of Quakers in the Philadelphia assembly election, but he got no encouragement or support. Proprietary supporters hoped that Isaac Norris II and Pemberton would duel over the succession to Speaker John Kinsey, Jr., in 1750, but such a quarrel never materialized. The most enduring split within the party was over the degree of intransigence to adopt toward the executive.

13. Tully, *William Penn's Legacy*, 226–27, for vote totals. For the cohesion index, see Appendix III.

14. Richard Peters to Thomas Penn, Oct. 20, 1748, in TPP. Calculations based on data in tables from Tully, *William Penn's Legacy*, 170–82, show 86 percent incumbency for the 1740s.

In 1743 and 1753 sizable proportions of the House advocated holding up the governor's salary until further concessions were forthcoming. In the first instance the withholders were not successful because the majority thought that Governor Thomas had been punished enough by being deprived of his salary for almost three years. In the later episode a bare majority voted to punish the inflexible Governor James Hamilton for adhering to proprietary instructions and refusing to expand the supply of paper currency. These were very minor differences among legislators and party leaders who almost invariably marched to the same drum.[15] For this first fourteen years the Quaker party operated under clearly understood principles, discipline, and lines of succession; its internal differences did not vex it, nor did its leadership falter.

When New Jersey's new governor, Lewis Morris, experienced opposition politician in New York, called his first election in 1738, he quickly discovered how it felt to be on the administration side, confronted by an opposition party. Fragmentary election reports indicate that a partisan antiadministration group contested the 1738 election in at least the counties of Essex, Monmouth, Burlington, and Gloucester. The Burlington election, one observer noted, was spirited but surprisingly nonviolent, for perhaps in contrast to earlier factional struggles there was no "using of Canes in a Hostile Manner on one another, being sensible that such a Practice, is inconsistent with the Freedom, which ought to subsist in our Elections." In Monmouth two groups calling each other "parties" bid for office. The opponents of the "court party" succeeded in branding it as plotting various evils; they elected a well-to-do Quaker farmer and a Dutch farmer of moderate property. The Dutch candidate won because party leaders believed that when he was "once Set Right there was no turning of him." The electors wanted determined, dependable, even stubborn representation. Because of, rather than in spite of, the absence of an election for eight years, they and the assemblymen elected in 1738 were in a mood to defend privileges, reform abuses, and oppose excessive executive power.[16]

When the new legislature met with Governor Morris, its full-blown partisan spirit astonished observers. Morris reported that "there grew so great a

15. Richard Bauman, *For the Reputation of Truth: Politics, Religion, and Conflict Among the Pennsylvania Quakers, 1750–1800* (Baltimore, 1971), 11; Illick, *Colonial Pennsylvania*, 192; Richard Peters to Thomas Penn, [fall, 1750?], Jan. 20, 1752, Sept. 11, Oct. 27, Nov. 6, 1753, in TPP; *Pa. Votes*, Oct. 17, Dec. 4, 1754.

16. *American Weekly Mercury* (Philadelphia), Oct. 19, 1738; *N.J. Votes*, Nov. 15, 16, 28, 1738; Jacob Dennis to Robert Hunter Morris, Nov. 13, 1738, in MP.

rancour among the members that they Shun'd the conversation of Each other Out of the house, and could not preserve the rules of common decency in it descending to downright Scolding, giving the lye, threatening to Spit in the faces & were (as I am inform'd) often very nigh getting together by the Ears." The proadministration side wanted full monetary support for Morris' administration, and the opposition hoped to restrict administrative funding. The latter side, though one-half the membership of the House, was as yet not united enough to withstand the former effectively. As one opposition partisan reported, "Three of our Members [were] at length prevail'd on, by continued Promises and Threatenings from the Court Party, that all would go well throughout the Province if the Governour was pleas'd." Regardless of the capitulation of these three oppositionists, Morris was greatly displeased by the partisan spirit shown. Accusing the members of "Supporting and Uniting of a Party" rather than acting for the common good, he sent them packing in March, 1739, and ordered a new election.[17]

Morris and other observers saw dimly through their eighteenth-century disdain of political contention what twentieth-century Americans would recognize as the workings of a legislative party. Bloc analysis applied to the roll call votes indicates that two well-defined groups were locked in contention. All but one member of the House can be placed in a bloc; the administration side had eleven members, the opposition twelve (until three were "prevail'd on"). Because the two sides were so evenly matched, the opposition party elected a Speaker of the House from the administration side to deprive its adversaries of one vote. Morris blamed the Quakers (his supporters against Cosby) for the opposition, which in the main was correct and would become characteristic of the opposition side in the New Jersey Assembly. As also was to become characteristic, the wealthy slightly favored the administration side. As Table 10 indicates, the House was divided by religious and regional rather than by economic or occupational characteristics.[18]

In the election of early 1740, the administration attempted a determined

17. Morris to Sir Charles Wager, May 10, 1739, in *NJA*, VI, 61–62; "W.J.," *A Letter to B.G. from One of the Members of Assembly of the Province of New-Jersey, Dissolved March 15, 1738, 9* (Philadelphia, 1739), 1; *N.J. Votes*, Apr. 6, 1740; Sheridan, *Lewis Morris*, 184–85.

18. Appendix I, for bloc analysis. In the 1738–1739 session only one administration bloc member ever agreed on a significant proportion of votes with one opposition bloc member. Morris to Sir Charles Wager, May 10, 1739, in *NJA*, VI, 61–62. Biographical sources listed in Chap. 2, n. 2 and n. 52, will be used for all text and tables describing the characteristics of New Jersey assemblymen.

TABLE 10

**Economic and Social Characteristics of
Party Members: New Jersey House, 1738–1739**

(*All tabulated figures are assembly terms*)

	Wealthy	Well-to-do	Middling
Administration	4	7	0
Opposition	3	7	2
Indeterminate			1

	Anglican	Presbyterian	Dutch Reformed	Quaker	Baptist	Lutheran
Administration	3	3	0	4	1	0
Opposition	0	0	4	7	0	1
Indeterminate				1		

	Central capital-town	West Jersey rural	East Jersey rural
Administration	8	3	0
Opposition	0	6	6
Indeterminate		1	

	Great landholder	Landowner	Farmer
Administration	3	4	1
Opposition	2	6	3

	Merchant	Shopkeeper/artisan	Lawyer	Unknown
Administration	2	1	0	
Opposition	1	0	0	
Indeterminate				1

lambda-*b*, partisanship and region = 0.67; and religion = 0.58; and occupation = 0.25; and wealth = 0.08

campaign to gain a majority for its side. The contending leaders circulated propaganda defending their stances during the last assembly.[19] In the one county poll for which figures are extant, the two sides mustered their supporters and fought a spirited contest. In Burlington County 62.1 percent of the probable qualified voters turned out when two administration supporters sought to oust the incumbents. They had the backing of most of the county

19. Lewis Morris republished his dissolution speech, *The Speech of His Excellency Lewis Morris, Esq; Capt. General and Governor in Chief of the Province of New Jersey &c. To the House of Representatives of the Said Province, on Thursday, March 15, 1738,9* (New York, 1739). On the assembly side was "W.J.," *A Letter to B.G.* Sheridan, *Lewis Morris,* 185–86.

elite, who sought patronage rewards for their support of the administration side. Of thirteen county justices whose votes were recorded in the poll book, only four supported both incumbents; of the forty-two past, present, and future members of the Board of Chosen Freeholders who voted, only twenty backed both incumbents. Large groups of voters of the same persuasion came to the polls together; these groups were most likely neighbors traveling in a body to the county seat to vote as neighborhood leaders had induced them. On the last two days of the five-day election, bands of voters from Burlington city, led by Richard Smith, Jr., and other prominent citizens of the town, came to the polls. They all plumped one vote only for the candidate who was at that point in the polling closest to overtaking the incumbents. Short-ticketing— voting for fewer candidates than there were vacancies—was considered unsporting; it must have been strong feelings of attachment to local leaders that persuaded a large portion of the electorate from the city to cast such votes.

Despite the devious tactics and despite all the influential notables arrayed against them, the incumbents together garnered 55.2 percent of the votes; 64.8 percent of the voters cast ballots for at least one (see Table 11). Their electoral adherents were unified, committed oppositionists whose votes defied the views of the county elite; 81.4 percent of those who voted for one opposition incumbent voted for the other. The cohesion index for the two winners was 0.972, indicating that the electorate was strongly partisan rather than compromising. Family ties engendered some of the strong cohesion. Of forty-two family groups of father-son, two-thirds cohered in voting for the same candidate. The election illustrates that inhabitants of local neighborhoods politically deferred to their leaders, but the pull of deference could not be extended over the entire county or even townships. The majority of the county magnates could not convince the bulk of the middling electorate to follow its lead.[20]

20. Thompson, ed., "Poll Book of an Election in 1739 [–40], Burlington County," 185–93. See Appendix III for voter turnout and the cohesion index. This election's results do not substantiate Purvis, *Proprietors, Patronage, and Paper Money*, 103, who asserts that gentry votes controlled elections. These neighborhood groups of voters were likely the local homogenous subculture groups that Thomas Bender, *Community and Change in America* (New Brunswick, 1978), 68–70, finds characteristic of the colonial period. Edward M. Cook, Jr., *The Fathers of the Towns: Leadership and Community Structure in Eighteenth Century New England* (Baltimore, 1976), 115–16, notes that the force of deference varied from town to town, as it did within this county. For a comparison with election of assistants in Connecticut, in which no deferential network encompassed the colony, Joy B. Gilsdorf and Robert R. Gilsdorf, "Elites and Electorates: Some Plain Truths for Historians of Colonial America," in *Saints and Revolutionaries: Essays on Early American*

TABLE 11

Vote Distribution: Burlington County, 1740

Incumbents (Mahlon Stacy, William Cook)	55.2%	(253)
Stacy—Samuel Woolman	8.1%	(37)
Stacy—Joshua Wright	(0)	
Cook—Woolman	3.9%	(18)
Cook—Wright	0.7%	(3)
Woolman—Wright	22.4%	(103)
Woolman (by plumpers)	9.6%	(44)
Total vote		458

The results of the other New Jersey elections, about which no details are known, were similar to that in Burlington, for when the House reassembled in April, 1740, its political alignment shifted slightly toward the opposition side. Virtually the only change from the previous House in social and economic characteristics was that the West Jersey landowning Quakers were more heavily oppositionist. The outbreak of war and the request that the colony supply the Cartagena expedition drew Quaker assemblymen and their constituents into the opposition camp, just as similar debates over military aid and defense preparations in Pennsylvania were solidifying the Quaker party.[21]

A dissolution and new election in 1743 helped Governor Morris and his allies not at all, for the opposition group quickly organized in several counties, adopted new election techniques, obtained strong backing, and was able to

History, ed. David D. Hall, John M. Murrin, and Thad W. Tate (New York, 1984), 224, 227. For comparison with the influence of local magistrates in Britain, Norma Landau, "Independence, Deference, and Voter Participation: The Behavior of the Electorate in Early Eighteenth-Century Kent," *Historical Journal,* XXII (1979), 570–71, which compares the 1713 and 1715 parliamentary elections. For comparison with neighborhood "opinion makers" of 1840 Virginia, Paul F. Bourke and Donald A. DeBats, "Identifiable Voting in Nineteenth-Century America: Toward a Comparison of Britain and the United States Before the Secret Ballot," *Perspectives in American History,* XI (1977–78), 278–85. Richard R. Beeman, "Deference, Republicanism, and the Emergence of Popular Politics in Eighteenth-Century America," *WMQ,* 3rd ser., XLIX (1992), 401–30, is a useful overview but vague regarding some middle-colony developments.

21. The number of opposition Quakers increased from seven of twelve to ten of thirteen; opposition West Jersey rural members from six of ten to ten of twelve; opposition landowners from six of ten to nine of twelve. Lambda-*b* in this session for the relation to partisanship of region = 0.73, of religion = 0.56, of occupation = 0.40, of wealth = 0.00. Sheridan, *Lewis Morris,* 190–93. *N.J. Votes,* June 18, 1740, records the opposition alignment against the council.

form a solid legislative bloc in the House. In three elections in the two years 1743–1745, the opposition completely routed the administration side. One reason was popular propaganda. It was likely Richard Smith, Jr., prominent Burlington Quaker merchant, who wrote an un-Quakerly, contentious answer to Robert Hunter Morris' defense of his father's administration. Smith observed that such replies "Some Say make the G....r dam.d Mad but they please the people so well that they are [passed?] among them."[22] In the 1744 election Smith acted as party leader, running a coordinated campaign in several counties. He kept in communication with allies in key districts on how the electorate was likely to vote. His opposition allies in Middlesex County forwarded overly optimistic reports that "all four Mellita Men in Midlesex are left out . . . we Expect the Same in Essex." In the next election, in 1745, Smith kept careful count of district election returns, as would any party manager, and reported that "only the 4 members of [Middlesex] County [were] dissenters."[23]

These frequent successive elections served only to increase the oppositionist majority in the assembly. Table 12 depicts the results for 1743. By 1745 the only major changes were on the administration side. Only Speaker Neville of the old cadre of proprietor-administration supporters was still a member in 1745. The others had probably given up in disgust, letting new members have a try at derailing the opposition's express train. It was fruitless. The strong relationship between partisanship and both religion and region prevailed during these assembly sessions. For the next three years Quakers, West Jersey rural members, and well-to-do landowners lined up on the opposition side. Smith exulted to his son John of party solidarity and domination; there was a "perfect good understanding" among the oppositionist majority, including those whom Smith termed "our duch Frds.," and "those few that are Contraminded are obligg'd to be Silent."[24]

22. Richard Smith, Jr., to John Smith, Oct. 18, 1743, in John Smith Correspondence, HSP; [Smith?], *The Note-Maker Noted, and the Observer Observed Upon; or, a Full Answer to Some Notes and Observations Upon the Votes of the House of Assembly of the Colony of New Jersey . . .* (Philadelphia, 1743); [Morris], *Extracts from the Minutes and Votes of the House of Assembly of the Colony of New-Jersey; Met in General Assembly at Burlington, on Saturday the 16th of October 1742. . . . To Which Are Added Some Notes and Observations Upon the Said Votes . . .* (Philadelphia, 1743). *N.J. Votes,* Oct. 17–27, 1743, records a contested election in Hunterdon, but nothing else is known of the 1743 election.

23. Richard Smith, Jr., to John Smith, Aug. 8, 1744, Mar. 22, 1745, in John Smith Correspondence, HSP.

24. Richard Smith, Jr., to John Smith, Oct. 28, 1743, Aug. 26, 1744, in John Smith Corre-

TABLE 12

**Economic and Social Characteristics of
Party Members: New Jersey House, 1743**

(All tabulated figures are assembly terms)

	Wealthy	Well-to-do	Middling	Unknown
Administration	3	2	0	1
Opposition	3	13	1	
Indeterminate				1

	Anglican	Presbyterian	Dutch Reformed	Quaker	Baptist	Lutheran	Unknown
Administration	2	2	1	0	0	0	1
Opposition	0	0	3	11	2	1	
Indeterminate	1						

	Central capital-town	West Jersey rural	East Jersey rural
Administration	6	0	0
Opposition	2	9	6
Indeterminate		1	

	Great landholder	Landowner	Farmer
Administration	3	3	0
Opposition	1	11	1

	Merchant	Shopkeeper/artisan	Lawyer
Administration	0	0	0
Opposition	2	1	1
Indeterminate		1	

lambda-*b*, partisanship and religion = 0.67; and region = 0.57; and occupation = 0.29; and wealth = 0.00

By 1745 the controlling group of the New Jersey Assembly was in effect a machine. Party unity was so strong that in the 1744 House all eighteen of the opposition assemblymen voted almost identically. Only the most determined partisanship could produce such unity through twenty-five roll calls. The proadministration group also cohered, but not nearly so strongly. Their leader, the haughty proprietor and administration supporter Samuel Neville, was

---

spondence, HSP. Lambda-*b* for the 1744 session for the relationship to partisanship of region = 0.33, of occupation = 0.33, of religion = 0.17, of wealth = 0.00. Lambda-*b* for the 1745 session for the relationship to partisanship of religion = 0.040, of region = 0.20, of occupation = 0.00, of wealth = 0.00.

made Speaker, "by which Means we weaken them a vote, altho we Gratify the ostentation of who is Chose to it," Smith explained. Smith revealed the majority's strong partisan feelings in noting that the opposition would rather have a larger voting bloc in the House than control of the Speaker's chair. Neville could only watch from his seat in exasperation as Smith and his allies maintained perfect unity and harmony within their legislative party.[25]

Major changes in the salient issues and the personnel of New Jersey politics weakened the opposition party in the House after 1745, but it remained, if not dominant, about evenly matched with the administration side. In 1746 a more conciliatory governor replaced the deceased Morris and the militia issue soon evaporated as the war with the French wound down. The new issues that now emerged concerned the privileges and landholding claims of the proprietors and great landholders. In 1746 land riots were staged by the Indian title claimants from Elizabethtown. In actuality the land disputes posed no threat to the government, though they were a considerable financial problem for the proprietors. Proprietors and councillors James Alexander and Robert Hunter Morris talked up the threat of the land rioters to convince the British government that it should intervene. Allegations that the mob and the rioters were in control of the assembly were sheer hyperbole, meant for British consumption to enlist home government support against the land claimants. That the issue was resolved by the courts, rather than by the political process or by violent action, shows that for most New Jersey constituents, except the proprietors and the land claimants, the controversy was not very significant. More meaningful to the populace was the issue of land taxation; for the first time in twenty-five years government expenses were outrunning income from the loan office interest and from duties. The House had to wrestle with the problems of fair apportionment among the counties and the rate of taxation of the large proprietary estates.[26]

25. Richard Smith, Jr., to John Smith, Aug. 26, 1744, in John Smith Correspondence, HSP; *N.J. Votes,* Apr.–Oct., 1745. When charted, the significant proportions of agreement among the members form an almost perfect eighteen by eighteen square, with 100 percent agreement among several members.

26. "A Brief State of the Facts, Concerning the Riots & Insurrections," in *NJA,* VII, 220; James Alexander to Cadwallader Colden, Jan. 20, 1748-9, in *NYHSC,* LXVIII, 2; Alexander and Robert Hunter Morris to Ferdinand John Paris, Dec. 23, 1748, in *NJA,* VII, 200. Purvis, "Origins of Agrarian Unrest in New Jersey," 600–627; Countryman, "'Out of the Bounds of the Law'" 48, 57; Horowitz, "New Jersey Land Riots," 31; New York *Gazette or the Weekly Post Boy,* Feb. 5, Mar. 5, 1770; Governor Belcher to the Lords of Trade, Apr. 21, 1749, in *NJA,* VII, 245–46; *N.J. Votes,* Oct. 18–19, 1749.

These issues influenced both the elections held between 1746 and 1751 and the partisan affiliation of sitting assemblymen. Quakers from West Jersey returned to the administration side now that the issue of military service was no longer current. Thus Richard Smith, Jr., two other Burlington Quakers, and three more from West Jersey counties went over to the administration, in effect returning to their political position of 1738–1742. The Middlesex-Burlington alliance was now restored. Merchants, well-to-do landowners, and West Jersey rural representatives also shifted toward the administration side. Essex County went into the opposition because of the strong antiproprietary feeling generated by the Indian title claimants.

The elections of 1746, 1749, and 1751 confirmed this change. They were held so frequently because Governor Jonathan Belcher wanted a House that would settle differences with the proprietors. Councillors Alexander and Morris, who pressed Belcher for action against the land rioters, were optimistic about their chances for electoral success in 1749 even though the cycle of dissolution and new election had not produced favorable majorities for Governor Lewis Morris. Councillor Morris wrote to James Alexander to lay his party's plans for the ensuing session: "I believe we shall have members enough to make motions in the House and perhaps to fourth & fifth such motions, and I submit it to you whether we should not think before hand of some motions proper to be made in the affair of the Money makers, Traitors, Rioters, &c." To gain sympathy and support, Alexander broadcast that the rioters had hopes of "Carrying the new [1749] Elections by violence." Both partisan leaders guessed wrong. "Cap Men and Mobmen" defeated "Wigmen and Gentlemen." Indeed, according to Morris and Alexander, the opposition party in the 1749 election campaign employed these very distinctions, "used . . . with great Success in East Jersey, and by which and other false & wicked Tales the Capmen and Mobmen were Chosen thro' East Jersey, Except in the City of Perth Amboy, so that the Assembly has a great Majority of Mob and Cap men in it." [27] Antiproprietary candidates, not actually "mobmen," prevailed in Middlesex and Somerset; Essex also remained oppositionist. During the 1751 elections administration party leaders made great political efforts to obtain an assembly more amenable to compromise, and their hard work pro-

27. Morris to Alexander, [Feb., 1748-9], in *NJA*, VII, 107–109. Morris here inaccurately but purposefully described the new Middlesex assemblyman, John Wetherill, a claimant by Indian title to four hundred undeveloped acres, as a "rioter." Alexander to John Coxe, May 2, 1748, in *NJA*, VII, 123; Alexander and Morris to Ferdinand John Paris, May 30, 1749, in *NJA*, VII, 263.

duced a significant shift. Two new members from Essex reversed the antiproprietary posture of that county when the land controversies died down; the election or reelection of conciliatory Quakers from Burlington, Gloucester, and Salem also contributed to a new compromising spirit. Neville's withdrawal may have been part of an agreement conjoined with the compromise effort; the intransigent proprietor would no longer berate the opposition from the Speaker's chair. After the 1746 and 1751 elections, the administration could claim a majority of one in the assembly. It numbered twelve, or half the House, while the opposition was one less, and one member was indeterminate. In 1749 the administration was reduced to nine; the opposi-

TABLE 13

**Economic and Social Characteristics of
Party Members: New Jersey House, 1746–1748**

(All tabulated figures are assembly terms)

	Wealthy	Well-to-do	Middling	Unknown
Administration	6	5	0	1
Opposition	4	5	2	
Indeterminate		1		

	Anglican	Presbyterian	Dutch Reformed	Quaker	Baptist	Lutheran
Administration	3	1	2	6	0	0
Opposition	0	2	2	4	2	1
Indeterminate				1		

	Central capital-town	West Jersey rural	East Jersey rural
Administration	6	4	2
Opposition	2	5	4
Indeterminate		1	

	Great landholder	Landowner	Farmer
Administration	1	4	2
Opposition	1	5	2
Indeterminate		1	

	Merchant	Shopkeeper/artisan	Lawyer
Administration	4	0	1
Opposition	2	0	1

lambda-*b*, partisanship and religion = 0.36; and region = 0.27; and wealth = 0.10; and occupation = 0.09

tion, now fifteen, gained no successes from its strong majority because the council blocked it (see Tables 13 and 14).[28]

TABLE 14

**Economic and Social Characteristics of
Party Members: New Jersey House, 1751–1754**
(*All tabulated figures are assembly terms*)

	Wealthy	Well-to-do	Middling
Administration	3	8	1
Opposition	6	5	0
Indeterminate		1	

	Anglican	Presbyterian	Dutch Reformed	Quaker	Baptist	Unknown
Administration	3	1	1	6	1	
Opposition	0	2	3	2	3	1
Indeterminate				1		

	Central capital-town	West Jersey rural	East Jersey rural
Administration	6	6	0
Opposition	2	3	6
Indeterminate		1	

	Great landholder	Landowner	Farmer
Administration	2	3	3
Opposition	1	5	2

	Merchant	Shopkeeper/artisan	Lawyer	Unknown
Administration	2	0	2	
Opposition	2	0	1	
Indeterminate	.			1

lambda-*b*, partisanship and religion = 0.50; and region = 0.50; and wealth = 0.25; and occupation = 0.17

28. Richard Smith, Jr., to John Smith, May 24, 1746, in John Smith Correspondence, HSP. Robert Hunter Morris to James Alexander, July 28, 1747, in *NJA,* VI, 473, inaccurately divorced the Quakers from the Middlesex group. For the 1749–1751 assembly, analysis of all roll call votes did not indicate partisan affiliation accurately. A large number of absences vitiated the analysis. Analysis of six of the fourteen roll calls, those on addresses to the governor, on issues involving the council, and on salaries, provides the basis for the assessment of partisan divisions. The administration side lost all Dutch support; the number of opposition Presbyterians increased from two of three to four of five. East Jersey rural opposition increased from four of six to six of six. Merchant administration supporters declined from four of six to two of four, opposition landown-

Richard Smith, Jr., characterized the opposition as "numbers of Stingey Creatures" who confronted the House with demands for paper money and attempted to withhold support from the government. Undoubtedly the opposition party held such views, but statistical analysis, as Table 13 shows, indicates that despite Quaker defections, religion remained the most important determinant of partisan affiliation in these three years. Anglicans lined up against Dutch Reformed, Presbyterians, and Baptists. Both sides continued to use the Speaker's post to consign one opponent vote to oblivion. In 1746 the administration majority elected oppositionist Robert Lawrence as Speaker in a turnabout both calculated and spiteful. Lawrence was a strong partisan in the House but a bit eccentric to be a major leader; he later claimed to have invented a mechanical device that defied gravity. When Lawrence later left the House temporarily, the opposition side got Neville reelected. In 1751 Charles Read of Burlington, newly elected, Anglican, a cousin of the Burlington Smiths, and successor to Richard Smith, Jr., became Speaker. He was influential with the Quakers who had looked to Smith for leadership, but he sided ideologically with the East Jersey proprietors; he favored paying Lewis Morris' back salary to his heirs (which the opposition side bitterly opposed and succeeded in preventing), and he reported Governor Belcher's private views to the council. Unlike his predecessors, he was both Speaker and majority party leader. Aaron Leaming, oppositionist partisan, testily and with much exaggeration summed up his political methods: "I have known the Governor & Council to do things against their inclinations to please him & the Assembly have often done so; He seemed to be their leader. During that time he took the whole disposal of all offices. He little consulted the merits of the person he preferred; the sole object was whither [*sic*] it suited his party principles."[29]

Although the proprietors and the council raved hysterically about the land

---

ers increased from five of thirteen to eight of thirteen, opposition well-to-do assemblymen increased from five of eleven to seven of twelve. Lambda-*b* in the 1749–1751 session for the relationship to partisanship of religion = 0.30, of occupation = 0.20, of region = 0.20, of wealth = 0.00.

29. Robert Lawrence to [?], July 22, 1763, in MP; Richard Smith, Jr., to John Smith, Oct. 16, 1751, Samuel Smith to John Smith, Dec. 14, 1753, both in John Smith Correspondence, HSP; Charles Read to Robert Hunter Morris, Apr. 22, 1749, Richard Saltar to Morris, Dec. 4, 1751, both in MP; Governor Belcher to Richard Partridge, May 20, 1752, in *NJA*, Vol. 8, Pt. 1, p. 61; Leaming, Diary, Nov. 14, 1775, in HSP; Carl R. Woodward, *Ploughs and Politicks: Charles Read of New Jersey and His Notes on Agriculture, 1715–1774* (New Brunswick, 1941), 142.

rioters, the opposition bloc rejected the drastic action that they demanded against the interlopers. Taxing the estates of these great landowners, treating them as the ordinary citizen was treated, not giving them special protection, was its concern. Through the sessions of two assemblies, from 1749 to 1752, it contested the administration on the matter of how heavily proprietary lands should be assessed for taxes. Each party evidently caucused on the specific tax assessment that it would support in the House, for in the roll call votes taken in October, 1751, on this issue, the House in nearly all cases was to choose between two assessment amounts per one hundred acres for each county—a high one supported by the opposition and a low one pushed by the administration in the interests of the proprietors. The opposition's united strength, in the about evenly divided assembly, prevailed in forcing the higher county assessments through the House.[30]

The opposition party was strong enough to take drastic measures to cow council and proprietors into agreeing to the higher assessment amounts. When, not surprisingly, the council amended the assembly's tax bill, the opposition moved to submit the bill directly to Governor Belcher, bypassing the council because the upper house should, according to parliamentary practice, have no right to amend money bills. Only Speaker Charles Read's casting vote prevented their action; but the near miss of this radical parliamentary maneuver compelled Speaker Read and other House leaders to work out a compromise that generally split the difference between the rates each party had demanded. The council, in real danger of being bypassed, had to accept the compromise tax bill. The opposition compelled the proprietors to pay more than they ever had intended but not as much as the majority thought they should.[31]

The major development in New Jersey legislative politics in this period was that of a strong opposition. It is no surprise that the colony possessed a united corps of administration supporters, seeking executive patronage and protection. But that the antiproprietary, the antimilitia, and the antiexpenditure elements should, in a rural colony of varied regions and peoples, be able to

30. For the assembly and the land riots, *N.J. Votes,* Feb. 16, 1747-8, Dec. 1–8, 1748; Belcher to the Duke of Bedford, June 24, 1749, in *NJA,* VII, 291. On the tax dispute, *N.J. Votes,* Mar. 16, 1748-9, Oct. 19, 1749, Feb. 23, 1749-50, Feb. 20, 1750-1, Oct. 12, 22, 23, 1751; Journal of the Governor and Council, Mar. 14, 1748-9, Feb. 21, 1749-50, Feb. 8, 22, 1750-1, in *NJA,* XVI, 127, 213, 248–49, 271–73.

31. *N.J. Votes,* Feb. 6, 11, 1752; Governor Belcher to the Lords of Trade, Aug. 8, 1752, in *NJA,* Vol. 8, Pt. 1, p. 151.

TABLE 15

**Assemblymen Adhering to and Shifting from Parties:
New Jersey House, 1738–1753**

Constant Administration	Constant Opposition	Changers	Indeterminate
42.7% (32)	38.6% (29)	12.2% (9)	6.7% (5)

form a coherent opposition indicates considerable political organization and electoral politicization. The opposition spiritedly maintained the antidefense stance of the colony, promoted economy in government, harassed governors, and prevented the proprietors from avoiding taxation in their landholdings. It showed its power at election time, particularly at its inception in 1738 and in the "capmen" versus "wigmen" election of 1749. In these elections and also in 1740 and 1744, party leaders such as Richard Smith, Jr., recruited allies, rallied the electorate, and encouraged campaigns in several counties. Even in the revival of the administration side after 1751 it maintained the allegiance of half or more of the assemblymen. In the 1720s fragmented factions and proprietary-family groups had characterized political activity; by the 1740s a two-party electoral and legislative alignment had replaced factional patterns.

The partisan consistencies of the 1738–1754 period are more notable than the shifts. As Table 15 shows, of the total number of House members serving, only 12.2 percent changed sides during this period. The cores of the constant groups remained intact throughout these years: on the administration side the Anglican proprietors from Perth Amboy, in the opposition party the representatives from Monmouth and Cape May counties, some Quakers, Baptists, and several Dutch. Even though many Quakers, including prominent leaders, shifted from the administration side to the opposition and then back to the administration, the group was chiefly in the opposition camp. From 1738 to 1751 Quaker oppositionists outnumbered Quaker administration supporters fifty-eight seats to eighteen. Localities and social groups maintained party continuity by electing representatives with certain characteristics who would take stances that had long been popular in particular districts. Partisan contention crystallized out of local traditions, religious affiliations, and ideological commitments.

New York partisanship, like that of Pennsylvania and New Jersey, took shape in response to issues of executive power, imperial demands, and defense. Yet the New York parties did not at first display the firm, uncompromising stances and the unity that characterized the parties in the other middle colonies in

TABLE 16

**Economic and Social Characteristics of
Party Members: New York House, 1737–1739**

(*All tabulated figures are assembly terms*)

	Wealthy		Well-to-do		Middling		Unknown
Morris	7		8		1		
Philipse	8		2		0		2

	Anglican	Presbyterian	Dutch Reformed	Congregational	Quaker	Unknown
Morris	5	0	7	2	1	1
Philipse	3	0	6	0		3

	New York City	East shore	West shore	Long Island	Staten Island
Morris	4	3	3	3	3
Philipse	1	2	3	1	5

	Great landholder	Landowner		Farmer
Morris	4	3		1
Philipse	5	2		0

	Merchant	Shopkeeper/artisan	Lawyer	Unknown
Morris	3	1	1	3
Philipse	1	0	1	3

lambda-*b*, partisanship and region = 0.17; and occupation = 0.11; and wealth = 0.10; and religion = 0.00. (Includes by-election results.)

the 1737–1753 period. They did not oppose defense measures with the fervor of the New Jersey and Pennsylvania oppositionist and Quaker parties. They did not have consistent enemies—proprietors or committed religious groups. Their strong tradition of party warfare, beginning in the Cosby era, shaped many of their stances and actions in the succeeding years. The two rival groups were ready for combat when Governor George Clarke in 1737 called the first general election in nine years. The governor hoped that a new House would take his side and ignore the clamors of the Morris party, which had opposed his succession to Cosby. The electorate, however, had seen enough of Cosby's friends. The "Country party" took control of the House from the "Court party," as James Alexander and Cadwallader Colden termed these groups, making a spirited contest in many electoral districts. It won the seats of New York City, those of two river counties, and several others. The incumbent Philipse-Clarke supporters were apparently taken by surprise, though in New York City they did regroup and get Adolph Philipse back in the House in a by-election in September, 1737, that was so furiously contested that several noses were bloodied.[32]

The Morris-Alexander party had a clear edge over what Lewis Morris, Sr., termed the "other party"; it had fifteen assemblymen on its side while uncle Adolph and nephew Frederick Philipse II mustered a dozen. As Table 16 shows, social and economic divisions between the parties were not great. The Morris side had a substantial majority in only two regions. The Philipse party had most of the wealthy. Most important were the traditional antipathies such as that between the Morris and Philipse groups in Westchester and constituent demands for new leadership that would repudiate what Cosby and his allies had symbolized.[33]

The House now pushed programs that marked an ideological shift: a land bank that would issue £40,000 in paper notes, a triennial act, publication of roll call votes, and, most important, a one-year salary appropriation for Governor Clarke. These were popular measures that essentially kept faith with the constituents who had put the new party in office. The Morris party was a true opposition party by any standard of the time. Instead of hypocritically seeking office on popular issues and then merely currying favor with the governor, as New York factions had done for the past thirty years, it took a clear stand on policy and, although willing to compromise with the governor, accomplished most of its platform goals.[34]

The New York opposition party got off to much the same strong start that the Quakers in Pennsylvania and the New Jersey opposition did. But the latter endured and grew stronger; in New York the Morris group faltered. The Philipse party decided that it could also appeal, or pretend to appeal, to a broad constituency. It affected a popular pose during the 1737–1738 sessions,

32. Postelection complaints to the House indicated party contests. *N.Y. Votes,* May 3, June 16, Sept. 6–Oct. 12, 1737; Colden, *History of Cosby's Administration,* in *NYHSC,* LXVIII, 351; Alexander to Colden, Apr. 6, 1739, in *NYHSC,* LI, 194. Colden reported to his wife, Sept. 11, 1737, in *NYHSC,* LI, 179, on the New York City election. Minutes of Committee of Privileges and Elections, Sept. 14–15, 1737, in Orange County Election Papers, NYHS.

33. Biographical sources listed in Chapter 2, notes 2 and 52, were used for all text and tables describing the characteristics of New York assemblymen.

34. *N.Y. Votes,* Nov. 24, 1737, Oct. 13, 1738; *N.Y. Laws,* II, 1036, III, 45; Colden, *History of Cosby's Administration,* in *NYHSC,* LXVIII, 351–55. Bonomi, *Factious People,* 135–37, has a very fine account of the achievements of the Morris party in this period. Also see White, *Beekmans of New York,* 110; Kammen, *Colonial New York,* 205.

claimed it wanted to pay Clarke only the half-salary of a lieutenant governor, and even suggested cutting the pay of Chief Justice James DeLancey. The ensuing election, after Governor Clarke dissolved the House in 1739 because the Morrisite majority would not comply with his demands for a five-year support act, was fought between two groups that attempted to appeal to popular sentiment and attack the governor's salary. In New York City the Morris side held an outdoor rally to solicit popular support for its nominees. It was able to nominate only two candidates, the incumbents Alexander and Cornelius Van Horne, brother-in-law of manor lord Philip Livingston, Sr. The other two incumbents from New York City, who had supported the Morris side, did not run, which shows that the party was not strong or well organized. Adolph Philipse and three allies, with merchant and Anglican backing, stood against the two. Both sides fought a heated propaganda battle over which had best represented the popular will. Traditional merchant support for Philipse and his allies won in New York City.[35]

In at least one other county the parties staged a hard-fought combat. The Philipse side turned out a united party vote for its candidates in Queens. Its unsuccessful Morrisite opponents, the uncle and nephew Hicks, polled a very strong party vote also; the cohesion index for those candidates was 0.907. Quakers in Queens formed a solid bloc for the Morris side. In upstate districts, the Philipse party combined its new antiadministration pose with its traditional appeal to wealthy landowners. The old elite ruling group convinced the voters to select the traditional leaders and reject the Morrisite upstarts. It succeeded in capturing whole districts, much to the dismay of the defeated James Alexander and of manor lord Philip Livingston. It took New York City, Albany, and the Hudson east shore. Wealthy and well-to-do manor lords and landowners predominated in its assembly delegation, as Table 17 indicates. The opposition included representatives from Long Island, Staten Island, and the west shore, indicating that the small farmer interest, traditional Morris backers, was its major constituency.[36]

---

35. *N.Y. Votes,* Oct. 19, 20, 1738; Lewis Morris, Sr., to Sir Charles Wager, May 10, 1739, James Alexander to the Lords of Trade, May 30, 1739, in *NJA,* VI, 67, 75–76; *Many of the Electors of the Two, to the Electors of the Four, Send Greeting* (New York, 1739). For Van Horne, Cynthia Anne Kierner, *Traders and Gentlefolk: The Livingstons of Colonial New York, 1675–1790* (Ithaca, 1992), 45.

36. Alexander to Cadwallader Colden, Apr. 6, 1739, in *NYHSC,* LI, 194; Philip Livingston, Sr., to Robert Livingston Jr., Mar. 24, 1738-9, in LP. For Queens election figures, Dinkin, *Voting in Provincial America,* 154. For the cohesion index, see Appendix III. For the disputed Ulster election, *N.Y. Votes,* Apr. 5, 1739.

TABLE 17

**Economic and Social Characteristics of
Party Members: New York House, 1739–1743**

(*All tabulated figures are assembly terms*)

	Wealthy	Well-to-do	Middling	Unknown
Philipse	8	6	2	1
Opposition	4	4	2	

	Anglican	Presbyterian	Dutch Reformed	Congregational	Unknown
Philipse	6	0	7	0	4
Opposition	3	0	6	1	

	New York City	Albany	East shore	West shore	Long Island, Staten Island
Philipse	4	4	6	1	2
Opposition	0	1	0	3	6

	Great landholder	Landowner	Farmer
Philipse	6	3	1
Opposition	2	2	2

	Merchant	Shopkeeper/artisan	Lawyer	Unknown
Philipse	3	2	0	2
Opposition	2	0	1	1

lambda-b, partisanship and region = 0.60; and occupation = 0.22; and religion = 0.10; and wealth = 0.00

The Philipse party, although more elitist than its rival, shed factional attributes. Rather surprisingly, given its earlier support of Cosby's arbitrary rule, it set about fulfilling its pledges to the electorate, showing that it had learned much from the Morris party about keeping faith with the voters. It resisted Clarke's efforts to procure support for a five-year term and granted him only a reduced salary as lieutenant governor, though it was not cut in half. Because the Philipse side appeared genuinely committed to carrying out the programs it had promised, it drew some of the elite from the Morris party. Lewis Morris, Jr., and two of his allies voted with it. New Yorkers regarded party affiliation as fluid; when parties took similar positions on major issues, even the leaders would cross to the other side.[37] In the summer of 1743, when

37. Clarke was fortunate not to have his salary cut in half; this motion passed in October, 1739, and came close again a year later (*N.Y. Votes*, Sept. 20, Oct. 2, 1739, Oct. 4, 1740, Nov. 20,

Clarke's successor, Governor George Clinton, called a new assembly election, the electorate showed little interest in making changes in the House.[38]

Despite losing strength to its rival, the opposition in the 1744 assembly sessions won one of its major points—retaining a high tax quota on New York City. Its west shore and Long Island small farmer constituents were the core of those who demanded the continuation of the unfair tax quota levied on New York County—49 percent of the revenue required, although the county contained only 14 percent of the colony's population and certainly much less than half its wealth. In vain did the Philipse party leaders—the city merchants, uncle Adolph and nephew Frederick, Jr., Philip Verplanck of Cortlandt manor—and their allies, Lewis Morris, Jr., and Robert Livingston, Jr., seek a fairer apportionment. The opposition group stood fast against changing the tax system. Only two of the eleven opposition members voted to relieve New York City's tax burden; over half the Philipse party rejected the lead of Adolph and Frederick and voted to maintain the 49 percent quota.[39]

The electorate endorsed the opposition side's stand on taxation in the election of 1745 after another dissolution ordered by Governor Clinton. As was often the case in other elections called after a hostile dissolution, the opposition side gained enough strength to control the House. Table 18 shows its numbers and composition. It reelected all its adherents, gained one new member, and won over three former Philipse supporters and one neutral assemblyman. Perhaps these members changed affiliation because of constituent pressure; they were from areas where small farmers were important and where

1741). Governor Clarke to the Board of Trade, June 13, 1740, in *DCHNY,* VI, 160. Katz, *Newcastle's New York,* 157, follows William Smith, Jr., in claiming that Chief Justice DeLancey "gained control of the lower house during the Clarke administration." DeLancey may have supported the Philipse leadership, but there is no direct evidence of his involvement in legislative matters.

38. New York City returned an opposition member, a Philipse rival was elected in Westchester, and two members shifted from the Philipse side. The opposition now stood at twelve members, the Philipse side was down to fourteen, and one was of indeterminate partisanship. *N.Y. Votes,* Sept. 27, Nov. 10–12, 1743, notes a contested election in Orange County. Clinton later wrote the Board of Trade, June 22, 1747, in *DCHNY,* VI, 354, that James DeLancey advised the dissolution because he wanted to oust Speaker Adolph Philipse. This is not credible; the Philipse-DeLancey alliance continued strong throughout this period, and Adolph remained Speaker. More Philipse assemblymen were of the wealthy in this session, and the opposition was chiefly of the well-to-do and middling. Lambda-*b* in this session for the relationship to partisanship of region = 0.50, of occupation = 0.40, of wealth = 0.25, of religion = 0.09.

39. *N.Y. Votes,* Sept. 4, 1744.

TABLE 18

**Economic and Social Characteristics of
Party Members: New York House, 1745–1746**

(*All tabulated figures are assembly terms*)

	Wealthy	Well-to-do	Middling	Unknown
Philipse	8	4	0	
Opposition	5	6	3	1
Indeterminate				1

	Anglican	Presbyterian	Dutch Reformed	Congregational	Unknown
Philipse	5	0	7	0	
Opposition	4	0	9	1	1
Indeterminate					1

	New York City	Albany	East shore	West shore	Long Island, Staten Island
Philipse	4	5	3	0	0
Opposition	0	0	3	4	8
Indeterminate				1	

	Great landholder	Landowner	Farmer
Philipse	5	2	0
Opposition	3	3	4

	Merchant	Shopkeeper/artisan	Lawyer	Unknown
Philipse	4	1	0	
Opposition	2	0	1	2
Indeterminate				1

lambda-*b*, partisanship and region = 0.75; and occupation = 0.42; and wealth = 0.25; and religion = 0.08. (Includes by-election results.)

opposition sentiment was strongest—Long Island and the upriver counties. The Philipse side countered by winning over one of the New York City representatives. The regional division, between on the Philipse side the city and Albany and on the opposition side Long Island, Staten Island, and the west shore, was very sharp. Not only was the Philipse party now in the minority, but it had lost its captain, Adolph, who, now eighty, had retired to be succeeded by one of his city merchant backers.[40]

After recouping its electoral fortunes, the opposition side majority sought

40. Katz, *Newcastle's New York,* 167–83, argues that James DeLancey was directing politics in

control of the Speaker's chair, continued high taxation of New York City, and control of military expenditures, for Britain was now at war with France. As successor to Speaker Philipse it elected David Jones of Queens. He had been a Philipse supporter in 1739, but by 1741 he had turned to voting with the opposition. In the previous assembly Jones firmly opposed Governor Clinton's attempts to control defense resources and appropriations, as would be expected of a popular opposition leader.[41] He also constantly opposed reducing the tax quota for New York City. Merchant allies of the Philipses and DeLanceys were demanding that the disproportionate tax burden on the city be reduced to be more in line with the city's population. Although under Speaker Jones's leadership the opposition held fast against any change in the tax quota apportionments for several months, it finally lost the second round in the struggle. In 1744 the Philipse party had split on the issue; in April, 1746, all its members, including those from Albany and its manor lord supporters, lined up in favor of reducing the tax quota formerly imposed on New York City and increasing those of certain back counties. Four members of the opposition broke ranks. They joined with the Philipse party to reject Speaker Jones's motion that the old quotas were equitable and to pass a bill lowering the city quota from 49 to 33.3 percent (see Table 19).[42]

The opposition party's continued stance against letting Governor Clin-

the House and had gotten Philipse ousted as Speaker. In actuality the assembly differed sharply with the DeLancey-dominated council. Also see Bonomi, *Factious People,* 167–68.

41. Governor Clinton to the Lords of Trade, June 22, 1747, in *DCHNY,* VI, 354, and Smith, *Continuation of the History of New York,* 65, both assume that Jones was a DeLancey henchman; this cannot have been true in 1746. Cadwallader Colden wrote to Dr. John Mitchell, July 6, 1749, in *NYHSC,* LXVIII, 26–27, that Jones was not "let into the Secrets of the Cabal." Later Jones's son would marry James DeLancey's daughter, and he would be appointed Supreme Court judge. DeLancey in-law John Watts, to General Robert Monckton, June 30, 1764, in *Letterbook of John Watts, Merchant and Councillor of New York,* January 1, 1762–December 22, 1765, *NYHSC,* LXI, 270, characterized him as a "scurvey fellow." Also see Colden to David Colden, July 5, 1759, in Letters on Smith's History, *NYHSC,* II, 206; Colden to the Board of Trade, Jan. 22, 1765, in Colden Letter Books, *NYHSC,* IX, 455; *DCHNY,* VIII, 185; Thompson, *History of Long Island,* III, 526–27; Flint, *Long Island Before the Revolution,* 150–52, 195.

42. *N.Y. Votes,* Sept. 4, 1744, Feb. 8, 1745-6, Apr. 25, 1746. See Benjamin H. Newcomb, "The Great Landholders and Political Power in Colonial New York and New Jersey," in *Working the Range: Essays on the History of Western Land Management and the Environment,* ed. John Wunder (Westport, 1985), 59–80. Population figures are interpolated from Gary B. Nash, "The New York Census of 1737: A Critical Note on the Integration of Statistical and Literary Sources," *WMQ,* 3rd ser., XXXVI (1979), 431; the 1737 census in *DCHNY,* VI, 133; and the 1756 census in E. B.

TABLE 19

Changes in Tax Apportionment: New York

County	Percent population 1745		Percent tax 1744	Percent tax 1746
New York	14.2	(10,509)	49.0	33.3
Albany	18.2	(13,520)	16.1	14.3
Westchester	12.8	(9,487)	5.1	5.5
Kings	3.4	(2,499)	3.9	5.8
Queens	13.2	(9,786)	5.5	11.2
Suffolk	12.0	(8,920)	5.2	10.0
Ulster	8.4	(6,232)	5.1	9.1
Orange	4.0	(2,956)	3.8	3.3
Dutchess	10.7	(7,940)	3.8	4.2
Richmond	3.1	(2,292)	2.6	3.1

ton have a free hand in administering the war effort against the French came to be the position of the whole assembly; the administration party almost completely collapsed. The opposition majority insisted on control of military appropriations, and in July, 1746, it succeeded in placing commissioners in charge of military expenditures.[43] When the projected British attack on Canada in 1746 was canceled, the assembly majority requested that the soldiers be disbanded and sent home, rather than be continued in winter encampment at great expense to the taxpayers and hardship to themselves. It refused to make further provision for them. Clinton rejected the request, obstinately retained the troops in camp, and, when the commissioners appointed by the assembly refused to furnish supplies, seized them from storehouses. The assembly's response to these high-handed acts was total political unity. By the end of November, 1746, partisan distinctions disappeared in the assembly; the political leaders on both sides forged a united front against the governor that would endure until he left office. As Henry Beekman reported in November, 1747, "We in the house of Assembly have perswadgen amongst us a Greed case of

O'Callaghan, ed., *The Documentary History of the State of New York* (4 vols.; Albany 1849–51), I, 696. For tax figures, *N.Y. Laws*, III, 404–405, 549, 579. Robert A. Becker, *Revolution, Reform, and the Politics of American Taxation, 1763–1783* (Baton Rouge, 1980), 43, and Countryman, *People in Revolution*, 83, note that the speculative holdings of manor lords were not taxed so they received a tax break despite the higher assessments on their counties.

43. *N.Y. Votes*, Feb. 13, 19, 1745-6, Apr. 9, 21–23, 25, June 4, 23, 27, July 9, 1746; *N.Y. Laws*, Feb. 27, 1745-6, July 15, 1746, III, 523, 595–98.

a Dissolution to Set up & Joyn so al to Come again in the same body if possible, time is come to such Crisis that Something must at all Events be tryd to Save our Country cas the Governour wil pase non of our Laws which are now before him." Roll call voting, a regular feature of New York assemblies for the past nine years, now virtually ended for the remainder of Clinton's term. Both Pennsylvania after 1742 and New Jersey from 1743 to 1746 experienced near complete one-party domination and resistance to the executive. The New York Assembly's stance against Clinton was even more solid. The Philipse party completely reversed itself because Clinton was proving himself to be impossible for a proadministration party to support. As well, the council refused to cooperate with the governor's plans to get the Six Nations to join in the attack on Canada, for it wished to maintain neutrality to preserve the Indian trade. Chief Justice and Councillor James DeLancey, perhaps for personal reasons, gave Governor Clinton little support. He seems to have played no role in the amalgamation of parties in the House, but his commissioning as lieutenant governor and his forming of a joint council-assembly committee in 1747 solidified the anti-Clinton stance of both legislative branches.[44]

The governor's response to his complete loss of credit with the legislature was partisan politics, punctuated by a succession of dissolutions and elections in 1748, 1750, and 1752. In 1748 Clinton's political efforts, aided by his ally Cadwallader Colden, were superficial and ineffectual. Colden made some effort in Orange and Ulster counties, and perhaps in Dutchess, but gained no assemblymen who supported Clinton. Unlike most previous elections, this contest was so one-sided in every district that not one election protest was carried to the assembly.[45]

By August, 1749, after the next prorogation, Clinton and Colden began

44. *N.Y. Votes*, Nov. 4, 26, 1746; Henry Beekman to Henry Livingston, Nov. 12, 1747, in "A Packet of Old Letters," *Yearbook, Dutchess County Historical Society* (1921), 32–33. *N.Y. Votes*, Oct. 19, Nov. 25, 1747, records that the House locked the door and put the key on the table to enforce unanimity while it discussed remonstrating with the governor. Two roll calls, *N.Y. Votes*, Oct. 24, 1748, Oct. 19, 1750, were taken between December, 1746, and Clinton's departure in 1753. Colden to Dr. John Mitchell, July 6, 1749, in NYHSC, LXVIII, 27. A law of December, 1746, in *N.Y. Laws*, III, 637–38, prohibited the further seizing of supplies. Bonomi, *Factious People*, 154–56. Katz, *Newcastle's New York*, 169–71, argues that in the spring of 1746 Clinton and DeLancey quarreled over the militia bill, and DeLancey, manipulating council and assembly, plotted to embarrass the governor so he would be ousted and DeLancey succeed. Perhaps DeLancey did so induce the council, but the legislative record indicates no such influence over the assembly.

45. Clinton to Newcastle, Feb. 13, 1747-8, in *DCHNY*, VI, 417. NYHSC, LII, 284–90, for Colden's collaboration with and defense of Clinton. Colden to Clinton, Jan. 14, [Jan.] (on Orange), Jan. 29, [Feb.], 1747-8, in NYHSC, LII, 333, LIII, 3, 7–8, LVI, 346–47.

building a party or at least a corps of followers. They hustled and bustled, making patronage appointments. The governor forged an alliance with the Morrises and James Alexander. Lewis Morris, Jr., had been a staunch opponent of Clinton—he had moved the publication of the assembly's remonstrance against the governor of November, 1747. But now interest overwhelmed ideology, as had happened in the Morris family before. Clinton promised Robert Hunter Morris, Lewis, Jr.'s, brother, that he should be lieutenant governor when Clinton managed to obtain DeLancey's removal. The Morrises and Alexander feared that DeLancey's executive power would jeopardize their land claims in northwest New Jersey. Their defection became a propaganda issue; a pamphlet pointedly noted that formerly they "pretended to very different Notions of Politicks, but finding Popularity the wrong Road to Elevation and Grandeur," they "prostrate themselves before the golden Image." In reply, writers on behalf of the governor's side argued against the excessive party zeal displayed by the assembly incumbents.[46]

All of Clinton's patronage, alliances, and propaganda availed nothing. In Westchester, Lewis Morris, Jr., in a close vote was ousted from the borough seat he had held since 1732. He belatedly tried to challenge manor lord Frederick Philipse II and his ally John Thomas in the county contest a few days later, and they overwhelmed him. The Morris interest was smashed because it had turned against the popular side, had not campaigned effectively in Westchester, and could not equal the combined Philipse-DeLancey influence. In the Queens election, both groups mustered their supporters in partisan fashion; they did not, as in Westchester, leave matters until the last minute. The cohesion indices for the two slates show that the electorate viewed them as partisan; that for the incumbents was 0.973, that for the Clintonian challengers was a solidly partisan 0.997. The governor's supporters were strongly unified, but there were too few of them; the incumbents garnered 61.5 per-

46. *N.Y. Votes,* Nov. 12, 1747, Oct. 19, 26, Nov. 12, 1748, July 5–18, Aug. 4, 1749, Nov. 6, 1753; Clinton to the Duke of Newcastle, Feb. 13, 1747-8, in *DCHNY,* VI, 417; John Livingston to Robert Livingston, Jr., Mar. 25, 1752, in LP; Memorial of the Council of Proprietors of East Jersey to Governor Belcher, Nov. 20, 1753, in *NJA,* Vol. 8, Pt. 1, pp. 217–19, 232; Kenney, *Stubborn for Liberty,* 137; Bonomi, *Factious People,* 160–61; Schwartz, *Jarring Interests,* 82, 140–41; *A Letter to the Freemen and Freeholders of the Province of New-York, Relating to the Approaching Election of Their Representatives,* 10. Clintonian pieces included *A Plain Answer from a Gentleman in Queen's County to a Familiar Letter from a Citizen of New York . . .* (New York, 1750); and *Queries Humbly Offered to the Freeholders in the County of Westchester* (New York, 1750). For Livingston family hostility to the "Reign" of "Morisania [sic]," Philip Livingston, Jr., to Robert Livingston, Jr., Nov. 29, 1751, Feb. 15, 1752, in LP.

cent of the vote. William Johnson failed to manage the Clinton side's campaign in Albany. None of the five potential candidates who backed Clinton was actually willing to stand against the incumbents.[47]

The 1752 election effort was likewise vigorous, but the results were the same. Clinton and his allies again conducted a widespread campaign. Both sides employed propaganda in New York City to rouse supporters. William Livingston took the popular side, writing on behalf of the Philipse-DeLancey party. The Clinton side betrayed its desperation when one of its propagandists accused the Indian trade commissioners appointed by the assembly of illicit relations with Native American women. The Clintonians succeeded only in Albany, where William Johnson made good his promise to discipline the incumbents, and got two new assemblymen elected. James Alexander anticipated a "great struggle" in Queens, but it was another resounding victory for the governor's opponents. Opposition leaders such as Henry Beekman of Dutchess County knew how to keep their backers happy. On election day he and fellow incumbent Henry Filkin felt obliged to provide food and drink for the voters. Beekman was to send six barrels of cider to "Several Houses of ours" and Filkin to "provid or furnish Beef, Pork, & Backin." Clinton's efforts through three elections proved that middle-colony governors had to cultivate electoral support carefully, as Beekman did; it could not be manufactured to order by a besieged governor and his few allies. By 1750, parties could not rise from small interest groups, as factions had fifty years previously. They had to be broadly based in both legislature and electorate.[48]

Partisanship in New York in the period 1737–1752 possessed frailties that

47. Richard Miller to William Johnson, July 31, 1750, "To the Voters of Canajoharie," [July, 1750], both in *The Papers of Sir William Johnson* (13 vols.; Albany, 1921–62), I, 293–94; Clinton to Cadwallader Colden, Feb. 9, 1749-50, in *NYHSC*, LIII, 189; Bonomi, *Factious People*, 162, 170. For Henry Beekman's fear of Clintonian opposition in Dutchess, White, *Beekmans of New York*, 206. For the cohesion index, see Appendix III.

48. James Alexander to Cadwallader Colden, Dec. 5, 1751, Feb. 15, 1752, in *NYHSC*, LIII, 303–304, 311. Klein, ed., *Independent Reflector*, introduction, 13, identifies William Livingston as the author of *A Letter to the Freeman and Freeholders of the City of New York; Relating to the Approaching Election of Representatives; Wherein the Several Papers That Have Lately Appeared on the Subject of Politicks, Are Briefly Considered; the Conduct of the Authors Exposed, and the Controversy Represented in Its True Light* (New York, 1752). No copy exists; it was answered by *An Answer to a Pamphlet, Entitled A Letter to the Freeman and Freeholders of the City of New York; Wherein Is Fully Shewn, the True Causes of the Defection of the Six Nations of Indians, with Some Historical Collections Never Yet Made Publick* (New York, 1752), 7–8, which made the accusations against the commissioners. John Ayscough to William Johnson, Jan. 3, 1752, in *Papers of Sir William Johnson*, IX, 86; Beekman to Henry Livingston, Jan. 23, 1752, in "A Packet of Old Letters," *Yearbook, Dutchess County Historical Society* (1921), 35.

indicate it was not as well developed as were parties in New Jersey and Pennsylvania. The principal difference in New York was that a substantial proportion of assemblymen, 26.1 percent, shifted their political allegiance during the period. Only 12.2 percent in New Jersey shifted; although there is no precise measure for the Pennsylvania House, the proportion shifting sides could not have been any larger than in New Jersey. Most assemblymen who changed sides became disillusioned with the administration or Philipse side. Eight assemblymen moved from the administration to the opposition position, largely as a result of the political tactics of Governor Clinton. Five shifted the other direction. Robert Livingston, Jr., in 1745 and Lewis Morris, Jr., in 1749 changed from the opposition to the administration side, though Livingston later returned to the unanimous assembly opposition to Clinton. Assemblymen neither drifted aimlessly from one partisan position to another, nor did they sell themselves to the highest bidder. The minority that moved from one bloc to the other was not for the most part exemplifying the often quoted observation of Philip Livingston the manor lord that partisan activity was merely self-serving: "We change Sides as Serves our Interest best not the Countries." Except for some opportunists like Lewis Morris, Jr., they knew that their constituents expected them to adhere to the legislative party that best fit the interests of that district (see Table 20).[49]

Traditional allegiances, local attitudes, and occupational status best explain partisan affiliation in New York in this period. Representatives of the middling farmers of Long Island formed much of the core of the opposition. As this side gained strength, it incorporated many of the Hudson Valley farmer representatives. The core administration group was the Philipse family members, other great landholders, and New York City and Albany trading interests. Others joined the cores and some switched sides as key issues aroused their concern.

The middle colonies in these fourteen years experienced two interconnected political developments: the institution of at least one strong party in each of the assemblies and the extension of party-directed political activity to the constituencies. The social and economic characteristics that influenced partisanship were somewhat different in each colony. In Pennsylvania and New Jersey religion played the greatest role. In New York and, secondarily in New Jersey, parties grouped regionally. Wealth and occupation were of

49. Livingston's remark to Jacob Wendell, July 25, 1737, is thoroughly analyzed in Bonomi, *Factious People,* 58, and also quoted in Katz, *Newcastle's New York,* 84, and Kammen, *Colonial New York,* 205.

TABLE 20

Assemblymen Adhering to and Shifting from Parties:
New York House, 1737–1746

Constant administration	Constant opposition	Changers	Indeterminate
34.8% (16)	37.0% (17)	26.1% (12)	(1)

lesser importance. The merchant-landowner clash in New York, prominent in factional development, was now subordinated to larger regional alliances concerned about taxation and other issues. Likewise, in New Jersey and Pennsylvania the parties found other important matters besides the paper money issue to unite them. Despite these differences, the general attitudes of administration and opposition parties in these colonies were parallel. The majority of representatives voted consistently over the period, the houses chose Speakers for partisan reasons, the members of the partisan groups readily gravitated to common positions on issues such as tax quotas and assessments, and the party leaders used influence and patronage to keep sympathizers in line. The factions out of which these parties grew had lacked these attributes and had taken fragmented positions on policy. The change from factions to more sophisticated political organizations made incomplete and halting progress. The Proprietary party in Pennsylvania and the administration party in New York showed little endurance. They would, however, soon be back in competition with their rivals.

Those election returns that are complete for specific contests illustrate the extent of the activity of the party in the electorate. Poll book evidence and the cohesion indices, calculated from the returns, reveal in the Philadelphia and Bucks elections of 1740 and 1742, the Lancaster election of 1742, the New York City local election of 1734, the Queens elections of 1739 and 1750, the Westchester election of 1750, and the Burlington election of 1740 strong partisan voting by the electorate.[50] Legislators and candidates posed for, appealed to, organized, and inspired the electorate. The techniques employed were yet primitive; these would develop as political experience accumulated.

50. For the cohesion index, see Appendix III. The poll book for the Burlington election of 1739–40 is the only full account for any New Jersey election for the period; that contest, although fully partisan, went unreported in the newspapers. The 1742 election in Chester was moderately partisan.

4
The Partisan System in Wartime, 1754–1764

The renewed conflict between Britain and France after 1754 caused political repercussions in the middle colonies that intensified partisan divisions. Each colony was threatened by French and Native American depredations in the 1754–1758 period; each was compelled, as part of its common obligation to the other colonies and to the empire, to bear a much greater burden than ever before in supplying men and material. Opposition parties were ideologically confronted with the problem of the extent to which administration demands for military support could practically be opposed, for unavoidable war came quickly upon the colonies and had to be fought. If an opposition remained intractable against defense measures, it could readily incur the wrath of both imperial government and constituents. Conversely, because military measures had suddenly become popular, the administration sides now had the opportunity to gain substantially greater electoral support.

A second important change was the development of a heightened religious and ethnic consciousness among the diverse middle-colony groups. Large-scale immigration during the first half of the eighteenth century included various peoples who demanded the status and protection that the Old World had denied them. By the 1750s and early 1760s these people had firmly arrayed themselves against cultural monopolization and discrimination and tied themselves to any established partisan group that would pay them heed. Consequently, both administration and opposition parties in the middle colonies had to adjust to more complex issues, to develop more finely the techniques of electoral politics, and to broaden their appeal so as to bring in these socially diverse groups. As a result, in New York and Pennsylvania effective political opposition revived in 1753–1754, and soon party contests became as heated as they had been in the early 1740s.

Religion now became much more significant in New York politics and ensured continual division between administration and opposition groups until the Revolution. When Anglicans proposed to establish King's College in

New York City, Presbyterians led by William Livingston and William Smith, Jr., of the *Independent Reflector*, attacked what they viewed as a plot by the established church to dominate the political and cultural life of the province. They appealed to the Dutch as fellow Calvinists to make common cause against the college and defend religious liberty. Allying with the religious groups were political leaders of the opposition to former governor Clinton. Speaker David Jones and William Nicoll II, both Long Islanders and Anglicans, joined Robert Livingston, Jr., in leading the opponents of the plan. As indicated by cluster-bloc analysis, the House divided into two parties. The newly formed opposition outnumbered the Philipse-DeLancey side fifteen to twelve. Richard Morris reported to his uncle Robert Hunter Morris in late 1754 that the "Reflector" interest was stronger than the "Church" interest. The opposition was not strong enough to wrest control of the college from DeLancey and his council, as Robert Livingston, Jr., tried to persuade the assembly to do, but it blocked extensive public financing of it.[1]

Although the restored opposition was launched by religious division, it soon contested issues that had nothing to do with religion. When in February, 1755, the House considered apportioning taxes for defense, the new opposition rejected a compromise effort by the administration side, led by Governor James DeLancey and composed of the old Philipse allies, and made substantial adjustments in the tax quotas for several counties. Roll call voting on the tax quota issue shows that the House divided almost exactly the same on this matter as it did on the King's College issue. Of the twenty-four assemblymen who voted on both issues (88.9 percent of the House), only three, all from Albany County, were not consistent in voting with one party or the other. The college issue and the tax issue were not intrinsically connected, but 87.5 percent of those voting treated both as party issues. The tax quota issue was also based on traditional regional alignments. The opposition party, as Table 21 shows, imposed heavier quotas on Westchester, Dutchess, and Albany than had been accepted in the tax compromise of 1746 and lowered those on Kings and Ulster, not only to come closer to an equitable apportionment but also

1. See Chapter 2 for the college controversy. Humphrey, *From King's College to Columbia*, 55–62. Nicoll's motion to weaken the dedication of lottery funds to the college passed. *N.Y. Votes*, Oct. 25, Nov. 6, 26, 28, 1754; *N.Y. Laws*, III, 614–15, 686–87; Richard Morris to Robert Hunter Morris, [Dec., 1754], in MP. William Smith Jr., in his *Continuation of the History of New York*, 142–43, identified elaborate linkages to DeLancey of all assemblymen elected in 1752, except Robert Livingston, Jr. Roll call analysis indicates that linkages did not control partisan alignments in the House.

TABLE 21

Tax Quota Changes: New York, 1755 (in percent)

	% of population, 1756	1746 tax quota	Administration proposal	1755 tax quota
Kings	2.9	5.8	—	4.8
Ulster	8.7	9.1	8.7	7.7
Westchester	13.3	5.5	5.4	10.0
Dutchess	15.3	4.2	4.2	8.6
Albany	18.8	14.3	—	16.6

because the former were centers of Philipse-DeLancey party support. The opposition party was bound together by an ideology incorporating hostility to special privilege for the college and for the religious group backing it and by aversion to a special tax break for certain favored counties in which its rival party was strong.[2]

The opposition refused to cooperate fully with Governors DeLancey and Charles Hardy in making financial arrangements and funding defense measures. That it was not entirely obstreperous, as it had been under Clinton, encouraged Hardy to allow it to continue for seven years, its full term. The governors accepted a moderate opposition that gave them part of what they wanted, rather than risk a dissolution during wartime that might produce a House full of extreme opponents.[3]

The opposition side saw in the dissolution of December, 1758, and the subsequent septennial election an opportunity for building a strong electoral coalition based on old rivalries, involvement of new religious groups, and dis-

2. *N.Y. Votes,* Feb. 11, Apr. 30, 1755. Population figures from O'Callaghan, ed., *Documentary History of the State of New York,* I, 696. See Table 19 for 1746 tax figures.

3. DeLancey to the Lords of Trade, Jan. 3, 1754, Mar. 8, 1755, in *DCHNY,* VI, 820–21, 941; *N.Y. Votes,* Apr. 12, 20, May 2–4, Nov. 12, 25, 28, 1754; *Journal of the Legislative Council of the Colony of New York* (Albany, 1861), Nov. 21, 1754, Feb. 15, May 3, 1755; Hardy to the Lords of Trade, Dec. 2, 1756, in *DCHNY,* VII, 201–203; Leslie V. Brock, *The Currency of the American Colonies: A Study in Colonial Finance and Imperial Relations* (New York, 1975), 333–42. Jack P. Greene, "The Seven Years War and the American Revolution: The Causal Relationship Reconsidered," *Journal of Imperial and Commonwealth History,* VIII (1980), 98, on the extent of New York's wartime contributions. [William Smith, Jr.], *The Watchman,* No. I (New York, 1770); and Smith, *A Review of the Military Operations in North-America, from the Commencement of the French Hostilities on the Frontiers of Virginia in 1753 to the Surrender of Oswego on the 14th of August 1756* (London, 1757; rpr. New York, 1770), 136–39, castigated Governor DeLancey's influence over the assembly during the war.

satisfaction with administration demands. The Morris family rejoined the opponents of Philipse and DeLancey. Lewis Morris, Jr., attempted to return to the House, but from Queens because Westchester was completely in the hands of his old adversaries. Most important was that the Livingston family as a group took the opposition side. As Robert Hunter Morris reported, "There had been for some time Past a Kind of Contention between the Livingstons & DeLanceys." Robert, Jr., had shifted to the opposition in the King's College controversy; brother William produced political propaganda against Anglican schemes. The family was worried that the government would not assist in quelling rioters and ejecting interlopers from manor lands. Merchants who were DeLancey supporters had competed with the Livingston brothers and their allies for government contracts. These clashes with the Philipse-DeLancey interest inspired at least four Livingston family members to stand for the assembly elections held around January 1, 1759.[4]

Concerted campaign efforts (of which no detailed record remains) resulted in the election of two Livingston brothers and two cousins: William and Philip, Jr., brothers of Robert, Jr., the manor lord, were elected from the manor and New York City respectively; the son of their uncle Robert of Clermont, Robert R. Livingston, together with Henry, son of their uncle Gilbert, won the Dutchess seats. They overcame Governor James DeLancey's coercive efforts; he reportedly exercised "his vengeance on his political opposers, by directing his creatures (the Officers of the Militia who were dependent on him) to detach them," that is, draft opponents for active duty. The four Livingston family members voted together as the core of a bloc that was essentially a continuation of the opposition party. As Table 22 shows, the difference between the two parties was now religious; Anglicans and Dutch Reformed confronted Presbyterians. The Livingston party lost support from larger landowners but garnered more backing from farmers. It dominated only the Hudson west shore, splitting Albany and the Long Island–Staten Island districts with the Philipse-DeLancey side. The Philipse-DeLancey party was now the majority party in the assembly, fourteen to thirteen, but the Livingston party contained such prominent assembly leaders that its influence surpassed its minority status.[5]

4. *N.Y. Votes,* Dec. 16, 1758, Feb. 2, 1759; Morris to [William] Walton, August, 1760, in MP; William Livingston to Robert Livingston, Jr., Feb. 4, 1754, in LP; Schwartz, *Jarring Interests,* 110–11; Lewis Morris, Jr., to Captain John Shirley, May 24, 1755, copy, Peter V. B. Livingston to William Alexander, July 9, 1755, both in William Alexander Papers, NYHS.

5. Livingston genealogies are in Kierner, *Traders and Gentlefolk,* 253–61. [Smith], *The Watch-*

The Livingston family's prominence in the House brought on a spirited election campaign in early 1761, when the assembly was dissolved after the death of George II in 1760. Robert Hunter Morris and his family were soon campaigning against their old rivals; he confidently predicted that "Philipse will be thrown out of West Chester County" and Lewis Morris III would gain control of Kings. The Livingston family members all stood for reelection except William, who withdrew in favor of nephew Peter R., heir to the manor. They also put up Abraham Yates in Albany, and several Livingstons campaigned for him. Robert Hunter Morris feared the expansion of Livingston power, but the Morris family and its allies sided with the Livingstons as the enemy of their enemies.[6]

In the New York City campaign, the Livingston leadership showed its inexperience in electoral politics and committed strategic errors. That party did not consider the city election to be very important until many of its supporters belatedly decided that they had a chance to oust the DeLancey candidates. At first Philip Livingston, Jr., accepted the initiative of James DeLancey, Jr., that he and the three New York incumbents stand as a unified ticket. The DeLancey city delegation majority of three to one would be preserved, for James was succeeding uncle Oliver, who had been named to the council. The four thus advertised their candidacy in the newspapers together and apparently expected no important rivals to appear against them. A large number of city voters, who may have been dissenters and who harbored anti-DeLancey sentiment, were dissatisfied with the ticket. Two other candidates quickly set up: merchant William Bayard and lawyer John Morin Scott. Scott was a Presbyterian who had assisted William Livingston and William Smith, Jr., in the *Independent Reflector* and was a strong Philipse-DeLancey opponent.

man, No. III (New York, 1770); *N.Y. Votes*, Mar. 1, 1759, Mar. 21–22, 1760. The Livingston family voted with its opponents to approve militia detachments, against which other oppositionist assemblymen voted. Three Livingstons quickly became leaders of the House; Philip, William, and Robert R. were top-ranking leaders. They surpassed their rivals in leadership positions, for Frederick Philipse III and Peter DeLancey were of only second-ranking leader status. See Appendix II for evaluation of leadership. Henry Livingston served on six committees, an above-average number. Bonomi, *Factious People*, 231, 237, is uncertain about the existence of a Livingston party before the later 1760s. Klein, "Prelude to Revolution in New York," 448–49, claims the Livingstons were in a majority in the House, 1759–1761.

6. *N.Y. Votes*, Mar. 10, 1761; Robert Hunter Morris to [William] Walton, August, 1760, Morris to General [?], Feb. 4, 1761, both in MP; Kenney, *Stubborn for Liberty*, 142–43; Alan Rogers, *Empire and Liberty: American Resistance to British Authority, 1755–1763* (Berkeley, 1974), 130–31.

TABLE 22

**Economic and Social Characteristics of
Party Members: New York House, 1759–1760**

(*All tabulated figures are assembly terms*)

	Wealthy	Well-to-do	Middling	Unknown
Philipse-DeLancey	7	6	2	
Livingston	5	5	1	2

	Anglican	Presbyterian	Dutch Reformed	Congregational	Quaker	Unknown
Philipse-DeLancey	6	0	7	0	1	1
Livingston	3	3	3	1	1	2

	New York City	Albany	East shore	West shore	Long Island, Staten Island
Philipse-DeLancey	3	3	4	1	4
Livingston	1	3	2	3	4

	Great landholder	Landowner	Farmer
Philipse-DeLancey	3	5	2
Livingston	2	3	4

	Merchant	Shopkeeper/artisan	Lawyer	Unknown
Philipse-DeLancey	4	0	0	1
Livingston	2	0	0	2

lambda-*b*, partisanship and religion = 0.36; and occupation = 0.27; and region = 0.15; and wealth = 0.00. (Includes by-election results.)

Many supporters of Philip Livingston, Jr., repudiated the coalition ticket and linked him with Bayard and Scott. The campaign became "spirited on both Sides"; the candidates agreed "not to open houses or give Liquor to the electors." Robert Hunter Morris predicted that the DeLancey side would go down to defeat, "the People as well in the Country as in the town shewing warm inclinations to oppose the friends of that Family."[7]

In New York City, the three relatives of Philip Livingston, Jr., who can be identified as voters, Lewis Morris III, and several hundred voters making up 28.4 percent of the electorate backed a Livingston-Bayard-Scott ticket that did not include DeLancey. Presbyterians, as identified by possession of Scotch names, voted for Scott and Bayard in greater numbers than did the total elec-

7. New York *Mercury,* Jan. 26, Feb. 2, 1761; [Smith], *The Watchman,* No. II (New York, 1770); Morris to General [?], Feb. 4, 1761, William Kelly to Morris, Feb. 22, 1761, both in MP.

torate. The three incumbents and James DeLancey, Jr., received about the same amount of support from the voters as did the Livingston party ticket. Because neither party had thoroughly canvassed the electorate, the plurality of voters, lacking organization and direction, did not form large voting blocs. Bayard edged out James DeLancey, Jr., but Scott, a lawyer without solid merchant backing, was unable to defeat either of the two Philipse-DeLancey incumbents.[8]

Both parties made some coordinated effort in the back counties. In Queens two Philipse-DeLancey and two opposition supporters engaged in the closest and hardest fought match in the colony's history; 86.6 percent of the qualified voters turned out. The Philipse-DeLancey party showed continued strength in Westchester. There the cohesion index for the incumbents affiliated with that side was 0.965, showing that voters associated them as party candidates. Despite considerable anti-DeLancey sentiment, the Morris candidates finished 230 votes behind their rivals. The Livingston party also lost in Kings and in a close Schenectady election. It campaigned hard in Albany but could only divide the delegation with the other side. As Sir William Johnson reported in disgust, politics there went on in the same "old Dutch Channel"; Livingston nominee Abraham Yates and Johnson's candidate were both defeated.[9]

The Livingston side held its House supporters in this election; all the assemblymen who voted with Robert R. Livingston on the major partisan questions in the previous session were returned, except for the Livingston manor representative, which change reflected no loss. As Table 23 indicates, Anglicans and Dutch Reformed chiefly lined up on the Philipse-DeLancey side. The Livingston side picked up important support from merchants, who formerly were more numerous in the Philipse-DeLancey ranks. The latter party also experienced a sizable decline in the number of wealthy assemblymen. The influence of region on partisanship increased slightly. The four Livingston family members continued to vote as a solid bloc, agreeing more than

8. *N.Y.C. Poll List, 1761.* See Chapter 2, note 28, for sources on the Presbyterian vote. The combined ticket of DeLancey and the three incumbents polled 434 votes; second was the Livingston-Bayard-Scott-Cruger combination with 165 votes; third was the Bayard-Scott combination with 151 votes. The winning combination was the choice of only 5.3 percent of the voters.

9. *N.Y. Votes,* Mar. 4, 12, Apr. 3, May 6, 9, Sept. 10, Dec. 1–9, 1761; New York *Mercury,* Mar. 2, 1761; Johnson to Cadwallader Colden, June 18, 1761, in *NYHSC,* LV, 43; Dinkin, *Voting in Provincial America,* 154; Varga, "Election Procedures in New York," 260–61. The Livingston side lost election protests in Queens and Schenectady and prevailed in Richmond.

TABLE 23

**Economic and Social Characteristics of
Party Members: New York House, 1761–1765**

(All tabulated figures are assembly terms)

	Wealthy	Well-to-do	Middling	Unknown
DeLancey	6	6	2	
Livingston	7	3	0	2
Indeterminate		1	1	

	Anglican	Presbyterian	Dutch Reformed	Congregational	Quaker	Unknown
DeLancey	6	0	6	1	0	1
Livingston	3	3	3	0	0	3
Indeterminate	1				1	

	New York City	Albany	East shore	West shore	Long Island, Staten Island
DeLancey	2	2	4	1	5
Livingston	2	3	2	3	2
Indeterminate					2

	Great landholder	Landowner	Farmer
DeLancey	3	3	3
Livingston	1	1	1
Indeterminate		1	1

	Merchant	Shopkeeper/artisan	Lawyer	Unknown
DeLancey	2	1	1	1
Livingston	7	0	0	2

lambda-*b*, partisanship and occupation = 0.50; and religion = 0.33; and region = 0.25; and wealth = 0.10. (Includes by-election results.)

75 percent of the time. The DeLancey side could claim fourteen adherents, two more than its opposition, but the Livingston party still provided the chief leaders of the House.[10]

The rise of the Livingston party, which in effect took over the bulk of the old opposition group, was the major change in the structure of New York partisanship in 1752–1765. Its party building was as yet very tentative. The Liv-

10. *N.Y. Votes,* Apr. 1, Dec. 3, 4, 7, 1761, Mar. 16, 1762, Dec. 2–14, 1763, Oct. 12, 1764, for the major issues that divided the parties. The lowest proportion of roll call agreement among the Livingston cousins was between Henry and Philip—77.8 percent; all others were in the 80 to 95 percent range.

ingstons were unable to organize the New York City voters in 1761. They were not as experienced in politics as had been the Morrises, James Alexander, or their rivals the Philipse and DeLancey families. That they supplied more vigor and leadership than opposition party assemblymen usually did was their major asset. The Philipse-DeLancey group seemed not to be concerned about the political challenge. Since 1739 that bloc had been generally solid, while its opponents often either merged with it or, like Clinton's few allies, waged hopeless political flank attacks.

Greater party solidification meant that assemblymen of the 1750s and early 1760s stayed aligned with their voting bloc more constantly than did their predecessors of the 1730s and 1740s. Twenty-two representatives constantly voted the Livingston-opposition side and twenty-one held fast to the Philipse-DeLancey party. During these three assemblies only seven members (13.5 percent) shifted parties, a smaller proportion than the number shifting in the 1737–1752 period. Partisan sentiment was becoming more enduring and more ingrained in New York's assembly.

New Jersey partisanship was more affected by the Great War for the Empire than was that of New York, but, as will be discussed later, less so than that of Pennsylvania. The opposition party refused in April, 1754, to grant any aid to Virginia in its conflict with the French. Quakers would not support military measures, and both they and the opposition party saw no need to be concerned about French incursions on the distant Ohio. Governor Belcher, displeased at the lack of cooperation, decided to risk a new election. Although the prospects of this tactic were not good, judging from past experience, it appeared the only way to prepare the colony for defense.[11]

During the two summer months of 1754 before the election of a new House, New Jersey experienced the most determined and conjoined political activity that it had seen in ten years. No direct record survives, but the electoral results indicate that a coordinated administration party campaign nominated new people, made a strong appeal to the voters, and elected its candidates in many districts. A New York newspaper reported contests in all northern districts except Perth Amboy, which was perennially safe for the administration side. Two new members came in from Essex. From Bergen, Somerset, and Hunterdon came five new assemblymen, replacing four of the opposi-

11. *N.J. Votes,* Apr. 27, 29, June 5, 14, 21, 1754. Donald L. Kemmerer, *Path to Freedom: The Struggle for Self-Government in Colonial New Jersey, 1703–1776* (1940; rpr. Cos Cob, 1968), 238–40, blames the unfulfilled demand for paper money, rather than religious scruples and traditional oppositionism, for the reluctance to support war measures.

tion group. The Dutch members from Bergen and Somerset had been generally in the opposition; new administration supporters replaced three of these. Both Hunterdon assemblymen—a Quaker administration supporter and one of the most consistent Baptist oppositionists—were ousted. Their replacements, a Presbyterian and a Dutch Reformed member, were instructed by an address of the inhabitants presented to them at the election site to vote for a militia act and for defense appropriations against French incursions.[12] One other important new administration member came in—a Quaker elected from Gloucester who opposed strict pacifism. These representatives changed the sentiment of the House.

The election did not result in victory for the administration party in all counties. Although an administration supporter put up a contest in Monmouth, the strong oppositionist incumbents were reelected. Pacifist Quaker voters of Burlington, Gloucester, and Salem counties each elected one new Quaker member who was more firmly on the side of the opposition than had been his predecessor. In the Middlesex election at New Brunswick a close party contest ensued, attracting over 80 percent of the qualified voters. John Wetherill, oppositionist incumbent, led the field, while his rival, administration leader Samuel Neville, defeated an obscure oppositionist opponent by only two votes. The cohesion index of the two oppositionist candidates was 0.931, indicating fairly strong partisan support for the oppositionist side. Throughout the colony the administration side had to fight hard for a thirteen-to-ten majority in the House in the most partisan election ever held there.[13]

Table 24 shows that religion, as generally before, was again the main determinant of partisanship in the assembly. The administration side lost nearly all of its West Jersey Quaker backing but picked up all the votes of the Dutch representatives. The Dutch, from northern counties vulnerable to attack, joined with the administration because they wanted action against hostile Native Americans. The number of Anglicans doubled; all were on the administration side. The north-south regional split, noted because it was based on attitudes toward defense, was almost perfectly partisan. The core of the minority in opposition remained intact. It included as usual the Monmouth and

12. New York *Gazette or the Weekly Post-Boy,* Aug. 5, 1754.

13. *Ibid.* See Appendix III for the Middlesex election vote total; this total was larger than the number of freeholders listed in the county in 1750. *N.J. Votes,* Oct. 15, 1754, notes that the opposition failed in a maneuver to get Neville expelled on the grounds that he was a supreme court justice.

TABLE 24

Economic and Social Characteristics of
Party Members: New Jersey House, 1754–1760

(*All tabulated figures are assembly terms*)

	Wealthy	Well-to-do	Middling	Unknown
Administration	7	6	1	2
Opposition	5	6	0	
Indeterminate	1			

	Anglican	Presbyterian	Dutch Reformed	Quaker	Baptist	Unknown
Administration	6	3	5	1	0	1
Opposition	0	2	0	7	2	
Indeterminate				1		

	Central capital-town	West Jersey rural	East Jersey rural	North	South
Administration	9	3	4	14	2
Opposition	1	8	2	1	10
Indeterminate	1				1

	Great landholder	Landowner	Farmer
Administration	5	3	3
Opposition	3	3	1

	Merchant	Shopkeeper/artisan	Lawyer	Unknown
Administration	2	0	2	1
Opposition	2	1	1	
Indeterminate	1			

lambda-*b*, partisanship and religion = 0.73; and region = 0.45; and occupation = 0.09; and wealth = 0.00

Cape May representatives, Wetherill of Middlesex, and five West Jersey Quakers who took the opposition side because of the issue of support for the war.[14]

The administration side consolidated its three-vote majority by making hard-core oppositionist Robert Lawrence the Speaker. This strategy quickly proved its merits when the House reversed by a twelve-to-eleven roll call the stance of the previous assembly on Governor Belcher's request for assistance.

14. Nicolosi, "Colonial Particularism," 88; Governor Bernard to the Lords of Trade, Mar. 21, 1759, in *NJA*, IX, 169; Lords of Trade to Governor Belcher, Mar. 27, 1751, in *NJA*, VII, 586; Samuel Smith to John Smith, July 30, 1751, in John Smith Correspondence, HSP. Northern districts are those north of Monmouth and Burlington counties, generally north of Trenton and the Raritan River.

Only gradually did the administration party build up its strength, for the opposition blocked most war measures at first. Not until the winter of 1755–1756, when Native American attacks threatened the colony, would the House comply with extensive imperial demands. Even then it was slow to raise troops, but by 1758 it had supplied those requested because the Dutch now supported the war effort and because, as Governor Francis Bernard noted in March, 1759, changes in both attitude and membership had reduced the number of "dissentients" to administration policy in the House. The result, as Robert Hunter Morris pointed out, was that the people of New Jersey "in proportion to their ability contributed as largely and seasonably towards the common cause as any of its neighbors." The opposition was in part mollified because to pay for the defense effort the governor and administration side were compelled to comply with one of its traditional demands: expansion of the paper money supply.[15]

When a new election was held in 1761, the administration party was firmly in control. In a campaign about which little is known but which was probably not very hotly contested, the opposition side lost three seats. Most indicative of the new appeal of the administration side was its victory in a Monmouth by-election in 1762; for the first time since party divisions began, an administration supporter won a contested election in that county.[16] Allied with it were the Dutch members and a couple of others in a moderate group that voted mostly with the administration core except for minor differences on the support of government. The Dutch members, who had shifted from the opposition to the administration side during wartime, voted to compromise between the support level the administration bloc demanded and that favored by the opposition. There was no essential difference in the compo-

15. *N.J. Votes,* Oct. 19, 1754, Mar. 28–31, 1757, Aug. 10, 1758, Mar. 9–10, 1759; Governor Belcher to William Pitt, May 11, 1757, in *NJA,* Vol. 8, Pt. 2, p. 250; Governor Bernard to the Lords of Trade, Aug. 10, 31, Sept. 15, 1758, Mar. 21, 30, 1759, in *NJA,* IX, 131–36, 138, 169–71; Morris to Henry Dagg, [1759], in MP. Although possessing 6.0 percent of the population of the thirteen colonies in 1760, as interpolated from U.S. Bureau of the Census, *Historical Statistics of the United States: Colonial Times to 1970* (Bicentennial ed.; Washington, D.C., 1975), 756, New Jersey contributed 10.17 percent of net colonial expenditures and had the third highest tax burden of any colony as a result of the war. In 1760 it raised about the same proportion of its quota of men as did the northern New England colonies and New York and many more than did Connecticut or Pennsylvania. Greene, "The Seven Years War and the American Revolution," 98; *Pa. Col. Recs.,* Sept. 21, 1763, IX, 48.

16. Gershom Mott to James Mott, Sr., Oct. 5, 1762, in John R. Williams Papers, Rutgers University Library, New Brunswick.

TABLE 25

**Economic and Social Characteristics of
Party Members: New Jersey House, 1761–1764**

(*All tabulated figures are assembly terms*)

	Wealthy	Well-to-do	Middling
Core administration	8	5	0
Moderate administration	4	1	1
Opposition	4	3	1
Indeterminate	1		

	Anglican	Presbyterian	Dutch Reformed	Quaker	Baptist
Core administration	7	4	0	2	0
Moderate administration	0	1	4	0	1
Opposition	0	2	0	4	2
Indeterminate				1	

	Central capital-town	West Jersey rural	East Jersey rural
Core administration	9	3	1
Moderate administration	0	2	4
Opposition	1	5	2
Indeterminate	1		

	Great landholder	Landowner	Farmer
Core administration	5	1	0
Moderate administration	1	3	2
Opposition	1	5	0
Indeterminate		1	

	Merchant	Shopkeeper/artisan	Lawyer
Core administration	2	2	3
Moderate administration	0	0	0
Opposition	2	0	0

lambda-b, partisanship and religion = 0.57; and occupation = 0.42; and region = 0.35; and wealth = 0.07. (Includes by-election results, 1762–1764.)

sition of these groups, taken together, and the composition of the administration bloc in the previous House. As Table 25 indicates, religion remained the most important determinant of partisanship. Region decreased in importance as the administration side gained popularity in all areas, including among West Jersey Quakers, now that the war appeared to be over. Anglicans, Presbyterians, the wealthy, the central capital-town group, the great landowners, and merchants were on that side in almost the same proportions as before.

Administration supremacy in the assembly meant that New Jersey politics became uncharacteristically tranquil. According to observers, "Party Feuds have subsided," and there were "no Parties existing in the Province. All is Peace and Quietness & likely to remain so," while "Harmony reigns in a considerable degree." In actuality, the legislative record shows that parties were not dissolved; astute governors took great pains to conciliate matters.[17]

In both New York and New Jersey the process of political change was similar. It was the election of new assemblymen, not switches in bloc by incumbents, that produced the major regroupings. As Table 26 shows, only eight New Jersey assemblymen out of thirty-eight changed sides in the period 1754–1765; three of these ambled into the moderate administration supporter group after 1761. Although this was a larger proportion than the 12.2 percent who shifted sides in the 1737–1754 period, it represented no real diminishing of partisan constancy. As was the case in the 1740s and early 1750s, the bulk of those who changed blocs (seven of eight) were Quakers or Dutch. Quakers changed only because of the peace testimony; seven adhered to the opposition throughout the period, while two went over to the administration side at the end of hostilities. The reason for the shifts in the Dutch viewpoint are not as evident; the Dutch counties elected new representatives in 1754, indicating that the old ones were not willing to change their party stance. Dutch assemblymen moved into the moderate administration bloc after 1761 probably to assert their independence from an Anglican-dominated party and to show that they could perform competently as legislators. Some of the Dutch assemblymen of the 1740s were obviously not able to participate and contribute adequately; their successors of the 1760s appear to have been more adept in language and legislative committee service.

In Pennsylvania, as in New York, one-party dominance could not endure in a changing society and soon ended; in Pennsylvania, as in New Jersey, an administration party revived because of the defense crisis and the unwillingness of the opposition party to respond to it. The Proprietary party got its opportunity to capitalize on the issue of defense in 1754, as did the New Jersey administration party. Only after long debate and over the deter-

---

17. "W.J.," *An Address to the Freeholders of New Jersey, on the Subject of Public Salaries* (Philadelphia, 1763), 11–12, which may have been written by Governor William Franklin; Franklin to the Lords of Trade, Aug. 8, 1765, in *NJA*, IX, 491; Smith, *History of New Jersey*, 488; William Logan to James Pemberton, Apr. 17, 1761, in Pemberton Papers, HSP. Larry R. Gerlach, "Soldiers and Citizens: The British Army in New Jersey on the Eve of the Revolution," *New Jersey History*, XCIII (1975), 6, believes that the 1761–1764 House was less willing than the previous one to support military expenditures.

TABLE 26

**Assemblymen Adhering to and Shifting from Parties:
New Jersey House, 1751–1765**

Constant administration	Constant opposition	Changers
50.0% (19)	28.9% (11)	21.8% (8)

mined resistance of a minority of strict pacifist Quaker members did the House approve a £15,000 contribution to the defense of Virginia.[18] To the Proprietary party, the strict pacifist Quakers appeared to be electorally vulnerable because of their intransigence; if they could be ousted and if the back counties could be politicized by proprietary influence and patronage, that party might come close to obtaining an assembly majority. Governor James Hamilton set the effort in motion when he rejected the bill appropriating £15,000 to aid the Virginia campaign, in effect claiming that the Quaker party had attached impossible conditions to the money bill in hopes that it would be rejected and strict Quaker consciences upheld. Constituents would now, the Proprietary party believed, blame Quaker pacifism and parsimony for the failure to prepare defenses against French encroachments.[19]

In contrast to New Jersey's prodefense administration party, Pennsylvania's Proprietary party had difficulty getting organized and making a serious challenge to the Quaker party. The party had been out of business too long and had lost the political habit. In mid-September, 1754, it attempted to marshal constituent support by calling a mass meeting in Philadelphia to nominate candidates for the Philadelphia seats. Nomination by an open meeting nicely contrasted with the Quaker party's method of candidate selection—in a caucus of a few party officeholders and merchant supporters—and was calculated to attract those who opposed control by a Quaker elite. Amateurishly, the party leaders apparently made little effort to direct the meeting, and those attending nominated a weak, partial slate. Only the four Philadelphia seats held by strict pacifists were contested. Only two of the meeting's candidates were proprietary supporters—an Anglican merchant and a rather

18. *Pa. Votes,* Apr. 5, May 8, Aug. 9, 13, 1754; Richard Hockley to Thomas Penn, Aug. 22, 1755, in TPP.

19. *Pa. Votes,* Aug. 16, 1754. The support bill provided for the expansion of the loan office and gave the governor no authority over disbursement of tax receipts. See Hutson, *Pennsylvania Politics,* 8–12.

obscure Anglican landowner. The meeting also put up former assembly-man Thomas Leech, who had led the counterattack on the sailors in 1742, and a Quaker merchant. Likewise, in Chester and Bucks the Proprietary party probably contested only one or two seats. Because major party leaders such as William Allen were so unpopular, the party had great difficulty fielding full slates.[20]

The experienced Quaker party easily turned back this feeble electoral effort. A proprietary supporter noted how Quaker party craftiness outmaneuvered its opposition: "They had all the Dutch to a man occasioned by false insinuations and even turn'd others of difft. Denomination who thought a Change absolutely necessary and the half-sheet of Political News that I inclose was sent down to Chester and Bucks County which had a great influence over the People who were striving for a Change there." The Proprietary party made an effective partisan appeal in Philadelphia; the cohesion index for its supporters was 0.980. But it was no match for the Quaker party, whose voters not only showed their great unity by a very high cohesion index—0.993—but as well turned out in much greater force. On average 970 more Philadelphia electors voted for the strict Quakers than for the Proprietary party. Throughout the colony thirty-four incumbents were returned; the two changes in seat occupants were of no partisan significance.[21]

The Proprietary party drew the same erroneous conclusion after the 1754 election that it drew after the 1740 election: electoral politics was of no avail, at least in the short run, in ousting its opponents. Its leaders decided on the same course of action that had proved fruitless in 1740–1741—protest to the British government against Quaker domination. Ceasing political activity in the midst of dire crisis—Braddock's defeat in July, 1755, and the resulting Native American incursions—gave Benjamin Franklin and his followers, including Quakers who would accept defensive war and non-Quaker opponents of the proprietors, every opportunity to take control. By persuading the assembly in late 1755 to agree to institute a voluntary militia and to pass a defense appropriation bill acceptable to Governor Robert Hunter Morris, Franklin made himself "prime minister" of the Quakers. When strict pacifist Quakers left the assembly under pressure of conscience, Franklin brought in antiproprietary backers from other denominations. He now had "Two

20. *Pennsylvania Gazette* (Philadelphia), Sept. 12, 19, 26, 1754. Nash, *Urban Crucible*, 199, points to electorate involvement in nominations as a major change.

21. Richard Hockley to Thomas Penn, Oct. 1, 1754, in TPP; Dinkin, *Voting in Provincial America*, 160. For the cohesion index, see Appendix III.

thirds of the Church" on his side. By the summer of 1756 Franklin very likely controlled eighteen of the thirty-six seats in the House. He had rebuilt the old Quaker party into an Assembly party that would uphold popular rights against proprietary prerogatives and prosecute the war against the French and their Indian allies.[22]

The Proprietary party appreciated the danger Franklin's maneuvering presented to its position. His new allies in the Assembly party, fiercely antiproprietary moderate Quakers and non-Quakers, would not be as vulnerable to political attack as were the strict pacifist Quakers. Rather than trust to a contest in the election of October, 1756, the Proprietary party tried compromise. Its leaders, including William Allen and James Hamilton, met with Franklin to arrange a joint ticket for Philadelphia County. The Proprietary party agreed to support four incumbents: Speaker Norris, lukewarm Quaker Joseph Fox, Anglican John Hughes, and Presbyterian Daniel Roberdeau. To this slate would be added four proprietary supporters new to the House. The compromise would frustrate any efforts by strict Quakers to win back their fading support and would forestall what portended to be a bitter election campaign.[23]

The compromise effort quickly unraveled. Franklin could not truly have intended to support the candidacy of Proprietary partisans while ignoring non-Quakers who were already members of the House or who strongly supported him. Incumbent Thomas Leech and lawyer Joseph Galloway, who in collaboration with William Franklin propagandized the Franklin cause, had better claims to seats than did any proprietary supporters. Franklin and the Quaker leaders remade the ticket, probably immediately before election day, to include these men. When the Proprietary party discovered that Franklin was not going to hold to the agreement, it altered its ticket, but because it had short notice it was able to field only a partial slate.[24]

The balanced Franklin-Quaker ticket and hard campaigning by Quaker

---

22. *Pa. Col. Recs.*, Nov. 24, 1755; *Pa. Votes,* Apr. 13, 1756; William Peters to Thomas Penn, Jan. 4, 1756, in TPP; Hutson, *Pennsylvania Politics,* 25–26; Richard Peters to Penn, Jan. 5, Apr. 29, June 3, 26, 1756, in TPP; Bockelman and Ireland, "Internal Revolution in Pennsylvania," 157–58. Franklin votes included those of the twelve members who supported his militia bill in April, 1756, those of five of the six new members, and his own.

23. Richard Peters to Penn, Sept. 16, 22, 1756, Jan. 10, 1757, in TPP; *Pennsylvania Journal* (Philadelphia), Sept. 30, 1756. Proprietary candidates were William Coleman, a proprietary placeman; Jacob Duché, who had been a 1754 candidate; Henry Pawling; and Phineas Bond, demonstrator for the Proprietary party defendants at the 1758 Moore-Smith trials (*Pa. Votes,* Jan. 11, 1758). On 1756 propaganda, Ketcham, "Franklin and Smith," 150–53.

24. Edward Shippen, Jr., to Edward Shippen, Sept. 19, 1756, in Thomas Balch, ed., *Letters and*

party stalwarts carried the day. That ticket did not do as well in 1756 as the Quaker party did in 1754. In 1756 it garnered 1,169 votes, but in 1754 the Quaker party had received 1,570. The lower total in the latter election was the result of the defection of the strict Quakers. But the turnout was much more than sufficient. The mean vote for the Proprietary party candidates in 1756 was 586, which was six votes fewer than in 1754. Franklin's maneuvers and its inactivity in 1755 weakened it. The cohesion index for the Proprietary party candidates in 1756 (0.943) was slightly smaller than in 1754 (0.980), probably because of the last-minute ticket arrangements in 1756. Franklin voters in 1756 had a cohesion index of 0.975, indicating a strong partisan response from the electorate, though not as strong as the Quaker party received in 1754 (0.993). Voters of other denominations, attracted to Franklin's reformed party, appear to have cast ballots *en bloc* for that ticket.[25]

In the back counties, where defense was the major issue, the Proprietary party was optimistic about its chances. Edward Shippen, Jr., confidently predicted to his father that their party was "pushing for a change in all the counties, and shall certainly carry it in some." Indeed it did in the more remote back counties. William Allen won two seats, in Cumberland and Northampton. Although he received only fourteen votes in the Philadelphia County election, his fellow Presbyterians in these counties had no qualms about electing a nonresident who would be ever-present in the capital to see to their interests. Allen chose Cumberland as the safest seat, for the antiproprietary Moravians might subsequently assert their strength and oust him in Northampton. Another nonresident, Philadelphia merchant and Proprietary partisan William Plumsted, was chosen in a by-election to replace Allen in Northampton "with a greater Concurrence of Votes than was ever known in the county before." The Proprietary party also won a York County seat. In Bucks it came close; it set up nominees for the six seats held by five Quaker and one

---

Papers Relating Chiefly to the Provincial History of Pennsylvania (Philadelphia, 1855), 64. For Galloway's propaganda efforts, "Humphrey Scourge," *Tit for Tat, or the Score Wip'd Off. Pennsylvania Journal* (Philadelphia), Mar. 25, Apr. 22, June 17, 1756; Ketcham, "Franklin and Smith," 150. Bruce R. Lively, "Towards 1756: The Political Genesis of Joseph Galloway," *Pa. Hist.*, XLV (1978), 133, argues that Franklin held to the agreement but that the Quakers overrode the compromise. Accepting this view means believing that Quaker leaders pushed Franklin's non-Quaker allies forward, while Franklin made no effort to get his own supporters nominated.

25. Richard Peters to Thomas Penn, Oct. 2, 1756, in TPP; Philadelphia vote totals in William Logan to John Smith, Jan. 10, 1757, in John Smith Correspondence, HSP. Logan noted that fewer Quakers voted than previously. For the cohesion index, see Appendix III.

Dutch Reformed incumbents. Both parties turned out committed adherents; the cohesion index for the Quaker party supporters was 0.974, that for the challengers was 0.972. The Quaker party squeaked through to a narrow victory; the difference between the mean vote on each side was 166. Conversely, in Chester and Lancaster the Proprietary party suffered disaster. Elections in Chester were conducted in the townships, not at the county seat; the entrenched Quaker party was consequently able to use its contacts in the localities and marshal the voters for its side. In Kennett Square, home of Assemblyman Nathaniel Pennock, Quaker incumbents received overwhelming support from the twenty-seven voters in attendance. The local voters were strongly pressed to maintain solidarity in balloting for assemblymen, county commissioner, and coroner but allowed a free choice in the nonparty contests for sheriff and local offices. In Lancaster the Proprietary party could find only reluctant candidates. James Hamilton thought it beneath a former governor to return to the House; Edward Shippen, Jr., at first declined. Belatedly, Shippen and one Stedman were induced to stand against three incumbents and a non-Quaker and were defeated.[26]

After 1756 the antiproprietary party can no longer accurately be termed the Quaker party but should be called by the name its leaders would later use—the Assembly party. It maintained important links with the antecedent Quaker party; Isaac Norris readily made the shift from Quaker party to Assembly party while remaining Speaker, for he agreed with Franklin and his followers both on the necessity of defense measures and on maintaining a firm challenge to proprietary prerogatives. Only a few other Quakers, particularly the Philadelphians Joseph Fox and Richard Pearne, exercised leadership roles. The thirteen Quakers who remained in the House (four strict ones resigned after the 1756 election) acquiesced in defense measures, although six of them had earlier opposed any militia law. Franklin's allies, Quaker and non-Quaker, directed the legislative process and awarded themselves numerous important commissions. As Table 27 indicates, Franklin had the backing of fourteen non-Quakers who voted for substantial military sup-

26. Edward Shippen, Jr., to Edward Shippen, Sept. 14, 19, 1756, in Balch, ed., *Letters and Papers*, 62–63; Rev. William Smith to [?] Vernon, Oct. 15, 1756, in Logan Papers, HSP; [Smith], *A Letter from a Gentleman in Philadelphia, to a Freeholder in the County Northampton* (Philadelphia, 1757), 1–3; election return, Bucks County, 1756, in Thomas L. Montgomery, ed., *Pennsylvania Archives*, 6th ser. (Harrisburg, 1906–1907), XI, 118–19; election return, Kennett Square, 1756, in Chester County Miscellaneous Manuscripts, HSP. For the cohesion index, see Appendix III.

TABLE 27

Religious and Partisan Composition:
Pennsylvania House, 1756

	Quaker	Non-Quaker Franklin	Proprietary	Unknown
Philadelphia County	3	5	0	
Philadelphia city	0	2	0	
Bucks	2	3	2	1
Chester	4	3	1	
Lancaster	2	2	0	
York	1	0	1	
Cumberland	1	0	1	
Northampton	0	0	1	
Berks	0	0	0	1

port, demanded the taxation of the proprietary estates, and hoped that proprietary prerogatives would be surrendered. Some were Anglicans, some were termed by their opponents "Quaker'd Presbyterians." In future assemblies Quaker religious principles would influence a few issues, but generally their politics became indistinguishable from those of their non-Quaker allies. The alliance was so solid and its supremacy so secure that Franklin could venture off on a mission to London for five years, leaving his lieutenants in charge and his own Philadelphia burgess seat vacant—held by him *in absentia* as a symbol of his party's dominance.[27]

The partisan efforts of 1756 proved to be the high-water mark of the Proprietary party for the next seven years. After winning two seats in by-elections in Chester and Bucks—of those that the four strict Quakers resigned—the party at the end of that year held six of thirty-six seats in the House. Regardless of its small size, its opponents were determined to suppress it by parliamentary trickery. Plumsted was in effect "weeded" for a year; the House kept his seat vacant while it conducted a lengthy investigation of alleged election irregularities. Finally, in September, 1757, it declared the election ille-

27. Richard Peters to Thomas Penn, Oct. 2, 1756, in TPP. Isaac Wayne, father of Mad Anthony, was an Anglican Assembly party supporter (*Pa. Votes*, Apr. 7, 1761). Pennsylvania met most of its defense responsibility, raising 2,800 men in 1758–1759, although raising only half its quota in 1760 (*Pa. Col. Recs.*, Sept. 21, 1763, IX, 48; Nash, *Urban Crucible*, 242). According to Greene, "The Seven Years War and the American Revolution," 98, its expenses amounted to almost 16 percent of all net colonial expenses, and its tax rate per adult white male was sixth highest among the colonies. The only assemblymen holding five or more commissions from the House were Franklin's party stalwarts from Philadelphia: John Hughes (twelve), John Baynton (eight), Joseph Galloway (seven), Joseph Fox (seven), William Masters (five), and Richard Pearne (five).

gal; nevertheless, Plumsted's constituents, aroused by a propaganda piece from the Reverend William Smith's pen, reelected him the next month. Plumsted got only one committee post in 1757–1758; William Allen was excluded from committee service until 1764 and never during his twenty years in the House was appointed to bring in a bill. Likewise, David McConnaghy of York never was designated to bring in a bill during his twelve years in the House. The other Proprietary party members were also kept twiddling their thumbs while the majority party monopolized the machinery of the assembly. Four of the six Proprietary partisans elected in 1756 were gone after 1758, including Plumsted, who was replaced by a German Moravian supporter of the Assembly party.[28]

It was not until 1764 that the Proprietary party again reorganized to mount a challenge to the Assembly party. Alleged executive duplicity and connivance with backcountry murderers of Indians convinced the Assembly party that the only salvation for Pennsylvania was royal government. On March 24, 1764, the House passed a "necklace of resolves" condemning the Penns and asserting that royal government should replace that of the proprietors.[29] The Proprietary party, determined to block this scheme, brought under its banner four groups. Presbyterians, Reformed and Lutheran Germans, and the backcountry joined the core of the party—the proprietary placemen and sympathizers. Both Presbyterian and German groups feared that they would lose important liberties if royal government came and Anglicanism were established. Backcountry settlers detested eastern Quaker defense and Indian policies. New men quickly replaced the old, ineffectual leadership based in the governor's circle; Samuel Purviance, Jr., Philadelphia merchant and Presbyterian, organized a network of correspondents in the back counties that com-

28. Election return, Bucks County, 1756, in Montgomery, ed., *Pennsylvania Archives*, 6th ser., XI, 118–19; *Pa. Votes*, Oct. 30, Dec. 10–11, 1756, Sept. 23, 1757, Jan. 11–24, 1758; Keith, *Provincial Councillors of Pennsylvania*, 169–70; J. Smith Futhey and Gilbert Cope, *History of Chester County, Pennsylvania, with Genealogical and Biographical Sketches* (Philadelphia, 1881), 274, 702; J. H. Battle, ed., *History of Bucks County, Pennsylvania; Including an Account of Its Original Exploration, Its Relation to the Settlement of New Jersey and Delaware; Its Erection into a Separate County, Also Its Subsequent Growth and Development, with Sketches of Its Historic and Interesting Localities, and Biographies of Many of Its Representative Citizens* (Philadelphia, 1887), 425–29. For roll calls identifying assemblymen as partisans, *Pa. Votes*, Apr. 7, 1761, Oct. 20–26, 1764. Isaac Norris to Benjamin Franklin, Nov. 21, 1758, in Labaree *et al.*, eds., *Franklin Papers*, VIII, 175; "Philo-Pennsylvanie," *A Serious Address to the Freeholders and Other Inhabitants of the Province of Pennsylvania* (New York, 1758), 16.

29. *Pa. Votes*, Mar. 7, 10, 19–20, 24, 1764; Franklin to William Strahan, Mar. 30, 1764, in Labaree *et al.*, eds., *Franklin Papers*, XI, 149; Hutson, *Pennsylvania Politics*, 87–90, 113–19.

peted with the Assembly party's system of coordinating its faithful House members for party work. New spokesmen as well soon appeared. In Philadelphia the chief voice of the party became John Dickinson, who had previously in the House sided with the Assembly party. Dickinson agreed with the religious and ethnic critics of the change of government that valuable liberties would be lost. The Proprietary party seized on what it thought would be a popular issue, the radical whig one of preserving the religious and political privileges of Pennsylvanians; it conveniently forgot that it traditionally had supported special privilege and land monopolization.[30]

By the summer of 1764 the Proprietary party could match the Assembly party speech for speech, pamphlet for pamphlet, slander for slander, even punch for punch, and, most important, candidate for candidate. Throughout most of the summer the two sides waged a monumental pamphlet war, remarkable for both principled argument and shameful scurrility. Dickinson and Galloway fought each other with speeches in the assembly and with their fists outside the State House. Uncharacteristically for the Proprietary party, candidates were now ready and willing to carry its banners. In Philadelphia city and county the leaders put up full slates. Purviance also gave special attention to Lancaster, where local Proprietary party leader James Burd, in-law of the powerful Shippen family, operated under his direction. The "Quakers & Mennonites having made a powerful Party," Purviance instructed Burd to contest three of the four seats. Burd was willing to try, claiming that the party had "on our side all the Lutheran & Calvanists Dutch with many others of the Germains [sic]." His more cautious Proprietary party allies apparently determined not to field a slate but to concentrate on the reelection of their incumbent assemblyman. In Northampton the Proprietary party put up a Scotch-Irish Presbyterian. Its incumbent supporters from York and Cumberland also stood. It may have contested some seats in Bucks and Chester but was weakest in these strongly Quaker counties.[31]

30. Hutson, *Pennsylvania Politics,* 152–57, 162–65; Newcomb, *Franklin and Galloway,* 85–86.

31. The ten Proprietary party candidates from Philadelphia included Assembly party members Isaac Norris and Joseph Richardson, John Dickinson, Presbyterian merchant and former Franklin supporter George Bryan, Henry Pawling, a candidate in 1756; Thomas Willing; Amos Strettle; Henry Harrison; and Germans Henry Keppele and Frederick Antis. See Labaree *et al.,* eds., *Franklin Papers,* XI, 390–91; Hutson, *Pennsylvania Politics,* 173–74; Purviance to Burd, Sept. 10, 1764, Burd to Purviance, Sept. 17, 1764, in Shippen Family Papers, APS; Emmanuel Carpenter to Edward Shippen, [1759], in Lancaster County Miscellaneous Papers, 1724–1772, HSP; *Pa. Votes,* May 28, Sept. 15, 1764; Joseph Shippen to Burd, Oct. 6, 1764, in Balch, ed., *Let-*

The great majority of the Assembly party remained determined in the face of this strong opposition to prevail in the election and push forward with the proposal for royal government. Although the issue caused Speaker Isaac Norris and Israel Pemberton, Jr., to defect, only a small minority of the Assembly party shared their view that charter rights were in jeopardy. After the House voted instructions to agent Richard Jackson, in May, 1764, to withdraw the petition for royal government if by it charter rights would be abridged, nearly all Assembly party leaders, Quaker and non-Quaker, backed the attempt to obtain the change. Only one Quaker assemblyman, from Bucks County, left the House in the 1764 election. Fifteen Quaker incumbents, all the Friends who were members except Norris and another who did not vote, stood up after the election to say yes to pursuing the change of government, appointing Franklin as agent in London, or both. Pemberton was hopeful rather than accurate in claiming that backcountry Friends were lukewarm to the change; historians William S. Hanna, James H. Hutson, and Alan Tully have interpreted that hope as fact, even though backcountry electoral results indicate strong party unity.[32]

In the back counties the party became more Quaker than before; in Chester a Quaker replaced an Anglican on the ticket, and in Lancaster the ticket probably contained four Quakers. The Proprietary party's appeal to non-Quakers in the back counties compelled the Assembly party to seek out reliable Quakers as candidates. In Philadelphia it experienced great difficulty in setting the

ters and Papers, 206–207; Rothermund, Layman's Progress, 101; Pennsylvania Gazette (Philadelphia), Oct. 19, 1764; Battle, ed., History of Bucks County, 652.

32. Pa. Votes, May 25, 1764; Pemberton to David Barclay, Sr., Nov. 6, 1764, in Pemberton Papers, HSP; Hutson, Pennsylvania Politics, 128–29, 170. Rural Quakers opposed the petitions for royal government before the assembly voted its restrictive instructions on the change. William Allen informed Thomas Penn, Oct. 21, 1764, in TPP, that the Quakers told back county Germans that it was the New Ticket that intended changing the government. Hutson cites this, Pennsylvania Politics, 170, as evidence of the urban Quakers deceiving the rural ones. William S. Hanna, Benjamin Franklin and Pennsylvania Politics (Stanford, 1964), 161; and Tully, "Quaker Party and Proprietary Politics," 84, 101, accept this statement as evidence of the duplicity and hypocrisy of Franklin and his Quaker allies. The story is implausible and would not be Allen's only reporting error. The Assembly party circulated so much propaganda for the change—including broadsides in German and Galloway's printed assembly speech, distributed by back county assemblymen—that it could not have intentionally falsified its basic position to any constituency. What the Old Ticket told the Germans was probably its stock appeal: the Proprietary party was intent on depriving them of their freedoms.

ticket. The party was forced to keep the defector Norris and the anti-Franklin Richardson on the Philadelphia slate, along with all other incumbents except Dickinson, because they were very well known and might attract wavering voters to the Old Ticket. Franklin stood for both his long-held burgess seat and Dickinson's seat in the county race, a tactic revealing both fear of losing and the lack of appealing candidates. Formerly the Proprietary party had to put up short slates, but now the Assembly party, under a battering attack, could not find all the strong nominees it needed.[33]

To recruit voters, party leaders broadcast a mixture of careful arguments about the issue of royal government and wild charges of gross behavior. Both helped to bring supporters to the election, but more important were the party canvassers—the White Oaks of the Assembly party in particular—who marshaled its constituents and led them to the polls. Treats dispensed by the governor of New Jersey himself, in aid of his father's candidacy, were an added inducement. The Proprietary party's hard work brought it victory in Philadelphia. It was a very narrow victory in the county, for only about 150 votes out of approximately 3,900 separated the twelve candidates who had opposition, but it was both convincing and precedent-shattering. About one thousand German voters provided the margin that put four of the six Proprietary party candidates in office and ousted both Franklin and Galloway. The experienced vote-gatherers of the Old Ticket should have been able to muster enough voters to overcome this German bloc, but they failed to bring in the number they needed. That thirty Assembly party supporters, just enough to change the result, arrived at the polls after the leaders agreed to close them epitomized the miscalculations and lapses in canvassing that led to the political disaster. Comparative election statistics show that the Assembly party got out the vote more effectively than it ever did before. It garnered a mean vote 47.0 percent larger than the estimated normal vote for Philadelphia County. The Proprietary party increased its estimated normal vote by threefold, an amazing achievement giving solid testimony to its resourceful and effective exploitation of the royal government issue. This party finally learned that partisan electoral politics was not a fruitless ritual in Pennsylvania but, given the right circum-

33. The Philadelphia incumbents were Fox, Galloway, Hughes, Rowland Evans, Plunkett Fleeson, and burgess Samuel Rhoads (Labaree *et al.*, eds., *Franklin Papers*, XI, 390–94). Quaker John Fairlamb replaced Anglican Isaac Wayne in Chester. Sources cited in note 31, this chapter, indicate that the probable Lancaster ticket was Quakers James Webb and James Wright, and likely Swiss Quakers Emmanuel and Jacob Carpenter.

stances and sufficient campaigning effort, could be an opportunity to gain political power.[34]

Elections in the city of Philadelphia, in Northampton, and in the more remote counties also went well for the New Ticket. Franklin was soundly drubbed in the city because his mechanic allies failed to counter Proprietary party propaganda and organization where it was most concentrated. The New Ticket's efforts did not meet with much success in the Quaker strongholds of Bucks and Chester or in Lancaster. Getting the one incumbent elected from Lancaster was only a modest achievement in a county where non-Quakers were numerous. Although the Proprietary party had done very well, by no means had it defeated its rival.[35]

When the House assembled later in October, the New Ticket proved to have fallen short of a majority. It controlled fifteen seats; its opponents had twenty-one. The New Ticket leaders, despite their success in persuading the electorate, could not win over any wavering assemblymen. In legislative politics they were confronted by old masters from the Assembly party. The Assembly party leaders by caucus and "cabal" mustered all the votes of their House members, except for two absentees, to send Franklin and the petition to London. Through seven roll calls the party members voted as a bloc. By contrast, the Proprietary party lost two defectors and three absentees. The New Ticket did not possess the cohesion, experience, or dedicated leadership that had ensured legislative triumph for the Old Ticket for many years.[36]

In contrast to the 1737–1753 period, this second period of party growth was one of balancing parties in the system. Many constituents perceived that the development of an intransigent opposition in New Jersey and of one-party dominance in both New York and Pennsylvania was unrepresentative, unstable, and unworkable. By 1764 a better balance prevailed in all three middle colonies. In both Pennsylvania and New Jersey revitalized administration parties forced essentially Quaker and oppositionist parties to give ground,

34. The estimated normal vote was 1,304 for the Assembly party and 653 for the Proprietary party; the actual mean vote was 1,917 for the former and 1,948 for the latter. The estimate was calculated using the election results for 1756, in which 37.3 percent of the qualified voters turned out, with 66.6 percent voting for Franklin's side and 33.4 percent for the Proprietary party candidates. For qualified voters, see Appendix III. Hutson, *Pennsylvania Politics*, 175, blames Old Ticket "mismanagement and complacency."

35. Hutson, *Pennsylvania Politics*, 171–72, seems correct in noting that there was no class division between parties in this election and no class union between city artisans and frontiersmen.

36. Benjamin Chew to Thomas Penn, Nov. 5, 1764, in TPP; *Pa. Votes*, Oct. 20, 25, 26, 1764.

and in New York the two fought on about even terms. For the proadministration parties in Pennsylvania and New Jersey, defense issues, incorporation of heretofore neglected groups, and administration party claims to uphold whig principles attracted more voters than in previous years.

Both the administration and opposition parties in the legislatures were now more stable; by 1765 the partisan cores in each of the middle colonies had remained intact in the same form they had taken in 1735–1740. As Philipse succeeded Philipse, DeLancey succeeded DeLancey, and Morris succeeded Morris among the New York leadership; Johnston succeeded Johnston on the East Jersey Council of Proprietors and one Quaker farmer succeeded another as representative of the southern and western counties; and as antiproprietary Anglicans took the reigns from antiproprietary Quakers in Pennsylvania politics, the partisan groups maintained much the same constituencies and elected the same sort of assemblymen. They had developed a continuity recognizable to and endorsed by their constituents. Although wartime prosperity and peacetime contraction meant difficult circumstances for many, party activity responded mostly to prosperity. Wartime contracts meant important patronage that generally sharpened political alliances and antagonisms. Peacetime hardship did not redound to any party's disadvantage. As the middle-colony economy experienced painful swings, religion clearly increased in importance to partisanship.

The competitiveness of the parties and the diversity of their composition required refinement in political techniques to gain voter support. In the urban centers party leaders cranked out propaganda, even hiring penmen to produce it in Philadelphia. The most important political piece of the period was probably the *Independent Reflector*. Not only was it well argued and well received, but it also had the practical effect of helping to break the DeLancey hold on New York politics, reviving the two-party system, and preparing the way for the leadership of the Livingstons in the 1760s. Pennsylvania political leaders soon decided, however, that propaganda should appeal to the viscera, a tactic that did no harm to the Proprietary party and would later be imitated in New York. Perhaps the more rural New Jersey voters were glad to be spared all this; in any event, their parties in the crucial election of 1754 mustered them and turned them out in large numbers without a spate of broadsides and pamphlets. Electioneering was a second development of the period. Here Pennsylvania forged ahead of the other colonies. Parties linked their efforts throughout most of the districts and devised methods of canvassing to bring large proportions of the eligible voters to the polls. In major campaigns

they offered treats and rewards. In New York and New Jersey the art of electioneering was as yet less developed, but the parties staged contests in
nearly all counties in crucial elections. Analysis of available voting returns
shows party success in the electorate. Cohesion indices for elections in Philadelphia County in 1754, 1756, and 1764; for Philadelphia city in 1764; for Bucks
in 1756; for Westchester and Queens in 1761; and for Middlesex in 1754 show
strong to lockstep partisan voting.[37] Partisan leaders still had much to learn
about winning elections; their inexperience showed clearly in New York
City in 1761. Their growing comprehension of electioneering techniques was
more often evident and would be more widely applied in the next ten years.

37. For the cohesion index, see Appendix III.

5

Partisanship in Imperial Crisis,
1765–1773

The imperial issues arising in 1764 and thereafter were so different from previous middle-colony experience that they could not be readily fitted into a partisan context at first. Although these issues convulsed the populace of the middle colonies, as they did in all thirteen, they did not immediately become partisan matters. In the period 1765–1768, the parties reacted to them only when they could be used as election issues. Administration and opposition groups in each middle colony would not automatically uphold or challenge British authority because upholding imperial taxation or defying it by active resistance were more extreme steps than were either concurring with or hampering the plans of a colonial governor. The parties often lagged behind the populace in taking action because they wanted to be assured that their officeholding or their electoral appeal would not suffer. In the period from 1769 to 1772, winning elections appeared to require them to adopt clearer stances on the issues arising from that resistance.

The passage of the Stamp Act in 1765 galvanized Americans in many colonies into rioting and boycotting in opposition to this unprecedented tax, but it had little immediate political effect except when it became involved in electoral politics. New York and New Jersey had no general elections in 1765–1767, and certainly no governor would call one so the voters could express their displeasure at British policy. In New York the Livingston party, which dominated the assembly leadership, assumed control of the legislature's actions against the Stamp Act with no complaint from its opponents.[1] Nor did New York's parties divide on the issue of resistance to the Mutiny Act in 1766. Livingston leaders in the House promoted moderate and nonviolent resistance without any opposition from those who favored street action. The New York City Sons of Liberty voted for Philip Livingston, Jr., in the next (1768) elec-

---

1. *N.Y. Votes*, Dec. 9, 1762, Apr. 19, Sept. 19, 1764, Nov. 20, 29, 30, Dec. 18, 1765; William Smith, Jr., to Philip Schuyler, Jan. 18, 1768, in Schuyler Papers, NYPL; Carl L. Becker, *The History of Political Parties in the Province of New York, 1760–1776* (1909; rpr. Madison, 1968), 27.

tion. The DeLancey party in that election campaign did attack John Morin Scott's alleged criticism of Patrick Henry's inflammatory anti–Stamp Act resolutions of 1765, but Scott's opposition to the tax itself had been firm and clear. Cadwallader Colden, reflecting the imperial viewpoint, appraised the Livingston and DeLancey sides as equally malevolent.[2]

Even though the combined moderate administration and strong administration groups in the New Jersey Assembly increased their majority via by-elections after 1761, they complied with constituent pressure to oppose the Stamp Act. In the first week in October, 1765, House members assembled in an extralegal meeting at an Amboy tavern to elect delegates to the Stamp Act Congress. All parties in the House were represented in approximate proportion to their assembly strength. The meeting chose three delegates from the large administration majority, but the minority opposition side voiced no objections. The House later reaffirmed the appointments made by the extralegal meeting, endorsed the resolutions of the Stamp Act Congress, formulated petitions of grievances to be sent to king, Lords, and Commons, and appropriated funds to support its agent in London in opposing the act, all without party division or dissent.[3] The political groups in the assembly like-

2. *N.Y. Votes,* June 19, 1766; John Cruger to Moses Franks, Apr. 22, June 13, 1767, in Cruger Letterbooks, NYHS; *N.Y. Laws,* IV, 947–48. Becker, *Political Parties in New York,* 57–58, implies that the 1767 appropriation of £4,500 for the troops, as per the Mutiny Act, was complaisant and extravagant, but the treasurer reported, *N.Y. Votes,* Nov. 25, 1766, spending £3,200 for supplies in July–November, 1766. Lee E. Olm, "The Mutiny Act for America: New York's Noncompliance," *NYHSC,* LVIII (1974), 188–214. William Smith, Jr., *Historical Memoirs,* ed. William H. W. Sabine (2 vols., 1956–58; rpr. New York, 1969–71), July 10, 1766, I, 33, asserts that DeLancey was "among the Sons of Liberty." Its leaders, Isaac Sears and John Lamb, had voted for DeLancey in 1761 (*N.Y.C. Poll List, 1761*). The radical anti-British group, according to Leopold S. Launitz-Schürer, Jr., *Loyal Whigs and Revolutionaries: The Making of the Revolution in New York, 1765–1776* (New York, 1980), 30–31, 34–38; Countryman, *People in Revolution,* 90; and Friedman, "New York Assembly Elections of 1768 and 1769," 7–8, frowned on Livingston moderation. Contrary to the accusations of "Philanthropos," *To the Freeholders and Freemen of the City and County of New York* (New York, 1768), 1, Scott published pieces in the New York *Gazette,* June 6, 13, 1765, attacking the Stamp Act and claimed he opposed the Virginia Resolves because they argued against external taxes. See Dillon, *New York Triumvirate,* 88–89, 117; Colden to Lord Mansfield, Jan. 29, 1768, in Colden Letterbooks, *NYHSC,* X, 155–56.

3. Gerlach, *Prologue to Independence,* 107, lists administration supporters Joseph Borden (Burlington), Cortland Skinner (Perth Amboy), and John Hart (Hunterdon) and oppositionists John Wetherill (Middlesex) and David Cooper (Quaker, Gloucester) in attendance, besides the Stamp Act Congress delegates elected: Speaker Robert Ogden (Essex), Hendrick Fisher (Somerset), and James Lawrence (Burlington City) (*N.J. Votes,* Nov. 29, 1765). *N.J. Votes,* June 27, 1766, accused Governor William Franklin of conspiring with Ogden to block the sending of delegates,

wise agreed in 1766 on advocating only partial compliance with British demands for supplies for quartered soldiers. Governor William Franklin reported to the Earl of Shelburne that assemblymen "look'd upon the Act of Parliament for Quartering Soldiers in America to be virtually as much an Act for laying Taxes on the Inhabitants as the Stamp Act." Wisely, the governor forbore pressing the House for compliance and even had to acquiesce in its rejection of particular army accounts because any strenuous demands for these supplies would give the oppositionist side an issue to use against him and his administration supporters.[4]

Pennsylvania reacted entirely differently because its populace had become highly politicized in 1764 and its two parties anticipated another electoral clash over the issue of royal government in 1765. The imposition of the new tax was a stroke of wonderful fortune for the Proprietary party, for the opponents of the change of government had argued during the election campaign of the year before that royal government would mean new exactions. Popular discontent with imperial measures now seemed likely to become strong electoral advantage. The Proprietary party hoped to combine resistance to the Stamp Act with settling political scores. Meanwhile, the Assembly party kept very quiet about the tax, opposed to it but fearful of being embarrassed by popular action against it. Because Franklin was soliciting in Britain for the change of government, his party could not afford to appear to foment opposition to imperial policy. Its Quaker supporters also wanted to avoid violent resistance. In an attempt to quiet agitation, Galloway anonymously argued that some taxation of America by Britain might be just.[5]

---

as did James Biddle, *To the Freeholders and Electors of the Province of Pennsylvania* (Philadelphia, 1765). William Franklin reported to his father, Apr. 30, 1766, in Labaree *et al.*, eds., *Franklin Papers*, XII, 256, that "I should have had my House pulled down about my Ears and all my Effects destroyed," had he not made his position on the Stamp Act Congress clear. Sheila L. Skemp, *William Franklin: Son of a Patriot, Servant of a King* (New York, 1990), 71–72, believes that Franklin made no opposition to appointing delegates.

    4. William Franklin to Shelburne, Dec. 18, 1767, in *NJA*, IX, 577 (Gerlach, *Prologue to Independence*, 403, corrects the date of this letter). Franklin told Shelburne that he strove to have the House include "the very Words of the Act of Parliament," but *N.J. Votes*, June 19–24, 1766, conveys no sense of this, and it is likely that Franklin dared make no such strong effort.

    5. [Hugh Williamson], *The Plain Dealer: or, a Few Remarks upon Quaker Politics, and Their Attempts to Change the Government of Pennsylvania, Number I* (Philadelphia, 1764), 17–18; Galloway to Franklin, June 7, 1766, Franklin to Charles Thomson, July 11, 1765, both in Labaree *et al.*, eds., *Franklin Papers*, XIII, 294, XII, 207–208; *Pennsylvania Journal* (Philadelphia), Aug. 29, 1765; Oaks,

Proprietary party propaganda would have been both accurate and shrewd in claiming that the Assembly party blundered into an untenable position by seeking favors from the British government at the very time that harsh imperial taskmasters attempted to tighten the reins and impose what appeared to be unconstitutional policies. But that party's attacks on the Old Ticket went too far; it attempted to make bad judgment appear to be calculated betrayal. It unwisely published charges that Benjamin Franklin had authored and promoted the Stamp Act and that William Franklin and Galloway attempted to prevent New Jersey and Pennsylvania from sending delegates to the Stamp Act Congress. The charges were neither true nor believed. The elder Franklin had opposed the act's passage, though he delayed in defending American resistance until late 1765. Galloway and William Franklin, fearful that fervent anti-British leaders such as John Dickinson might dominate the extralegal congress, remained neutral on participation in it. These extreme, groundless charges made the Assembly party appear wrongfully injured and its foes seem wild and irresponsible.[6] Proprietary party leaders also unwittingly politicized the electorate against themselves when their adherents planned riot against stamp distributor John Hughes and other alleged supporters of the Stamp Act, including the absent Franklin. Only two weeks before the October 1 election, Galloway and the Assembly party leaders turned out some eight hundred of the White Oaks and other supporters to put down any violence. That such a body could be mustered so quickly shows that a large part of the populace thought that the New Ticket was too extreme in its accusations and threats.[7]

"Philadelphia Merchants and the Origins of American Independence," 409; Hutson, *Pennsylvania Politics,* 196–201.

6. James Biddle, *To the Freeholders and Electors of the Province of Pennsylvania* (Philadelphia, 1765). Galloway's party divided on the question; Quaker members voted against sending delegates to the Stamp Act Congress, as noted in an election broadside published by Christopher Sauer, reprinted in Donald F. Durnbaugh, ed., *The Brethren in Colonial America: A Source Book on the Transplantation and Development of the Church of the Brethren in the Eighteenth Century* (Elgin, 1967), 385. Galloway to Franklin, [Nov., 1765], Hughes to Franklin, Sept. 10–11, 1765, Franklin to William Franklin, Nov. 9, 1765, all in Labaree *et al.,* eds., *Franklin Papers,* XII, 377–78, 265–66, 361–65; Samuel Purviance, Jr., to James Burd, Sept. 20, 1765, in Thomas Balch, ed., *Letters and Papers Relating Chiefly to the Provincial History of Pennsylvania* (Philadelphia, 1855), 208; *To the Freeholders and Other Electors of Assembly Men, for Pennsylvania* (Philadelphia, 1765), answered these charges. Gerlach, *Prologue to Independence,* 108–109.

7. Samuel Wharton to Franklin, Oct. 13, 1765, Galloway to Franklin, Sept. 20, 1765, both in Labaree *et al.,* eds., *Franklin Papers,* XII, 315, 270.

As befit its assumed image as the party of order, opposed to riots and aloof from agitation on imperial matters, the Assembly party kept its electoral ticket of 1764 essentially intact in 1765. Most of the nominees in Philadelphia and the back counties were the party's Quaker and Anglican stalwarts. It made two major changes. From Philadelphia County a German Anglican was nominated; the party recognized that its rival had attracted German voters with its German candidates in the 1764 contest and hoped to lure some of these voters away. The second change was that stamp distributor John Hughes was omitted of necessity. As Galloway later told William Franklin in a rare, candid characterization of his partisan allies, Hughes's name on the ticket would "ruin our Party."[8]

In nominating its candidates the Proprietary party also continued its strategy of 1764, to combine Germans, Presbyterians, proprietary supporters, backcountry voters, and, in this election, those who wanted to do something about the Stamp Act. It put up full slates in most of the back counties, except Lancaster. In Philadelphia city and county the candidates included the incumbents, another German, two Anglicans, and a Dutch Reformed. Only a heterogeneous coalition had any chance against the entrenched majority party.[9]

As the party managers had learned from the 1764 election, propaganda combined with personal efforts to round up voters was the path to victory. Although Isaac Hunt plumbed new depths of vulgarity in his attacks on Proprietary party leaders, most political energy was devoted to canvassing. Par-

8. The Assembly party ticket included Isaac Norris, Joseph Richardson, Joseph Fox, Rowland Evans, Thomas Livezay, Henry Pawling (who quit the Proprietary party), Michael Hillegas the German Anglican, and Galloway. James Pemberton challenged the incumbent "Envious Pres——n," George Bryan, in the city election. The incumbents from Chester and Bucks all ran again on the Assembly party ticket; the Lancaster County ticket was probably the same all-Quaker ticket as in 1764. Election return, Philadelphia City and County, Bucks, Chester, and Lancaster Counties, 1765, Samuel Wharton to William Franklin, Sept. 29, 1765, both in Franklin Papers, APS. James Pemberton to John Fothergill, Dec. 28, 1765, in Pemberton Papers, HSP. On Hughes, Galloway to William Franklin, Sept. 13, 1766, in Franklin Papers, APS.

9. Edward Burd to James Burd, Sept. 18, 1765, Samuel Purviance to James Burd, Sept. 20, 1765, both in Balch, ed., *Letters and Papers,* 207, 209. Norris was again on both tickets. Dickinson was put on the ticket at the last minute and perhaps without his permission. Incumbent German Henry Keppele was important to the ticket. Anglican Robert Strettle and German Frederick Antis tried again. New to the ticket were Anglican merchants Rodman Conyngham and Isaac Jones and Dutch Reformed Jacob Winey. In Philadelphia city incumbent Thomas Willing ran unopposed (Election return, Philadelphia, Bucks, Chester, Lancaster, 1765, in Franklin Papers, APS).

tisan Quakers Thomas Wharton and Hugh Roberts worked harder than they
ever had in any previous election. The stalwart White Oaks used their antiriot
defense organization to bring in new voters. These were normally apathetic
constituents, probably basically sympathetic to the Assembly party but requiring extra persuasion and even threats to be induced to come to the polls.
Some may have been more readily persuaded because they were amenable
to repudiating the Stamp Act violence ascribed to Proprietary partisans. Workers for the New Ticket were also industrious; they marched six hundred Lutherans to the polls to vote for Germans Henry Keppele and Frederick Antis
and the other New Ticket nominees.[10]

Colossal efforts by the Assembly party leaders reversed the disaster of the
previous year. Approximately five hundred more voters appeared in the
Philadelphia city and county elections than in 1764. During the three days,
October 1–3, that the polls stayed open, over 80 percent of the qualified voters appeared voluntarily or were lured or dragged in. In the county election
the Assembly party candidates received the votes of nearly all of the five hundred new voters. The difference between the mean Assembly party candidate
vote and the mean Proprietary party candidate vote was 494 votes. The mean
Proprietary party candidate vote in 1765 was 12 votes less than it was in
1764; substantially maintaining its vote through the latter election was not
sufficient for victory. In Bucks, Chester, and Lancaster the Assembly party was
completely and decisively victorious. Proprietary party leader Samuel Purviance, Jr., urged his Lancaster County lieutenant to broadcast that he would
counter any Assembly party trickery by sending his voters to the polls "with
a good Shilely" to "thrash the Sheriff every Inspector Quaker & Minonist
[Mennonite] to Jelly," but this was vain bluster when compared with the canvassing and vote-collecting of the Assembly party. The Proprietary party delegation in the House was reduced to only eight members, five of whom were
from the remote western and northern counties. The smashing of Proprietary party power in Pennsylvania was one of the largest electoral turns in
colonial politics, particularly because it came at a time when those resisting
imperial authority in other colonies were gaining in popularity.[11]

10. Hunt wrote nine pieces; the most vulgar and insulting were *The Substance of an Excersise
Had This Morning in Scurrility-Hall, No. 1* [*sic*] (Philadelphia, 1765), 4–5; and "Jack Retort," *A Humble Attempt at Scurrility* (Philadelphia, 1765), 40. Thomas Wharton to Benjamin Franklin, Oct. 5,
1765, in Labaree *et al.*, eds., *Franklin Papers*, XII, 290–91. See Chapter 2, note 54, for sources on
the White Oaks. Rothermund, *Layman's Progress*, 104.

11. Election returns, Philadelphia County, 1764, Philadelphia, Bucks, Chester, Lancaster,

The election in Philadelphia was a repudiation of radical or violent resistance to the Stamp Act. The same White Oaks who mustered against violence were the party workers who won the election. Voters regarded Assembly party leaders, especially Galloway, as moderates who would oppose rash action. Dickinson lost about 3 percent of his 1764 support, perhaps because of his activism. The strenuous canvassing that won the election for the Assembly party pulled in enormous and unprecedented vote totals only because the voters were convinced that the traditional antiproprietary party would protect their interests, as it always had, and not venture into violent resistance. By propaganda and industrious politicking the Assembly party defused the dangerous issue of the Stamp Act at the same time that it frustrated what appeared to be the opportunistic radicalism of its opponents.[12]

The Proprietary party learned little from its failure to make the Stamp Act an election issue. It tried this tactic again in 1766. Extracts from letters of Galloway and Hughes, forwarded to Franklin in England, were discovered there and soon reprinted as preelection propaganda. The only new revelation in these letters was that Galloway was the author of the anonymous piece signed "Americanus" of August, 1765, which advocated negotiation rather than resistance. These disclosures resulted in the most pointed, direct, and concentrated propaganda barrage ever to appear during a Pennsylvania election campaign. Its aim was to smear Galloway as no ally of Franklin but an opponent of his views on imperial taxation. The "Americanus" piece was compared to Franklin's *Examination Before Commons* to show how Galloway in effect supported the Stamp Act. Another broadside was titled *Six Arguments Against Chusing Joseph Galloway an Assemblyman at the Ensuing Election.* The ideology of resistance to Britain was now clearly confronting that of acquiescence to imperial demands.[13] And Galloway was confronted directly by his arch-rival

---

1765, in Franklin Papers, APS. Also see Appendix III. Purviance to James Burd, Sept. 20, 1765, in Shippen Family Papers, HSP. Only in Berks did an Assembly party incumbent lose; John Ross, Philadelphia colleague of Franklin, who had represented the county for three years, was ousted by a German Proprietary partisan (*Pa. Votes,* Oct. 15, 1765).

 12. Galloway to Franklin, [Nov., 1765], June 7, 1766, in Labaree *et al.*, eds., *Franklin Papers,* XII, 377–78, XIII, 292; *Pa. Votes,* June 6, 1766; *Pennsylvania Gazette* (Philadelphia), Sept. 18, 1766; Edmund S. Morgan and Helen M. Morgan, *The Stamp Act Crisis: Prologue to Revolution* (Rev. ed.; New York, 1963), 206, 223–24.

 13. Cadwalader Evans to William Franklin, Dec. 7, 1766, in Franklin Papers, APS; Galloway to Franklin, Sept. 20, 1765, Hughes to Franklin, extracts, Sept. 8–17, 1765, both in Labaree *et al.*, eds., *Franklin Papers,* XII, 269–70, 264–66; *Pennsylvania Journal* (Philadelphia), Sept. 18, 25, 1766;

Dickinson. The Proprietary party put up only its leader and another candidate in Philadelphia County to oppose the alleged Stamp Act advocate and the German incumbent. Dickinson also stood in the city, for the party leaders were very anxious to return him to the House and gain there a clear voice advocating their position.[14]

Despite all its strategic calculation, the New Ticket propaganda and electioneering proved unappealing and unavailing. Samuel Purviance, Jr., planned the strategy but then left town before election day. The Germans docilely returned to the Assembly party fold. Voter turnout slipped about 1,350 electors in the Philadelphia County poll and about 550 in the city. Perhaps the electorate was tired of hard-fought contests year after year. By the summer of 1766 the Assembly party was confident of victory so the White Oaks did not canvass as fiercely as in preceding years. Galloway got about 550 fewer votes than he did in 1765, but Dickinson and Keppele each got 790 fewer votes. The city contest was tighter; Dickinson lost a close race.[15]

Governor John Penn and the Proprietary party leaders believed that they had come to the end of the road in the electoral struggle over the change of government. The governor lamented to his uncle that the "Quakers" were invincible politically. The Assembly party may have sensed that this was true; but rather than offer conciliation and compromise it appeared anxious to crush its rivals as completely as possible. The ultrapartisan Galloway replaced the conciliatory Joseph Fox as Speaker. The new Speaker, William Franklin, and Thomas Wharton were determined to prevent the Proprietary party from ever again gaining a propaganda advantage over their party and thereby recouping its strength. They installed William Goddard as printer of the *Pennsylvania Chronicle*. This avowedly party newspaper enabled them readily, freely, and in a timely manner to fire broadsides at the governor and other political opponents and to keep the party's version of the issues before the

---

Six Arguments Against Chusing Joseph Galloway . . . (Philadelphia, 1766); *Friends, Brethren, and Countrymen* (Philadelphia, 1766).

14. Also in Philadelphia County Henry Keppele opposed Michael Hillegas. Dickinson opposed John Ross in the city. Willing declined reelection (*Pennsylvania Journal* [Philadelphia], Sept. 25, 1766). Election return, Philadelphia City and County, October, 1766, in Franklin Papers, APS; Flower, *John Dickinson*, 59.

15. Purviance to Ezra Stiles, Nov. 1, 1766, in Dexter, ed., *Itineraries and Miscellanies of Ezra Stiles*, 554; Galloway to Franklin, June 7, 1766, in Labaree *et al.*, eds., *Franklin Papers*, XIII, 296; also see Appendix III. Election returns, Philadelphia, 1764, Philadelphia, Bucks, Chester, Lancaster, 1765, Philadelphia, 1766, in Franklin Papers, APS.

electorate. The *Chronicle* produced the desired results for about two years. It carried reprints of the party's most important propaganda— Benjamin Franklin's press essays written for the London newspapers. It also carried condemnations of proprietary government, which allowed two backcountry hoodlums, who savagely murdered ten Native Americans, to escape. It blasted John Dickinson, who, the Assembly party leaders feared, might in 1768 attempt a political comeback.[16] The result of this Assembly party resurgence was that throughout the province in the elections of 1767, 1768, and 1769, in which 108 seats were at stake, there were only fourteen changes— only one in Philadelphia city and county. William Allen lamely explained to Thomas Penn that his party's intent in abjuring contests was to convince the majority party that proprietary supporters were truly conciliatory and not grasping for power.[17] The party that in 1764 rebuilt itself to assert principles of freedom from centralized power and greater liberty for the citizens from British impositions had now largely been forced to retire, having lost the ideological battle to its rival's policy of greater centralization and circumspect resistance to impositions and having lost the electoral battle to its rival's superior politicking.

By 1769 in the other middle colonies as well as Pennsylvania imperial issues became bound up with parties and electoral contests. The imposition of the Townshend duties and the continuing controversy over supplying British troops readily became party matters when New Jersey and Pennsylvania conducted elections in the late 1760s and early 1770s. In 1770 and 1772 elections, these colonies experienced substantial political realignments. New York parties realigned on imperial issues as a result of, not during, the 1769 election in that colony.

Refraining from involvement in imperial issues worked well for the As-

16. John Penn to Thomas Penn, Nov. 12, 1766, in TPP. William Goddard, *The Partnership* (Philadelphia, 1770), 5–6, describes the founding of the newspaper. *Pennsylvania Chronicle* (Philadelphia), Aug. 8–15, 15–22, 1768, for attacks on Dickinson. Rowe, "Frederick Stump Affair," 259–88.

17. Galloway to Franklin, Oct. 17, 1768, in Labaree *et al.*, eds., *Franklin Papers*, XV, 229–30; Jasper Yeats to James Burd, Sept. 8, 1768, Edward Shippen to Burd, Sept. 16, 1768, William Atlee to Burd, Sept. 20, 1768, all in Shippen Family Papers, APS; Yeats to Burd, Sept. 17, 19, 1769, in Balch, ed., *Letters and Papers*, 221–24; Bockelman, "Politics in Lancaster County," 51–52; Allen to Thomas Penn, Oct. 8, 1767, in TPP, quoted in Hutson, *Pennsylvania Politics*, 151. James Pemberton reported to John Fothergill, July 8, 1766, Oct. 20, 1768, in Pemberton Papers, HSP, that the "Spirit of Party" was stilled in Philadelphia. Brooke Hindle, *The Pursuit of Science in Revolutionary America, 1735–1789* (Chapel Hill, 1956), 122–39, shows how in 1766–1768 each party captured its own learned society.

sembly party in 1765 and 1766 because it was able to convince constituents that the Proprietary party was too radical. But in 1768, Galloway and most of the Assembly party leaders were overly cautious about petitioning Parliament against the taxes imposed by the Townshend Acts. Meanwhile, John Dickinson and Charles Thomson led mass meetings and urged the adoption of nonimportation, which Philadelphia merchants implemented in March, 1769. The Assembly party ignored the resistance movement; no assemblyman was a member of the committee to enforce nonimportation.[18] This temporizing cost its leaders political support in 1769 and led to major changes in the party's structure in 1770. Many merchants demanded that nonimportation be ended, while advocates for resistance and those mechanics who profited from less British competition supported its continuance. Merchant and assemblyman Joseph Richardson was attacked in the press as one of the opulent who had advocated breaking the agreement. Printer William Goddard, having fallen out with his politician partners, castigated Speaker Galloway for his criticism of the *Farmer's Letters,* his opposition to Stamp Act resistance, and his insults of Germans. Artisans accused a corrupt "juncto" of monopolizing nominations and allowing those who were only lukewarm toward resistance to Britain, like Richardson and Galloway, to continue to hold their seats. Disgusted with their party leadership that had not strongly supported the boycott, the White Oaks and mechanics abandoned their old alliance with Quaker merchants—an alliance that had dominated Philadelphia politics since 1756. They repudiated the Assembly party ticket in the 1770 election and chose Dickinson as city burgess, tailor Joseph Parker as county assemblyman, and four artisans for city offices. Galloway, through cajolery and the exertion of considerable influence, barely managed election from a Bucks County rotten-borough seat.[19]

18. *Pa. Votes,* Feb. 20, May 10, 1768; David L. Jacobson, *John Dickinson and the Revolution in Pennsylvania* (Berkeley, 1965), 60–63. On the composition of the committee, Ryerson, *The Revolution Is Now Begun,* 68–78. Also see Merrill Jensen, *The Founding of a Nation: A History of the American Revolution, 1763–1776* (New York, 1968), 261, 271, 285–86.

19. *Pennsylvania Gazette* (Philadelphia), Sept. 27, 1770; Goddard, *The Partnership,* 11, 16, 69–72; *A German Freeholder to His Countrymen* (Philadelphia, 1770); Galloway to Franklin, Sept. 27, 1770, in Labaree *et al.,* eds., *Franklin Papers,* XVII, 228; "A Bucks County Man," *A True and Faithful Narrative of the Modes and Measures Pursued at the Anniversary Election, for Representatives, of the Freemen of the Province of Pennsylvania, Held at Newtown, in and for the County of Bucks, on Monday the First Day of October, Anno Domini 1770* (Philadelphia, 1771), 5; Flower, *John Dickinson,* 94; Olton, *Artisans for Independence,* 43, 50–57. Israel Jacobs and Samuel Rhoads were two other antiresistance Quakers elected in 1770.

This beginning of the "mechanic revolution" in Philadelphia was limited but portentous. It did not eliminate all antiboycott merchants from power. It did not extend outside Philadelphia County, for only two other seats changed hands in 1770. It did not knock Speaker Galloway from his lofty perch. Yet it did mark the beginning of attacks on old "juncto" control in Philadelphia. In the next year mechanic voters retired four pro-British and antiresistance candidates and gave the greatest support to those nominees who had most strongly favored nonimportation. A couple of the old "juncto" assemblymen remained, owing more to the inertia of incumbency than to politicking. Galloway complained to Franklin after the 1772 election that in Philadelphia no political organizers made an effort to get out the Assembly party vote; many of their old allies "would not take the trouble to walk to the State House" polling place. Once the party had reigned supreme in Philadelphia and demolished all challengers; now it was ripped asunder. It was following the path of the moribund Proprietary party that, as Galloway noted, had not stirred in recent elections and competed only in Lancaster County.[20]

The more anti-British elements in Philadelphia either neglected or disdained the opportunity to capitalize on the fragmentation of the old Assembly party. In 1772 they organized the Patriotic Society to contest elections with the "juncto," but this group did not adopt the pattern of party organization or the techniques traditional in Philadelphia balloting. In the 1772 election it failed to prepare tickets in advance or conduct a thorough campaign for its nominees. The election-day broadside of the Patriotic Society pleaded that each "Gentleman who approves of the above List, will please to write a few Spare Tickets, to furnish his Friends with." Assembly party leaders who in past elections had furnished Germans with hundreds of written tickets must have winced at the irony of this inept campaigning; they had patented the techniques but lost the popular base on which to employ them, while their opponents, with great potential for popular support, neglected the very tools

20. Ryerson, *The Revolution Is Now Begun*, 185, is fullest on the "mechanic revolution." Election return, 1771, Philadelphia and Chester counties, in William Franklin to Thomas Wharton, Sept. 21, 1771, in William Franklin Manuscripts, 1768–1772, Society collection, HSP. Ryerson, *The Revolution Is Now Begun*, 271, 273–74, provides identification of candidates Peter Knight and Joseph Pascall, conservative merchants. Samuel Potts and John Ross were pro-British former assemblymen. Galloway to Franklin, Sept. 27, 1770, Oct. 12, 1772, in Labaree *et al.*, eds., *Franklin Papers*, XVII, 434, XIX, 331; Jasper Yeats to James Burd, Sept. 20, 1773, Oct. 6, 1773, in Balch, ed., *Letters and Papers*, 231–32; Joseph Shippen, Jr., to James Burd, Oct. 6, 1764, in Shippen Family Papers, APS; Matthias Slough to [Jasper Yeats], June 26, 1775, in Society Collection, HSP.

that would have put them in unchallenged command. The result was that the Patriotic Society failed to elect Dickinson and Thomson, though it did successfully promote seven less controversial candidates.[21] In the 1773 Philadelphia election an antiresistance coalition of proprietary supporters and vestiges of the old "juncto" had enough energy to outmaneuver the Patriotic Society. This more politically astute combination put the absent Franklin, whose vast popularity ensured his election, against (probably) Charles Thomson. At the cheap price of one assembly seat the antiresistance side kept out an undesirable agitator.

Because Quakers, particularly in Chester and Bucks counties, remained attached to it out of traditional loyalty, and because the Patriotic Society could not get its leaders elected, the old Assembly party majority still predominated in the House. It continued Galloway as Speaker, much to the chagrin of his opponents; in turn, he kept the support of Quaker members by awarding them important committee posts.[22] The remote back counties elected several Presbyterians who were Assembly party opponents, but they were outnumbered.

The nonimportation crisis of 1770 had initiated a realignment that temporarily changed Pennsylvania politics from a structured, ordered partisan system, both in the assembly and among the electorate, to one composed of three weak parties: two vestigial and one embryonic. The majority and minority parties in the House in 1765 had maintained partisan commitment and obeyed designated leaders; by 1774 one of these operated only locally, the other limped along primarily supported by traditional allegiances and the influence of the Speaker of the House, and a third new one, the most alive, hesitated in seizing its opportunity. Pennsylvania politics was drastically altered in these years and would soon be more so.

New Jersey's political realignment, like that in Pennsylvania, came during elections held amid controversy. This realignment did not wreck the old parties and begin a new organization, as in Pennsylvania, but remade and revitalized the opposition. The 1769 election, virtually a septennial one, saw some

21. *Pennsylvania Gazette* (Philadelphia), Aug. 19, 1772; *Fellow Citizens and Countrymen* (Philadelphia, 1772). This broadside expressed the fear that its candidates, if elected, could do nothing "in an Assembly where a great Majority would oppose them." Galloway told Franklin, Oct. 12, 1772, in Labaree *et al.*, eds., *Franklin Papers*, XIX, 331, that Goddard came close to victory, but he was not listed on the printed ticket.

22. *Pennsylvania Chronicle* (Philadelphia), Oct. 11–18, 1773; Ryerson, "Portrait of a Colonial Oligarchy," 123, 128, 131.

slight gains for the opposition party, but, more important, strengthened anti-British sentiment in the House. Several counties demanded representatives who would take a stronger anti-British posture. After the election, the freeholders instructed them on these issues. The Monmouth County instructions were probably composed by some relatively inarticulate local leader and later refined by a more educated person. The Gloucester County election turnover, after which the freeholders also instructed the assemblymen, well symbolized the change. Former assemblyman David Cooper was cautious and unappreciative of the constitutional issues at stake in the imposition of the Townshend duties. His replacement, John Hinchman, was an anti-British Quaker and the assemblyman most outspoken against the Townshend Acts. Except for this instance, it is not certain that the new members were more anti-British than those they succeeded, but the new members as a group were more anti-British than their incumbent colleagues, offering greater resistance to supplying British troops. That one-half the House was not reelected strongly suggests that the electorate consciously voted to replace the overly cautious with those who would take a more anti-British stance. The opposition party increased to eight members, its size in 1761. It gained two farmers and held the support of Quakers and Baptists as before. As Table 28 indicates, religion remained most important in determining partisanship in the House.[23]

It was after the election, in instructing their representatives, that the voters showed their anti-British colors most clearly. Gloucester, Middlesex, and Monmouth county voters directed their assemblymen in October, 1769, to continue to oppose the Townshend Acts and to refuse to supply quartered troops. Further instructions in 1771 enjoined assemblymen to refuse to pay the army supply accounts.[24] The House resisted full payment of army accounts through-

23. [Draft of instructions, Monmouth County, 1769], in Holmes Family Papers, Rutgers University Library, New Brunswick; Instructions of the Board of Justices and Freeholders, and other principal inhabitants, to Robert Friend Price and John Hinchman, Gloucester County, Oct. 3, 1769, in Stewart Collection, Rowan College Library, Glassboro; David Cooper to Samuel Allinson, Nov. 21, 1768, in Samuel Allinson Papers, Rutgers University Library, New Brunswick. Determination of parties is based on cluster-bloc analysis and on roll calls on the civil list and on supplying British troops. *N.J. Votes,* Oct. 18, 1769, Oct. 23, 25, 26, 1770, Apr. 19, 20, May 3, 31, Dec. 10, 20, 1771, Aug. 28, 1772, Dec. 18, 1773. For Hinchman, E. Alfred Jones, *The Loyalists of New Jersey: Their Memorials, Claims, Etc. from English Records,* Collections of the New Jersey Historical Society, X (Newark, 1927), 97. Purvis, *Proprietors, Patronage, and Paper Money,* 105, suggests that the nonreturning assemblymen voluntarily retired.

24. New York *Journal or General Advertiser,* Oct. 19, 1769; Instruction of Board of Justices & Freeholders, and other principal inhabitants, to Robert Price and John Hinchman, October 3,

out 1770 and 1771. In October, 1770, Governor Franklin, by persuading three Quakers to change their votes, got about one-half of the amount requested. In May, 1771, the House refused to make any allowance; Franklin reported to Hillsborough that the assemblymen calculated "by their Refusal they should recommend themselves to the Bulk of the Common People and so secure their Elections." By December, 1771, the governor's pleadings again induced three members to change their votes so that about one-third of the sum he first demanded was approved. As governor and assembly teetered on the edge of a major confrontation over imperial policy, Franklin believed that he had no choice but to humor the House by what was in reality a triennial dissolution in 1772.[25]

The New Jersey electorate had too many concerns and confronted too many issues to have a peaceful and inconsequential election in 1772. Opposition to quartering charges; demands for a loan office; resentment against the high fees and other abuses perpetrated by lawyers that caused antilawyer outbreaks in Monmouth County in 1769–1770; and the apparent negligence of East Jersey Treasurer Stephen Skinner, who kept the public money in a wooden chest in a first-floor room with windows in his Perth Amboy home, in allowing over £6,500 to be stolen by burglars in June, 1768, all combined to make the 1772 contest the most spirited since 1754. Candidates who were both supporters of strong resistance to Britain and opponents of Governor Franklin's administration appeared in many districts, even in "safe" Perth Amboy. The hotly contested Amboy election, with its extremely heavy turnout, and in which a newcomer defeated an East Jersey proprietor who later became a loyalist, was symbolic of the popular determination to band together to thrust out antiresistance and unresponsive incumbents.[26]

1769, in Stewart Collection, Rowan College Library, Glassboro; Instructions to Richard Hartshorne and Edward Taylor, October, 1769, Holmes Family Papers, Rutgers University Library, New Brunswick; Gerlach, *Prologue to Independence,* 156, 160–65, 431. Aaron Leaming of Cape May broadcast details of the crisis to constituents in a very long and very anti-British statement (Aaron Leaming to his constituents, May 26, 1771, in Stewart Collection, Rowan College Library, Glassboro). Instructions of Hunterdon County Freeholders, May 28, 1771, in *NJA,* X, 269–73; William Franklin to the Earl of Hillsborough, June 1, 1771, in *NJA,* X, 298.

25. *N.J. Votes,* Oct. 23, 25, 26, 1770, Apr. 19–20, May 31, Dec. 7, 18, 20, 1771; Franklin to Hillsborough, Feb. 12, Sept. 29, 1770, June 1 (quoted), Dec. 27, 1771, in *NJA,* X, 150–52, 201, 298–99, 322–23; Journal of the Governor and Council, Feb. 21, 1772, in *NJA,* XVIII, 278–79.

26. *N.J. Votes,* Oct. 10–17, 1770; Larry R. Gerlach, "Politics and Prerogatives: The Aftermath of the Robbery of the East Jersey Treasury in 1768," *New Jersey History,* XC (1972), 136–37. Appendix III gives figures on the Perth Amboy election.

TABLE 28

**Economic and Social Characteristics of
Party Members: New Jersey House, 1769–1772**

(*All tabulated figures are assembly terms*)

	Wealthy	Well-to-do	Middling	Unknown
Administration	9	6	1	1
Opposition	4	3	1	1

	Anglican	Presbyterian	Dutch Reformed	Quaker	Baptist
Administration	4	5	2	5	1
Opposition	0	2	1	3	3

	Central capital-town	West Jersey rural	East Jersey rural
Administration	6	8	3
Opposition	2	4	3

	Great landholder	Landowner	Farmer
Administration	4	4	1
Opposition	1	5	2

	Merchant	Shopkeeper/artisan	Lawyer
Administration	4	1	3
Opposition	0	1	0

lambda-b, partisanship and religion = 0.33; and occupation = 0.22; and region = 0.00; and wealth = 0.00. (Includes by-election results.)

This election confirmed the rule that many colonial governors, including Franklin, knew all too often applied: dissolution helped only the opposition. No administration supporter gained a seat at the expense of the opposition, nor did any opposition member convert to the administration side. That party declined in force from sixteen of twenty-four members in 1769 to eleven of thirty after 1772. Three of these were of the six assemblymen from counties newly permitted to elect their own representatives, three others were of the ten replacements elected, and only five of those who had been administration supporters in the previous House were reelected. The much-reduced administration group was confronted by a moderate and an extreme opposition. The moderate opposition, unlike the moderate administration group of the 1761–1768 House, voted against the administration side on most major issues. Six new assemblymen, including three from the newly privileged counties, and one incumbent were in this group. The extreme opposition numbered twelve, including five incumbent oppositionists, two former administration supporters, and five new assemblymen.

This New Jersey election was the most striking victory for the middling sort heretofore in middle-colony politics. In the very heated Perth Amboy poll and eight others, the voters chose farmers with moderate property. Of these nine, seven had never served before. The increase in the number of representatives with moderate holdings was unprecedented; in each of the three previous elections no more than two assemblymen with moderate property holdings had been chosen. New Jersey voters, bolder than those of any other middle colony, in these critical times believed that new men, closer to the people, from an underrepresented social order, deserved their opportunity to govern. As Table 29 indicates, traditional religious affiliations with partisanship and the new activism of the middling held forth in this assembly. Quakers and Baptists all returned to the opposition side. The majority of middling assemblymen and farmers in the House were in the moderate or extreme opposition. The blending of these sources of opposition produced the most antiadministration House in any of the middle colonies in the period 1769–1775.

Confrontation with Governor Franklin quickly bloomed as the opposition bloc in the House turned its attention to the negligence of the East Jersey treasurer. Franklin refused to dismiss Treasurer Skinner and appoint a replacement. Petitions and instructions, supposedly from constituents but probably solicited by oppositionist leaders, filled the table and pressed cautious assemblymen to push for Skinner's ouster. The treasurer's brother Cortland Skinner was, in the tradition of New Jersey politics, minority Speaker and powerless to stop the House. On February 19, 1774, the House took seven roll call votes condemning Skinner, and he resigned within the week. The episode solidified the strength of the oppositionists and primed them for the more intense resistance against Britain that was to come.[27]

Imperial issues took longer to affect New York parties than was the case with its two southern neighbors because in that colony ideological and religious divisions between the parties, which in Pennsylvania and New Jersey contributed to attitudes on imperial issues, were not as sharp. Neither the Liv-

27. *N.J. Votes,* Aug. 28, 1772, Sept. 10–26, 1772. Dec. 2–21, 1773, Feb. 15–19, 26, Mar. 3, 9, 1774, Feb. 4–8, 1775; Cortland Skinner to Philip Kearney, Dec. 5, 1773, in *NJA,* X, 414. Gerlach, "Politics and Prerogatives," 154, counts forty petitions against Skinner, signed by three thousand freeholders. "Draft of Instructions," in *NJA,* X, 417–18, seems to be a model for use in various constituencies.

TABLE 29

**Economic and Social Characteristics of
Party Members: New Jersey House, 1772–1775**

(*All tabulated figures are assembly terms*)

	Wealthy	Well-to-do	Middling	Unknown
Administration	3	5	3	1
Moderate opposition	1	4	1	1
Extreme opposition	2	5	5	
Indeterminate				1

	Anglican	Presbyterian	Dutch Reformed	Quaker	Baptist
Administration	3	6	3	0	0
Moderate opposition	0	2	0	4	1
Extreme opposition	1	4	1	4	2
Indeterminate					1

	Central capital-town	West Jersey rural	East Jersey rural
Administration	4	3	5
Moderate opposition	1	6	0
Extreme opposition	3	6	3
Indeterminate	1		

	Great landholder	Landowner	Farmer
Administration	1	2	5
Moderate opposition	1	1	2
Extreme opposition	0	5	5

	Merchant	Shopkeeper/artisan	Lawyer
Administration	1	1	2
Moderate opposition	0	1	2
Extreme opposition	2	0	0
Indeterminate	1		

lambda-b, partisanship and religion = 0.32; and occupation = 0.26; and region = 0.16; and wealth = 0.06. (Includes by-election results.)

ingston nor the DeLancey parties paid attention to the Townshend duties during the election of March, 1768. Historian Patricia U. Bonomi has viewed the 1768 election as a contest between two parties with different ideologies and stances on imperial issues: the DeLancey side as the "popular Whigs," more in sympathy with the fervent anti-British resistance leaders, and the Livingston party as the moderate Whig group. Although she asserts that Philip Livingston, Jr., won in 1768 "despite a strong popular Whig tide," she has not perceived which way the tide flowed. Livingston received the votes of all the identified Sons of Liberty and of all men who later would become officials in the revolutionary and new state governments of New York. James DeLancey, Jr., received only six of eleven identified Sons of Liberty votes and support from eighteen of thirty-three future officials.[28] In fact, the election was between two parties that did not differ on imperial issues, though they did differ in religion and on who could best represent local districts. No issue had emerged in the legislature that divided the parties or the people. The nine reported contests in the 1768 election—the largest number known for any election in colonial New York—indicate that each party made a concerted effort to capture an evenly divided House, not to make policy changes.[29]

The DeLancey party made its strongest effort in New York City, where it hoped to recapture the majority of the representatives. It put up no incumbents but nominated three men who would have strong appeal to important constituencies: James DeLancey, Jr., Jacob Walton, and James Jauncey. All were merchants. DeLancey was the nephew of two councillors, Walton the nephew of one. Jauncey was a prominent Presbyterian, nominated to draw dissenter votes away from the Livingston party, which was generally supported by that denomination. The Livingston party stayed with its incumbents, Philip Livingston, Jr., and William Bayard, who had generally voted together. Presbyterian lawyer John Morin Scott again ran as a Livingston ally. More calculation than was usual for New York went into the formulation of these tickets; New York political leaders were just beginning to appreciate the value of religious balance. Pennsylvanians would view the choice of candidates for religious or ethnic appeal as commonplace.[30]

Just as party strategy was careful in selecting suitable candidates, so were the parties lavish in their efforts at persuasion and influence. DeLancey supporters purchased hundreds of meals, bottles of wine, and bowls of punch

28. Bonomi, *Factious People*, 239–46, 254 (quoted). Recent studies such as Kierner, *Traders and Gentlefolk*, 186–88, follow Bonomi's analysis. For names of Sons of Liberty, Herbert M. Morais, "The Sons of Liberty in New York," in *The Era of the American Revolution*, ed. Richard B. Morris (New York, 1939), 273; and Pauline Maier, *From Resistance to Revolution: Colonial Radicals and the Development of American Opposition to Britain, 1765–1776* (New York, 1972), 303. For names of later revolutionary and state officials, Becker, *Political Parties in New York*, 185, 206, 232, and Countryman, *People in Revolution*, 313–25. These were traced in *N.Y.C. Poll List, 1768*.

29. Contested elections occurred at least in New York City, Albany, Richmond, Queens, Westchester County and Borough, Dutchess, Orange, and Cortlandt (*N.Y. Votes*, Oct. 29, 1768).

30. Roger J. Champagne, "Family Politics Versus Constitutional Principles: The New York Assembly Elections of 1768 and 1769," *WMQ*, 3rd ser., XX (1963), 66.

TABLE 30

Results of Canvassing Efforts: New York City, 1768

	% 1768 voters for candidate held from 1761		1761 voters who switched to candidate
DeLancey	50.9	(356)	220
Livingston	40.4	(432)	203
Scott	34.9	(252)	140
Bayard	22.8	(181)	114

to treat the thirsty. So on a lesser scale did Amos Dodge, a house carpenter standing as an independent in imitation of his betters, though he spoiled the effect by voting for himself, which no gentleman would ever do. Oliver De-Lancey "posted himself in the broad way," seeking votes for his nephew by "coaxing or bullying." These measures were probably more effective than De-Lancey propaganda efforts, which were mostly negative attacks on lawyers, particularly Scott. The Livingston side could not match its opposition's influence, though its campaigners probably purchased treats also. Nor did it have a propaganda advantage; its defenses of Scott and subtle jabs at De-Lancey were not as spirited or voluminous as the DeLancey output. The Livingston party relied too much on the reputation of Philip Livingston, Jr., and neglected to use the efficient tactics its rivals employed.[31]

The hardworking party faithful turned out the largest vote ever in the city, a 32.7 percent increase over 1761. The new voters did not support any one candidate; they seem to have flocked to the treats. The serious voters, those who had voted in 1761, were the key to the election. As Table 30 shows, the party canvassers brought back to the polls the majority of those who had voted for James DeLancey, Jr., in 1761. No other candidate received such a high level of support from repeat voters. Assiduous canvassing also encouraged other voters of 1761 to switch allegiance to DeLancey in larger numbers than those switching to other candidates. The joint appeal of the De-Lancey candidates was mutually reinforcing.

Walton and DeLancey shared 1,017 voters, 84.5 percent of DeLancey's

31. New York *Mercury,* Feb. 22, Mar. 21, 1768. Charles Evans, *American Bibliography* (14 vols., 1903–1909; rpr. New York, 1941), IV, 129, reports notice of Dodge's now lost broadsides. The *N.Y.C. Poll List, 1768,* shows that Dodge voted for himself and William Bayard. Derek M. Hirst, *The Representation of the People? Voters and Voting in England Under the Early Stuarts* (Cambridge, Eng., 1975), 113, finds no candidate voting for himself between 1604 and 1640. [Smith], *The Watchman,* No. II, reported on Oliver DeLancey.

total. Jauncey may have helped DeLancey with the Presbyterian and Scotch-Irish vote, for he did considerably better among that group in 1768 than in the previous election, though not nearly as well as did Livingston and Scott. The DeLancey appeal to merchants and tradesmen and to Anglicans and some Presbyterians bespoke a successful coalition that reasserted traditional DeLancey control of the city.[32]

The Livingston party effort was valiant but unsuccessful. All the Livingston family members and Lewis Morris III voted for both Livingston and Scott. More than one-fifth of all voters (20.4 percent) cast short ballots—a partisan strategy—for Livingston and Scott. Three Livingston cousins and other supporters voted for Bayard. Philip Livingston, Jr., led all candidates; he showed wide appeal among all voters. Not only did he do well with Presbyterians, but he also had the backing of the Sons of Liberty and others of anti-British sentiment. His triumph did not carry Scott and Bayard to victory. He received one-third of his support from voters who split their tickets between him and the DeLancey allies. These voters refused to support Scott and Bayard. Of identifiable groups, only the Scotch-Irish backed Scott. Dutch and mechanic voters gave him about the same support as did the general electorate, and only four of eleven Sons of Liberty voted for him, perhaps because of the propaganda attacking his stand on the Stamp Act. Probably more persuasive were the broadsides from "Merchants' Hall" and "Tradesmen's Hall." The former proclaimed that "No man will Vote for a Lawyer, unless he prefers the Craft of the Law, to the Business of MERCHANTS." The latter identified the interest of the "leather aprons" with that of traders. Even Livingston partisan Robert Morris termed Scott's candidacy ill-advised for a "trading city." Bayard's poor electoral showing, the worst of any incumbent in any recorded middle-colony election, may have resulted from his pro-British sentiments—he was later a loyalist refugee. He received little support from Sons of Liberty or future state officers.[33]

Elections in Pennsylvania, where new voters of particular religious and eth-

32. *N.Y.C. Poll List, 1761; N.Y.C. Poll List, 1768.* Table 32 reports the mechanic support for both the DeLanceys and the Livingstons.

33. *N.Y.C. Poll List,* 1768; *Merchants' Hall* (New York, 1768); "Mr. Axe and Mr. Hammer," *A Card;* Morris quoted by Bonomi, *Factious People,* 244–45. "A Whip for the American Whig, No. 10," in New York *Gazette and Weekly Mercury,* Apr. 28, 1768, claimed that Scott headed a Presbyterian "Faction." Harrington, *New York Merchant on the Eve of the Revolution,* 134–35; William Bayard to [son], Feb. 16, 1790, in Emmet Collection, NYPL. Bayard's vote total declined by 26.5 percent from 1761 to 1768. There is no record of any pro-British statement or action by Bayard in the assembly journals or the election propaganda.

nic groups turned out in blocs, were considerably better managed than in New York. Treats got people to turn out in both cities; canvassing in Philadelphia got a great majority of them to vote *en bloc* for linked party candidates, while New York voters often split their tickets. Vote garnering was a highly developed art in the Quaker city, less so in New York.

In the back county elections, as in the city, the Livingston ticket had little success because of local issues and weak candidates. In Dutchess, the tenants on the estates of Livingston relatives and backers opposed landlord domination of politics, rejected Robert R. Livingston, and elected two merchants allied with the DeLancey side.[34] In Orange County a lawyer attacked by DeLancey antilawyer propaganda finished last, as in Queens did Presbyterian cleric Abraham Keteltas, who too clearly reflected the religious orientation of the Livingston party.[35] The election resulted in the voters sending to the new assembly six firm DeLancey partisans, eleven moderate DeLancey sympathizers, eight committed Livingston advocates, and two neutrals. As Table 31 shows, religion again strongly influenced partisan differences. The Livingston party needed to capitalize on its religious difference from the DeLancey party with better organization, better propaganda, and a concentrated effort to rally voting blocs if it were to compete effectively with its rival.

Imperial issues confronted the new assembly when Governor Henry Moore, after giving the House its longest recess since 1736, finally summoned it in October, 1768. Moore hoped to put off the inevitable consideration of the circular letter from the Massachusetts House of Representatives, but the demonstrators in the streets, merchants before the House, and instructions

34. Robert R. Livingston to Robert Livingston, Jr., Feb. 21, 1768, LP. Tenant discontent was evident the next year; thus it probably best explains the outcome. Peter R. Livingston to Philip Schuyler, Mar. 27, 1769, in Schuyler Papers, NYPL. Colden told the Earl of Hillsborough, Apr. 25, 1768 in Colden Letter Books, *NYHSC,* X, 168, that Livingston had "lost the esteem of the Freeholders."

35. *N.Y. Votes,* Oct. 29, Nov. 10–18, 1768. In Westchester borough, John DeLancey barely outpolled Lewis Morris III, who complained that the sheriff illegally barred four of his voters. Jonathan Landon to Robert Morris, Mar. 13, 1768, in MP. "Philanthropos," *To the Freeholders and Freemen of New York,* 1, attacked Livingston lawyer candidates in several counties. New York *Mercury,* Mar. 21, 1768. Albany politicians agreed to divide the two seats between the two sides. Only in the manor of Cortlandt did a Livingston ally take a formerly DeLancey seat. Abraham Ten Broeck to James Duane, Feb. 22, 1768, in Duane Papers, NYHS. Jacob Judd, ed., *Correspondence of the Van Cortlandt Family of Cortlandt Manor, 1748–1800* (Tarrytown, 1977), 4–8, Vol. II of *Van Cortlandt Family Papers,* 4 vols. Helen W. Reynolds, *Dutch Houses in the Hudson Valley Before 1776* (New York, 1929), 305.

TABLE 31

**Economic and Social Characteristics of
Party Members: New York House, 1768**
(All tabulated figures are assembly terms)

	Wealthy	Well-to-do	Middling	Unknown
Livingston	5	2	0	1
DeLancey	7	8	1	1
Indeterminate	1		1	

	Anglican	Presbyterian	Dutch Reformed	Congregational	Quaker	Lutheran	Unknown
Livingston	0	4	3	0	0	0	1
DeLancey	8	1	5	1	0	1	1
Indeterminate	1				1		

	New York City	Albany	East shore	West shore	Long Island, Staten Island
Livingston	1	3	1	3	0
DeLancey	3	2	5	1	6
Indeterminate					2

	Great landholder	Landowner	Farmer
Livingston	2	2	0
DeLancey	2	2	3
Indeterminate			1

	Merchant	Shopkeeper/artisan	Lawyer	Unknown
Livingston	3	0	1	
DeLancey	7	2	0	1
Indeterminate			1	

lambda-b, partisanship and religion = 0.57; and region = 0.38; and wealth = 0.14; and occupation = 0.10

from constituents in New York City and Queens compelled the assembly to respond favorably to Massachusetts' request that all colonies petition Parliament against the Townshend duties. The problem for the House was to comply with the letter without incurring an inconvenient dissolution. Neither party wanted to lose the bills of this session or to face another election so soon. The DeLancey allies on the council opposed dissolution; that party in the House was pleased with its majority as it stood. The Livingston minority was satisfied to retain its important leadership posts — especially that of Speaker Philip Livingston, Jr. — and its amicable relations with the governor. The House therefore devised a nonpartisan process for petitioning Parliament, answering Massachusetts, and getting essential legislation passed. On November 8 it ordered a petition to the British government against the Townshend duties drawn up, in effect complying with the Massachusetts letter. On December 10 Livingston supporter Philip Schuyler proposed that the assembly explicitly reply to the sister colony after passing important bills to avoid losing necessary legislation in a hasty dissolution. Once these passed, the House would then enter Schuyler's resolutions about replying to Massachusetts on the journals as adopted unanimously. The House approved this plan, over the objections of a few DeLanceyites. All assemblymen agreed that in the event of a dissolution and new election, "all the Members [were] to fare alike in Point of Reputation," meaning that no party was to claim that it was more avid in opposition to the Townshend duties or in support of Boston than was its rival. Although some DeLancey legislators dissented on Schuyler's plan, the majority concurred, for most assemblymen did not intend to make resistance to Britain an election issue.[36]

Dissolution in early January, 1769, which Governor Moore dared not forgo proclaiming, gave the Livingston party the opportunity to regain a majority, which it too avidly seized. In New York City the Livingston leaders sought at least parity with the DeLancey party. They proposed that, instead of jointly putting up the incumbents, each party should name two candidates for the four seats. The strategists anticipated that the DeLancey side would nominate the popular DeLancey and Walton and the Livingston party would nominate Philip Livingston, Jr., and John Morin Scott. This plan would compel the De-Lancey side to swallow the unpalatable Scott and to abandon the loyal Jauncey—

36. Smith, *Historical Memoirs*, Nov. 18–21, Dec. 10, 13 (quoted), 1768, May 21, 1769, I, 46–49, 51; New York *Journal*, Nov. 17, Dec. 1, 1768; *N.Y. Votes*, Nov. 3–18, 23, Dec. 9, 12, 14–16, 28, 31, 1768, Jan. 2, 1769; Moore to Hillsborough, Jan. 4, 1769, in *DCHNY*, VIII, 144. For the scholarly debate on the responsibility for dissolution, Champagne, "Family Politics Versus Constitutional Principles," 70–71; Olson, "New York Assembly," 24; Friedman, "New York Assembly Elections of 1768 and 1769," 14. Both *An Answer to the Foolish Reason That Is Given for Re-choosing the Old Members, to Wit, That They Passed Certain Resolves, Agreeable to the Instructions Given Them by Some of Their Constituents* (New York, 1769), 2; and *As a Scandalous Paper Has Appeared, Stiled an Answer . . . , Calculated to Asperse the Character of Three of the Late Members, Candidates in the Ensuing Election, It Is Necessary for the Satisfaction of the Public, to Give a True Narrative of Their Conduct in the Late House of Assembly, Respecting Some Matters Which Are Grossly Misrepresented* (New York, 1769), 2, note that two DeLancey assemblymen from the city laid wagers that the House would not be dissolved. "Honestus," *An Anecdote of a Certain Candidate, for the Ensuing Election* (New York, 1769), and *The Freeholder, No. III: The Conclusion of the Answers, to the Reasons* (New York, 1769), charged that even before the dissolution a "Juncto" had declared that new candidates would be set up in New York City, but in fact the tickets were not set until a week after the dissolution. Colden's comment to George Grenville, Jan. 6, 1769, Colden Letterbooks, in *NYHSC*, X, 82, that both groups wanted a dissolution "to gain or preserve popularity," seems inaccurate.

"at all Costs Jauncey must go to the Wall this time," vowed Peter R. Livingston. He appeared especially vulnerable because he admitted that he had paid for votes in 1768. Replacing him with Scott would give the Livingston party another strong leader in the House and jeopardize the DeLancey majority.[37]

The DeLancey side quickly rejected the substitution of Scott for Jauncey; the Livingston strategists in turn refused DeLancey overtures to support the incumbents. They put up a new slate, including Philip Livingston, Jr., his brother Peter Van Brugh Livingston, Theodorus Van Wyck, and Scott. The DeLancey party found an equally strong candidate to stand with the three incumbents on its ticket: John Cruger, brother of a councillor, former assemblyman, and opponent of burdensome British regulation, who consented to serve again only if the DeLancey party made him Speaker of the House. The candidates on these tickets were more firmly allied than were those in the 1768 election; the two tickets were more clearly partisan rivals than any New York City tickets had been since 1739.[38]

Although propagandists focused personal attacks on Jauncey and Scott and "Leather Aprons" were exhorted to elect merchants not lawyers, as they had been in 1768, the campaign also incorporated religious, ethnic, and imperial issues. Livingston party propagandists took up a cause that had occupied the presses for the past nine months but previously was not partisan: opposition to an Anglican bishop. Because it was largely Anglican, the DeLancey party made a handy target for those opposed to the expansion of Anglican power. The Livingston side, with all Presbyterian and Dutch Reformed candidates, appealed to dissenters to stand fast against domination of the colony by Anglicans. Its propaganda alleged that Anglicans, when bolstered by a bishop, would begin the persecution of dissenters, that an Anglican-dominated government would not charter dissenting churches, and that Anglican churches would acquire glebe lands by fraud. In reply, the DeLancey side castigated "Independents" as intolerant and turbulent and indicted the Presbyterians for greedily seeking the revenues of the established church for them-

37. *The Freeholder, No. III*, 4; Robert R. Livingston to Philip Schuyler, Jan. 28, 1769, Peter R. Livingston to Schuyler, Jan. 16, 1769, both in Schuyler Papers, NYPL.

38. Philip Livingston, *To the Freeholders and Freemen, of the City and County of New York* (New York, 1769), asserted that he had been popularly drafted. Henry and John Cruger to Moses Franks, Apr. 22, 1767, in Cruger Letterbook, NYHS; John Stevens to Lord Stirling, Jan. 28, 1769, in William Alexander Papers, NYHS. John Cruger claimed he wanted to "avoid all Occasion of Heat and Party Spirit, at a Time when so much depends on our Union and Harmony," in his *To the Freeholders and Freemen of the City and County of New York* (New York, 1769).

selves. It also charged Livingston supporters with insulting Germans and Irish. Imperial issues entered the campaign when the DeLancey party broke the pledge that all incumbents were to be accounted supporters of the assembly's stance on the Massachusetts letter. It falsely charged that Philip Livingston, Jr., was "a great Prerogative Man." It also denounced Scott for his 1765 opposition to Virginia's resolutions against the Stamp Act. In reply, the Livingston side not only took full credit for passing Schuyler's resolutions but also alleged that DeLancey assemblymen had delayed the approval of petitions against the Townshend Acts. Attacks on Scott's character, that he cheated a poor man out of his wages and danced with and kissed other men, were probably not believed.[39]

This bitter election campaign saw the most reported use of unabashed coercion, chiefly by the DeLancey party. A broadside alleged that "many of the poorer People . . . deeply felt the aristocratic Power, or rather the intolerable Tyranny of the great and opulent, who . . . have openly threatened them with the loss of their Employment, and to arrest them for debt, unless they gave their Voices as they were directed." Sir William Johnson allegedly sent threatening letters to his "Dependants . . . in order to intimidate them to vote as he wanted them." DeLancey partisan Isaac Sears admitted telling baker Andrew Marschalk that it was "probable" he would not be continued as flour inspector if he voted for John Morin Scott, but if he voted against Scott he would receive greater preferment. The Livingston side warned that its opponents would employ "threats and terror" but claimed it was ready for them. The arrogant Peter R. Livingston confidently boasted to Philip Schuyler that "we have by far the best part of the Brusers on our side who are determined to use force if they [the DeLanceyites] use any foul play." In fact, the "Brusers" were not in evidence during the election, unlike Philadelphia's White Oaks, who prevented any violence against the Assembly party.[40]

39. John Morin Scott, Peter V. B. Livingston, and Theodorus Van Wyck, *To the Freeholders and Freemen of the City and County of New York* (New York, 1769); Peter R. Livingston to Philip Schuyler, Jan. 16, 1769, in Schuyler Papers, NYPL; *A Seasonable Advertisement to the Freeholders and Freemen of the City of New York, and All the Real Friends to Liberty, and Lovers of Their Country* (New York, 1769); "Impartial," *To the Dissenting Electors of All Denominations* (New York, 1769); *The Freeholder, No. I: Answers to the Reasons, Lately Published by the Independents, in Support of Their Malicious Construction* (New York, 1769); *The Freeholder, No. II: A Continuation of the Answers, to the Reasons* (New York, 1769); *The Freeholder, No. III;* New York *Gazette and Weekly Mercury,* Jan. 16, 1769; *An Answer to the Foolish Reasons,* 1–2; *As a Scandalous Paper Has Appeared, Stiled an Answer to the Foolish Reasons,* 2; John Morin Scott, untitled broadside, Jan. 9, 1769 (New York, 1769); *A Contrast: Read My Fellow Citizens and Judge for Yourselves* (New York, 1769).

40. Untitled broadside, Jan. 8, 1770 (New York, 1770); *Seasonable Advertisement to the Freehold-*

Middle-colony political parties seeking votes in a city were compelled to make both propaganda pitches and threats in the hope of persuading a few needed voters, but in this election, as in most by the 1760s, what counted was party affiliation and canvassing. Party solidarity on the DeLancey side and wavering and ticket splitting on the Livingston side brought victory to the former. Slightly over half (50.8 percent) of the voters chose the straight DeLancey ticket; 30.3 percent voted the straight Livingston ticket. The highest proportion of straight ticket votes in the two previous city elections was 30.0 percent. Bringing new voters to the polls was not as important to the DeLancey side as was recapturing those who had voted in 1768. DeLancey and Walton held on to 65 to 66 percent of their 1768 vote, and those voters made up over 70 percent of their 1769 vote. This core bloc determined the outcome of the election. Jauncey held 501 of his 1768 voters, 57.1 percent of his 1769 total, and he swung more of the 1768 voters (213) to his camp than did any other candidate. Cruger's prominence added considerable strength to the ticket. The DeLancey triumph in New York City was a team victory.[41]

The candidates on the DeLancey ticket complemented each other; those on the Livingston ticket dragged the leader, Philip Livingston, Jr., down to defeat. The party strategists hoped for a "vast deal of Cross Voting" or ticket splitting, but they completely misjudged the political spirit and efficiency of their opponents. Only 15.4 percent of the voters split tickets, and almost 40 percent of these voted for three DeLancey candidates. Peter Van Brugh Livingston and Van Wyck, running a poor seventh and eighth, added no electoral support to the ticket. The vote for Philip Livingston was basically the Scott vote of 1768; the same 440 voters of 1768 who voted for Scott in 1769 made up 66.1 percent of Livingston's 1769 vote total (666). Voters choosing both Livingston and Scott in 1769 totaled 595, 89.3 percent of the total Livingston vote and 92.1 percent of the total Scott vote. The Livingston party's strongest support came from Presbyterians. Religiously oriented propaganda turned out alarmed Presbyterians but also lined up the Anglicans against them. The Livingston loss was an example of the coattails effect in reverse; the supposedly more popular candidate did not induce his supporters to vote for others on the ticket, but the ticket attracted in the main only the supporters

ers and Freemen, and Peter Van Schaack to Henry Van Schaack, Jan. 29, 1769, in Hawks Manuscripts, NYHS; Isaac Sears, untitled broadside, Jan. 24, 1769 (New York, 1769); *N.Y.C. Poll List, 1769;* Livingston to Schuyler, Jan. 16, 1769, in Schuyler Papers, NYPL.

41. *N.Y.C. Poll List, 1768; N.Y.C. Poll List, 1769.*

of a controversial and less popular candidate while repelling former supporters of the most popular candidate.[42]

Although historians Patricia Bonomi and Gary Nash assert that in 1769 city artisans were coerced into voting for the DeLancey ticket and against Philip Livingston and his allies, close analysis of the poll lists and the lists of freemen shows that this was not the case. Voters in New York City displayed considerable resistance to coercion, perhaps encouraged by the anti-British movement to stand up for their rights. Baker Marschalk refused to be intimidated, informed the city of this threat, and voted the Livingston ticket. Elite pressure did not scare the mechanics from coming to the polls, although Nash asserts that it did. The vote totals supplied in Table 32, correcting those published in 1967 by Roger Champagne and used by Nash and Bonomi, show that mechanic participation grew from 54.3 percent (803/1,449) in 1761 to 54.5 percent (1,049/1,923) in 1768 and 57.8 percent (877/1,515) in 1769. The mechanic voters of 1768 who failed to appear in 1769 were a minority (40.4 percent, 269/667) of the total number of voters of 1768 failing to reappear at the polls in the following year. The decline in mechanic participation affected both the Livingston and DeLancey parties about equally. On the DeLancey side, 44.3 percent (148/244) not returning in 1769 were mechanics; on the Livingston side a very slightly smaller proportion (43.4 percent, 85/195) were artisans. Vote tallies show that mechanics were less likely to refrain from voting, even when electoral conflicts and cross pressures were strong or when elections came inconveniently in successive years, than were all other voters. As Table 32 shows, artisans supported the Livingston side more strongly than did the general populace and more strongly than had artisans in the two previous elections. Mechanics gave the party 35.8 percent of their votes; the proportion garnered from the general electorate was 32.2 percent. This proportion of mechanic votes for the Livingston party was larger than that obtained by the party in 1768 (30.0 percent) by more than five percentage points. Masons proclaimed their support for the Livingston side; no artisan group announced for its DeLancey opposition.[43]

42. *N.Y.C. Poll List, 1769;* Peter R. Livingston to Philip Schuyler, Jan. 16, 1769, in Schuyler Papers, NYPL.

43. Nash, *Urban Crucible,* 367, compares total mechanic votes in 1768 and 1769 for Philip Livingston (Nash writes "Robert") to show he was defeated in 1769 owing mainly to the loss of mechanic votes and argues that the more than 300 mechanics who voted in 1768 but not in 1769 (actually 269 mechanics) were scared away by the publication of the 1768 poll lists. Bonomi, *Factious People,* 254, concludes that "it may indeed have been the common people who held the bal-

TABLE 32

Comparison of Mechanics and All Voters:
New York City Elections, 1761–1769

	DeLanceyites		Livingstons		Split	
1761 election						
Mechanics (N = 803)	36.9%	(296)	27.8%	(223)	35.4%	(284)
All voters (N = 1,449)	33.8%	(490)	30.1%	(436)	36.1%	(523)
1768 election						
Mechanics (N = 1,049)	39.2%	(411)	30.0%	(315)	30.8%	(323)
All voters (N = 1,923)	38.2%	(735)	28.7%	(552)	33.1%	(636)
1769 election						
Mechanics (N = 877)	49.5%	(434)	35.8%	(314)	14.7%	(129)
All voters (N = 1,515)	51.6%	(781)	32.2%	(488)	16.2%	(246)

New Yorkers active in the anti-British resistance did not indicate by their choices that they agreed on which party was likely to favor strong resistance. Of the nine probable Sons of Liberty who voted in 1769, six chose DeLancey and three Livingston, dividing between the parties in about the same proportion as did the general electorate. Of the future revolutionary and state leaders who voted, nineteen supported Livingston and twelve backed De-Lancey. That these voters did not as a group make a clear party choice indicates that imperial issues were inconsequential in the election, as was the case in 1768. No imperial crisis divided the populace—the merchants from the artisans—as it did in Pennsylvania in 1770. Historians have too readily seen ideology and interest groups as most influential in this election, but what counted most, as it did in Pennsylvania in the mid-1760s, was partisan organization and electoral campaigning.[44]

---

ance of power" and won the 1769 election for the DeLancey side. *N.Y.C. Poll List, 1768,* lists ten more mechanics than did Roger J. Champagne, "Liberty Boys and Mechanics of New York City, 1764–1774," *Labor History,* VIII (1967), 132, for 1768. The *N.Y.C. Poll List, 1769,* lists 99 more than does Champagne. It also lists 47 more voters of both 1768 and 1769 than does Champagne. Mechanics were identified in *Burghers and Freemen, NYHSC,* XVIII. For other colonial and revolutionary era successive elections in which the second saw a great falloff in turnout, Edmund S. Morgan, *Inventing the People: The Rise of Popular Sovereignty in England and America* (New York, 1988), 303. After Marschalk revealed this threat, Isaac Sears, untitled broadside, Jan. 24, 1769 (New York, 1769), admitted he had approached the baker. Gerard Bancker asserted to Lord Stirling, Jan. 28, 1769, in William Alexander Papers, NYHS, that the 1769 election "was conducted with Order and Regularity." Howard B. Rock, *Artisans of the New Republic: The Tradesmen of New York City in the Age of Jefferson* (New York, 1979), 51–55, notes coercion attempts in the 1790s.

44. See note 28, this chapter, for identification of these voters.

The back county elections were also hard-fought campaigns because the Livingston side hoped to recoup losses, while the DeLancey partisans targeted key seats. After propaganda skirmishes and diligent campaigning by both sides, Dutchess County remained in the DeLancey camp. In Orange the De-Lancey side elected a new assemblyman, John DeNoyelles, who would prove to be one of its chief spokesmen in the House. The DeLanceyites hoped that Sir William Johnson could muster the voters necessary to unseat Philip Schuyler in Albany, but the Lord of the Mohawks found this impossible in a midwinter election. In a rare electoral contest in Suffolk, Livingston partisan and later revolutionary war general Nathaniel Woodhull defeated a DeLancey supporter. And in Westchester borough Lewis Morris III finally defeated John DeLancey by four votes in a poll marred by charges of fraud and corruption. The election produced a gain of two seats for the Livingston side, but the De-Lancey side held a sixteen-to-ten advantage.[45]

As it had been since the 1750s and the rise of the new opposition, religion remained strongly associated with party divisions. The denominational alignment in the House remained about the same as in 1768 except that the non-Dutch dissenters joined the Livingston side. Regional divisions and economic circumstances remained less significant than religion, as had been the case in recent elections.[46]

Whig ideology and imperial issues began to play important roles in New York politics only in the aftermath of this bitterly fought election. Livingston opposition and persistence offended the majority party, so it lashed back at its rival with an old Walpolean tactic—"weeding the House." In April and May, 1769, the DeLanceyites hoed out Philip Livingston, Jr., elected from the Livingston manor seat, and Lewis Morris III on the grounds that they were nonresidents of the districts that elected them. In the case of Morris the charge was patently fraudulent, the ejection motion passed by one vote, and the DeLancey majority, to save appearances, had to stage a questionable

45. *An Address to the Freeholders of Dutchess County, by a Fellow Freeholder and Inhabitant* (New York, 1769), 1–2; New York *Gazette and Weekly Mercury*, Feb. 20, 1769; Peter R. Livingston to Philip Schuyler, Jan. 23, Feb. 27, 1769, William Smith, Jr., to Schuyler, Feb. 11, 1769, Sir William Johnson to Schuyler, Jan. 17, 1769, all in Schuyler Papers, NYPL; Peter Van Schaack to Henry Van Schaack, Jan. 27, 1769, in Hawks Manuscripts, NYHS; Johnson to Colden, Jan. 26, 1769, in *NYHSC*, LVI, 151. Bonomi, *Factious People*, 256, has a lively summary of the Westchester election.

46. Lambda-b for the relationship to partisanship of religion = 0.50, of region = 0.33, of wealth = 0.25, and of occupation = 0.10. One Lutheran and one Quaker were added to the Livingston side. The DeLancey party lost two votes from Albany and the Schenectady member. It also gained two middling farmers from Long Island.

scrutiny of the Westchester election after Morris was dismissed. The House also refused to seat Philip's successor, cousin Robert R. Livingston.[47] De-Lanceyites, moreover, sought to block any patronage benefits for Livingston adherents. Peter DeLancey vowed "he wishes himself Damned . . . if Ever a Morris or Hunt should have the nominating or putting in any officer even a Constable" in Westchester.[48]

In the face of palpably unscrupulous and destructive partisan tactics, the Livingston party had nowhere to turn but to the people. It retreated to the higher ground of political principle in hopes that popular support would follow. The party argued that its victimization in the denial to Westchester borough and Livingston manor of the right of representation showed the need for greater fairness and openness in the political process. Peter R. Livingston, advocating political reforms, became very much a radical Whig for an heir to a manor. Both Livingston and DeLancey election propaganda had endorsed opening assembly debates to the public, but it was the Livingston side that kept its pledge after the election, seeking to allow the admission of spectators. It pursued this reform to put on display how the DeLancey bloc was persecuting Philip and Robert R. Livingston. Peter R. Livingston asserted to his father that the majority was powerless to block the change; it was "heartily tired of having open doors but know not how to gett them shut."[49]

47. Smith, *Historical Memoirs*, May 20, 1769, I, 67. Hill, *Growth of Parliamentary Parties*, 51; Romney Sedgwick, *The House of Commons, 1715–1754: The History of Parliament* (2 vols.; London, 1970), I, 14; Peter R. Livingston to Robert Livingston, Jr., Apr. 3, 14, May 1, 15, 29, 1769, James Duane to Robert Livingston, Jr., June 1, 1769, all in LP; *N.Y. Votes*, Apr. 12, 20, May 17, 18, Nov. 24, Dec. 21, 1769, Jan. 25, 1771, Feb. 5, 1772, Jan. 26, 1774; Robert R. Livingston, *Address of Mr. Justice Livingston, to the House of Assembly, in Support of His Right to a Seat* (New York, 1769). Bonomi, *Factious People*, 259 and n., deals thoroughly with the nonresidency question. DeNoyelles tried to have Abraham Ten Broeck ejected from the Rensselaerwyck seat on the grounds of nonresidency, but failed because Ten Broeck was legal guardian of the patroon. *N.Y. Votes*, Dec. 29, 1769.

48. The two losers in the Orange County election of 1769 had the temerity to challenge De-Lancey henchman John DeNoyelles and his cohort in demanding a scrutiny. The one loser who pursued his claim—the other feared reprisal and withdrew his petition—not only lost the protest but was assessed costs of £80 by the assembly, a unique and outrageous mulcting. Peter R. Livingston to Philip Schuyler, Feb. 6, 1769, in Schuyler Papers, NYPL; *N.Y. Votes*, Apr. 5, 7, 18, 25, 29, 1769, Jan. 16, 1772. On patronage, Jonathan Landon to Robert Morris, Mar. 2, 1769, in MP. Smith, *Historical Memoirs*, May 29, Sept. 13, Oct. 17, 1769, I, 54–55, 67–68.

49. Philip Schuyler and William Walton went out to fight a duel, which was called off on the field of honor. Jonathan Landon to Robert Morris, Nov. 2, 1769, in MP. William Franklin reported the intended duel to his father, May 11, 1769, in Labaree *et al.*, eds., *Franklin Papers*, XVI, 129. "Philanthropos," *A Few Observations on the Conduct of the General Assembly of New York, for*

When a motion that elections be by ballot was introduced in the House in late 1769, the Livingston party adopted the issue as its own. The elite party leaders manufactured a petition drive in support of the reform. Peter R. Livingston wrote his father the manor lord that he should enlist supreme court justice Robert R. Livingston "to draw such a one as you and he approve of and git it as there is time enough signed by all the freeholders in the Manor." They showed no concern that ballot reform might dilute the lord's sway over his tenants; using the issue to rally the city populace against the DeLancey party was more crucial to the Livingston side. That party's newfound ideology was persuasive. Sons of Liberty leaders joined it, organizing mass meetings and circulating petitions. Passions ran high; violence flared at one mass meeting. This helped to press the House to action; a few DeLancey members fell in with all the Livingston bloc in voting for the ballot bill, but the measure was defeated on the second reading in January, 1770, by Speaker Cruger's casting vote. Although the support of some Livingstons for ballot reform waned during the Revolution, when mechanics and tenants demanded it, in 1769 and 1770 the party saw it as a matter of principle, an attraction for new supporters, and a jab at the DeLancey side.[50]

Its whig position in these ideological causes led the Livingston party to take the popular side in imperial controversies. In its opposition to the supply of quartered troops, which it developed by the end of 1769, the party grew closer in touch with constituents' demands, became willing to take the anti-British side publicly, and even endorsed radical attacks on the assembly. The Livingston legislators made no protest when £1,800 was appropriated to support the quartered troops in May, 1769, but in December they voted to pay the expenses only out of the interest arising from a loan office, when one was permitted by the Crown. This would have stopped the troop supply, at least temporarily. When the Livingston plan failed to pass, Alexander McDougall's bombshell manifesto inflamed the "betrayed inhabitants" against the House for voting the funds and led to demonstrations and to fights between soldiers

Some Years Past, Addressed to the Freemen and Freeholders of the City and Province (New York, 1768), 5; *Address to the Freeholders of Dutchess County*, 1; Peter R. Livingston to Robert Livingston, Jr., Apr. 24, May 1, 1769, LP. Kierner, *Traders and Gentlefolk*, 155, notes Livingston's character.

50. Peter R. Livingston to Robert Livingston, Jr., May 15, Dec. 23, 25, 1769, Feb. 5, 1770, all in LP; New York *Gazette and Weekly Mercury*, Apr. 17, 24, 1769; *N.Y. Votes*, Dec. 22, 1769, Jan. 9, 1770; Untitled broadside, Jan. 8, 1770. Robert Livingston, Jr., asserted that four hundred voters acted at his direction. Smith, *Historical Memoirs*, May 13, June 11, 1777, II, 136, 157.

and townspeople at Golden Hill and Nassau Street in January, 1770. Livingston partisans took up McDougall's cause, portraying him as a martyr to DeLancey oppression when the assembly majority jailed him in February, 1770. Peter R. Livingston donated ground for the Sons of Liberty to erect their liberty pole when the city fathers refused to provide a site. The Sons, persuaded by both Livingston favors and McDougall's attack on the DeLancey majority, now allied with the Livingston party. Former DeLancey backer Isaac Sears, leader of the Sons, switched sides. The anti-British artisans blamed the merchant allies of the DeLancey party for the abrogation of nonimportation in the summer of 1770, and they gravitated to the Livingston camp.[51]

By the fall of 1773, eight years after the Stamp Act crisis, imperial issues had become so pervasive and divisive that they had reshaped the partisan groups in the middle colonies, preserving many traditional aspects but at the same time introducing radical departures from the ordinary course of politics. One partisan group in each colony now possessed a determined anti-British viewpoint and showed its commitment to resistance to imperial impositions. The Patriotic Society, with a strong resistance ideology but both unable and unprepared to be a true party in the style of the old Assembly party; the Livingston party, badly bloodied by the DeLanccy group but yet unbowed; and the greatly revived New Jersey opposition all advocated American rights, and all were gaining more popular support. Artisans and farmers were considerably more political and partisan by 1773 than they were ten years before. The proportion of mechanics in New York City who voted partisan (unsplit) tickets increased from 64.7 percent in 1761 to 85.3 percent in 1769. New Jersey farmers in the 1772 election showed that they wanted to be represented in the assembly by those of their own economic group. A conjunction of compelling ideological issues and the realization that they were economically and politically dominated by elite great landowners and merchants inspired their political activity. Although shaken by events, the parties retained their essential unity, much as they had since the late 1730s. In New Jersey from 1764 to 1773 only 5.3 percent of the assemblymen changed from

---

51. Alexander McDougall, *To the Betrayed Inhabitants of the City and Colony of New York* (New York, 1769); Peter R. Livingston to Philip Schuyler, Feb. 27, 1769, William Smith, Jr., to Schuyler, June 25, 1769, both in Schuyler Papers, NYPL; *N.Y. Votes,* May 12, Dec. 15, 29, 30, 1769, Dec. 13, 1770; Cadwallader Colden to the Earl of Hillsborough, Jan. 6, 1770, in *DCHNY,* VIII, 199–200; Jonathan Landon to Robert Morris, Mar. 24, 1770, in MP; Peter R. Livingston to Robert Livingston, Jr., Feb. 5, 1770, in LP. For the links between McDougall and the Livingston party, Kierner, *Traders and Gentlefolk,* 192–95.

TABLE 33

**Assemblymen Adhering to and Shifting from Parties:
New Jersey House, 1764–1773**

Constant administration	43.9%	(25)
Constant opposition–moderate opposition	33.3%	(19)
Change to or from moderate group	12.3%	(7)
Change to or from party extremes	5.3%	(3)
Indeterminate	5.3%	(3)

TABLE 34

**Assemblymen Adhering to and Shifting from Parties
New York House, 1764–1773**

Constant administration–DeLancey	48.7%	(19)
Constant opposition–Livingston	35.9%	(14)
Changers	15.4%	(6)

one extreme party to the other; in New York 15.4 percent changes sides (see Tables 33 and 34). In the next two and one-half years middle-colony partisan groups would have to face even more serious crises that challenged their coherence and ideology.

6
Parties and the Revolution, 1774–1776

The break with Britain and the formation of new governments severely tested party utility, structure, and appeal in the middle colonies. Revolutions are often potent solvents for political organizations and even for basic political traditions. In Pennsylvania, New Jersey, and New York the Revolution caused great changes in the parties; some were dissolved, and some were drastically reshaped. The realignment is not surprising given the power of the revolutionary crisis. What was significant was that the basic ideas and practices of partisan competition—party alignment in the legislature, the involvement of the electorate, canvassing and electioneering, ideological propaganda—survived to flourish after the Revolution.

New Jersey's opposition party, having captured the assembly in 1772, remained dominant in it and in the revolutionary governing apparatus that took shape in 1774–1775. When the House appointed a Committee of Correspondence in February, 1774, probably following the example of New York, it chose mostly anti-British oppositionists. None of those few assemblymen who favored full support for quartered troops and only two administration supporters were on the committee of nine.[1] New Jersey inhabitants maintained the same political balance when they chose extralegal county committees in the summer of 1774 to meet in a provincial convention in July to elect and instruct delegates to the projected Continental Congress. Twenty-eight of the thirty 1772 assemblymen served on the county committees. Only six of the eleven committees were chaired by House members. Only two of these chairmen were of the administration side or Quakers because the committees avoided appointing any who might not be fervently committed to resistance.[2]

1. *N.J. Votes,* Jan. 20, Feb. 8, 1774. Stephen Crane of Essex and Hendrick Fisher of Somerset were the two administration supporters. Franklin may have dissuaded the House from at first responding to the request of the Virginia Burgesses to form such a committee; it was the slowest colonial assembly, except for Pennsylvania, to take action, but it did respond enthusiastically. See Gerlach, *Prologue to Independence,* 195–96.

2. Gerlach, *Prologue to Independence,* 195–96, 206–15, 448–52. Only Speaker Cortland Skinner and a Quaker from Monmouth did not serve on the committees.

The anti-British opposition hardly wavered when in early 1775 Governor Franklin tried to get the assembly to petition separately from the Continental Congress. Seven members wished to delay consideration of the approval of the actions of the Congress, but oppositionist leader James Kinsey, aided outside the House by Continental Congress delegates William Livingston and John DeHart, persuaded it to approve Congress' resolves unanimously. The House agreed to petition separately, but not differently, from Congress. The petition, probably written by Livingston, was a strong denunciation of British policy, to which administration leader and House Speaker Cortland Skinner, later the colony's most militant loyalist besides Franklin, voiced vigorous dissent. Franklin had no better luck in dampening the oppositionist mood of the assembly after Lexington and Concord, even though some Quaker political leaders abandoned their involvement in the resistance against Britain. When he called the House in session to consider Lord North's reconciliation proposals, it quickly rejected them. For good measure, the oppositionists challenged Franklin directly, for the first time in his administration, by initiating an inquiry into the governor's alleged report to the Earl of Dartmouth that only "artful management" had induced the House to approve the actions of Congress. Franklin then sent the House home, for its oppositionist and anti-British majority could not be curbed.[3]

When this assembly ended, although another and final session would be held at the end of 1775, the colonial political parties faded away. Not surprisingly, the administration party collapsed with the rebuff to Franklin's pro-British efforts. As resistance to Britain turned more toward independence, most of its assemblymen either became loyalists or abandoned political activity. The leader of the administration side, Speaker Cortland Skinner, and three other strong administration supporters became loyalist sympathizers. The other eight members of the administration bloc in 1772 began service in the Provincial Congresses in May, 1775, in the military forces, or as delegates to the Continental Congress. Only three continued in these posts, one in the Provincial Congress and two in the military forces, through June, 1776, when the final Provincial Congress voted for independence and the formation of a new government. Four other administration supporters from earlier assembly sessions also participated in these revolutionary matters; but all

3. *N.J. Votes,* Jan. 13, 24, 25, Feb. 3, 13, May 16, 18, 20, 1775; Franklin to the Earl of Dartmouth, Feb. 1, 1775, Franklin to Joseph Galloway, Mar. 12, 1775, in *NJA,* X, 537, 575–76. Kinsey opposed the petition as adopted, favoring a draft of his own. Only Joseph Barton, later an officer in the New Jersey loyalist militia, dissented from the inquiry into Franklin's report.

except John Hart, the signer of the Declaration of Independence, left before June, 1776.[4]

More significant was the demise of the opposition party, which had espoused the whig principles of restricted government authority on which resistance to Britain was based. It failed because many of its leaders left politics for religious, not ideological, reasons. Six of the eight Quakers in the House, all members of the oppositionist side, quit active politics when war broke out in April, 1775. Another, James Kinsey, was not reelected as Continental Congress delegate in early 1776, when independence was in the offing. These Quakers had been the leadership and inspiration of the oppositionist group. Only six oppositionist 1772 assemblymen out of nineteen continued to serve in the Provincial Congress of June, 1776. Five of them supported most of the measures—the ouster of Governor Franklin and the formation of a new state government—that were the major business of this last Provincial Congress.[5]

Although the opposition party was slightly more numerous in the revolutionary government than its rival, its presence was probably meaningless. The Provincial Convention of 1774 and the successive Provincial Congresses of 1775–1776 had many more members than did the old colonial assembly. The first two congresses had more than eighty members each, and the third and fourth each had fifty to fifty-one members, but only an average of fourteen colonial assemblymen attended any of them. The fifth had sixty-five members, but only nine of them were former assemblymen. The new men who were members of the Provincial Convention and the Provincial Congresses were too preoccupied with new matters to continue old politics, though they had very likely taken sides in previous assembly elections. They had to superintend the war effort, raise money and men, and face new requests from constituents.[6]

4. Gerlach, *Prologue to Independence*, 370–79. Jones, *Loyalists of New Jersey*, identifies Cortland Skinner, Nathaniel Pettit, Joseph Barton, and John Demarest as loyalists and Thomas P. Hewlings as accused of loyalist sentiments. Demarest was the lone 1772 administration supporter who continued to serve in the Provincial Congresses until after July, 1776.

5. Besides the thirteen oppositionist assemblymen accounted for in the text, one served in several of the first four Provincial Congresses, leaving in 1776; one was a military officer; two died; and two could not be traced. Gerlach, *Prologue to Independence*, 370–79; Hinshaw, *Encyclopedia of Quaker Genealogy*, III. Only one Quaker, John Hinchman, is identified as a Loyalist by Jones, *Loyalists of New Jersey*. *N.J. Prov. Cong. Votes*, June 14, 16, 21, 22, July 2, 3, 1776. The oppositionists who persisted were Congress president Samuel Tucker, John Combs, John Wetherill, John Mehelm, Theophilus Elmer, and Edward Taylor. Taylor did not fully support the formation of a new government.

6. The Provincial Convention of 1774 was about four times as large as the colonial assembly. All but two 1772–1775 assemblymen served in it. *N.J. Prov. Cong. Votes, passim.*

Voters were now excited by revolutionary issues and the possibility of radical change. For this they turned to the Provincial Congress. Several towns petitioned for taxpayer or householder suffrage. Others pleaded for the suspension of suits for debt and the taxing of both lawyers and money loaned at interest. Measures such as these had never been part of any partisan program; they were new business raised under new circumstances. The Provincial Congress was slow in moving toward independence and ignored important reform proposals. Nevertheless, constituents believed that the colony now had a more representative and responsive legislature that would redress newly voiced grievances.[7] Controversy over these new issues, not over the old divisions between administration and opposition parties, was what mattered to the voters after 1775.

Only in one instance did the old politics intrude on the new *de facto* government. At Governor Franklin's call the assembly met in November, 1775, to transact routine business and also to reassess the colony's attitude toward imperial relations. The leaders of the Provincial Congress—President Samuel Tucker and former president Hendrick Fisher—attended. Only two assemblymen who were congress members failed to participate. Provincial Congress leaders did not yet wish to declare the legitimate colonial legislature defunct. They wanted the House to remain viable because its existence demonstrated a commitment to demanding redress of imperial grievances and remaining loyal to the Crown. Most New Jersey citizens had a different viewpoint about the continuance of the old assembly than did their leaders. None petitioned it for important political reforms because they believed it should be powerless. The principal petitions that the House received were from Quaker counties—Monmouth, Burlington, and Gloucester—against independence and alteration of the government.[8] The two party cores—oppositionist Quakers and pro-British administration leaders—united in proposing to send a separate petition to the king. The purpose was not to make independent concessions to Britain but to avert the final break that Quakers and incipient loyalists feared. A visit from a committee of the Continental Congress, chaired by John Dickinson, quickly convinced the assembly that the united front behind the congress had to be maintained. The episode illustrated that the assembly was superfluous and unrepresentative. Nearly three-fourths (73.3 per-

7. *Ibid.*, May 24, 1775, Aug., 1775, Oct. 4, 6, 9, 12, 19, 1775, Feb. 16, 1776, June, 1776; New York *Journal,* Sept. 28, 1775.

8. *N.J. Votes,* Nov. 16–28, 1775. Some Quaker petitioners had their own revolutionary idea—freeing the slaves.

cent) of the 1772 House—all but five oppositionists, one administration supporter, and three military officers—temporarily or permanently abandoned
political activity soon after this.[9]

The new state government incorporated members of the colonial assembly if they had not been neutralist or negative toward the American side.
Twenty-two former assemblymen of 1772–1775 continued or returned to service in legislative office during the period 1776–1786. They appear to have
been comfortable in the new political environment, or at least they were able
to make the necessary political adjustments. Their constituents elected them
to almost the same number of terms to which they elected the new legislators, showing that the old hands continued to be regarded highly—but not
too highly, for few of the old assemblymen led the new House, and none
served as governor or other high officeholder. Legislators and other leaders
created new parties on different bases. The issues of an inflation-racked economy, burdensome taxation, and greater support for a central government
now beleaguered the state. The new parties that arose to deal with these issues, the Localists and Cosmopolitans of Jackson T. Main's formulation, had
no direct links with the previous colonial partisan groups. Yet their system was
cut from the same cloth as was that of the colonial administration and opposition parties and as would be that of their mass party successors.[10]

The party collapse in New Jersey was in part replicated in Pennsylvania politics in the years immediately before independence. The existing political
groups broke apart, religious scruples forced assemblymen to quit politics,
new men came to power, and new issues changed the context of politics. The
major difference was that new parties became such bitter rivals in 1776 and
afterward that partisanship became even more intense than it was in the 1760s.
No one could have predicted such changes in partisanship in 1773, for the
Proprietary party was inactive, the Assembly party was concerned only with
maintaining office, and the new Patriotic Society abjured partylike methods.

---

9. *Ibid.*, Nov. 28, 30, Dec. 5, 1775; Notes on Dickinson's Speech, in *NJA*, X, 689–91; Flower,
John Dickinson, 141–42.

10. Main, *Political Parties Before the Constitution*, 159–61, 164–66, 170, 173, 426–32. Gerlach,
Prologue to Independence, 363, incorrectly identifies assemblyman John Combs as a loyalist. Combs
served in the 1782 legislature; a loyalist of the same name but younger is noted in Jones, *Loyalists of New Jersey*, 47. A survey of the legislative council and assembly journals for 1776–1786 shows
that 50.0 percent of the old assemblymen (N = 18) and 38.6 percent of the new members served
only one term; 22.3 percent of the old members and 28.3 percent of the new members served
more than three terms.

The events of late 1773 and the first half of 1774 sparked Philadelphia to form committees and prepare for the Continental Congress. Joseph Galloway maintained control of the Continental Congress delegation. In the congress he pushed, but failed to get adopted, his plan of union that was seen as too compromising of American rights. Galloway's opponents in the Patriotic Society made his caution and his party's "Juncto," which dominated the assembly, their main causes in challenging the old leadership in the October, 1774, election. In this election they began the first comprehensive partisan campaign to capture Philadelphia city and county since 1770, supporting John Dickinson in the county and Charles Thomson and Thomas Mifflin in the city. The old Assembly party had just enough life remaining to defend itself. It combined with proprietary supporters and pacifist Quakers in Philadelphia to nominate and campaign for antiresistance Quakers. In Philadelphia city former Proprietary party leader Thomas Willing and Quaker former assemblyman Edward Penington stood as opponents of Mifflin and Thomson.[11]

Thomson bore the brunt of the political attacks; a broadside charged that he was not only seditious but had "sacrificed our Friend Dr. Franklin, by spreading abroad his *private* letters." Just as in 1766 the Proprietary party had claimed that Franklin and Galloway were at odds, now the Assembly-Quaker-Proprietary combination claimed that Thomson had betrayed everyone's hero. Neither time was the electorate fooled; Thomson won a narrow victory over Willing. Quakers in the city were little help to Penington, who finished far behind. Dickinson also won handily over the opposition of those whom John Adams termed "Broadbrims." Yet the Quakers and the Assembly party remnants remained formidable. Philadelphia County divided between the Patriotic Society and the old "Juncto." None of the incumbent antiresistance Quakers was defeated, but one of the incumbent anti-British assemblymen was left out. The backcountry representation changed hardly at all. In Bucks County cautious and even neutralist Quakers were chosen, although one strict Quaker refused to serve. In Chester "Mad Anthony" Wayne entered politics with a circulated handbill declaring for the election of assemblymen who would help the colony "withstand and ward off the Impending blows big with the fate of British America."[12]

11. Ryerson, *The Revolution Is Now Begun*, 69, 81–86, 189, details the composition of the committees. *Ibid.*, 62, believes that the choice of delegates was based on districts and seniority of assemblymen; but Galloway apparently wanted few strict Quakers on the delegation, so several from Bucks County who were senior to some of the appointees were passed over.

12. *Friends, Countrymen, and Fellow Electors* (Philadelphia, 1774). Oaks, "Philadelphia Mer-

Despite the continued divisions in the assembly, the Patriotic Society gained strength after the election, while the Assembly party continued to unravel. In the Philadelphia balloting for its Committee of Observation in mid-November, 1774, a carefully selected anti-British and proresistance, or "radical-mechanic," ticket easily defeated the nominees hastily set up by a Quaker, merchant, antiresistance, "moderate-conservative" group. Meanwhile, Galloway suffered successive defeats in the assembly. In October, 1774, he was ousted as Speaker; new members Dickinson, Thomson, and Wayne helped to change the "Ballance" against him. Symbolizing his loss of power, an old Assembly party member nominated his successor. In March, 1775, the House majority rejected Galloway's proposal to send a separate petition to Britain. In this effort only the Bucks County Quakers remained loyal to their old leader and his disintegrating party. All but one of the Chester County Quakers voted against him; Galloway railed at them for their desertion. Of the fourteen current assemblymen who had been stalwarts of the old Assembly party since the 1760s, seven voted against the separate petition. The Assembly party, a continuous political group since its Quaker party antecedents took shape in 1739, shattered beyond repair. Its longtime chieftain, "great Champion of the Party" as Thomas Penn had once called him, could only rage helplessly and quit politics in disgust.[13]

After Galloway's defeat and the split of the Assembly party, the Patriotic Society became Pennsylvania's strongest political group, though it too would soon fragment. In the October, 1775, election it campaigned to eliminate nonresistance Quakers from the House, encountering little competition, for six of its Philadelphia County nominees were unopposed. Yet it was still re-

chants and the Origins of American Independence," 427–28, gives vote totals for Philadelphia city: Mifflin, 1,105; Thomson, 670; Willing, 631; Penington, 266. Flower, *John Dickinson,* 113–14; John Adams to Abigail Adams, Oct. 7, 1774, in L. H. Butterfield, ed., *Adams Family Correspondence* (Cambridge, Mass., 1963–), I, 165; "A Freeman of Chester County," draft handbill in Wayne Papers, HSP.

13. Thomas Wharton to Samuel Wharton, Nov. 16, 1774, in Thomas Wharton Letter Book, HSP. Ryerson, *The Revolution Is Now Begun,* 94–96, identifies the new committee election as a major event in the "mechanic revolution." John Adams to Abigail Adams, Oct. 7, 1774, in Butterfield, ed., *Adams Family Correspondence,* I, 165; George Read to Gertrude Read, Oct. 16, 1774, in Paul H. Smith, ed., *Letters of Delegates to Congress, 1784–1789* (21 vols. to date; Washington, D.C., 1976–), I, 204. Galloway and Dickinson were both nominated as Speaker; neither had the votes to win. William Edmunds of Northampton nominated Edward Biddle. *Pa. Votes,* Oct. 14, 1774, Mar. 4, 9, 1775; Penn to Benjamin Chew, Sept. 10, 1762, in TPP.

luctant to act like a party; its leaders were unable to arrange the ticket. They thrust Thomson out as burgess so Franklin could have his old seat back, though he never occupied it. Thomson shifted his candidacy to Philadelphia County, although eight proresistance candidates were already running. Allied with them were those Quaker incumbents from Chester who had deserted Galloway. The remnants of the old Assembly party were very weak but still alive. Only one of its incumbents ran in Philadelphia; three would not stand again. In Bucks, however, the antiresistance group remained solid; seven strict Quakers stood for the House.[14]

The compelling issues of resistance and war and the encouragement of hot committee elections generated great enthusiasm for political participation in Philadelphia. The 1775 election attracted the largest proportion of voters since 1766, despite the small number of contested seats. A substantial number of Friends turned out to make sure that the one strict Quaker in the election won. Support for this minority candidate was symbolic—the Quaker constituency had not yet abandoned its principles, even now that war was on. The high Quaker turnout also was meant to indicate to the proresistance candidates that they should not rush headlong into precipitate action, for the Quaker element still had some political force. The election of the Quaker candidate over Thomson and another proresistance committeeman was chargeable also to the Patriotic Society's reluctance to canvass and electioneer. It failed to turn out the three hundred or so additional voters for the proresistance candidates that would very likely have made the difference. The former Assembly party leaders knew how to canvass to win elections; the proresistance leaders showed little relish for the task.[15]

The antiresistance Quakers lost Philadelphia, but they maintained their traditional political superiority in Bucks. Here the Quaker contingent rolled to complete victory; one non-Quaker assemblyman was even compelled to vote the Quaker line. No gains accrued for the anti-British side in Chester; no more strict Quakers were elected, but Wayne was ousted by an antiresist-

14. Ryerson, *The Revolution Is Now Begun*, 103–104. Unopposed Patriotic Society candidates were incumbents Dickinson, Hillegas, George Gray, and Joseph Parker and military officers Thomas Potts and Samuel Miles. Robert Morris, artisan committee candidate in August; committeeman Thomas Pryor; Thomson; and strict Quaker incumbent Jonathan Roberts contested for the other two seats. *Ibid,*, 136, believes that the city "radicals" opposed Morris, but this is unlikely; his voting record in the subsequent assembly was anti-British and proresistance.

15. For voter turnout, Appendix III. Ryerson, *The Revolution Is Now Begun*, 137, for election figures.

ance Anglican.[16] Of the districts outside Philadelphia, only in Lancaster did the antiresistance advocates lose a seat they formerly held. Quaker determination to continue the political struggle after the most prominent Quaker candidates had retired and during a time when numerous Quakers defected from the denomination because of disagreement with the strict peace testimony shows how strongly that group was committed to partisan activity. Quakers had little concern that the chance of blocking or even dampening American resistance was now very slight; they kept up political action as they had for many years because they fervently believed that their pacifist, nonresistance principles were being directly violated.

Further political fragmentation disrupted old party affiliations when the assembly met in October, 1775. Americans had been fighting British soldiers for more than six months, and the idea of independence began to jar colonial minds. The proresistance group split into supporters and opponents of independence. The anti-independence side, including nine antiresistance Quakers remaining in the House and eleven proresistance anti-independence allies of John Dickinson, outnumbered the pro-independence contingent. Both pro and anti-independence sides recognized that each lacked a clear mandate; therefore, both were agreeable to enlarging the assembly by seventeen members, making a total of fifty-eight. The pro-independence advocates believed they could win about sixteen of the new seats, which, added to their fourteen or so members, would give them an absolute majority. The anti-independence side would need to capture only three to four of the new seats, those of Philadelphia city, to ensure its dominance.[17]

The election of additional Philadelphia representatives to the assembly, set for May 1, 1776, was, in the view of the participants, a true party struggle between "two general denominations of persons, Independents and Tories, or, if you please, Traitors." The former was part of the Patriotic Society, combined with the militia and the mechanics. "Independents" was an accurate appellation, but its opposition was not truly "Tory" or "Traitor." That side consisted of Dickinson's supporters combined with those elements in the old Assembly and Proprietary parties that had opposed the Patriotic Society since 1772. Both contenders continued the hallowed Pennsylvania political tradi-

---

16. Paul David Nelson, "Anthony Wayne: Soldier as Politician," *PMHB*, CVI (1982), 466–67.

17. Only two of Dickinson's allies were from outside the eastern counties—from Berks and Lancaster; of the pro-independence members, ten were from western counties. Calculations of size of delegation and seats needed by each party are based on the few roll calls and votes in *Pa. Votes*, Oct. 30, Nov. 17, 1775, Mar. 13, 14, Sept. 24, 1776.

tion of issuing fervent propaganda. In 1764–1766 Pennsylvanians had been treated to the arguments, blasts, and diatribes of Benjamin Franklin, William Franklin, Galloway, Isaac Hunt, and Hugh Williamson; now Thomas Paine, James Cannon, Benjamin Rush, Thomas Young, and even Sam Adams from Boston engaged in a propaganda onslaught. Twenty-seven pieces advocating independence appeared in the press to bolster that side's campaign. The Independent party planned to contest the election on issues, not personalities, a scruple that its predecessors had often violated.[18]

In previous campaigns the old Assembly and Proprietary parties generally had highlighted issues, but they also had taken pains to construct tickets incorporating popular individuals or representatives of certain interests. The Independents neglected this strategy; they chose rather obscure candidates. Only one former assemblyman, Daniel Roberdeau, stood. The other nominees had played important roles in the resistance movement but were only recently prominent. One reason that the Independents found it difficult to establish a strong ticket was that major leaders such as Franklin were occupied in Congress or the army. Lower-ranking revolutionaries could not muster the same popular appeal that the prominent but unavailable leaders could. The links of the anti-independence group with the old Proprietary party were strong; it set up as candidates for the new Philadelphia seats old Proprietary party leader Thomas Willing; Andrew Allen, who was son and son-in-law of William Allen and Governor John Penn; Alexander Wilcocks, proprietary supporter and a member of the city corporation; and Samuel Howell, a lapsed Quaker merchant. All the anti-Independent nominees had considerable influence and connections; they were wisely chosen.[19]

As in previous Philadelphia elections, not only the issues or the prominence of the candidates but mainly the political efforts of the competing parties determined the result. The parties needed a persuasive, arm-tugging canvass to get voters, however interested they might be in the issues and the candidates, to come to the polls and cast ballots. In 1776 the Quaker-Assembly-Proprietary party combination canvassed the Quakers diligently and, in the manner of the old White Oak allies of the Assembly party, went door-to-door to search out voters among the lower orders. The Independent party used two com-

18. *Four Letters on Interesting Subjects* (Philadelphia, 1776). Ryerson, *The Revolution Is Now Begun,* 166–73, summarizes the newspaper debates.

19. Ryerson, *The Revolution Is Now Begun,* 173; David Hawke, *In the Midst of a Revolution* (Philadelphia, 1961), 76. Independent party candidates were George Clymer, Frederick Kuhl, Owen Biddle, and Roberdeau.

mittees: the Philadelphia Committee of Observation, dominated by proindependence leaders and heavily staffed by artisans; and the Committee of Privates, representing and acting for the common soldier. These aided in recruiting the voters they affected to represent, but not as thoroughly as the elite bosses of the Assembly party organization had done in the past. The Independents seemed much less interested in getting out the vote; they expected that the ticket would win on the issues. Like the Patriotic Society in 1770–1772, they failed to see the need for hard canvassing. Christopher Marshall, a leader of the Independents, passed most of his time in meetings planning the ticket and on election day posted himself at the State House to distribute ballots for his side. He spent only a few hours out on the streets.[20]

The issues turned out the committed party voters. The cohesion indices for the supporters of each ticket are very high—0.988 for the Independent party and 0.987 for the anti-Independents. The Independent managers found voters who were strongly committed to their side, but they made little effort to canvass a decisive number and to bring them to the polls. They came close; fifty-two more straight ticket votes for the losing side would have elected their other three candidates. Only George Clymer of that side won, by a dozen votes over the lowest-ranking anti-independence candidate. An efficient political machine, thoroughly canvassing a city of less than two square miles, should have and did in the past bring out more voters than appeared in this election. From 1764 through 1766 the party managers had turned out from 61.9 to 82.5 percent of the eligible voters. The failure to turn out more than 56.7 percent of the electorate, a conspicuous neglect of tried-and-true electoral techniques, led the Independent party to defeat. By contrast, the mésalliance of Quaker pacifism and proprietary supporters' reverence for authority—two ancient enemies—found just enough renewed energy to elect three of its candidates, Allen, Howell, and Wilcocks, and temporarily block the rush toward independence. Later events would prove that the election result was not an accurate reflection of the sentiment of the Philadelphia constituency.[21]

The result in the back counties was the reverse of that in Philadelphia. Probably only two of the thirteen new back county seats were won by anti-Inde-

20. Christopher Marshall, Diary, Apr. 18, 21, 28, May 1, HSP. Hawke, *In the Midst of a Revolution*, 22–29, analyzes carefully the propaganda and tactics of both sides.

21. For the turnout, Appendix III. Vote totals were Howell, 941; Clymer and Allen, 923; Wilcocks, 921; Willing, 911. Roberdeau was last with 890. Mean for the anti-Independents was 924, for the other side, 905.

pendents. Nine of the new backcountry assemblymen were later active in the revolutionary provincial convention or the state government. Overall, they reflected the plurality of sentiment for independence. That the newly elected assemblymen very likely divided about ten to five for independence indicates that the idea of a final break had widespread appeal and probably the support of a clear plurality.[22]

The election of new members produced an even division in the House between the pro- and anti-independence assemblymen. The addition of ten new members to the incumbent pro-independence contingent and the return of another to the House brought that party's effective total to twenty-four or twenty-five. The anti-independence bloc was composed of eight of the Quaker antiresistance group, five antiresisters who had not voted in key 1775 roll calls, seven who followed John Dickinson in supporting resistance but opposing independence, and the five new anti-independence representatives. Eight other assemblymen were either absent or voted indeterminately.[23]

The advocates of independence, including the leaders of the Philadelphia Committee of Inspection, of the militia, and of the Committee of Privates, believed that the popular will had been frustrated rather than expressed in the election. Most discouraging was that their carefully produced propaganda campaign did not work in the city election; the people did not respond to reasoned, compelling arguments; they did not turn out en masse to support independence, while canvassers for the anti-independence side brought in nearly all possible sympathizers. Traditional attachments had even a greater hold in Chester and Bucks. Quaker leaders dominated politics constantly in these counties, and the coming of war had done little to shake their grip. Many Quakers had dropped out of politics, but not enough to permit the plurality that demanded independence to have its way. The people's will would have to be given expression outside the unrepresentative assembly and outside the electoral system that the old party leaders still managed.

---

22. Back county anti-Independents were a Quaker of York and proprietarian James Allen, brother of the new Philadelphia burgess Andrew Allen, from Northampton County. Ryerson, *The Revolution Is Now Begun*, 174, 226, argues that the backcountry was largely for independence. Hawke, *In the Midst of a Revolution*, 61–62, claims that when thirteen of these representatives signed a report, supporting the anti-independence Committee of Safety in its dispute with the captains of Pennsylvania's row galley navy, they were acting as "moderates" not Independents. On their post-1776 service, *Journal of the House of Representatives of the Commonwealth of Pennsylvania* (Philadelphia, 1782), 49.

23. *Pa. Votes*, June 8, Sept. 24, 1776.

To bring about the new government required considerable coordinated political activity. A carefully staged mass meeting attended by four thousand people generated revolutionary fervor in Philadelphia. Political leaders from the metropolis journeyed to the interior towns to rally support. The rallying of the electorate, the direct contacts, the canvassing for support that the anti-British and pro-independence group had previously disdained or halfheartedly attempted were now employed without stint. Had as much effort been spent in Philadelphia before the election for the additional assemblymen, had four thousand been turned out for the Independent party candidates instead of fewer than one thousand, the effort to implement a new government would have been unnecessary. Soon the call for a provincial conference to vote for independence and set in motion the formation of a new government rang out throughout Pennsylvania. The anti-Independents could not repeat their earlier electoral victory. They tried to solicit support but found it weak except in the Quaker strongholds of Bucks and Chester. By mid-June, 1776, the House was powerless; independence and a new government, fruits of a "mechanic revolution," were soon to replace the old order.[24]

With the triumph of the independence advocates the parties of Pennsylvania's late colonial period—the Assembly party and the Patriotic Society—came to an end. After the new state constitution was promulgated in September, 1776, two strong, competitive parties quickly formed, following the model of the Assembly and Proprietary parties of the 1760s. The great changes in Pennsylvania parties accelerated, rather than diminished, the new state's partisan spirit and habit that since 1739 had become ingrained in Pennsylvania's political culture. The electorate expected an annual partisan struggle, replete with propaganda and desperate canvassing. The party breakdown that occurred in 1770–1775 was only a temporary decline of organized partisanship. The new post-1776 parties would avidly contest elections, passing on the practices of fervent partisanship to their successors, the first national parties of the 1790s. Pennsylvania before and after 1776 led in developing party rivalry later characteristic of the nineteenth century.

William Smith, Jr., councillor and prominent Livingston party leader in New York, predicted in 1773 that partisanship there would travel the same road that the parties of New Jersey and Pennsylvania were to travel: decay and splintering. "Our Domestic Parties will probably die, & be swallowed up in the general Opposition to the Parliamentary Project of raising the Arm of

24. Ryerson, *The Revolution Is Now Begun*, 217–18.

Government by Revenue Laws," he asserted; the issues generated by imperial conflict would likely dwarf the party rivalry of Livingstons and DeLanceys. This prophecy was half correct, for one party did die. The other survived, in that its leaders and supporters remained connected, much as they had been in the colonial period, until after independence. Likewise, the surviving party generally maintained its ideological principles during this period.[25]

The Livingston party leaders were those first called upon to direct New York City's resistance to the dutiable tea in October, 1773. Chosen as members of the city Committee of Correspondence were Philip Livingston, Jr., Alexander McDougall, and perennial candidate John Morin Scott. DeLancey assemblymen were pointedly ignored. Of the twelve probable committee members, six had voted the Livingston ticket in 1769 and one had turned to that party in 1770; four were DeLancey adherents and one had not voted. No effort was made to balance this committee socially even though the mechanics showed force in the streets and at mass meetings. Merchants and lawyers, most people agreed, should continue to lead.[26]

The political imbalance on the committee quickly shifted even more to the Livingston side when the four DeLancey supporters quit the committee, as did one Livingston backer, for they feared violent opposition to landing the tea. It mattered not to the DeLancey partisans that perhaps three-fourths of the city's inhabitants approved of opposing the landing of the tea. They would not defy the government for the sake of popularity. The DeLanceyites returned to the cautious proadministration stance that characterized that party's history under Governors Cosby, Clarke, and DeLancey. When the potential for violence in the seaport was again nearing the boiling point, its leaders conveniently forgot that they had pushed hard against the Stamp Act and the Townshend duties. After its 1769 debacle, the Livingston side had advocated

25. William Smith, Jr., *Historical Memoirs*, ed. William H. W. Sabine (2 vols., 1956–58; rpr. New York, 1969–71), Oct. 13, 1773, I, 156. Launitz-Schürer, *Loyal Whigs and Revolutionaries*, 97, and Bernard Mason, *The Road to Independence: The Revolutionary Movement in New York, 1773–1777* (Lexington, Ky., 1966), 9, 41, make too much of this prediction. In this chapter I avoid the terms *conservative* and *radical*, used by Becker, *Political Parties in New York*, 184–85, 191, in a confusing manner, failing to delineate conservatism from loyalism; and also used by Countryman, *A People in Revolution*, 138.

26. Smith, *Historical Memoirs*, Dec. 17, 18, 1773, I, 161–62. The committee roster is in Mason, *Road to Independence*, 15, and includes Livingston voters or supporters Philip Livingston, Jr., Scott, McDougall, John and Samuel Broome, David Van Horne, and former DeLanceyite Isaac Sears. DeLanceyites were Isaac Low, Leonard Lispenard, Abram Walton, and Francis Lewis. John Lamb was the nonvoter. *N.Y.C. Poll List, 1769*.

the ideas of fair representation and ballot reform; it was wholly consistent in also advocating resistance to parliamentary infringements. It probably had better contact with the public pulse, for "Sears, McDougal & al" were believed to be plotting with "Mechanics at Beer-Houses." The ideological distance between the parties would widen as resistance intensified.[27]

When, in May, 1774, news of the severe punishment of Boston arrived, the Livingston side quickly allied with a self-proclaimed Committee of Mechanics, composed largely of its supporters, which also favored spirited resistance. Both the DeLanceyites, fearful of the Livingston anti-British stance and of a "mechanic revolution," and the Livingston-mechanic side put up rival slates of candidates for an expanded city Committee of Correspondence. The DeLanceyite slate included fifty city inhabitants, among whom DeLancey supporters outnumbered Livingston supporters about two to one. Its twenty-three incipient loyalists about equaled those of strong anti-British sentiment. The Livingston-mechanic ticket numbered twenty-five, was about evenly divided between the parties, and contained only five nominees who were later loyalists. DeLanceyite leaders dominated the mass meeting that chose their ticket, although the meeting added one Livingston-mechanic nominee to the list. The DeLancey majority on the committee then selected a Continental Congress delegation composed of three DeLancey supporters and two Livingston backers. The Livingston-mechanic group tried to substitute Leonard Lispenard and McDougall for two of the DeLanceyites and insisted on strong statements of resistance, but was unheeded. The mechanics temporarily lost control of the effort to oppose Britain. When a severe crisis loomed, the majority of "respectable" city inhabitants relied principally on the traditional DeLanceyite leadership, not on the Livingston and artisan upstarts.[28]

27. Smith, *Historical Memoirs*, Dec. 18, 22, 1773, I, 162–63; Becker, *Political Parties in New York,* 111.

28. Smith, *Historical Memoirs*, May 18–19, 1774, I, 186–87. Mason, *Road to Independence*, 23 n., 32 n., 39 n.; Becker, *Political Parties in New York*, 120 n., 123 n., 135 n., 198 n.; and *N.Y.C. Poll List, 1769*, indicate that the known members of the Committee of Mechanics were six Livingston and three DeLancey voters. The DeLancey ticket appears to have been composed of twenty DeLancey voters, twelve Livingston voters, and eighteen ticket-splitters or nonvoters. The Livingston-mechanic ticket contained eleven Livingston voters and nine DeLancey voters. Mason, *Road to Independence*, 27 n., counts thirty-seven DeLanceyites and fourteen Livingston supporters on the committee. DeLancey candidates for Congress were Isaac Low, John Alsop, and James Duane; delegate Philip Livingston, Jr., was Duane's wife's uncle and also uncle of the wife of the fifth delegate, John Jay. Launitz-Schürer, *Loyal Whigs and Revolutionaries,* 114–15, believes the two parties arranged a compromise. Mason, *Road to Independence,* 28 n., 31–35, doubts that any elec-

The DeLancey party also prevented the backcountry from becoming involved in the resistance efforts. That side controlled five assembly delegations from outside New York City, while the Livingston side controlled only two. The latter party, joined by the artisans, called for a Provincial Congress in July, 1774, in hopes that it could use such a meeting to direct the resistance movement throughout the colony, but the back counties showed no interest. In Poughkeepsie, town center for Dutchess County, the leading citizen, an Anglican lawyer who was an in-law of DeLanceyite assemblyman Leonard Van Kleek, influenced the townspeople to refrain from any action in response to the call for a congress, and he kept his town inactive until after the battles of Lexington and Concord. DeLancey supporters in the back counties relied on important Anglican contingents who evinced loyalist sympathies and on apathetic and apolitical small farmers and tenants who were reluctant to do anything.[29]

The results of the Continental Congress provided a rallying point for the Livingston-mechanic side. The Livingston leaders and the artisans demanded a new large Committee of Observation to enforce the Continental Association in New York City. The old Committee of Correspondence dissolved, and a committee of sixty members replaced it in November, 1774.[30] The new committee had thirty-one new members and twenty-nine who were retained from the fifty-one of the old committee. Of the new members, Livingston supporters outnumbered DeLancey supporters about two to one. This change probably gave the Livingston side a bare majority. The ideological and social composition of this new committee was significantly different from the old; it contained half the number of future loyalists (twelve) that the committee of fifty-one did, and it included three times as many artisans (fifteen) as did its predecessor.[31]

---

tion was actually held and believes that the Livingston side gave way to the DeLancey side for the sake of colonial unity. Becker, *Political Parties in New York*, 120–36, finds Livingston-mechanic behavior "inexplicable."

29. Becker, *Political Parties in New York*, 136–41, explains the inactivity of the back counties in ideological rather than partisan terms. Jonathan Clark, "The Problem of Allegiance in Revolutionary Poughkeepsie," in *Saints and Revolutionaries*, ed. Hall, Murrin, Tate, 288–89, 305; Tiedemann, "Communities in the Midst of the American Revolution," 58, 69; Philip Ranlet, *The New York Loyalists* (Knoxville, 1986), 141–42.

30. Duane to Samuel Chase, Dec. 29, 1774, Duane to Thomas Johnson, Dec. 24, 1774, Duane, "Notes for a Speech in Congress, [May 23–25, 1775], in Smith, ed., *Letters of Delegates to Congress*, I, 277–80, 280–82, 391–95; William Smith, Jr., to Philip Schuyler, Nov. 22, 1774, in Schuyler Papers, NYPL.

31. Becker, *Political Parties in New York*, 168; Mason, *Road to Independence*, 38 n., 39.

Back county response to the Continental Congress now became more enthusiastic for the Livingston side. Albany, Ulster, and Suffolk, in which that party held four, two, and one seats respectively, were the only counties outside the city to comply with the Association. In Queens and Westchester, where the other two Livingston assemblymen held seats, local leaders attempted to organize committees of observation. In the rural counties dominated by DeLanceyites almost nothing in support of the Congress was done, and in at least two of these counties loyalist leaders staged anti-Congress demonstrations. The basic political orientation of a county—Livingston or DeLancey—largely determined whether it would support Continental Congress resistance measures.[32]

The DeLanceyite-backcountry opposition to Congress unexpectedly gained its major triumph in the January, 1775, assembly session. The Livingston-mechanic side was confident after its gains in the city that, as William Smith, Jr., put it, "the Current will set all one Way for Liberty." DeLanceyite councillors and House leaders apparently agreed. Counting votes the evening of January 9, 1775, just before the session was to open, they anticipated that the nine Livingston partisans and five defectors, probably from Suffolk, Queens, Kings, Westchester, and Dutchess, would affirm support for Congress. Delegates from the northernmost counties would not attend this winter session, and the DeLancey side would muster only eleven supporters.[33]

Traditional politics proved to be stronger than either party had anticipated, for the DeLancey majority held together to push through the House separate petitions to king, Lords, and Commons that, unlike New Jersey's separate petition, sharply deviated from the statements of rights adopted by the Continental Congress. In vain did the Livingston leaders try to amend the petitions to echo the resolutions and petitions of the Congress. A solid bloc of fourteen DeLancey supporters never wavered from the party position through nineteen roll calls on the three petitions. Indeed, eight DeLancey members voted precisely the same on all roll calls that had to do with imperial matters. Of the twenty-one DeLancey partisans in the House, only two bolted to the opposition over imperial issues. The Livingston party was even more tightly knit—in one of thirty-eight roll calls one Livingston supporter voted with the DeLancey side; in every other instance it presented a phalanx of opposition.

32. Becker, *Political Parties in New York*, 169–73; and Countryman, *A People in Revolution*, 104–108, report back county events without reference to partisan affiliation.

33. Smith to Schuyler, Nov. 22, 1774, in Schuyler Papers, NYPL; Smith, *Historical Memoirs*, Jan. 10, 1775, I, 208.

But it was only five strong; two members went home perhaps in disgust at the majority's hostility to Congress' actions.[34]

For the first time in its long history, the DeLancey party rejected representing most of its constituents; its votes on imperial issues either defied them or took advantage of their apathy. The leaders of the party convinced their followers that the whig-loyalist position of compromise and moderation had to be substituted for the ideology of resistance. Whig-loyalism found British policy unjust but hesitated to take decisive or determined action against it. With the tide of public opinion running strong for determined resistance, the DeLancey leaders concluded that they had lost the allegiance of the populace, that their political careers were at an end if they could not bring their constituents to their viewpoint, and that if their ship were to swamp in this rip it would be with pro-British and proadministration flags flying high.[35]

As the DeLancey party maneuvered itself into political oblivion, its Livingston rivals, losers in the assembly roll calls, became victors in the contest for the support of the New York electorate. Now that the DeLanceyites had rendered the assembly useless, the Livingston leadership moved to replace it with a provincial convention that would elect suitable delegates to the Continental Congress. DeLanceyite leaders tried to block the convention elections; Frederick Philipse III and Isaac Wilkins failed to do so in Westchester, but Christopher Billop, lord of the manor of Bentley on Staten Island, succeeded. In late March and early April, 1775, six of the eight Livingston members of the assembly were elected to the convention, along with four former Livingston assemblymen and five other known Livingston supporters.[36] The

34. *N.Y. Votes,* Jan. 26, Feb. 16–17, 23, Mar. 3, 8, 24, 1775. Jack N. Rakove, *The Beginnings of National Politics: An Interpretive History of the Continental Congress* (New York, 1979), 67–68, for DeLanceyite James Duane's views.

35. For the term *whig-loyalist,* William Benton, *Whig-Loyalism: An Aspect of Political Ideology in the American Revolutionary Era* (Rutherford, 1969). The British bribed printer James Rivington and two Anglican clerics and were alleged to have paid assemblymen James DeLancey, Jr., Frederick Philipse III, and John Rapalje one thousand guineas each for their votes (Mason, *Road to Independence,* 50–53). Launitz-Schürer, *Loyal Whigs and Revolutionaries,* 143–44, notes the arguments against the likelihood of bribery.

36. *Am. Arch.,* II, 351–57; Smith, *Historical Memoirs,* Mar. 18, 1775, I, 214. Launitz-Schürer, *Loyal Whigs and Revolutionaries,* 146–55, is best on the convention. Livingston delegates to the convention included Philip Schuyler, Abraham Ten Broeck, Woodhull, Charles DeWitt, George Clinton, Zebulon Seaman, Philip Livingston, Jr., Robert R. Livingston, Henry Wisner, Lewis Morris III, Abraham Yates, Jay, McDougall, Isaac Roosevelt, and Abraham Brasher. The only DeLancey partisan from the assembly to be elected was Simon Boerum of Kings, who had deserted his bloc on the petition issue. Former DeLancey supporters Duane, Lispenard, and Francis Lewis

convention selected as Continental Congress delegates seven Livingston partisans, three DeLancey deserters, and one DeLanceyite who opposed independence. The minority party in the assembly had in a few weeks transformed itself into the majority party in New York's extralegal governing bodies.[37]

News of the fighting in Massachusetts slowed the ascendance of the Livingston-mechanic-Liberty Boys alliance, but only temporarily. Its tickets for the elections in April, 1775, to a Provincial Congress and an enlarged city Committee of Observation were defeated. Livingston partisans still outnumbered the DeLancey side in the Congress delegation and the city committee, but there were six future loyalists in the former and nineteen out of one hundred on the new committee. From the back counties only five known Livingston supporters won election—three fewer than had been in the provincial convention. New Yorkers were uncertain about electing strong anti-British advocates when war was looming. By October, however, they saw that they needed activist leadership. The Provincial Congress, sprinkled with lukewarm DeLanceyites and timid merchants, proved too cautious. Pressure from anti-British constituents compelled it to call a new election in October, 1775. It broadened the suffrage outside New York County (but retained the *viva voce* poll) to gain both wide popular support and new delegates who were more avidly prorevolutionary. This broader electorate, reacting to the poor performance of the previous Congress, chose seven known Livingston supporters, including two family members, and retired all known DeLanceyites.[38]

Because the Provincial Congress was firmly in the hands of the avid revolutionaries, Governor William Tryon turned to the assembly as a possible rival to the extralegal government, hoping that its majority might take up the conciliatory proposals of Lord North, which had arrived after the last assembly had been prorogued. Because the septennial term of the House would expire in early 1776, Tryon, on January 2, called a new election.[39]

The revolutionaries had no major objection to the resuscitation of the

had probably deserted by this time. The only other known DeLancey partisans elected to the convention were Alsop and Abraham Walton.

37. *Am. Arch.*, II, 355–57. Delegates were Philip and Robert R. Livingston, Schuyler, Clinton, Morris, Wisner, Jay; DeLancey deserters Boerum, Duane, Lewis; and Alsop, whose views are noted in Ranlet, *New York Loyalists*, 7.

38. Smith, *Historical Memoirs*, Apr. 29, 1775, I, 222–23; *Am. Arch.*, II, 1241–42, III, 580, IV, 384; Becker, *Political Parties in New York*, 211, 230–32; *N.Y.C. Poll List, 1769.*

39. Smith, *Historical Memoirs*, Dec. 4–31, 1775, I, 251–56; Mason, *Road to Independence*, 129–31.

assembly, with a transfusion of Livingston blood. John Jay and Alexander Mc-Dougall, although believing that a convention with full constitutional authority should replace the House, realized that the populace was not ready for such an extremity. James Duane predicted to his father-in-law that the "Whiggs" would win all but two counties. As soon as the dissolution became known, Duane's new allies in the Livingston party began campaigning. Broadsides and newspaper articles exhorted the inhabitants to choose candidates who would support both resistance and political reforms. The Liberty Boys controlled ticket selection in the city, nominating three of the present Continental Congress delegates and McDougall. The latter's candidacy symbolized how immensely New York politics had changed in the six years since he had been jailed by the House for his political views. The pro-British DeLancey merchant group in the city dared not put up an opposing ticket; it had to accept Congress delegate John Alsop as its one representative. Though Duane expected Queens and Richmond to vote loyalist, only Richmond returned both DeLancey incumbents. The only other incumbent DeLanceyite elected was Dirck Brinkerhoff of Dutchess, who had served in the first Provincial Congress. Among the new assemblymen, only Alsop and Oliver DeLancey, Jr., of Westchester borough adhered to that party. Five DeLancey assemblymen faced thirteen known Livingston supporters and ten others who were undoubtedly prorevolutionary. Six Livingston incumbents; the vindicated Philip Livingston, Jr.; Robert R. Livingston, Jr., who won back his father's old seat in Dutchess; Lewis Morris III, in the seat held by the Frederick Philipses for fifty years; McDougall; Livingston nephew-in-law Jay; Abraham and Robert Yates from Albany and Schenectady; nine members of the second Provincial Congress; and one county committee chairman constituted the "Whigg" bloc. Small wonder that the House never met; the Tryon-DeLancey plan to outflank the Provincial Congress had completely failed. Now only the British army could help the New York loyalists.[40]

The Livingston party retained control of the third Provincial Congress; belatedly, cautiously, but surely moved toward independence; and participated

40. Duane to Robert Livingston, Jr., Jan. 25, 1776, in Duane Papers, NYHS; Jay to McDougall, Dec. 8, 1775, in Smith, ed., *Letters of Delegates to Congress*, II, 457; Smith, *Historical Memoirs*, Jan. 8, 1776, I, 256–57; New York *Mercury*, Feb. 19, 1776; *Am. Arch.*, IV, 383–86; Mason, *Road to Independence*, 130–31. Loyalist-dominated Queens did not elect any delegates to the second Congress. In January, 1776, its loyalists were disarmed and arrested, and it elected to the third Congress in May, 1776, the same men it elected to this assembly. Becker, *Political Parties in New York*, 242, 250, attaches little importance to the assembly election.

in writing a state constitution that instituted a property qualification for new voters in New York City and promised eventual ballot reform. Its members remained prominent throughout the Revolution and the 1780s. Of the fifty men from New York City who served in the Provincial Congress or state legislature between 1775 and 1786, twenty-five had been Livingston voters of 1769, eight had been DeLancey voters, and four had split their ballots. During the first years of the new state, Livingston leaders George Clinton and Pierre Van Cortlandt were respectively governor and lieutenant governor, and Robert R. Livingston, Jr., was chancellor. All the Livingston partisans elected to the House in 1768, 1769, and 1776, except two, held high office in the state or in the military forces during and after the Revolution. Only two old DeLancey assemblymen held high office; at least fourteen became loyalists.[41] The Livingston party ideology and common bonds developed in the electoral and assembly battles of the colonial period bridged the calamitous war years and helped to shape New York State politics. Political historians of New York from Carl Becker in 1909 to Edward Countryman in 1981 have not sufficiently noted the continuing influence and significant contribution of this colonial political party.

The Livingston party structure could not remain precisely as it had been, with governmental forms, interest groups, and major issues almost all entirely different from the pre-1776 world. Some old Livingston leaders now contested against each other for office. New legislative and electoral parties formed. The artisans became an interest separate from the Livingston leadership in May, 1776, splitting on the issues of independence and suffrage under the new government. Throughout the 1780s and later the artisans alternately coalesced with and challenged former Livingston leaders in New York City. The "mechanic revolution" had achieved less political power for New York artisans than for those in Pennsylvania. Regardless of the fundamental, neces-

---

41. Countryman, *A People in Revolution*, 313–25; *N.Y.C. Poll List, 1769*. Zebulon Seaman, who changed his name to Williams to obtain a maternal inheritance, is listed by Alexander C. Flick, *Loyalism in New York During the American Revolution* (New York, 1901), 32. Jacobus Mynderse remains untraced. Dirck Brinkerhoff and John Coe were the DeLanceyite survivors. Only 5.8 percent of New York City voters in 1769 could be identified as loyalists from a sample derived from Lorenzo F. Sabine, *Biographical Sketches of Loyalists of the American Revolution, with an Historical Essay* (2 vols.; 1864; rpr. Port Washington, 1966); and from Gregory Palmer, *Biographical Sketches of Loyalists of the American Revolution* (Westport, 1984). This offers some needed statistical confirmation to the view of Ranlet, *New York Loyalists*, 186, that loyalism was not strong in New York. Chi-square calculation for the relationship between loyalism and voting the straight DeLancey ticket was 0.11, insignificant at the 0.05 level with 1 df.

sary realignment of partisan groups, the colonial experience bequeathed to the new state a basic party framework and partisan habits that were readily adapted to the new postrevolutionary situation.[42]

By the end of the Revolution partisanship was deeply implanted in the political life of the middle states. Voters there would now expect from elected officials an ideological position shared by a group of supporters, consistent voting in the legislature, and efforts to solicit constituent backing. Those of the wealthier classes would contribute financial support to election efforts. Officeholders and political workers would propagandize the cause and search out voters to incorporate more and more different groups. Quakers, loyalists, and others who dropped out at the Revolution were too different ideologically; Germans, artisans, and farmers who supported the anti-British effort, although socially different, were recruited and welcomed. The strength of the parties in the electorate increased during the 1760s and remained high during the turmoil of the 1770–1776 period. The cohesion indices of the elections in Philadelphia County in 1765 and 1766, in Philadelphia city in 1776, and in Queens and Dutchess in 1768, and the poll list for the New York City election of 1769 show that partisanship remained fervent and was spreading in those colonies. The elections of committees in Philadelphia and New York, 1774–1776, illustrate that the middling artisan group was becoming more politicized. Although their degree of partisanship cannot be evaluated precisely, New Jersey inhabitants were both participating heavily and demanding an enlarged suffrage.[43] The integration of new members and the broadening and strengthening of party bases ensured the survival of the partisan system and charted the way for its activities in later national politics.

42. New York *Mercury,* Apr. 8, 1776; "Mechanics in Union," untitled broadside (New York, 1776); "The Watchman," *To the Inhabitants of the City and County of New York* (New York, 1776); "The Sentinel," *To the Inhabitants of the City and County of New York* (New York, 1776); "A Sober Citizen," *To the Inhabitants of the City and County of New York* (New York, 1776); Mason, *Road to Independence,* 149–65. Staughton Lynd, "The Mechanics in New York Politics," *Labor History,* V (1964), 232, overstates the possibility of mechanic-elite confrontation. Countryman, *A People in Revolution,* 196–97, 248, 261, 269, 271, 288; Main, *Political Parties Before the Constitution,* 124. Main and Countryman agree that a two-party system operated in New York in the 1780s but differ on precisely what the parties were.

43. For the cohesion index, see Appendix III. Weaker partisanship was evident in the cohesion indices for Chester and Bucks elections of 1765 and for Westchester of 1768. There are no sufficient tabulations of New Jersey elections in this period.

Conclusion

One should not assume from the vigorous middle-colony political activity recounted here that politics was the most important aspect of life in these provinces. Making a living—working the farm, expanding one's trade, keeping accounts, providing professional services—and tending to family responsibilities all made peremptory demands on people's time. Leisure activities that did not require preparation, attendance, detailed work, long conferences, public contact, contention with associates, travel in bad weather, and the painful thrust of responsibility or blame were undoubtedly more attractive than was politics. People attended religious services more commonly than they did political events. Some undoubtedly shirked, just as some deserted in wartime or avoided volunteering. Some undoubtedly were repelled, for political activity at best was contentious and upsetting, at worst bitter, embarrassing, or even brawling. The hard-fought elections—requiring planning, canvassing, mass meetings, patronage, propaganda, treats, and threats; the election day turnout of on average from 40 to 70 percent of the qualified voters in middle-colony districts; and the organized, consistent legislative coalitions demonstrate that public attention to politics was, despite all impediments, widespread. Partisan politics in the middle colonies was not merely a corrupt juggle rigged by bribery, a fearful response by an intimidated electorate, or an empty ritual in which the lower orders danced to tunes played by their betters; it was meaningful, purposeful, and rewarding to many of the participants regardless of their economic circumstances. The lower orders might vote as their powerful neighbors advised them, but they paid scant attention to deferential expectations of the colonial elite. The start that the middling sort got in politics in the middle colonies enabled them to take a greatly enlarged and more independent role.[1]

Partisanship was related to and affected by the economic ideas and practices of the colonists, yet it was not simply a superstructural appendage to the economy. It grew from religious and ethnic affiliations yet went beyond the promotion of ethnocultural purity. It acted as a vehicle and amplifier for ide-

---

1. For voter percentages for districts and counties, see Appendix III.

ological positions yet remained apart from unduly narrow viewpoints. It was part of all of these other aspects of colonial life yet stood alone as a separate compartment of activity.

The effect of economic ideas and conditions on middle-colony political groups was not starkly deterministic but indirect and muted. Continued economic growth and the development of a large market for imported consumer goods helped to increase the size of merchant and landholder elites and to develop an economically diverse society. The middle-colony farmer, mechanic, merchant, lawyer, or landholder, determined to thrive in the growing competitive market economy, believed that his political capital was his vote, which he should spend wisely, just as he shrewdly traded the fruits of his labor. He might ally with others to bring about some policy implementation or change, just as he joined with his hands and servants or his neighbors to get cargoes to port or crops to market. The small farmer who was only tangentially involved in the world of expanding individual enterprise was nevertheless often drawn into the political network by his more assertive neighbors. Local community ties and community loyalties led some middle-colony voters to the polls, but the ties to political views and to parties extending beyond the isolated locality were probably more influential by 1776.[2]

The specific short-range economic changes of the 1700–1776 period—cycles of wartime prosperity and postwar recession, credit crises and business failures in Britain and America—and the emerging structural problems including increases in wealth inequalities and the growth of a poor class in the cities, did not create parties and added only slightly to the intensity of political battles. Competition in the marketplace did not provoke undying rivalries of elite against mass or merchant against artisan. Indeed, it inspired principally interchange and only infrequently antagonism. As individuals or particular interests coalesced toward a shared position in the larger partisan body, they discovered views they held in common with others and through a process analogous to market bargaining arrived at mutually satisfactory policy positions. Because middle-colony parties strove to build effective combinations, they brought in those of diverse economic interests. Not all were welcome—the unfree could not qualify, nor could many of the poorer sort. Farmers and artisans, however, expanded their roles. Although at first ma-

2. C. B. McPherson, *The Political Theory of Possessive Individualism: Hobbes to Locke* (Oxford, 1962), esp. 267–73. James T. Lemon, "Comment on James A. Henretta's 'Families and Farms: *Mentalities* in Pre-Industrial America,'" *WMQ*, 3rd ser., XXXVII (1980), 688–96; Joyce Appleby, "The Social Origins of American Revolutionary Ideology," *JAH*, LXIV (1977–78), 949–51.

nipulated as demonstrators and vote-chasers, by the 1770s they were interacting on a more equal basis with elite leaders, participating in political realignments, and obtaining a larger share of offices.[3]

The example of the artisans illustrates that partisanship was liveliest in the large urban areas, though even small Perth Amboy could have a hot election. In cities party leaders crossed paths and figurative swords constantly. Propaganda attacks at election time were a daily bill of fare at taverns. City dwellers harbored far greater political antagonisms toward their neighbors than did the more isolated inhabitants of placid rural communities. Because of these antagonisms, because merchants and lawyers were prepared to spend cash on vigorous political campaigns, and because the economic prominence and educational attainments of city political leaders helped to make them legislative leaders, the city contests were more important than those of the backcountry. It would, however, be an error to assume that the backcountry was merely a cipher in partisan calculations. The hurly-burly and din of the market penetrated rural areas in both economic and political contexts. Back counties usually nominated candidates without central direction, but party managers from the central districts often coordinated crucial campaigns and organized canvassing throughout the colony. Very important political battles were fought outside the cities and towns—for instance, in Bucks and Lancaster, Pennsylvania; in Hunterdon and Gloucester, New Jersey; and in Queens and Westchester, New York. The backcountry often held the key to politics; in Pennsylvania it was the hotbed of independence sentiment and in New Jersey the base of the opposition group.

Economic factors provided much of the basis for political activity, but the motivation for and the direction of party politics were largely the products of ideology, particularly that associated with religious denominations. Middle-colony partisanship grew up nurtured by religious diversity. Unfriendly competition between these groups led many of them into partisan activity. Ethnocultural differences and rivalries aroused partisan passions, inspired and channeled organized politicking, and brought voters to the polls and demonstrators into the streets. During this period ethnically and religiously exclusive communities tore down many of the barriers between themselves and outside society and in a partisan spirit readily allied with or took

---

3. Gary B. Nash, "Artisans and Politics in Eighteenth-Century Philadelphia," in *Origins of Anglo-American Radicalism*, ed. Jacob and Jacob, 162–82, emphasizes the economic motivation of artisans.

up the cudgels against neighboring communities. Religious groups generally did not believe that political activity violated strict confessional standards; they participated with only occasional restraint. As religious and ethnic groups grew more self-conscious and active, the elite political strategists, by balancing tickets and by arousing these groups against their traditional adversaries, engineered their incorporation into the parties.[4]

Parties used ideological appeals to attract those who were not members of defined groups, whose enthusiasm was not generated by a special interest but had to be cultivated. They shifted from economic to ideological appeals when they found the latter to be more persuasive. Parties that employed a strong religious basis to their campaigns broadened their appeal by emphasizing ideology. Groups that forwarded particular economic demands tried to show that these were for the good of society at large by appropriating applicable ideological principles. Whig ideological principles received generally strong endorsement and widespread subscription, though seriousness of commitment varied greatly among individual political leaders. The major promoters of whig ideas were the oppositionist political groups, particularly the Livingston party and the Quaker-Assembly parties. Administration sides were less consistent in their adherence to such ideas but did proclaim that they too were Whigs when it served their purposes. Both the DeLancey and Livingston sides in the hard-fought 1760s elections in New York asserted that they were the true defenders of liberty, as did the Assembly and Proprietary parties of Pennsylvania in the middle of that decade.[5]

Partisanship in the middle colonies made an important contribution by giving candidates and voters political orientation in times of crisis and perplexity. When a middle-colony inhabitant enlisted in a partisan cause he was seeking a better definition of his place in society. The components that contributed to partisanship—religion, ethnicity, region, occupation, wealth—were the principal definers of place in the early years of colonization, but as society became more complex, these categories appeared too exclusive for many citizens. By the 1760s political group identification had become meaningful for a significant proportion of the electorate. As political issues became more salient with the growth of American resistance to Britain, parties served more and more to assist middle colonials to find their places. By the early

4. Schwartz, "*Mixed Multitude*," provides a different interpretation of religious group relations in Pennsylvania.

5. Bonomi, "Middle Colonies," 85, suggests that middle-colony politics was simply a contest for office.

1770s voters would readily deem themselves DeLanceyites, or supporters of the Patriotic Society, or backers of the New Jersey opposition side. The intensity of identification varied, but in many cases, particularly that of the DeLanceys and Livingstons, it served to tag supporters with ideological leanings to which they adhered through the crises of 1774–1776. The acceptance of partisanship as identification accompanied the broadening of political groups to encompass and even supplant other categories of social groupings. When the two consummate middle-colony political bosses, Joseph Galloway and Samuel Purviance, Jr., in 1766 separately referred to "our Party," each meant that he and his supporters were members in common and believed themselves identified by the organization.[6] Although elite lawyers and merchant leaders did not consider White Oaks or Liberty Boys to be their equals, their party also belonged to the people who worked and voted for it. Middle-colony parties functioned as integrators for individual demands, community needs, ethnic protections, religious views, and traditional principles, some or all of which the individual member of the party could appropriate as defining himself.

The ideal political type in the middle colonies was not a Country party gentleman who virtuously and disinterestedly donated his efforts to public service. Middle colonists believed that there was no essential difference between the ideal disinterested political leader and the partisan acting from enlightened self-interest. The truly disinterested person was likely to be a rare specimen; those of enlightened self-interest populated political landscapes. The latter could serve the polity just as effectively and fairly as could the supposedly disinterested person, provided that his interest was truly enlightened, not rapacious or bigoted. A James Alexander or Israel Pemberton, Jr., could be greedy for land or shortchange creditors and at the same time promote whiggish political principles. Not subscribing to the perfectionist view of political man but also unconvinced that only unscrupulous, cunning, or graspingly ambitious representatives could best check governors of the same ilk, middle-colony voters were willing to settle for political leaders who attended to their own interests but also gave the public good high priority.

Assemblymen in each colony believed party grouping to be a meaningful organizing principle for the lower houses. They found continued allegiance

---

6. Patricia U. Bonomi, *Under the Cope of Heaven: Religion, Society, and Politics in Colonial America* (New York, 1986), 179 and n. 49, notes Purviance's "modern conception of political organization and electioneering."

to a legislative bloc functional and comfortable and increasingly through the latter part of the eighteenth century committed themselves to a common bond with their like-minded colleagues. The proportion of assemblymen changing sides declined over the forty years before 1776 in both New York and New Jersey—from 12.2 to 5.9 percent in New Jersey and from 26.1 to 15.3 percent in New York. In the relatively small legislatures of these colonies members could not readily escape or ignore the persuasive efforts of the House leaders. Nor could they dodge inquiries of constituents by pleading that they had little influence among many members. They could not easily remain neutral and noncommittal but were compelled to be involved in partisan contention.[7]

Partisan differences boiled over out of the assemblies to heat up the electorate. Detailed election reports, poll books, and cohesion indices calculated from tallies for thirteen Pennsylvania elections, eight New York elections, and two New Jersey elections show strong partisanship. For five of the eight other elections for which complete voting figures are available, the cohesion indices and poll books show a moderate partisanship. No election returns for any known contested poll show a disorganized electorate that was uninfluenced by some party electioneering.[8] The electorate fairly consistently held to partisan groupings, it remained alert and receptive to political intelligence, and some members undertook specialized tasks at election time. Tradition dominated many electoral districts. Three or four in each colony rarely if ever deviated from their partisan positions, electing men of much the same stance time after time. These districts were not monolithic in their political affiliation, for there is evidence of several hard-fought contests in them, but the winning side was almost always the incumbent partisan group. In other districts—the majority of them—where the political pendulum swung more widely, parties appealed to particular groups that they thought would be friendly. The success of these appeals in part depended on specific circumstances, but each party could usually maintain the allegiance of a core of support that it had assembled over the years. In those districts where contests were regular, voters got into the party habit. Partisan voters expected to be reassured by their side's propaganda, to be canvassed, and to be led to the polls

7. See Robert Zemsky, *Merchants, Farmers, and River Gods: An Essay on Eighteenth Century American Politics* (Boston, 1971), 290–99, for the different mode of operation of a large colonial legislature. Sidney Verba, *Small Groups and Political Behavior: A Study of Leadership* (Princeton, 1961), 22–26; A. Paul Hare, *Handbook of Small Group Research* (2nd ed.; New York, 1976), 24–40.

8. For the cohesion index and election tallies, see Appendix III.

by their local leaders; they participated in large numbers when party managers used these techniques. They saw these not as intrusions on their time but as part of their obligation to the community. Electors did not want their votes scattered in the wind; they wanted to cast them efficiently, based on the direction or suggestion of a party. Seldom were large numbers of voters ignorant of election issues. In crucial elections middle-colony voters were deliberately made partisan and grouped themselves behind candidates with whom they identified: during these campaigns parties were firmly in the electorate.

Middle-colony parties were surprisingly competitive and enduring. The competition flagged at times but soon revived. In Pennsylvania it was squelched by the strong dominant party until issues mobilized the competition. In New York the ineptitude of Governor Clinton caused the collapse of party rivalry, but it reappeared after his departure. In New Jersey imperial controversy brought the opposition back after its decline in the early 1760s. In no case did complete one-party domination or chaotic fragmentation prevail for long. In New Jersey both administration and opposition parties were continuous throughout the forty years before the Revolution. The Quaker-Assembly parties and the Philipse-DeLancey parties exhibited like continuity. The realignments of the late 1730s, the mid-1750s, and the early 1770s were much like those of later American politics, giving renewed strength and inspiration to one of the contending parties. Only when war with Britain broke out and the issues became overpowering, when in New Jersey and Pennsylvania 40 to 50 percent of the assemblymen retired from politics at the coming of the Revolution, did parties disintegrate or basically change form.

The middle-colony example induced other states to refine partisan practices as their new polities developed after the Revolution. Except for Rhode Island in the 1750s and 1760s, other colonies did not experience partisanship to the extent that New York, New Jersey, and Pennsylvania did. No other colony had such long-enduring party conflicts. In others, legislative blocs were not so clearly polarized or continuous, elections were not so heartily contested, partisan techniques were not so finely formulated. By the end of the 1780s, legislatures and electorates in the other states in emulation of their middle-state neighbors developed parties of the same general character. In each state, legislative blocs established policy positions, though Massachusetts was the only state besides the middle states and Rhode Island to exhibit party organization. Legislative blocs appeared in the Confederation Congress, but they had little connection to the strong state parties of Pennsylvania and New York or to the blocs in the other states. Even if the Congress blocs were more than fluid, small, and primitive, as historian Jack N. Rakove has characterized them, they were short-lived and without popular bases. National political parties would have to be grounded in popular electoral contests and in state organizations, just as middle-colony parties had thrust down their roots.[9]

Although historians disagree on precisely when and on what issues the first battle lines of national partisanship became most clearly drawn in Congress, there is no doubt that legislative parties were contending by the mid-1790s. These parties derived their modes of action and styles of conduct not from the blocs of the Confederation Congress but from the examples of the colonial and state legislatures. Commonly held views forged strong bonds among congressmen of very different origins, constituent bases, and perceptions. Information channeled to constituents tied them to the partisan frameworks. Party newspapers trumpeted the virtues of one side and castigated the foibles of the other. None of this would have been out of place in the earlier middle-colony systems, with their legislators firmly committed to partisan sides, their distribution of speeches and other propaganda to voters, and such party organs as the *Pennsylvania Chronicle*. Through the Federalist and Jeffersonian periods the middle states continued to predominate in party competitiveness. By the late 1790s New York City and Philadelphia had the most advanced party organizations, though their two-party systems languished by 1820. New Jersey partisan activity increased more slowly, but by 1812 its party leaders developed election machinery to a high point. Only Massachusetts and Maryland exhibited election campaigns and partisan organization that equaled or surpassed those in the middle states.[10]

9. Sydney V. James, *Colonial Rhode Island: A History* (New York, 1975), 294–313, discusses the partisan electoral tactics of the Ward and Hopkins groups. David Curtis Skaggs, *Roots of Maryland Democracy, 1753–1776* (Westport, 1973), 20–24, 89, 92–95, though employing the terms *Court* and *Country* parties, reports a limited franchise, gentry domination, and no electoral partisanship. Formisano, *Transformation of Political Culture*, 26–27, finds little party development in colonial Massachusetts, agreeing with Van Beck Hall, *Politics Without Parties: Massachusetts, 1780–1791* (Pittsburgh, 1972). John G. Kolp, "The Dynamics of Electoral Competition in Pre-Revolutionary Virginia," *WMQ*, 3rd ser., XLIX (1992), 660–65, finds electoral competition and voter turnout declining in the 1750–1775 period. For developments in the 1780s, Main, *Political Parties Before the Constitution*, 398. Rakove, *Beginnings of National Politics*, 248, 324. In contrast, H. James Henderson, *Party Politics in the Continental Congress* (New York, 1974), 350–51, delineates three periods—1775–1780, 1780–1784, and 1784–1788—in which different blocs formed and dominated.

10. Hoadley, *Origins of American Political Parties*, 187–91, finds true parties in Congress after

The mass political parties of the Jackson era owed much to their prerevolutionary forerunners; these tendencies of the earlier period became the heart and soul of the party systems of the nineteenth century. Middle-colony partisanship played a large part in generating what historian Joel H. Silbey calls the partisan imperative, the disposition of nineteenth-century Americans to see politics wholly in partisan terms. Legislative blocs became hardened by party labeling—sometimes using family names as did middle-colony parties—and by party discipline in roll calls. Party leaders became more adept at sustaining party regularity in committee formation and in legislative voting, though models and precedents can be found in series of middle-colony roll calls that were as lockstep as those in nineteenth-century legislatures.[11] The party in the electorate likewise became a very disciplined organization. Party labeling served ubiquitously as an important badge of identification; Mark Twain in *Tom Sawyer, Detective,* portrayed Tom and Huck Finn being questioned closely as to whether the deaf and dumb stranger was "Baptis' or Methodis', Whig or Democrat." The broadening of the electoral base, which some earlier middle-colony politicians would have found appalling and others would have welcomed, meant primarily that more new men had to be incorporated into the political structure, and more rapidly, than had been slowly and cautiously absorbed by the colonial partisan groups. The middle-colony parties had managed to incorporate them quite effectively as long as the new recruits and the old elite shared generally common views. The strong national parties in the second party system combined interest groups in much

---

1796. Ronald P. Formisano, "Federalists and Republicans: Parties, Yes—Systems, No," in *The Evolution of American Electoral Systems,* ed. Paul Kleppner *et al.* (Westport, 1981), 52, 55, 66–68, 73, is skeptical of the sophistication of partisan activity in this period. Alan Taylor, " 'The Art of Hook and Snivey': Political Culture in Upstate New York During the 1790s," *JAH,* LXXIX (1992–93), 1379, notes the role and limitations of parties there. For other states see Bohmer, "The Maryland Electorate and the Concept of a Party System in the Early National Period," 151; Norman K. Risjord, *Chesapeake Politics, 1781–1800* (New York, 1978); and James H. Broussard, "Party and Partisanship in American Legislatures: The South Atlantic States," *Journal of Southern History,* XLIII (1977), 45–46.

11. Joel H. Silbey, *The Partisan Imperative: The Dynamics of American Politics Before the Civil War* (New York, 1985), 55–56. William G. Shade, "Political Pluralism and Party Development: The Creation of a Modern Party System, 1815–1852," in *Evolution of American Electoral Systems,* ed. Kleppner, 80, notes use of family names. See Peter Swenson, "The Influence of Recruitment on the Structure of Power in the U.S. House, 1870–1940," *Legislative Studies Quarterly,* VII (1982), 1–36, on partisan roll calls.

the same manner as did their predecessors. Very large proportions of the qualified voted in both colonial and nineteenth-century elections. The same proportion of white adult males turned out in the hotly contested Queens election of 1761 as did in the presidential election of 1828—56.3 percent; in the colonial election this was 87 percent of the qualified voters. Eighty to 90 percent of the qualified turned out in two New Jersey elections in 1772, the Philadelphia County election of 1765, and the Lancaster election of 1742; these equaled the high turnouts in the 1840 presidential contest and in later nineteenth-century elections.[12] Middle-colony politicians and the more sophisticated party organizations of the later period produced large voter turnouts because their strategies and techniques were similar.

Nineteenth-century mass parties had no greater capacity for endurance than did middle-colony parties; they also experienced realignment at critical intervals. The Whigs lasted some twenty years—about the same length of time as the Franklin-Galloway Assembly party in Pennsylvania and a shorter period than the Philipse-DeLancey party in New York. Party realignments of the 1850s, 1890s, and 1930s were manifestly the results of grave crises or dislocations, just as were middle-colony realignments of the 1750s and 1770s. Neither these earlier parties nor the modern Democrats and Republicans have been impervious to major pressures from outside. Modern parties are undoubtedly deeper rooted and probably able to withstand shocks that would have overturned the earlier organizations, but the difference is one of degree, not of kind. Sometimes middle-colony parties succumbed to hurricanes, but they, like modern counterparts, weathered moderate storms with little trouble. In foul weather they battened the hatches and, when the blow was over, put on full sail again, just as do late twentieth-century parties.

12. Gienapp, " 'Politics Seems to Enter into Everything,'" 15–69; Whitman H. Ridgway, *Community Leadership in Maryland, 1790–1840: A Comparative Analysis of Power in Society* (Chapel Hill, 1979), 15–16, 29, 100–111. William N. Chambers, *Political Parties in a New Nation: The American Experience, 1776–1809* (New York, 1963), 32, notes that roughly 25 percent of adult white males voted before 1798 and 26.5 percent voted in the presidential election of 1824. There were important state variations; Risjord, *Chesapeake Politics*, 519, finds about 70 percent adult white male participation in crucial elections in one county, 1797–1800. Between 1840 and 1900 presidential election turnout ranged from 69.6 to 81.8 percent (U.S. Bureau of the Census, *Historical Statistics of the United States, Colonial Times to 1970* [Bicentennial ed.; Washington, D.C., 1975], Pt. 2, pp. 1071–72; Kleppner, *The Third Electoral System*). Walter Dean Burnham, "The Appearance and Disappearance of the American Voter," in *Electoral Participation: A Comparative Analysis*, ed. Richard Rose (Beverly Hills, 1980), 46–48, 67–68, discounts the claim that electoral fraud accounts for large-scale voter participation in this period.

The principal difference between the middle-colony party and the mass party of nineteenth-century America was organization. Professionals now ran a structured institution that functioned continuously, not only at election time. These organizations were more sophisticated and disciplined than were the loosely combined parties that middle-colony leaders geared up several weeks before election day. Their bosses, who were party leaders first and officeholders secondarily, operated a much more efficient machine than did Peter R. Livingston, Thomas Wharton, or Richard Smith, Jr. Yet these earlier amateurs, for short periods, mobilized passive constituents into active partisan workers and voters, using some of the same techniques that nineteenth-century bosses employed.

The "political church," as Paul Kleppner has termed the parties of the late nineteenth century, developed from the middle-colony connection between partisanship and religion. Parties continued to draw their membership from those of certain religious dispositions, just as middle-colony parties had done. By the 1870s one side moralized about drink, condemned its opponents for trying to control the educational system, and generally roused the righteous against some evil. The other defended local or states' rights against government interference. Party zealots demanded almost the same faith commitment as did religious proselytizers. The Great Depression of the twentieth century injected crucial economic issues into politics, which overshadowed ethnocultural ones but never completely erased them. The religious and moralistic dimension of politics has remained important in the late twentieth century.[13]

The partisan system that originated in the mid-eighteenth century in the middle colonies still retains its functional relevance to the modern state. Wealthy leaders employ more sophisticated methods than did Galloway, Thomas Wharton, Amos Dodge, or Oliver DeLancey in the "broad way" but still seek out individual voters. Propaganda efforts build on middle-colony precedents but far surpass them in selling candidates and evoking positive responses to emotional issues. A considerable proportion of the electorate claims to support parties by volunteer work, financial contributions, and other activities.[14] This long-lived American institution is not likely soon to be con-

13. Paul Kleppner, *Who Voted? The Dynamics of Electoral Turnout, 1870–1980* (New York, 1982), 80. Kleppner summarizes his views on this period very completely and precisely in his "Partisanship and Ethnoreligious Conflict: The Third Electoral System, 1853–1892," in *Evolution of American Electoral Systems*, ed. Kleppner, 131–41.

14. Sidney Verba and Norman Nie, *Participation in America: Political Democracy and Social Equal-*

signed to the scrap heap, despite the recent growth of independent sentiment.

Perhaps the hardest questions are whether parties should be abandoned, whether they truly serve the public interest, and whether they always have and will be mechanisms for exploitation. In the middle colonies parties concerned themselves with espousing ideas of liberty, protection, and effective government without truly attempting to deal with the problems of the callous treatment of the helpless, the deprivation of the lower class, and the stark brutality mustered to discipline forced labor. Moral questions raised and stances taken by nineteenth-century parties were sometimes of the greatest consequence, as was the stance against slavery, but were in most cases tangential to real social needs. Twentieth-century parties, despite declines in voter turnout, have been more (but not sufficiently more) responsive to real problems than were their predecessors. Parties in the United States will probably remain a compromised institution: partly bound to hegemonic capitalism, partly dedicated to amelioration of social conditions, partly manipulative of many misled voters, partly composed of assertive, idealistic groups who want fundamental redirection. One hopes for the party for virtue that Franklin wished to found but probably has to settle for Peter Van Schaack's resigned acceptance of formidable parties that guarded against each other. Middle colonists would agree with modern critics that partisanship was frustrating, obstructionist, and sordid. Yet they found it necessary, inevitable, innovative, and sometimes even honorable and redeeming—in short, an institution all too human.

---

ity (New York, 1972), 79–80, notes that 11 to 15 percent of the population is very active politically.

Appendix I:
Analysis of Roll Call Voting

The primary method of roll call analysis employed in this study to determine party affiliation is Rice-Beyle cluster-bloc analysis. Each assemblyman is paired with every other assemblyman to determine whether they voted the same or differently on each roll call. The pairing or comparison is made for each assembly from general election to general election. A percentage of agreement for each pair is calculated. A high percentage of agreement among a group of legislators, or most members of a group, indicates that they form a partisan bloc. The method is described in Lee F. Anderson, Meredith W. Watts Jr., and Allen R. Wilcox, *Legislative Roll Call Analysis* (Evanston, 1966), 59–75. The percentage levels that represent significant agreement among pairs of legislators for various numbers of roll calls have been calculated by Peter Willetts, "Cluster-Bloc Analysis and Statistical Inference," *American Political Science Review*, LXVI (1972), 569–82. Batinski, *New Jersey Assembly*, 77–90, prints cluster-bloc results for the New Jersey House that are derived by somewhat different methods than are used here. Main, *Political Parties Before the Constitution*, also employs cluster-bloc analysis. This method seems appropriate for the size of the colonial assemblies and the number of roll calls.

All 521 roll calls for New Jersey and 510 for New York were analyzed, even those that appeared to duplicate earlier roll calls. (Purvis, *Proprietors, Patronage, and Paper Money*, 112, counts 498 New Jersey roll calls; Batinski, *New Jersey Assembly*, 75, counts 544.) The basic premise for the decision to use all votes was that because they were relatively rarely taken, they all must have been important. Generally roll calls were taken at the request of a member. Few or none were taken on trivial matters. The 4.2 percent of New Jersey roll calls and the 10.6 percent of New York roll calls that were essentially repetitive were included in this study because these roll calls were probably demanded in the hope that during the series of votes some erstwhile committed partisans would change their minds because of pressure or ideological considerations. Each roll call was in actuality selected by legislators as a device to test whether their party would hold together on an important issue or whether the opponent's party would fragment. Constituents, reviewing the legislative journals, would likely insist that representatives adhere to the major ideas advocated by their political group. When researchers arbitrarily choose which roll calls to analyze, their research may lose objectivity. Hoadley, *Origins of American Political Parties,* 237, reports that he used all roll calls for his study of the U.S. Congress, 1789–1803; as he states, "because any scheme of exclusion or weighting would be difficult to justify all votes have been included here." Mary P. Ryan, "Party Formation in the United States Congress, 1789 to 1796: A Quantitative Analysis," *WMQ,* 3rd ser., XXVIII (1971), 528, and H. James Henderson, "Quantitative Approaches to Party Formation in the United States Congress: A Comment," *WMQ,* 3rd ser., XXX (1973), 311, obtain different results by using different criteria for selecting roll calls.

The percentages of agreement found significant at the 0.05 level by Willetts, "Cluster-Bloc Analysis," indicate the boundaries and composition of the blocs. These percentages range from a necessary 100 percent agreement on five roll calls to 55.6 percent on 250 roll calls. Other researchers have arbitrarily chosen various proportions: Batinski, *New Jersey Assembly,* 75–76, and Risjord, *Chesapeake Politics.* 573–74, set 70 percent as the lower limit of agreeing pairs to be placed in a bloc; Henderson, "Quantitative Approaches," 311, used two-thirds.

To verify the cluster-bloc analysis, votes on key administration-opposition issues were used: confronting the governor or council, paying official salaries, printing legal tender paper money, making military appropriations, settling election disputes, deciding on religious matters, and levying taxes. Only in one instance—the New York 1759–1760 assembly, did the two procedures not generally agree. In three cases, the 1740–1742, 1746–1748, and 1749–1751 New Jersey assemblies, the combined methods resolved ambiguities about three or four assemblymen. Purvis, *Proprietors, Patronage, and Paper Money,* 261–75, identifies more than two blocs in nearly all assembly sessions. He employs a method that takes into account the probability of a legislator's voting in the majority or minority, that omits some votes, and that analyzes separate sessions rather than from election to dissolution. The most enduring bloc was a Perth Amboy–Burlington coalition. The analysis of cluster blocs in Batinski, *New Jersey Assembly,* 53, 143–45, 191, 210–11, differs with that presented here particularly in regard to the assemblies of 1740–1742, 1746–1748, and those after 1751, primarily because his cutoff of 70 percent excludes significant agreement when roll calls number more than 28. Although he finds "no class divisions that cut across the several categories of policy," he does postulate a "country" position.

To evaluate the influence of the variables religion, region, wealth, and occupation on partisanship, the statistical measures lambda-*b*, chi-square, and phi are used. Lambda-*b* measures the strength of the relationship between that variable and partisanship; it ranges between 0 and +1. The lambda-*b* calculations for each variable's relationship to partisanship can be compared. Chi-square measures the significance of the relationship between a specific variety of the variable (*e.g.*, Quaker as a variety of religion) and a specific party but does not compare the strength of relationships. Phi, which is derived from chi-square and the number of cases, ranges from -1 to +1 in the statistical calculations employed here and compares the strength of those relationships chi-square finds significant. See Charles M. Dollar and Richard J. Jensen, *Historian's Guide to Statistics: Quantitative Analysis and Historical Research* (New York, 1971), 71–85.

Appendix II:
Analysis of Participation of Assemblymen

PENNSYLVANIA

Top rank

Criteria for inclusion were holding the post of Speaker or serving on an average of at least five bill committees per year of service and on an average of at least one standing committee per year of service.

W. Allen	J. Hughes	I. Norris II
E. Biddle	A. James	J. Pemberton
J. Dickinson	J. Kinsey	S. Rhoads
J. Fox	J. Langhorne	G. Ross
B. Franklin	T. Leech	S. Shoemaker
J. Galloway	W. Masters	John Wright, Sr.
A. Hamilton	T. Mifflin	T. Willing
M. Hillegas	J. Morton	

Allen did not qualify quantitatively because of partisan bias against him but is included because of other evidence of his leadership. Top-rank members constituted 9.9 percent (N = 233) of the total assemblymen serving.

Second rank

Criteria for inclusion were service on an average of at least one bill committee per year and on an average of at least one standing committee per two years.

G. Ashbridge	G. Bryan*	C. Cooper
B. Bartholomew	W. Callender	J. Douglas
J. Baynton	B. Chapman	P. Fleeson
John Brown	W. Clymer*	G. Gray

*Served only one term.

R. Hayes
J. Hockley*
C. Humphries
S. Kearsley
Jos. Kirkbride, Jr.
J. Kirkbride III*
T. Livezay
S. Miles
E. Morgan
J. Parker
R. Pearne

I. Pearson
I. Pemberton, Sr.
I. Pemberton, Jr.*
E. Penington*
J. Richardson
D. Roberdeau
H. Roberts
W. Rodman
J. Ross
J. Saunders
John Smith

J. Stretch
A. Strettle*
A. Strickland
E. Warner
Jos. Watson
A. Wayne*
P. Worrall
John Wright, Jr.
H. Wynkoop
T. Yardley*

Second-rank members constituted 18.8 percent of the assemblymen.

Inactive

Criteria for inclusion were service on an average of one bill committee or less for eight years, service on no more than an average of one standing committee per year of membership, and service of more than one year in the House.

John Armstrong
Jos. Armstrong
J. Ash
J. Blackburn
T. Blacklege
S. Brown
J. Byers
T. Canby
T. Chandler
J. Davis
W. Edmunds

J. Evans
J. Ewing
B. Field
D. Houghland
M. Hughes
W. Hughes
S. Hunter
R. Lewis
T. Linley
D. McConnaghy
T. Minshall

J. Pennock, Jr.
W. Peters
J. Shaw
P. Shepherd
James Smith
M. Starr
T. Tatnall
C. Van Horne
G. Van Sant
F. Yarnall

Inactives constituted 14.2 percent of the total number of assemblymen. Tully, *William Penn's Legacy*, 186, 229 n. 59, calculates almost the same proportion of leaders—29.8 percent—for the years 1727–1755. He employs a different method and does not distinguish between top and second-rank leaders.

*Served only one term.

NEW YORK

Top rank

Criteria for inclusion were service as Speaker or chair of at least an average of three committees of the whole per year.

J. Alexander	H. Holland	L. Morris, Jr.
W. Bayard	J. Jauncey	W. Nicoll II
C. Brush	D. Jones	A. Philipse
G. Clinton	D. Kissam	P. Richards
J. Cruger	Ph. Livingston	Ph. Schuyler II
James DeLancey, Jr.	R. R. Livingston	J. Watts
J. DeNoyelles	W. Livingston	

Top-rank leaders constituted 17.4 percent of the total number of assembly-men (N = 115).

Second rank

Criterion for inclusion was chair of at least an average of two committees of the whole during three years.

H. Beekman	P. R. Livingston	Ph. Schuyler I
C. Billop	R. Livingston, Jr.	B. Seaman
D. Clarkson	J. Moore	A. Ten Broeck
H. Cruger	W. Nicoll III	J. Thomas
D. Delancey	F. Philipse II	Jer. Van Rensselaer
C. DeWitt	F. Philipse III	J. Walton
S. Gale, Jr.	E. Platt	N. Woodhull
S. Johnson		

Second-rank leaders constituted 19.1 percent of the total number of as-semblymen.

Inactive

Criteria for inclusion were chairing no committees of the whole, an average service of less than one bill committee or standing committee per year, and service of more than one year in the House.

A. Bradt	H. Hansen	T. Snediker
J. Bruyn	J. Hardenburg	J. Tappan
M. DePue	J. Jansen	C. Ten Eyck
P. Douw	J. Lott	J. Tur Boss
H. Filkin	P. Micheaux	D. Vandervere
H. Frey	J. Mynderse	J. B. Van Rensselaer
A. Gaasbeck-Chambers	A. Pawling	J. Van Slyck
T. Gale	D. Purdy	S. Wells
A. Glen		

Inactives constituted 21.7 percent of the assemblymen.

NEW JERSEY

Top rank

Criteria for inclusion were service as Speaker or as chair of at least one committee of the whole.

J. Bonnell	W. Hancock	R. Ogden
W. Cook	R. Hude	C. Read
J. Cooper	A. Johnston	R. Smith, Jr.
S. Crane	L. Johnston	C. Skinner
J. Eatton	R. Lawrence	M. Stacy
T. Farmar	A. Leaming, Jr.	G. Vrelandt
H. Fisher	S. Neville	

Top-ranking assemblymen constituted 14.6 percent of the total (N = 137).

Second rank

Criteria for inclusion were service on an average of at least one standing committee and two bill committees per year of service.

J. Bullock	James Kinsey	B. Smith
J. Hart	J. Lawrence	A. Smyth
R. Hartshorne	J. Mehelm	A. Sykes
A. Hewlings	R. Price	E. Taylor
John Hinchman	J. Reading	S. Tucker
J. L. Johnston	T. Rodman	J. Wetherill
P. Kearney	J. Shepherd	J. Yard

Second-rank leaders constituted 15.3 percent of the assemblymen serving.

Inactive

Criteria for inclusion were service on an average of one bill committee or less per year of service, on an average of four standing committees or less per five years of service, and service of more than one year in the House.

R. Bradbury	J. Hand	J. Reeve
J. Brick	James Hinchman	J. Rolph
J. Brick, Jr.	J. Hoghland	N. Stilwell
J. Camp	B. Holme	C. Vandevere
S. Clement	E. Hopkins	R. Van Gieson
S. Clement, Jr.	J. Ladd	T. Van Horne
D. Demarest	T. Leonard	J. Van Middleswart
D. Dey	J. Mickle	G. Van Neste
D. Doughty	W. Mickle	D. Van Veghten
E. Eldridge	P. Middaugh	C. Van Vorst
J. Ellis	J. Peace	R. Wood
H. Gerritse	N. Pettit	

Inactives constituted 25.5 percent of the total assemblymen.
Purvis, "Social Origins of New Jersey Assemblymen," 605, lists forty-one leaders; thirty of them are included in the above lists. Batinski, *New Jersey Assembly*, 67–70, lists thirty-one activists; twenty-two are listed above. He also identifies eighty-six backbenchers but does not take into account length of tenure.

Appendix III:
Voter Participation and Partisanship

NEW JERSEY

Perth Amboy	90% of adult white males (a.w.m.)
Middlesex	50% "
Somerset	64% "
Essex	70% "
All others	60% "

New Jersey Elections

District	Year	Voters	a.w.m.	Qualified	Voters/ a.w.m.	Voters/ qualified
Hunterdon	1738	194	1,349	809	14.4%	24.0%
Burlington	1739–40	458	1,229	737	37.3%	62.1%
Middlesex	1754	694	1,700	850	40.8%	81.6%
Cape May	1761	113	329	197	34.4%	57.4%
Gloucester	1766	60	1,611	967	3.7%	6.2%
Perth Amboy	1772	284	323	291	87.9%	97.6%
Somerset	1772	1,000	1,915	1,226	52.2%	81.6%

For Hunterdon, Purvis, *Proprietors, Patronage, and Paper Money*, 101. Purvis gives somewhat different figures for the Burlington vote totals and for the populations of Middlesex, Cape May, and Perth Amboy. For Middlesex, Somerset, Essex: Dinkin, *Voting in Provincial America*, 45, 177; New York *Gazette*, Aug. 5, 1754, May 25, 1772. For Perth Amboy: McCormick, *History of Voting in New Jersey*, 63; and New York *Journal*, Apr. 2, 1772. For all others: Donald L. Kemmerer, "The Suffrage Franchise in Colonial New Jersey," *Proceedings of the New Jersey Historical Society*, LII (1934), 169; and Chilton Williamson, *American Suffrage from Property to Democracy, 1760–1860* (Princeton, 1960), 29; Thompson, ed., "Poll Book of Election in 1739 [-40], Burlington County," 187–93; Leaming, Diary, Mar. 14, 1761, HSP; David Cooper to Samuel Allinson, Jan. 26, 1766, Samuel Allinson Papers, Rutgers University Library, New Brunswick. McCormick, *History of Voting in New Jersey*, 43–44, posits that actual suffrage was universal because qualifications were ignored on election day.

NJA, VI, 242–44, X, 452–53; and Stella H. Sutherland, *Population Distribution in Colonial America* (1936; rpr. New York, 1966), 99, were used to calculate the numbers of qualified voters and adult white males. For all colonies, adult white males are assumed to be 0.215 of the total white population. This is based on figures for the 1770s from Alice Hanson Jones, *American Colonial Wealth: Documents and Methods* (2nd ed., 3 vols.; New York, 1978), III, 1790; and Robert V. Wells, *The Population of the British Colonies in America Before 1776: A Survey of Census Data* (Princeton, 1975), 92, 117.

NEW YORK

New York County	100% of adult white males
Westchester County	50% "
All others	65% "

New York City Elections

Year	Voters	Qualified (a.w.m.)	Voters/qualified
1734 (local)	442	1,529	28.9%
1737	812	1,437	56.5%
1739	633	1,534	43.0%
1745	177	1,827	9.7%
1761	1,449	2,661	51.5%
1768	1,923	3,532	54.7%
1769	1,515	3,657	41.4%

mean of aggregated percentages of voters/a.w.m.   =41.2%.
median of aggregated percentages of voters/a.w.m. =43.0%.

Queens County Elections

Year	Voters	a.w.m.	Qualified	Voters/a.w.m.	Voters/qualified
1737	726	1,635	1,063	44.4%	68.3%

Year	Voters	a.w.m.	Qualified	Voters/a.w.m.	Voters/qualified
1739	728	1,654	1,075	44.0%	67.7%
1748	800	1,517	986	52.7%	81.1%
1750	755	1,480	962	51.0%	78.5%
1761	678	1,864	1,212	36.4%	55.6%
1761	1,050	1,864	1,212	56.3%	86.6%
1768	871	1,817	1,181	47.9%	73.8%

	Voters/a.w.m.	Voters/qualified
mean of aggregated percentages	47.5%	73.2%
median of aggregated percentages	47.9%	73.8%

Westchester County Elections

Year	Voters	a.w.m.	Qualified	Voters/a.w.m.	Voters/qualified
1733	420	1,279	640	32.8%	65.6%
1750	589	2,298	1,149	25.6%	51.3%
1761	476	3,406	1,703	14.0%	28.0%
1768	739	3,901	1,951	18.9%	37.9%

	Voters/a.w.m.	Voters/qualified
mean of aggregated percentages	22.8%	45.7%
median of aggregated percentages	22.3%	44.6%

New York—Various Counties

County	Year	Voters	a.w.m.	Qualified	Voters/a.w.m.	Voters/qualified
Albany	1739	636	2,027	1,318	31.4%	48.3%
Ulster	1748	117	890	534	13.2%	21.9%
Richmond	1761	151	412	268	36.7%	56.3%
Dutchess	1769	1,296	4,422	2,874	29.0%	45.1%
Westchester Borough	1769	114				
Schenectady (local)	1747	24		252 (taxpayers)		9.5%

Klein, *Politics of Diversity*, 23–25; Dinkin, *Voting in Provincial America*, 43–44, 154–56; Bonomi, *Fac-*

tious People, 114, 162; New York *Mercury,* Mar. 2, 1761, Mar. 21, 1768; Cadwallader Colden to Governor George Clinton, Jan. 29, 1747–8, in *NYHSC,* LIII, 7–8. *N.Y.C. Poll List, 1761: N.Y.C. Poll List, 1768; N.Y.C. Poll List, 1769;* New York *Gazette,* Feb. 20, 1769; New York *Weekly Journal,* Sept. 30, 1734; Election return, 1747, in Schenectady Manuscripts and Tax list, 1737–1748, NYHS. Dinkin underestimates the number of adult white males qualified in New York County because he misinterprets the figures in Champagne, "Liberty Boys and Mechanics in New York City," 125. Philip S. Foner, *Labor and the American Revolution* (Westport, 1976), 24, argues that poor mechanics could not vote. Qualified voters and adult white males are estimated from *DCHNY,* V, 929, VI, 133, 392, 550, VIII, 457; O'Callaghan, ed., *Documentary History of the State of New York,* I, 697; Gary B. Nash, "The New York Census of 1737: A Critical Note on the Integration of Statistical and Literary Sources," *WMQ,* 3rd ser., XXXVI (1979), 431.

PENNSYLVANIA

Philadelphia city	63.8% of adult white males, 1737
	50.3% " , 1776
Philadelphia County	58.6% " , 1737
	53.4% " , 1775
Bucks, Chester counties	55% "
Lancaster, York counties	60% "
Northampton	73% "
All others	65% "

Philadelphia City Elections

Year	Voters	Population	a.w.m.	Qualified	Qualified/ a.w.m.	Voters/ a.w.m.	Voters/ qualified
1737	238	9,000	1,935	1,235	63.8%	12.3%	19.3%
1742	600	10,000	2,150	1,330	61.8%	27.9%	45.1%
1751	831	14,000	3,010	1,838	61.1%	27.6%	45.2%
1752	730	14,500	3,118	1,869	59.9%	23.4%	39.1%
1757	603	16,500	3,548	2,068	58.3%	16.9%	29.2%
1758	183	17,000	3,655	2,140	58.5%	5.0%	8.6%
1764	1,490	19,700	4,236	2,345	55.4%	35.2%	63.5%

1765	1,973	20,100	4,322	2,392	55.3%	45.6%	82.5%
1766	1,512	20,600	4,429	2,441	55.1%	34.1%	61.9%
1774	1,336	29,000	6,235	3,002	48.1%	21.4%	44.5%
1775	775	30,000	6,450	3,326	51.6%	12.0%	23.1%
1776	1,900	31,000	6,665	3,350	50.3%	28.5%	56.7%

	Voters/a.w.m.	Voters/qualified
mean of aggregated percentages	24.2%	43.2%
median of aggregated percentages	25.5%	44.9%

Discrepancies in the trend of decrease of the proportion of qualified voters are due to inconsistent data on taxables.

Philadelphia County Elections

Year	Voters	a.w.m.	Qualified	Qualified/ a.w.m.	Voters/ a.w.m.	Voters/ qualified
1727	787	3,201	1,793	56.0%	24.6%	43.9%
1728	971	3,381	1,867	55.2%	28.7%	52.0%
1730	622	3,643	2,050	56.3%	17.1%	30.3%
1732	904	3,910	2,210	56.5%	23.1%	40.9%
1734	821	4,277	2,424	56.7%	19.2%	33.9%
1735	1,097	4,436	2,639	59.9%	24.7%	41.6%
1736	719	4,594	2,712	59.0%	15.7%	26.5%
1737	904	4,753	2,785	58.6%	19.0%	32.5%
1738	1,306	4,911	2,858	58.2%	26.6%	45.7%
1739	555	5,049	2,916	57.8%	11.0%	19.0%
1740	1,832	5,185	2,997	57.8%	35.3%	61.1%
1741	1,151	5,358	3,097	57.8%	21.4%	37.2%
1742	1,843	5,616	3,237	57.6%	32.8%	56.9%
1743	1,028	5,856	3,366	57.5%	17.6%	30.5%
1750	2,004	7,464	4,266	57.2%	26.8%	47.0%
1751	1,473	7,660	4,396	57.4%	19.2%	33.5%
1752	948	7,837	4,465	57.0%	12.1%	21.2%
1754	2,181	8,126	4,604	56.7%	26.8%	47.4%
1755	1,236	8,821	4,674	56.4%	14.9%	26.4%
1756	1,770	8,437	4,743	56.2%	21.6%	37.3%

1757	785	8,614	4,854	56.4%	9.1%	16.2%
1758	1,567	8,790	4,964	56.4%	17.8%	31.6%
1761	950	9,206	5,225	56.7%	10.3%	18.2%
1764	3,874	9,586	5,287	55.2%	40.4%	73.3%
1765	4,363	9,865	5,441	55.2%	44.2%	80.2%
1766	3,019	10,166	5,596	55.0%	29.7%	53.9%
1771	1,300	12,208	6,500	53.2%	10.6%	20.0%
1775	3,122	13,928	7,439	53.4%	22.4%	42.2%

	Voters/a.w.m.	Voters/qualified
mean of aggregated percentages	22.2%	39.3%
median of aggregated percentages	21.2%	35.6%

Bucks County Elections

Year	Voters	Taxables (a.w.m.)	Qualified	Voters/ a.w.m.	Voters/ qualified
1738	522	2,500	1,375	20.9%	38.0%
1739	382	2,500	1,375	15.3%	27.8%
1740	670	2,500	1,375	26.8%	48.7%
1742	990	2,500	1,375	39.6%	72.0%
1756	1,280	3,080	1,694	41.5%	75.6%
1765	1,450	3,161	1,739	45.9%	83.6%

	Voters/a.w.m.	Voters/qualified
mean of aggregated percentages	31.7%	57.6%
median of aggregated percentages	33.2%	60.4%

Chester County Elections

Year	Voters	Taxables (a.w.m.)	Qualified	Voters/ a.w.m.	Voters/ qualified
1737	724	2,532	1,418	28.6%	51.1%
1738	963	2,627	1,471	36.7%	65.5%
1739	864	2,722	1,524	31.8%	56.8%

Year	Voters	Taxables (a.w.m.)	Qualified	Voters/a.w.m.	Voters/qualified
1740	700	2,817	1,578	24.8%	44.3%
1742	1,000	3,007	1,684	33.3%	59.4%
1765	1,150	5,090	2,850	22.6%	40.4%

	Voters/a.w.m.	Voters/qualified
mean of aggregated percentages	29.6%	54.1%
median of aggregated percentages	30.2%	54.0%

Lancaster County Elections

Year	Voters	Taxables (a.w.m.)	Qualified	Voters/ a.w.m.	Voters/ qualified
1737	753	2,461	1,477	30.6%	51.0%
1738	1,019	2,560	1,536	39.8%	66.3%
1740	1,010	2,761	1,657	36.6%	61.0%
1741	1,150	2,858	1,715	40.2%	67.1%
1742	1,565	2,957	1,774	52.9%	88.2%
1749	1,000	3,652	2,191	27.4%	45.6%
1757	709	5,004	3,002	14.2%	23.6%
1765	2,925	6,077	3,646	48.1%	80.2%

	Voters/a.w.m.	Voters/qualified
mean of aggregated percentages	36.2%	60.4%
median of aggregated percentages	38.3%	63.7%

York County Elections

Year	Voters	Taxables (a.w.m.)	Qualified	Voters/ a.w.m.	Voters/ qualified
1756	1,248	2,741	1,645	45.5%	75.9%
1757	1,106	2,885	1,731	38.3%	63.9%

Dinkin, *Voting in Provincial America,* 160; *American Weekly Mercury* (Philadelphia), Sept. 29–Oct. 6, 1737, Sept. 28–Oct. 5, 1738, Sept. 27–Oct. 4, 1739; Tully, *William Penn's Legacy,* 93, 225–26; J. Thomas Scharf and Thompson Westcott, *History of Philadelphia, 1609–1884* (3 vols., Philadelphia, 1884), I, 218; William Logan to John Smith, Jan. 10, 1757, in John Smith Correspondence,

HSP; Montgomery, ed., *Pennsylvania Archives,* 6th ser., XI, 118–19; Labaree *et al.*, eds. *Franklin Papers,* XI, 391–92, XII, 290–92, XIII, 447; Election returns, Philadelphia, 1764, Philadelphia, Bucks, Chester, Lancaster, 1765, Philadelphia, 1766, in Franklin Papers, APS; William Franklin to Thomas Wharton, Sept. 21, 1771, enclosure, in Society Collection, HSP; Oaks, "Philadelphia Merchants and the Origins of American Independence," 155; Ryerson, *The Revolution Is Now Begun,* 137, 173. In 1756, twenty-seven of ninety-six Kennett Square freeholders voted, as reported in Chester County Miscellaneous Papers, HSP. For city voters as 75 percent of taxables, Williamson, *American Suffrage from Property to Democracy,* 33–34. For taxables, Proud, *History of Pennsylvania,* II, 275 n.; Nash, *Urban Crucible,* 407–408; Evarts B. Green and Virginia D. Harrington, *American Population Before the Federal Census of 1790* (New York, 1932), 117–19. Calculations of adult white males in Philadelphia city were made from my estimates for the total population. These are between those of P. M. G. Harris, "The Demographic Development of Colonial Philadelphia in Some Comparative Perspective," *Proceedings of the American Philosophical Society,* CXXXIII (1989), 274, and of John K. Alexander, "The Philadelphia Numbers Game: An Analysis of Philadelphia's Eighteenth-Century Population," *PMHB,* XCVIII (1974), 324, which are higher; and the lower ones of Nash, *Urban Crucible,* 407–408; and of Sharon V. Salinger and Charles Wetherell, "A Note on the Population of Pre-revolutionary Philadelphia," *PMHB,* CIX (1985), 385. Smith, *The 'Lower Sort,'* 205–206, accepts Harris' figures. Williamson, *American Suffrage from Property to Democracy,* 34, and Dinkin, *Voting in Provincial America,* 44, assume that the number of adult white males outside Philadelphia city is equal to the reported taxables. For Philadelphia County the adult white male population is estimated by adding the Philadelphia city estimates to the total of county noncity taxables; the qualified voters are estimated by adding the total city qualified voters to 55 percent of the county noncity taxables.

A useful measure of the strength of partisanship among the electorate is a cohesion index that measures how strongly the supporters of one party coalesced behind all the candidates (with opponents) running on that ticket. To employ this it must first be determined by literary or roll call evidence, independently of vote totals, which candidates were of the same party. The cohesion index is then calculated for these candidates from the vote totals that they garnered. The calculation is made by first dividing the standard deviation of the votes of the allied candidates by the mean of the vote totals. This quotient will range from 0 to 1. It represents the variation among the candidate vote totals; to convert it to a robust measure of cohesion it is subtracted from 1. The statistic appears to be a good indicator of partisan solidarity in elections that are known to have generated party strife. When tested by data from elections reported in poll books—there are only four such—the cohesion indices and the poll books independently show the solidarity of party support, though the cohesion indices do not correlate exactly with poll book results. The 1739-40 Burlington election poll book shows that 81.4 percent of the voters who voted for either of the two allied winners voted for both. The cohesion index calculated solely from the vote totals is 0.971. Conversely, only 49.8 percent of the supporters of either of the two losers in this election voted the straight ticket, and the cohesion index for these voters was a low 0.689. The poll list results of the 1769 New York City election show that 80.4 percent of the voters who tended toward the winning DeLancey side voted a straight ticket; the cohesion index calculated from only the vote totals was a strong 0.970. The Livingston opponents garnered a lower straight ticket proportion—71.8 percent—and a lower but still meaningful cohesion index—0.890. The 1768 New York City election poll list shows that 75.1 percent of those who voted for either James DeLancey, Jr., or William Walton voted for both; the cohesion index of these voters was 0.988. In the 1761 New York City election the literary evidence indicates that many voters did not identify candidates with tickets; both the poll list results and calculation of a cohesion index show little partisanship. This empirical evidence indicates that when candidates are running as a ticket, a cohesion index of 0.92 or above is a strong indication of a solid partisan response—that 75 percent of their combined supporters voted the straight ticket. A cohesion index of less than 80 percent indicates weak partisanship; one of less than 70 percent indicates very little organized partisan activity.

COHESION INDICES FOR KNOWN PARTISAN ELECTIONS

Strong partisanship

Phila. County 1740   Quaker—0.991, Prop.—0.968
Phila. County 1754   Quaker—0.993, Prop.—0.980
Phila. County 1756   Quaker—0.975, Prop.—0.943
Phila. County 1764   Assembly—0.969, Prop.—0.946
Phila. County 1765   Assembly—0.978, Prop.—0.970
Phila. County 1766   Assembly—0.986, Prop.—0.967
Phila. city 1764   Assembly—0.976, Prop.—0.961
Phila. city 1776   Independ.—0.974, Prop.—0.977
Bucks 1740   Quaker—0.950, Proprietary—0.924
Bucks 1742   Quaker—0.981, Proprietary—0.973
Bucks 1756   Quaker—0.974, Proprietary—0.972
Lancaster 1742   Quaker—0.997

Lancaster 1765   Proprietary—0.925 (Assembly—0.763)

N.Y.C. 1768   DeLancey—0.988

N.Y.C. 1769   DeLancey—0.970, Livingston—0.890

Queens 1739   Philipse—0.916, Opposition—0.907

Queens 1750   Opposition—0.973, Clinton—0.997

Queens 1761   Opposition—0.988

Queens 1768   DeLancey—0.923

Westchester County 1750   Opposition—0.970

Westchester County 1761   Philipse-DeLancey—0.965

Middlesex 1754   Opposition—0.931

Burlington 1740   Opposition—0.971

Moderate partisanship

Phila. County 1742   Quaker—0.847 (disrupted by riot)

Chester 1742   Quaker—0.855

Queens 1768   Livingston—0.860

Westchester 1768   DeLancey—0.893

Dutchess 1768   DeLancey—0.900 (Livingston—0.720)

Weak partisanship

Bucks 1765   Quaker—0.724

Chester 1765   Assembly—0.743

Lancaster 1740   Quaker—0.715

Bibliography of Secondary Sources

Adams, Willi Paul. *The First American Constitutions: Republic Ideology and the Making of the State Constitutions in the Revolutionary Era*. Translated by Rita and Robert Kimber. Chapel Hill, 1980.

Ahlstrom, Sydney. *A Religious History of the American People*. New Haven, 1972.

Alexander, John K. "Deference in Colonial Pennsylvania and That Man from New Jersey." *Pennsylvania Magazine of History and Biography*, CII (1978), 422–36.

———. "The Philadelphia Numbers Game: An Analysis of Philadelphia's Eighteenth-Century Population." *Pennsylvania Magazine of History and Biography*, XCVIII (1974), 314–24.

———. *Render Them Submissive: Responses to Poverty in Philadelphia, 1760–1800*. Amherst, 1980.

Anderson, Lee F., Meredith W. Watts, Jr., and Allen W. Wilcox. *Legislative Roll-Call Analysis*. Evanston, 1966.

Appleby, Joyce. "The Social Origins of American Revolutionary Ideology." *Journal of American History*, LXIV (1977–78), 935–58.

Archdeacon, Thomas J. *New York City, 1664–1710: Conquest and Change*. Ithaca, 1976.

Bailyn, Bernard. "A Comment [on Greene, 'Political Mimesis . . .']." *American Historical Review*, LXXV (1969), 361–63.

———. *The Origins of American Politics*. New York, 1968.

Balmer, Randall. *A Perfect Babel of Confusion: Dutch Religion and English Culture in the Middle Colonies*. New York, 1989.

Batinski, Michael C. *The New Jersey Assembly, 1738–1775: The Making of a Legislative Community*. Lanham, 1987.

———. "Quakers in the New Jersey Assembly, 1738–1775: A Roll-Call Analysis." *Historian*, LIV (1991–92), 65–78.

Battle, J. H., ed. *History of Bucks County, Pennsylvania; Including an Account of Its Original Exploration, Its Relation to the Settlement of New Jersey and Delaware; Its Erection into a Separate County, also Its Subsequent Growth and Development, with Sketches of Its Historic and Interesting Localities, and Biographies of Many of Its Representative Citizens*. Philadelphia, 1887.

Bauman, Richard. *For the Reputation of Truth: Politics, Religion, and Conflict Among the Pennsylvania Quakers, 1750–1800*. Baltimore, 1971.

Becker, Carl L. *The History of Political Parties in the Province of New York, 1760–1776*. 1909; rpr. Madison, 1968.

Becker, Laura L. "Diversity and Its Significance in an Eighteenth-Century Pennsylvania Town." In *Friends and Neighbors: Group Life in America's First Plural Society*, edited by Michael Zuckerman. Philadelphia, 1982.

Becker, Robert A. *Revolution, Reform, and the Politics of American Taxation, 1763–1783.* Baton Rouge, 1980.

Beeman, Richard R. "Deference, Republicanism, and the Emergence of Popular Politics in Eighteenth-Century America." *William and Mary Quarterly*, 3rd ser., XLIX (1992), 401–30.

Bender, Thomas. *Community and Social Change in America.* New Brunswick, 1978.

Benson, Lee, Joel H. Silbey, and Phyllis F. Field. "Toward a Theory of Stability and Change in American Voting Patterns: New York State, 1790–1970." In *The History of American Electoral Behavior*, edited by Joel H. Silbey, Allan G. Bogue, and William H. Flanagan. Princeton, 1978.

Benton, William. *Whig-Loyalism: An Aspect of Political Ideology in the American Revolutionary Era.* Rutherford, 1969.

Bockelman, Wayne L. "Local Government in Colonial Pennsylvania." In *Town and County: Essays on the Structure of Local Government in the American Colonies*, edited by Bruce C. Daniels. Middletown, 1978.

———. "Local Politics in Pre-Revolutionary Lancaster County." *Pennsylvania Magazine of History and Biography*, XCVII (1973), 45–74.

Bockelman, Wayne L., and Owen S. Ireland. "The Internal Revolution in Pennsylvania: An Ethnic-Religious Interpretation." *Pennsylvania History*, XLI (1974), 125–59.

Bodle, Wayne. "The Myth of the Middle Colonies Reconsidered: The Process of Regionalization in Early America." *Pennsylvania Magazine of History and Biography*, CXIII (1989), 527–48.

Bohmer, David. A. "The Maryland Electorate and the Concept of a Party System in the Early National Period." In *The History of American Electoral Behavior*, edited by Joel H. Silbey, Allan G. Bogue, and William H. Flanagan. Princeton, 1978.

Bonomi, Patricia U. *A Factious People: Politics and Society in Colonial New York.* New York, 1971.

———. "A Just Opposition: The Great Awakening as a Radical Model." In *The Origins of Anglo-American Radicalism*, edited by Margaret Jacob and James Jacob. London, 1984.

———. "Local Government in Colonial New York: A Base for Republicanism." In *Aspects of Early New York Society and Politics*, edited by Jacob Judd and Irwin H. Polishook. Tarrytown, 1974.

———. "The Middle Colonies: Embryo of the New Political Order." In *Perspectives on Early American History: Essays in Honor of Richard B. Morris*, edited by Alden T. Vaughan and George Athan Billias. New York, 1973.

———. *Under the Cope of Heaven: Religion, Society, and Politics in Colonial America.* New York, 1986.

Bonomi, Patricia U., and Peter R. Eisenstadt. "Church Adherence in the Eighteenth-Century British American Colonies." *William and Mary Quarterly*, 3rd ser., XXXIX (1982), 245–86.

Bourke, Paul F., and Donald A. DeBats. "Identifiable Voting in Nineteenth-Century America: Toward a Comparison of Britain and the United States Before the Secret Ballot." *Perspectives in American History*, XI (1977–78), 259–88.

Boyer, Lee R. "Lobster Backs, Liberty Boys, and Laborers in the Streets: New York's Golden Hill and Nassau Street Riots." *New-York Historical Society Quarterly*, LVII (1973), 281–308.

Bradley, James E. *Religion, Revolution, and English Radicalism: Nonconformity in Eighteenth-Century Politics and Society.* Cambridge, Eng., 1990.

Brewer, John. *Party Ideology and Popular Politics at the Accession of George III.* Cambridge, Eng., 1976.

Bridenbaugh, Carl. *Cities in Revolt: Urban Life in America, 1743–1776.* 1955; rpr. New York, 1964.

———. *Cities in the Wilderness: The First Century of Urban Life in America.* 1938; rpr. New York, 1964.

———. *Mitre and Sceptre: Transatlantic Faiths, Ideas, Personalities, and Politics, 1689–1775.* New York, 1962.

Bridenbaugh, Carl, and Jessica Bridenbaugh. *Rebels and Gentlemen: Philadelphia in the Age of Franklin.* 2nd ed. New York, 1962.

Brobeck, Stephen. "Revolutionary Change in Colonial Philadelphia: The Brief Life of the Proprietary Gentry." *William and Mary Quarterly*, 3rd ser., XXXIII (1976), 410–34.

Brock, Leslie V. *The Currency of the American Colonies: A Study in Colonial Finance and Imperial Relations.* New York, 1975.

Broussard, James H. "Party and Partisanship in American Legislatures: The South Atlantic States." *Journal of Southern History*, XLIII (1977), 39–58.

Brown, Richard Maxwell. "Violence and the American Revolution." In *Essays on the American Revolution*, edited by Stephen G. Kurtz and James H. Hutson. Chapel Hill, 1973.

Browning, Reed. *Political and Constitutional Ideas of the Court Whigs.* Baton Rouge, 1982.

Burnham, Walter Dean. "The Appearance and Disappearance of the American Voter." In *Electoral Participation: A Comparative Analysis*, edited by Richard Rose. Beverly Hills, 1980.

———. "The System of 1896: An Analysis." In *The Evolution of American Electoral Systems*, edited by Paul Kleppner *et al.* Westport, 1981.

Burr, Nelson R. *The Anglican Church in New Jersey.* Philadelphia, 1954.

Carter, Katherine D. "Isaac Norris II's Attack on Andrew Hamilton." *Pennsylvania Magazine of History and Biography*, CIV (1980), 139–61.

Chambers, William N. "Party Development and the American Mainstream." In *The American Party Systems: Stages of Political Development*, edited by William N. Chambers and Walter Dean Burnham. 2nd ed. New York, 1975.

———. *Political Parties in a New Nation: The American Experience, 1776–1809.* New York, 1963.

Champagne, Roger J. *Alexander McDougall and the American Revolution in New York.* Schenectady, 1975.

———. "Family Politics Versus Constitutional Principles: The New York Assembly Elections of 1768 and 1769." *William and Mary Quarterly,* 3rd ser., XX (1963), 57–79.

———. "Liberty Boys and Mechanics of New York City, 1764–1774." *Labor History,* VIII (1967), 115–35.

Charlot, Jean. "Political Parties: Toward a New Theoretical Synthesis." *Political Studies,* XXXVII (1989), 352–61.

Clark, J. C. D. *The Dynamics of Change: The Crisis of the 1750s and English Party Systems.* Cambridge, Eng., 1982.

———. "A General Theory of Party, Opposition, and Government, 1688–1832." *Historical Journal,* XXIII (1980), 295–325.

Clark, Jonathan. "The Problem of Allegiance in Revolutionary Poughkeepsie." In *Saints and Revolutionaries: Essays on Early American History,* edited by David D. Hall, John M. Murrin, and Thad W. Tate. New York, 1984.

Cohen, Norman H. "The Philadelphia Election Riot of 1742." *Pennsylvania Magazine of History and Biography,* XCII (1968), 306–19.

Colden, Cadwallader. "History of William Cosby's Administration as Governor of the Province of New York and of Lieutenant Governor George Clarke's Administration Through 1737." *Collections of the New-York Historical Society,* LXVIII (1935), 281–355.

Colley, Linda. *In Defiance of Oligarchy: The Tory Party, 1714–1760.* London, 1982.

Cook, Edward M., Jr. *The Fathers of the Towns: Leadership and Community Structure in Eighteenth Century New England.* Baltimore, 1976.

Cornly, Isaac. "Sketches of the History of Byberry in the County of Philadelphia, with Biographical Notices of Some of the First Settlers, and Other Distinguished Inhabitants of the Neighborhood." *Memoirs of the Historical Society of Pennsylvania,* Vol. II (1827), Pt. 1, pp. 165–203.

Countryman, Edward. " 'Out of the Bounds of the Law': Northern Land Rioters in the Eighteenth Century." In *The American Revolution: Explorations in the History of American Radicalism,* edited by Alfred F. Young. De Kalb, 1976.

———. *A People in Revolution: The American Revolution and Political Society in New York, 1760–1790.* Baltimore, 1981.

———. "The Revolutionary Transformation of New York." In *New Wine in Old Skins: A Comparative View of Socio-Political Structures and Values Affecting the American Revolution,* edited by Erich Angermann, Marie-Luise Frings, and Herman Wellenreuther. Stuttgart, 1976.

Crowther, Simeon J. "A Note on the Economic Position of Philadelphia's White Oaks." *William and Mary Quarterly,* 3rd ser., XXIX (1972), 134–36.

Cushing, Thomas, and Charles E. Sheppard. *History of the Counties of Gloucester, Salem, and Cumberland, New Jersey, with Biographical Sketches of Their Prominent Citizens.* Philadelphia, 1883.

Cutcliffe, Stephen H. "Sideling Hill Affair: The Cumberland County Riots of 1765." *Western Pennsylvania Historical Magazine,* LIX (1976), 39–53.

Dangerfield, George. *Chancellor Robert R. Livingston of New York, 1746–1813.* New York, 1960.

Dargo, George. "Parties and the Transformation of the Constitutional Idea in Revolutionary Pennsylvania." In *Party and Political Opposition in Revolutionary America,* edited by Patricia U. Bonomi. Tarrytown, 1980.

Dexter, Franklin B. *Biographical Sketches of the Graduates of Yale College, with Annals of the College History.* 6 vols. New York, 1885–1912.

Diamondstone, Judith M. "The Government of Eighteenth-Century Philadelphia." In *Town and County: Essays on the Structure of Local Government in the American Colonies,* edited by Bruce C. Daniels. Middletown, 1978.

Dickinson, H. T. *Liberty and Property: Political Ideology in Eighteenth-Century Britain.* London, 1977.

Dillon, Dorothy R. *The New York Triumvirate: A Study of the Legal and Political Careers of William Livingston, John Morin Scott, and William Smith, Jr.* New York, 1949.

Dinkin, Robert J. *Voting in Provincial America: A Study of Elections in the Thirteen Colonies.* Westport, 1977.

Doerflinger, Thomas M. "Philadelphia Merchants and the Logic of Moderation." *William and Mary Quarterly,* 3rd ser., XL (1983), 197–226.

————. *A Vigorous Spirit of Enterprise: Merchants and Economic Development in Revolutionary Philadelphia.* Chapel Hill, 1986.

Dollar, Charles M., and Richard J. Jensen. *Historian's Guide to Statistics: Quantitative Analysis and Historical Research.* New York, 1971.

Duverger, Maurice. *Political Parties: Their Organization and Activity in the Modern State.* Translated by Barbara and Robert North. 2nd ed. New York, 1963.

Egnal, Marc. *A Mighty Empire: The Origins of the American Revolution.* Ithaca, 1988.

————. "The Pattern of Factional Development in Pennsylvania, New York, and Massachusetts, 1682–1776." In *Party and Political Opposition in Revolutionary America,* edited by Patricia U. Bonomi. Tarrytown, 1980.

Flick, Alexander C. *Loyalism in New York During the American Revolution.* New York, 1901.

Flint, Martha B. *Long Island Before the Revolution: A Colonial Study.* 1896; rpr. Port Washington, 1967.

Flower, Milton E. *John Dickinson: Conservative Revolutionary.* Charlottesville, 1983.

Foner, Philip S. *Labor and the American Revolution.* Westport, 1976.

Formisano, Ronald P. "Deferential-Participant Politics: The Early Republic's Political Culture, 1789–1840." *American Political Science Review,* LXVIII (1974), 473–87.

————. "Federalists and Republicans: Parties, Yes—Systems, No." In *The Evolution of American Electoral Systems,* edited by Paul Kleppner *et al.* Westport, 1981.

————. *The Transformation of Political Culture: Massachusetts Parties, 1790s–1840s.* New York, 1983.

Friedman, Bernard. "The New York Assembly Elections of 1768 and 1769: The Disruption of Family Politics." *New York History,* XLVI (1965), 3–42.

————. "The Shaping of the Radical Consciousness in Provincial New York." *Journal of American History*, LVI (1970), 781–801.

Frost, J. William. *A Perfect Freedom: Religious Liberty in Pennsylvania*. Cambridge, Eng., 1990.

————. *The Quaker Family in Colonial America: A Portrait of the Society of Friends*. New York, 1973.

Futhey, J. Smith, and Gilbert Cope. *History of Chester County, Pennsylvania, with Genealogical and Biographical Sketches*. Philadelphia, 1881.

Gerardi, Donald F. M. "The King's College Controversy, 1753–1756, and the Ideological Roots of Toryism in New York." *Perspectives in American History*, XI (1977–78), 147–96.

Gerlach, Larry R. "Anglo-American Politics in New Jersey on the Eve of the Revolution." *Huntington Library Quarterly*, XXXIX (1975–76), 291–316.

————. "Politics and Prerogatives: The Aftermath of the Robbery of the East Jersey Treasury in 1768." *New Jersey History*, XC (1972), 133–68.

————. *Prologue to Independence: New Jersey in the Coming of the American Revolution*. New Brunswick, 1976.

————. "'Quaker' Politics in Eighteenth-Century New Jersey: A Documentary Account." *Journal of the Rutgers University Library*, XXXIV (1970), 1–12.

————. "Soldiers and Citizens: The British Army in New Jersey on the Eve of the Revolution." *New Jersey History*, XCIII (1975), 5–36.

Gienapp, William E. "'Politics Seem to Enter into Everything': Political Culture in the North, 1840–1860." In *Essays on American Ante-Bellum Politics, 1840–1860*, edited by Stephen E. Mazlish and John J. Kushna. College Station, 1982.

Gilje, Paul A. *The Road to Mobocracy: Popular Disorder in New York City, 1763–1834*. Chapel Hill, 1987.

Gilsdorf, Joy B., and Robert R. Gilsdorf. "Elites and Electorates: Some Plain Truths for Historians of Colonial America." In *Saints and Revolutionaries: Essays on Early American History*, edited by David D. Hall, John M. Murrin, and Thad W. Tate. New York, 1984.

Gough, Robert J. "Can a Rich Man Favor Revolution? The Case of Philadelphia in 1776." *Pennsylvania History*, LXVIII (1981), 235–50.

————. "The Myth of the 'Middle Colonies': An Analysis of Regionalization in Early America." *Pennsylvania Magazine of History and Biography*, CVII (1983), 393–419.

Green, Evarts B., and Virginia D. Harrington. *American Population Before the Federal Census of 1790*. New York, 1932.

Greenberg, Douglas. "The Middle Colonies in Recent American Historiography." *William and Mary Quarterly*, 3rd ser., XXXVI (1979), 396–427.

Greene, Jack P. "Changing Interpretations of Early American Politics." In *The Reinterpretation of Early American History*, edited by Ray Allen Billington. New York, 1968.

————. "The Growth of Political Stability: An Interpretation of Political Development in the Anglo-American Colonies." In *The American Revolution: A Heritage of Change*, edited by John Parker and Carol Urness. Minneapolis, 1975.

———. "Interpretive Frameworks: The Quest for Intellectual Order in Early American History." *William and Mary Quarterly*, 3rd ser., XLVIII (1991), 515–30.

———. "Legislative Turnover in British America, 1696 to 1775: A Quantitative Analysis." *William and Mary Quarterly*, 3rd ser., XXXVIII (1981), 442–63.

———. *Peripheries and Center: Constitutional Development in the Extended Politics of the British Empire and the United States, 1607–1763*. Athens, Ga., 1986.

———. "Political Mimesis: A Consideration of the Historical and Cultural Roots of Legislative Behavior in the British Colonies in the Eighteenth Century." *American Historical Review*, LXXV (1969), 337–60.

———. "Reply [to Bailyn, 'A Comment . . .']." *American Historical Review*, LXXV (1969), 364–67.

———. "The Seven Years War and the American Revolution: The Causal Relationship Reconsidered." *Journal of Imperial and Commonwealth History*, VIII (1980), 85–105.

Guzzardo, John C. "Democracy Along the Mohawk: An Election Return, 1773." *New York History*, LVII (1976), 31–52.

Hall, Van Beck. *Politics Without Parties: Massachusetts, 1780–1791*. Pittsburgh, 1972.

Hanna, William S. *Benjamin Franklin and Pennsylvania Politics*. Stanford, 1964.

Hare, A. Paul. *Handbook of Small Group Research*. 2nd ed. New York, 1976.

Harrington, Virginia D. *The New York Merchant on the Eve of the Revolution*. New York, 1935.

Harris, P. M. G. "The Demographic Development of Colonial Philadelphia in Some Comparative Perspective." *Proceedings of the American Philosophical Society*, CXXXIII (1989), 262–304.

Hawke, David. *In the Midst of a Revolution*. Philadelphia, 1961.

Henderson, H. James. "The First Party System." In *Perspectives on Early American History: Essays in Honor of Richard B. Morris*, edited by Alden T. Vaughan and George Athan Billias. New York, 1973.

———. *Party Politics in the Continental Congress*. New York, 1974.

———. "Quantitative Approaches to Party Formation in the United States Congress: A Comment." *William and Mary Quarterly*, 3rd ser., XXX (1973), 307–23.

Henretta, James A. *The Origins of American Capitalism: Collected Essays*. Boston, 1991.

Hill, B. W. *The Growth of Parliamentary Parties, 1689–1742*. London, 1976.

Hindle, Brooke. *The Pursuit of Science in Revolutionary America, 1735–1789*. Chapel Hill, 1956.

Hinshaw, William Wade. *Encyclopedia of American Quaker Genealogy*. Vols. II and III of 6 vols. Ann Arbor, 1938.

Hirst, Derek M. *The Representative of the People? Voters and Voting in England Under the Early Stuarts*. Cambridge, Eng., 1975.

Hoadley, John F. *Origins of American Political Parties, 1789–1803*. Lexington, Ky., 1986.

Hofstadter, Richard. *The Idea of a Party System: The Rise of Legislative Opposition in the United States, 1780–1840.* Berkeley, 1969.

Holmes, Geoffrey. *British Politics in the Age of Anne.* New York. 1967.

Horowitz, Gary S. "New Jersey Land Riots, 1745–1755." In *Economic and Social History of Colonial New Jersey,* edited by William C. Wright. Trenton, 1974.

Howe, Adrian. "The Bayard Treason Trial: Dramatizing Anglo-Dutch Politics in Early Eighteenth-Century New York City." *William and Mary Quarterly,* 3rd ser., LXVII (1990), 57–89.

Humphrey, David C. *From King's College to Columbia, 1746–1800.* New York, 1976.

Hutson, James H. "An Investigation of the Inarticulate: Philadelphia's White Oaks." *William and Mary Quarterly,* 3rd ser., XXVIII (1971), 3–25.

———. *Pennsylvania Politics, 1746–1770: The Movement for Royal Government and Its Consequences.* Princeton, 1972.

———. "Rebuttal." *William and Mary Quarterly,* 3rd ser., XXIX (1972), 136–42.

Illick, Joseph E. *Colonial Pennsylvania: A History.* A History of the American Colonies in Thirteen Volumes. New York, 1976.

Ireland, Owen S. "The Crux of Politics: Religion and Party in Pennsylvania, 1778–1789." *William and Mary Quarterly,* 3rd ser., XLII (1985), 453–75.

Jacobsen, Douglas C. *An Unprov'd Experiment: Religious Pluralism in Colonial New Jersey.* Brooklyn, 1991.

Jacobson, David L. *John Dickinson and the Revolution in Pennsylvania.* University of California Publications in History, LXXVIII. Berkeley, 1965.

James, Sydney V. *Colonial Rhode Island: A History.* A History of the American Colonies in Thirteen Volumes. New York, 1975.

Jeffrey, Thomas E. *State Parties and National Politics: North Carolina, 1815–1861.* Athens, Ga., 1989.

Jensen, Merrill. *The Founding of a Nation: A History of the American Revolution, 1763–1776.* New York, 1968.

Jewell, Malcolm E., and Samuel C. Patterson. *The Legislative Process in the United States.* New York, 1966.

Jones, Alice Hanson. *American Colonial Wealth: Documents and Methods.* 2nd ed. 3 vols. New York, 1978.

Jones, E. Alfred. *The Loyalists of New Jersey: Their Memorials, Claims, Etc. from English Records.* Collections of the New Jersey Historical Society, X. Newark, 1927.

Jordan, David W. *Foundations of Representative Government in Maryland, 1632–1715.* Cambridge, Eng., 1987.

———. "God's Candle Within Government: Quakers and Politics in Early Maryland." *William and Mary Quarterly,* 3rd ser., XXXIX (1982), 628–54.

Judd, Jacob. "A Loyalist Claim, the Philipse Estate." In *The Loyalist Americans: A Focus on Greater New York,* edited by Robert A. East and Jacob Judd. Tarrytown, 1975.

———. "New York: Municipality and Province." In *Aspects of Early New York Society and Politics,* edited by Jacob Judd and Irwin H. Polishook. Tarrytown, 1974.

Kammen, Michael G. *Colonial New York: A History.* A History of the American Colonies in Thirteen Volumes. New York, 1975.

Katz, Stanley M. *Newcastle's New York: Anglo-American Politics, 1732–1753.* Cambridge, Mass., 1968.

Keith, Charles P. *The Provincial Councillors of Pennsylvania Who Held Office Between 1733 and 1776, and Those Earlier Councillors Who Were Some of the Chief Magistrates of the Province, and their Descendants.* Philadelphia, 1883.

Keller, Clair W. "The Rise of Representation: Electing County Officeholders in Colonial Pennsylvania." *Social Science History,* III (1979), 139–66.

Kelley, Robert. *The Cultural Pattern in American Politics: The First Century.* New York, 1979.

Kemmerer, Donald L. *Path to Freedom: The Struggle for Self-Government in Colonial New Jersey, 1703–1776.* 1940; rpr. Cos Cob, 1968.

———. "The Suffrage Franchise in Colonial New Jersey." *Proceedings of the New Jersey Historical Society,* LII (1934), 166–73.

Kenney, Alice P. *Stubborn for Liberty: The Dutch in New York.* Syracuse, 1975.

Ketcham, Ralph. "Benjamin Franklin and William Smith: New Light on an Old Philadelphia Quarrel." *Pennsylvania Magazine of History and Biography,* LXXXVIII (1964), 142–63.

Kierner, Cynthia Anne. *Traders and Gentlefolk: The Livingstons of Colonial New York, 1675–1790.* Ithaca, 1992.

Kim, Sun Bok. *Landlord and Tenant in Colonial New York: Manorial Society, 1664–1775.* Chapel Hill, 1978.

Kishlansky, Mark. "The Emergence of Adversary Politics in the Long Parliament." *Journal of Modern History,* XLIX (1977), 617–40.

Klein, Milton M. "Corruption in Colonial America." *South Atlantic Quarterly,* LXXVIII (1979), 57–72.

———. "New York in the American Colonies: A New Look." In *Aspects of Early New York Society and Politics,* edited by Jacob Judd and Irwin H. Polishook. Tarrytown, 1974.

———. *The Politics of Diversity: Essays in the History of Colonial New York.* Port Washington, 1974.

———. "Prelude to Revolution in New York: Jury Trials and Judicial Tenure." *William and Mary Quarterly,* 3rd ser., XVII (1960), 439–62.

Kleppner, Paul. "Partisanship and Ethnoreligious Conflict: The Third Electoral System, 1853–1892." In *The Evolution of American Electoral Systems,* edited by Paul Kleppner *et al.* Westport, 1981.

———. *The Third Electoral System, 1853–1892: Parties, Voters, and Political Cultures.* Chapel Hill, 1979.

———. *Who Voted? The Dynamics of Electoral Turnout, 1870–1980.* New York, 1982.

Kolp, John G. "The Dynamics of Electoral Competition in Pre-Revolutionary Virginia." *William and Mary Quarterly,* 3rd ser., XLIX (1992), 652–74.

Lacey, Douglas R. *Dissent and Parliamentary Politics in England, 1661–1669.* New Brunswick, 1969.

Landau, Norma. "Independence, Deference, and Voter Participation: The Behavior of the Electorate in Eighteenth-Century Kent." *Historical Journal*, XXII (1979), 561–83.

Landsman, Ned. "Revivalism and Nativism in the Middle Colonies: The Great Awakening and the Scots Community in East New Jersey." *American Quarterly*, XXXIV (1982), 149–64.

Langford, Paul. *The Excise Crisis: Society and Politics in the Age of Walpole*. Oxford, 1975.

Launitz-Schürer, Leopold S., Jr. *Loyal Whigs and Revolutionaries: The Making of the Revolution in New York, 1765–1776*. New York, 1980.

———. "Whig-Loyalists: The DeLanceys of New York." *New-York Historical Society Quarterly*, LVI (1972), 179–98.

Leder, Lawrence H. *Robert Livingston, 1654–1728, and the Politics of Colonial New York*. Chapel Hill, 1961.

Leiby, Adrian C. *The Revolutionary War in the Hackensack Valley: The Jersey Dutch and the Neutral Ground*. New Brunswick, 1962.

Lemisch, Jesse, and John K. Alexander, "The White Oaks, Jack Tar, and the Concept of the 'Inarticulate.'" *William and Mary Quarterly*, 3rd ser., XXIX (1972), 109–34.

Lemon, James T. *The Best Poor Man's Country: A Geographical Study of Early Southeastern Pennsylvania*. Baltimore, 1972.

———. "Comment on James A. Henretta's 'Families and Farms: *Mentalities* in Pre-Industrial America.'" *William and Mary Quarterly*, 3rd ser., XXXVII (1980), 688–96.

Levitt, James H. *For Want of Trade: Shipping and the New Jersey Ports, 1680–1783*. Newark, N.J., 1981.

Lewis, Walker. "Andrew Hamilton and the He-Monster." *William and Mary Quarterly*, 3rd ser., XXXVIII (1981), 268–94.

Lively, Bruce R. "Towards 1756: The Political Genesis of Joseph Galloway." *Pennsylvania History*, XLV (1978), 117–38.

Lokken, Roy N. *David Lloyd: Colonial Lawmaker*. Seattle, 1959.

Lynd, Staughton. "The Mechanics in New York Politics." *Labor History*, V (1964), 225–46.

McAnear, Beverly. "Mr. Robert R. Livingston's Reasons Against a Land Tax." *Journal of Political Economy*, XLVIII (1940), 63–90.

McCormick, Richard P. *The History of Voting in New Jersey: A Study in the Development of Election Machinery*. New Brunswick, 1953.

McDonald, Forrest, and Ellen Shapiro McDonald. "The Ethnic Origins of the American People, 1790." *William and Mary Quarterly*, 3rd ser., XXXVII (1980), 179–99.

McPherson, C. B. *The Political Theory of Possessive Individualism: Hobbes to Locke*. Oxford, Eng., 1962.

Maier, Pauline. *From Resistance to Revolution: Colonial Radicals and the Development of American Opposition to Britain, 1765–1776*. New York, 1972.

Main, Jackson Turner. *Political Parties Before the Constitution*. Chapel Hill, 1973.

———. *The Social Structure of Revolutionary America*. Princeton, 1965.

Marietta, Jack D. *The Reformation of American Quakerism, 1748–1783.* Philadelphia, 1984.

Mark, Irving. *Agrarian Conflicts in Colonial New York, 1711–1775.* 2nd ed. Port Washington, 1965.

Martin, James K. *Men in Rebellion: Higher Governmental Leaders and the Coming of the American Revolution.* New Brunswick, 1973.

Mason, Bernard. *The Road To Independence: The Revolutionary Movement in New York, 1773–1777.* Lexington, Ky., 1966.

Mass, Sister Mary Martin, R.S.M. "The Hicks Family as Quakers, Farmers, and Entrepreneurs." Ph.D. dissertation, St. John's University, 1976.

Moore, David Cresap. *The Politics of Deference: A Study of the Mid-Nineteenth Century English Political System.* New York, 1976.

Morais, Herbert M. "The Sons of Liberty in New York." In *The Era of the American Revolution,* edited by Richard B. Morris. New York, 1939.

Morgan, Edmund S. *Inventing the People: The Rise of Popular Sovereignty in England and America.* New York, 1988.

Morgan, Edmund S., and Helen M. Morgan. *The Stamp Act Crisis: Prologue to Revolution.* Rev. ed. New York, 1963.

Morris, Ina K. *Morris' Memorial History of Staten Island, New York.* 2 vols. New York, 1898–1900.

Morris, Richard B. *Government and Labor in Early America.* New York, 1946.

Murrin, John M. "English Rights as Ethnic Aggression: The English Conquest, the Charter of Liberties of 1683, and Leisler's Rebellion in New York." In *Authority and Resistance in Early New York,* edited by William Pencak and Conrad Edick Wright. New York, 1988.

———. "The Great Inversion, or Court Versus Country: A Comparison of the Revolutionary Settlements in England (1688–1721) and America (1776–1816)." In *Three British Revolutions: 1641, 1688, 1776,* edited by J. G. A. Pocock. Princeton, 1980.

———. "Political Development." In *Colonial British America: Essays in the New History of the Early Modern Era,* edited by Jack P. Greene and J. R. Pole. Baltimore, 1984.

Nadelhaft, Jerome J. "Politics and the Judicial Tenure Fight in Colonial New Jersey." *William and Mary Quarterly,* 3rd ser., XXVIII (1971), 46–63.

Nash, Gary B. "Artisans and Politics in Eighteenth-Century Philadelphia." In *The Origins of Anglo-American Radicalism,* edited by Margaret Jacob and James Jacob. London, 1984.

———. "The New York Census of 1737: A Critical Note on the Integration of Statistical and Literary Sources." *William and Mary Quarterly,* 3rd ser., XXXVI (1979), 428–35.

———. *Quakers and Politics: Pennsylvania, 1681–1726.* Princeton, 1968.

———. "The Transformation of Urban Politics, 1700–1765." *Journal of American History,* LX (1973–74), 605–32.

———. *The Urban Crucible: Social Change, Political Consciousness, and the Origins of the American Revolution.* Cambridge, Mass., 1979.

Nelson, Paul David. "Anthony Wayne: Soldier as Politician." *Pennsylvania Magazine of History and Biography*, CVI (1982), 463–81.

Newcomb, Benjamin H. *Franklin and Galloway: A Political Partnership.* New Haven, 1972.

———. "The Great Landholders and Political Power in Colonial New York and New Jersey." In *Working the Range: Essays on the History of Western Land Management and the Environment*, edited by John Wunder. Westport, 1985.

Nicolosi, Anthony. "Colonial Particularism and Political Rights: Jacob Spicer II on Aid to Virginia, 1754." *New Jersey History*, LXXXVIII (1970), 69–88.

Oaks, Robert F. "Philadelphia Merchants and the Origins of American Independence." *Proceedings of the American Philosophical Society*, CXXI (1977), 407–36.

Olm, Lee E. "The Mutiny Act for America: New York's Noncompliance." *New-York Historical Society Quarterly*, LVIII (1974), 188–214.

Olson, Alison Gilbert. *Anglo-American Politics, 1660–1775: The Relationship Between Parties in England and Colonial America.* New York, 1973.

———. "Eighteenth-Century Colonial Legislatures and Their Constituents." *Journal of American History*, LXXIX (1992–93), 543–67.

Olson, James S. "The New York Assembly, the Politics of Religion, and the Origins of the American Revolution, 1768–1771." *Historical Magazine of the Protestant Episcopal Church*, XLIII (1974), 21–28.

Olton, Charles S. *Artisans for Independence: Philadelphia Mechanics and the American Revolution.* Syracuse, 1975.

[Onderdonk, Henry Jr., *et al.*]. *History of Queens County, New York, with Illustrations, Portraits, and Sketches of Prominent Families and Individuals.* New York, 1882.

Palmer, Gregory. *Biographical Sketches of Loyalists of the American Revolution.* Westport, 1984.

Parsons, William T. "The Bloody Election of 1742." *Pennsylvania History*, XXXVI (1969), 290–306.

Phillips, John A. *Electoral Behavior in Unreformed England: Plumpers, Splitters, and Straights.* Princeton, 1982.

Plumb, J. H. *The Origins of Political Stability: England, 1675–1725.* Boston, 1965.

Pocock, J. G. A. "The Classical Theory of Deference." *American Historical Review*, LXXXI (1976), 516–23.

———. *The Machiavellian Moment: Florentine Political Thought and the Atlantic Republican Tradition.* Princeton, 1975.

———. *Politics, Language, and Time: Essays on European Political Thought and History.* New York, 1971.

Pointer, Richard W. *Protestant Pluralism and the New York Experience: A Study of Eighteenth-Century Religious Diversity.* Bloomington, 1988.

Pole, J. R. *Political Representation in England and the Origins of the American Republic.* New York, 1966.

Pomfret, John E. *The New Jersey Proprietors and Their Lands, 1664–1776.* Princeton, 1964.

Prewitt, Kenneth. *The Recruitment of Political Leaders: A Study of Citizen-Politicians.* Indianapolis, 1970.

Proud, Robert. *The History of Pennsylvania, in North America, from the Original Institution and Settlement of That Province, Under the First Proprietor and Governor William Penn, in 1681, Till After the Year 1742.* 2 vols. Philadelphia, 1797–98.

Purvis, Thomas L. "The European Ancestry of the United States Population, 1790." *William and Mary Quarterly,* 3rd ser., XLI (1984), 85–101.

―――. "'High-Born, Long-Recorded Families': Social Origins of New Jersey Assemblymen, 1703 to 1776." *William and Mary Quarterly,* 3rd ser., XXXVII (1980), 592–615.

―――. "The New Jersey Assembly, 1722–1776." Ph.D. dissertation, Johns Hopkins University, 1979.

―――. "Origins and Patterns of Agrarian Unrest in New Jersey, 1735 to 1754." *William and Mary Quarterly,* 3rd ser., XXXIX (1982), 600–627.

―――. *Proprietors, Patronage, and Paper Money: Legislative Politics in New Jersey, 1703–1776.* New Brunswick, 1986.

Rakove, Jack N. *The Beginnings of National Politics: An Interpretive History of the Continental Congress.* New York, 1979.

Ranlet, Philip. *The New York Loyalists.* Knoxville, 1986.

Ridgway, Whitman H. *Community Leadership in Maryland, 1790–1840: A Comparative Analysis of Power in Society.* Chapel Hill, 1979.

Risjord, Norman K. *Chesapeake Politics, 1781–1800.* New York, 1978.

Robbins, Caroline. "Discordant Parties: A Study of the Acceptance of Party by Englishmen." *Political Science Quarterly,* LXXIII (1958), 505–29.

―――. *The Eighteenth Century Commonwealthman: Studies in the Transmission, Development, and Circumstance of English Liberal Thought from the Restoration of Charles II Until the War with the Thirteen Colonies.* 2nd ed. New York, 1968.

Rock, Howard B. *Artisans of the New Republic: The Tradesmen of New York City in the Age of Jefferson.* New York, 1979.

Rogers, Alan. *Empire and Liberty: American Resistance to British Authority, 1755–1763.* Berkeley, 1974.

Rothermund, Dietmar. *The Layman's Progress: Religion and Political Experience in Colonial Pennsylvania, 1740–1770.* Philadelphia, 1961.

Rowe, G. S. "The Frederick Stump Affair, 1768, and Its Challenge to Legal Historians of Early Pennsylvania." *Pennsylvania History,* XLIX (1982), 255–88.

Ryan, Dennis P. "Landholding, Opportunity, and Mobility in Revolutionary New Jersey." *William and Mary Quarterly,* 3rd ser., XXXVI (1979), 571–92.

Ryan, Mary P. "Party Formation in the United States Congress, 1789 to 1796: A Quantitative Analysis." *William and Mary Quarterly,* 3rd ser., XXVIII (1971), 523–42.

Ryerson, Richard Alan. "Portrait of a Colonial Oligarchy: The Quaker Elite in the Pennsylvania Assembly, 1729–1776." In *Power and Status: Officeholding in Colonial America,* edited by Bruce C. Daniels. Middletown, 1986.

―――. *The Revolution Is Now Begun: The Radical Committees of Philadelphia, 1765–1776.* Philadelphia, 1978.

Sabine, Lorenzo F. *Biographical Sketches of Loyalists of the American Revolution, with an Historical Essay*. 2 vols. 1864; rpr. Port Washington, 1966.

Salinger, Sharon V., and Charles Wetherell. "A Note on the Population of Pre-revolutionary Philadelphia." *Pennsylvania Magazine of History and Biography*, CIX (1985), 367–86.

Sartori, Giovanni. *Parties and Party Systems: A Framework for Analysis*. Cambridge, Eng., 1976.

Scharf, J. Thomas. *History of Westchester County, New York, Including Morisania, King's Bridge, and West Farms, Which Have Been Annexed to New York City*. Philadelphia, 1886.

Scharf, J. Thomas, and Thompson Westcott. *History of Philadelphia, 1609–1884*. 3 vols. Philadelphia, 1884.

Schlenther, Boyd Stanley. *Charles Thomson: A Patriot's Pursuit*. Newark, Del., 1990.

Schoonmaker, Marius. *The History of Kingston, New York*. New York, 1888.

Schultz, Ronald. "The Small-Producer Tradition and Artisan Radicalism in Philadelphia, 1720–1810." *Past and Present*, CXXVII (1990), 84–116.

Schwartz, Philip J. *The Jarring Interests: New York's Boundary Makers, 1664–1776*. Albany, 1979.

Schwartz, Sally. *"A Mixed Multitude": The Struggle for Toleration in Colonial Pennsylvania*. New York, 1987.

Sedgwick, Romney. *The House of Commons, 1715–1754: The History of Parliament*. 2 vols. London, 1970.

Seligman, Lester G., Michael R. King, Chong Lin Kim, and Roland C. Smith. *Patterns of Recruitment: A State Chooses Its Lawmakers*. Chicago, 1974.

Shade, William G. "Political Pluralism and Party Development: The Creation of a Modern Party System, 1815–1852." In *The Evolution of American Electoral Systems*, edited by Paul Kleppner *et al.* Westport, 1981.

Sheridan, Eugene R. *Lewis Morris, 1671–1746: A Study in Early American Politics*. Syracuse, 1981.

Silbey, Joel H. *The Partisan Imperative: The Dynamics of American Politics Before the Civil War*. New York, 1985.

Sills, David, ed. *International Encyclopedia of the Social Sciences*. New York, 1968. S.v. "Party Systems," by Harry Eckstein.

Skaggs, David Curtis. *Roots of Maryland Democracy, 1753–1776*. Westport, 1973.

Skemp, Sheila L. *William Franklin: Son of a Patriot, Servant of a King*. New York, 1990.

Smith, Billy G. "Death and Life in a Colonial Immigrant City: A Demographic Analysis of Philadelphia." *Journal of Economic History*, XXXVII (1977), 863–89.

———. *The "Lower Sort": Philadelphia's Laboring People, 1750–1800*. Ithaca, 1990.

Smith, Joseph H., and Leo Hershkowitz. "Courts of Equity in the Province of New York: The Cosby Controversy, 1732–1736." *American Journal of Legal History*, XVI (1972), 1–50.

Smith, Samuel. *The History of the Colony of Nova-Caesaria, or New-Jersey; Containing, an Account of Its First Settlement, Progressive Improvements, the Original and Present Consti-*

tution, and Other Events to the Year 1721. With Some Particulars Since; and a Short View of Its Present State. Burlington, 1765.

Smith, William, Jr. *Continuation of the History of New York. Collections of the New-York Historical Society,* IV (1829).

Sorauf, Frank J. "Political Parties and Political Analysis." In *The American Party Systems: Stages of Political Development,* edited by William N. Chambers and Walter Dean Burnham. New York, 1975.

Sosin, J. M. *English America and Imperial Inconstancy: The Rise of Provincial Autonomy, 1696–1715.* Lincoln, 1985.

Speck, W. A. *Tory and Whig: The Struggle in the Constituencies, 1701–1715.* London, 1970.

Stillwell, John E. *Historical and Genealogical Miscellany: Data Relating to the Settlement of Colonial New York and New Jersey.* 5 vols. New York, 1903–32.

Stokes, Isaac Newton Phelps. *The Iconography of Manhattan Island.* 6 vols. New York, 1915–28.

Sutherland, Stella H. *Population Distribution in Colonial America.* 1936; rpr. New York, 1966.

Swenson, Peter. "The Influence of Recruitment on the Structure of Power in the U.S. House, 1870–1940." *Legislative Studies Quarterly,* VII (1982), 1–36.

Sylvester, Nathaniel Bartlett. *History of Ulster County, New York, with Illustrations and Biographical Sketches of Its Prominent Men and Pioneers.* 2 Pts. Philadelphia, 1880.

Taylor, Alan. "'The Art of Hook and Snivey': Political Culture in Upstate New York During the 1790s." *Journal of American History,* LXXIX (1992–93), 1371–96.

Teaford, Jon C. *The Municipal Revolution in America: Origins of Modern Urban Government, 1650–1825.* Chicago, 1975.

Thompson, Benjamin F. *History of Long Island from Its Discovery and Settlement to the Present Time.* 3rd ed. 3 vols. New York, 1918.

Tiedemann, Joseph S. "Communities in the Midst of the American Revolution: Queens County, New York, 1774–1775." *Journal of Social History,* XVIII (1984), 57–78.

———. "A Revolution Foiled: Queens County, New York, 1775–1776." *Journal of American History,* LXXV (1988–89), 417–44.

Tully, Alan. "Constituent-Representative Relationships in Early America: The Case of Pre-Revolutionary Pennsylvania." *Canadian Journal of History,* XI (1976), 139–54.

———. "Ethnicity, Religion, and Politics in Early America." *Pennsylvania Magazine of History and Biography,* CVII (1983), 491–536.

———. "Quaker Party and Proprietary Politics: The Dynamics of Politics in Pre-Revolutionary Pennsylvania, 1730–1775." In *Power and Status: Officeholding in Colonial America,* edited by Bruce C. Daniels. Middletown, 1986.

———. *William Penn's Legacy: Politics and Social Structure in Provincial Pennsylvania, 1726–1755.* Baltimore, 1977.

Varga, Nicholas. "The Development and Structure of Local Government in Colonial New York." In *Town and County: Essays in the Structure of Local Government in the American Colonies,* edited by Bruce C. Daniels. Middletown, 1978.

————. "Election Procedures and Practices in Colonial New York." *New York History,* XL (1960), 249–77.

Verba, Sidney. *Small Groups and Political Behavior: A Study of Leadership.* Princeton, 1961.

Verba, Sidney, and Norman Nie. *Participation in America: Political Democracy and Social Equality.* New York, 1972.

Ver Steeg, Clarence L. *The Formative Years, 1607–1763.* New York, 1964.

Wacker, Peter O. *Land and People: A Cultural Geography of Preindustrial New Jersey: Origins and Settlement Patterns.* New Brunswick, 1975.

Wainwright, Nicholas B. "William Denny in Pennsylvania." *Pennsylvania Magazine of History and Biography,* LXXXI (1957), 170–98.

Wallace, Michael. "Changing Concepts of Party in the United States: New York, 1815–1828." *American Historical Review,* LXXIV (1968), 453–91.

Walton, Gary M., and James F. Shepherd. *The Economic Rise of Early America.* New York, 1979.

Walton, Joseph S. *John Kinsey, Speaker of the Pennsylvania Assembly and Justice of the Supreme Court of the Province.* Philadelphia, 1900.

Wellenreuther, Herman. "The Political Dilemma of the Quakers in Pennsylvania, 1681–1748." *Pennsylvania Magazine of History and Biography,* XCIV (1970), 135–72.

————. "The Quest for Harmony in a Turbulent World: The Principle of 'Love and Unity' in Colonial Pennsylvania Politics." *Pennsylvania Magazine of History and Biography,* CVII (1983), 537–76.

Wells, Robert V. *The Population of the British Colonies in America Before 1776: A Survey of Census Data.* Princeton, 1975.

Wendel, Thomas. "The Keith-Lloyd Alliance: Factional and Coalition Politics in Colonial Pennsylvania." *Pennsylvania Magazine of History and Biography,* XCII (1968), 289–305.

White, Philip L. *The Beekmans of New York in Politics and Commerce, 1647–1877.* New York, 1956.

Wilkenfeld, Bruce M. "The New York City Common Council, 1689–1800." *New York History,* LII (1971), 249–73.

Willetts, Peter. "Cluster-Bloc Analysis and Statistical Inference." *American Political Science Review,* LXVI (1972), 569–82.

Williamson, Chilton. *American Suffrage from Property to Democracy, 1760–1860.* Princeton, 1960.

Wolf, Stephanie Grauman. *Urban Village: Population, Community, and Family Structure in Germantown, Pennsylvania, 1683–1800.* Princeton, 1976.

Woodward, Carl R. *Ploughs and Politics: Charles Read of New Jersey and His Notes on Agriculture, 1715–1774.* New Brunswick, 1941.

Zemsky, Robert. *Merchants, Farmers, and River Gods: An Essay on Eighteenth-Century American Politics.* Boston, 1971.

Index